The Art and Science of Technical Analysis

The Art and Science of Technical Analysis

Market Structure, Price Action,
and Trading Strategies

ADAM GRIMES

WILEY

John Wiley & Sons, Inc.

Published by John Wiley & Sons, Inc., Hoboken, New Jersey.
Published simultaneously in Canada.

Charts generated with the TradeStation platform and code in EasyLanguage format are used with permission. © TradeStation Technologies, Inc. 2001–2011, All rights reserved.

For general information on our other products and services or for technical support, please contact our Customer Care Department within the United States at (800) 762-2974, outside the United States at (317) 572-3993 or fax (317) 572-4002.

Wiley also publishes its books in a variety of electronic formats. Some content that appears in print may not be available in electronic books. For more information about Wiley products, visit our web site at www.wiley.com.

Library of Congress Cataloging-in-Publication Data:

Grimes, Adam, 1973–
   The art and science of technical analysis : market structure, price action, and trading strategies / Adam Grimes.
      pages cm. – (Wiley trading series ; 544)
   Includes bibliographical references and index.
   ISBN 978-1-118-11512-1 (cloth); ISBN 978-1-118-22427-4 (ebk);
   ISBN 978-1-118-23814-1 (ebk); ISBN 978-1-118-26247-4 (ebk)
 1. Investment analysis.   I. Title.
   HG4529.G75 2012
   332.63'2042–dc23

                                                                    2012000874

Printed in the United States of America

*To my wife Betsy. Without her unfailing love and support
I could have accomplished nothing.*

Contents

Preface

The book you are holding in your hands is the product of nearly two decades of my study and experience as a trader, covering the full span of actively traded markets and time frames. I owe much to authors and traders who have come before me, for no one produces anything significant in a vacuum. I would not have been successful without the help and guidance of my mentors, but I learned many of the lessons here from my own mistakes. In some ways, this work represents a radical break from many of the books that have preceded it, and I hope it encourages you to question much of the traditional thinking of technical analysis.

This book does not present a rigid system to be strictly followed, nor a set of setups and patterns that can be assembled at the trader's whim. Rather, it offers a comprehensive approach to the problems of technically motivated, directional trading. The book is structured to be read from beginning to end, but individual sections and chapters stand on their own. Through the entire work, deliberate repetition of important concepts helps to build a complete perspective on many of the problems traders face. The tools and techniques must be adapted to the trader's personality and business situation, but most will find a firm foundation between these covers.

There are some underlying themes, perhaps not expressed explicitly, that tie this work together, and they may be surprising to many readers: *Trading is hard.* Markets are extremely competitive. They are usually very close to efficient, and most observed price movements are random. *It is therefore exceedingly difficult to derive a method that makes superior risk-adjusted profits,* and it is even more difficult to successfully apply such a method in actual trading. Last, *it is essential to have a verifiable edge in the markets*—otherwise no consistent profits are possible. This approach sets this work apart from the majority of trading books published, which suggest that simple patterns and proper psychology can lead a trader to impressive profits. Perhaps this is possible, but I have never seen it work in actual practice.

This book is divided into four parts:

- Part One begins with a look at some of the probability theory supporting the concepts of successful trading. Next comes an in-depth look at a specific approach to chart reading that focuses on clarity and consistency lays the foundation for building and understanding of price patterns in markets. This section concludes with an overview of the Wyckoff market cycle, which is already well known in the literature of technical analysis.

- Part Two focuses on the details of trends, trading ranges, and critically, the transitions from one to the other in considerable detail. This is a deep look at the underlying foundation of price movements, and there is information here that, to my knowledge, has never appeared in print before.
- Part Three might appear, at first glance, to be the meat of this book, as it includes specific trading patterns and examples of those patterns applied to real markets. It also advocates a way of looking at indicators and other confirming factors that requires a deep understanding of the nuances of these tools. One of the key elements of any trading plan is how the trader sizes the trade and manages the position as it develops; these elements are also covered in considerable depth. Much attention is devoted to the many risks traders will encounter, both from the market and from themselves. Though most traders are going to be tempted to turn directly to this section, remember that these patterns are only the tip of the spear, and they are meaningless unless they are placed within the context provided by Parts One and Two.
- Part Four is specifically written for the individual trader, and begins by focusing on elements of psychology such as cognitive biases and issues of emotional control. Chapter 11 takes a look at many of the challenges developing traders typically face. Though it is impossible to reduce the trader development process to a one-size-fits-all formula, the majority of traders struggle with the same issues. Most traders fail because they do not realize that the process of becoming a trader is a long one, and they are not prepared to make the commitment. This section concludes with a look at some performance analysis tools that can help both the developing and the established trader to track key performance metrics and to target problems before they have a serious impact on the bottom line.
- Last, there are three appendixes in this work. The first appendix is a trading primer that will be useful for developing traders or for managers who do not have a familiarity with the language used by traders. Like any discipline, trading has its own idioms and lingo, an understanding of which is important for effective communication. The second expands on the some specific details and quirks of moving averages the MACD, which are used extensively in other sections of this book. The last appendix simply contains a list of trade data used in the performance analysis of Part Four.

This book is written for two distinct groups of traders. It is overtly addressed to the individual, self-directed trader, either trading for his or her own account or who has exclusive trading authority over a number of client accounts. The self-directed trader will find many sections specifically addressed to the struggles he or she faces, and to the errors he or she is likely to make along the way. Rather than focusing on arcane concepts and theories, this trader needs to learn to properly read a chart, and most importantly, to understand the emerging story of supply and demand as it plays out through the patterns in the market.

Though this book is primarily written for that self-directed trader, there is also much information that will be valuable to a second group of traders and managers who do not approach markets from a technical perspective or who make decisions within an institutional framework. For these traders, some of the elements such as trader psychology may appear, at first glance, to be less relevant, but they provide a context for all market action. These traders will also find new perspectives on risk management, position sizing, and pattern analysis that may be able to inform their work in different areas.

The material in this book is complex; repeated exposure and rereading of certain sections will be an essential part of the learning process for most traders. In addition, the size of this book may be daunting to many readers. Once again, the book is structured to be read and absorbed from beginning to end. Themes and concepts are developed and revisited, and repetition is used to reinforce important ideas, but it may also be helpful to have a condensed study plan for some readers. Considering the two discrete target audiences, I would suggest the following plans:

- Both the individual and the institutional trader should page through the entire book, reading whatever catches their interest. Each chapter has been made as self-contained as possible, while trying to keep redundancy to an absolute minimum.
- After an initial quick read, the individual trader should carefully read Chapters 1 and 2, which provide a foundation for everything else. This trader should probably next read Part Four (Chapters 11 and 12) in depth, paying particular attention to the elements of the trader development process. Next, turn to Chapters 6 and 10, which focus on often-misunderstood aspects of risk and position sizing. Two important aspects of the book are missed on this first read: in-depth analysis of market structure and the use of confirming tools in setting up and managing actual trades. These are topics for deeper investigation once the initial material has been assimilated.
- For the institutional trader, Chapter 1 is also a logical follow-up to a quick read. Next, Chapter 2 would provide a good background and motivation for the entire discipline of technical analysis. Chapters 8 and 9 will likely be very interesting to this trader. For managers who are used to thinking of risk in a portfolio context, there are important lessons to be learned from a tactical/technical approach to position and risk management. Last, many of these readers will have an academic background. Chapters 2 through 5 would round out this trader's understanding of evolving market structure.

Following both of these study plans, it is advisable to then begin again from the beginning, or perhaps to turn to the parts of the book not covered in these shorter plans and pick up what you have missed. Intellectually, the material can be assimilated fairly quickly, but flawless application may remain elusive for some time. Additional materials supporting this book, including a blog updated with examples and trades drawn from current market action, are available at my web site and blog, www.adamhgrimes.com.

The title of this book is *The Art and Science of Technical Analysis*. Science deals primarily with elements that are quantifiable and testable. The process of teaching a science usually focuses on the development of a body of knowledge, procedures, and approaches to data—the precise investigation of what is known and knowable. Art is often seen as more subjective and imprecise, but this is not entirely correct. In reality, neither can exist without the other. Science must deal with the philosophical and epistemological issues of the edges of knowledge, and scientific progress depends on inductive leaps as much as logical steps. Art rests on a foundation of tools and techniques that can and should be scientifically quantified, but it also points to another mode of knowing that stands somewhat apart from the usual procedures of logic. The two depend on each other: Science without Art is sterile; Art without Science is soft and incomplete. Nowhere is this truer than in the study of modern financial markets.

ADAM GRIMES
September 2011
New York, New York

Acknowledgments

First, to Linda Raschke: I owe you a debt I can never repay—who would have thought your kindness that began with answering a simple e-mail so many years ago would have had such a profound impact on someone's life?

Jose Palau, you played a seminal role in helping me crystallize the ideas for this book. There were times in our arguments that I wanted to punch you, and I'm sure it was mutual. In the end, much of what is good in this book came from those discussions, and, as you said, "there is no spoon."

There have been many others along the way who have challenged my thinking with new ideas and helped to drive out imprecision and errors in my trading. To Larry Williams, Mark Fisher, Chris Terry, Ralph Vince, Chuck LeBeau, Victor Niederhoffer, Michael Gunther, Louis Hazan, Mark D. Cook, David McCracken, Doug Zalesky, and Andrew Barber, thank you. Andrew Karolyi and Ingrid Werner, you expanded my thinking and opened my mind to new possibilities.

The first draft of this book was produced in 45 days, but then the real work began. Henry Carstens, David Dyte, and Dr. Brett Steenbarger provided invaluable guidance in the early stages of this project, and helped me to see some of the problems from many perspectives. Perry Kaufman provided some good quantitiative insights and critique. Travis Harbauer, you were the best intern imaginable. Being willing to get on a train at 10:00 p.m. on a Friday night with a flash drive is far above and beyond the call of duty! And Aimin Walsh—how (and why) does someone meticulously proofread a 900-page manuscript in a single week while having a real life, a job, and, presumably, sleeping sometime in between? My mother, Lila Grimes, persevered in reading and editing early versions of this manuscript, a difficult task but a valuable perspective from someone not familiar with the subject matter. Thank you also to my small army of interns who proofread, crunched numbers, and made a thousand small improvements to my work: Benjamin Shopneck, Ethan Tran, Austin Tran, and Fred Barnes. This project would have taken far longer, and the finished work would have been much weaker, without your contributions. Thank you so much to all of you.

I probably would have put off writing this book much longer if not for the encouragement of Mike Bellafiore. His advice, to "make a book that will be a gift to the trading community," guided my actions at every step.

Last, but certainly not least, Kevin Commins and Meg Freeborn at John Wiley & Sons, your work supporting a first-time author was fantastic. Thank you for dealing with my questions and for navigating the complexity of this manuscript so well. It has been a joy working with you.

PART I

The Foundation of Technical Analysis

CHAPTER 1

The Trader's Edge

If you would be a real seeker after truth, it is necessary that at least once in your life you doubt, as far as possible, all things.

—René Descartes

There is something fascinating and mesmerizing about price movements in actively traded markets; academics, researchers, traders, and analysts are drawn to study markets, perhaps captivated as much by the patterns in the market as by the promise of financial gain. Many people believe that price changes are random and unpredictable; if this were true, the only logical course of action would be to avoid trading and to invest in index funds. This is, in fact, what a significant number of financial advisers recommend their clients do. On the other hand, there are analysts and traders who believe that they have some edge over the market, that there is some predictability in prices. This camp divides into two groups that historically have been diametrically opposed: those who make decisions based on *fundamental* factors and those who rely on *technical* factors. Fundamental analysts and traders make decisions based on their assessment of value, through an analysis of a number of factors such as financial statements, economic conditions, and an understanding of supply/demand factors. Technical traders and analysts make decisions based on information contained in past price changes themselves.

Our work here concerns the latter approach. Few traders make decisions in a vacuum; technical traders may consider fundamental factors, and fundamental traders may find that their entries and exits into markets can be better timed with an understanding of the relevant elements of market structure, money flows, and price action. Most traders find success with a hybrid approach that incorporates elements from many disciplines, and there are very few purely technical or fundamental decision makers. The key distinction, for us, is that technically motivated traders acknowledge the primacy of price itself. They know that price represents the end product of the analysis and decision

3

making of all market participants, and believe that a careful analysis of price movements can sometimes reveal areas of market imbalance that can offer opportunities for superior risk-adjusted profits. Building the tools for that analysis and learning how to apply them is the purpose of this book.

DEFINING A TRADING EDGE

Most of the time, markets are efficient, meaning that all available information is reflected in asset prices, and that price is a fair reflection of value. Most of the time, prices fluctuate in a more or less random fashion. Though a trader may make some profitable trades in this type of environment purely due to random chance, it is simply not possible to profit in the long run; nothing the trader can do will have a positive effect on the bottom line as long as randomness dominates price changes. In theory, in a true zero-expectancy game, it should be possible to trade in a random environment and to break even, but reality is different. Trading accounts in the real world suffer under the constant drag of a number of trading frictions, transaction costs, errors, and other risks. Together, these create a high hurdle that must be overcome in order to break even. It is even possible for a trader to work with a positive expectancy system and still lose a significant amount of money to the vig.

Newer traders especially are often drawn to focus on elements of performance psychology and positive thinking. There is an entire industry that caters to struggling traders, holding out hope that if they could just get their psychological issues resolved, money would flow into their trading accounts. However, this fails to address the core problem, which is that most traders are doing things in the market that do not work. Excellent execution, risk management, discipline, and proper psychology are all important elements of a good trading plan, but it is all futile if the trading system does not have a positive expectancy. These are essential tools through which a trading edge can be applied to the market, and without which a trader is unlikely to succeed in the long run. However, none of these is a trading edge in itself.

A *positive expectancy* results when the trader successfully identifies those moments where markets are slightly less random than usual, and places trades that are aligned with the slight statistical edges present in those areas. Some traders are drawn to focus on high-probability (high win rate) trading, while others focus on finding trades that have excellent reward/risk profiles. Neither of these approaches is better than the other; what matters is how these two factors of probability and reward/risk ratio interact. For instance, it is possible to be consistently profitable with a strategy that risks many times more than what is made, as long as the win rate is high enough, or with a much lower percentage of winning trades if the reward/risk ratio compensates. In all cases, the trading problem reduces to a matter of identifying when a statistical edge is present in the market, acting accordingly, and avoiding market environments that are more random. To do this well, it is essential to have a good understanding of how markets move and also some of the math behind expectancy and probability theory.

Expected Value

Expected value (or *expectancy*) is a term from probability theory that every good trader and gambler understands intuitively. For our purposes, we need to define a number of scenarios that each have a precisely defined payout (or loss), and we also need to be able to quantify the probabilities of each scenario occurring. If we are analyzing actual trading records, this can be as simple as calculating summary statistics for historical trades, but the problem is much more complicated on a look-forward basis because we have to make assumptions about how closely future conditions are likely to resemble history. Furthermore, we also need to make sure that our calculations include every possible outcome so that the probabilities sum to 1.0; this is sometimes difficult in real-world applications where unforeseeable outlier events may lurk in the future. Leaving these practical considerations aside for a moment and focusing on the underlying math, multiplying the payout of each scenario by the probability of each scenario occurring creates a probability-weighted average of the payouts, which is also called the expected value.

The Expected Value Formula

Formally, for k possible scenarios, each with a payoff of x and associated probability p, the expected value E() is defined as:

$$E(X) = x_1 p_1 + x_2 p_2 + \cdots + x_k p_k$$

or, in alternate notation:

$$E(X) = \sum_{i=1}^{k} x_i p_i$$

Consider a simplified example where a trader can either make or lose 1 point with 50 percent probability of either outcome. In this example, the relevant math is: $E(X) = .5(1) + .5(-1) = 0$. It is important to understand precisely what expectancy tells us, which, in the case of a simplified trading or game of chance scenario, is the average amount we should win or lose on each trial. Furthermore, and this is very important, like many things in the field of probability, expectancy is valid only over a fairly large sample size. Even though our trader was playing a zero expectancy game, it is entirely possible that the trader could have had many wins or losses in a row, and could actually have accumulated a significant gain or loss at some point. In fact, it is very likely this *will* happen because random data tends to have many more strings of runs than most people would expect. Over a larger sample, it is likely that the actual value realized will begin to converge on the theoretical expected value, but distortions can and do occur.

The bottom line is that you must have an edge. If you are not trading with a statistical advantage over the market, everything else is futile. Nothing will help. Discipline, money management, execution skills, and positive thinking add great value in support of an actual edge, but they are not edges in themselves. From a statistical standpoint, the definition of an edge is simple: can you properly identify entry and exit points in the market so that, over a large sample size, the sum of the profit and loss (P&L) from your winning trades is greater than the sum of your losing trades? The question then becomes: how do you find, develop, refine, and maintain an edge? There are many answers to that question; this book shows one possible path.

Where Does the Edge Come From?

Many of the buying and selling decisions in the market are made by humans, either as individuals, in groups (as in an investment committee making a decision), or through extension (as in the case of execution algorithms or "algos"). One of the assumptions of academic finance is that people make rational decisions in their own best interests, after carefully calculating the potential gains and losses associated with all possible scenarios. This may be true at times, but not always. The market does not simply react to new information flow; it reacts to that information as it is processed through the lens of human emotion. People make emotional decisions about market situations, and sometimes they make mistakes. Information may be overweighted or underweighted in analysis, and everyone, even large institutions, deals with the emotions of fear, greed, hope, and regret.

In an idealized, mathematical random walk world, price would have no memory of where it has been in the past; but in the real world, prices are determined by traders making buy and sell decisions at specific times and prices. When markets revisit these specific prices, the market *does* have a memory, and we frequently see nonrandom action on these retests of important price levels. People remember the hopes, fears, and pain associated with price extremes. In addition, most large-scale buying follows a more or less predictable pattern: traders and execution algorithms alike will execute part of large orders aggressively, and then will wait to allow the market to absorb the action before resuming their executions. The more aggressive the buyers, the further they will lift offers and the less they will wait between spurts of buying. This type of action, and the memory of other traders around previous inflections, creates slight but predictable tendencies in prices.

There is no mystical, magical process at work here or at any other time in the market. Buying and selling pressure moves prices—only this, and nothing more. If someone really wants to buy and to buy quickly, the market will respond to the buying and sellers will raise their offers as they realize they can get a better (higher) price. Similarly, when large sell orders hit the market, buyers who were waiting on the bid will get out of the way because they realize that extra supply has come into the market. More urgency to sell means lower prices. More buying pressure means higher prices. The conclusion is logical and unavoidable: buying and selling pressure must, by necessity, leave patterns in the market. Our challenge is to understand how psychology can shape market structure and price action, and to find places where this buying and selling pressure creates opportunities in the form of nonrandom price action.

The Holy Grail

This is important. In fact, it is the single most important point in technical analysis—the holy grail, if you will. *Every edge we have, as technical traders, comes from an imbalance of buying and selling pressure.* That's it, pure and simple. If we realize this and if we limit our involvement in the market to those points where there is an actual imbalance, then there is the possibility of making profits. We can sometimes identify these imbalances through the patterns they create in prices, and these patterns can provide actual points around which to structure and execute trades. Be clear on this point: we do not trade patterns in markets—we trade the underlying imbalances that create those patterns. There is no holy grail in trading, but this knowledge comes close. To understand why this is so important, it is necessary to first understand what would happen if we tried to trade in a world where price action was purely random.

FINDING AND DEVELOPING YOUR EDGE

The process of developing and refining your edge in the market is exactly that: an ongoing process. This is not something you do one time; it is an iterative process that begins with ideas, progressing to distilling those ideas to actionable trading systems, and then monitoring the results. Midcourse corrections are to be expected, and dramatic retooling, especially at the beginning, is common. It is necessary to monitor ongoing performance as markets evolve, and some edges will decay over time. To be successful as an individual discretionary trader means committing to this process. Trading success, for the discretionary trader, is a dynamic state that will fluctuate in response to a multitude of factors.

Why Small Traders Can Make Money

This is an obvious issue, but one that is often ignored. The argument of many academics is that you can't make money trading; your best bet is to put your money in a diversified fund and reap the baseline drift compounded over many years. (For most investors, this is not a bad plan for at least a portion of their portfolios.) Even large, professionally managed funds have a very difficult time beating the market, so why should you be able to do so, sitting at home or in your office without any competitive or informational advantage? You are certainly not the best-capitalized player in the arena, and, in a field that attracts some of the best and brightest minds in the world, you are unlikely to be the smartest. You also will not win by sheer force of will and determination. Even if you work harder than nearly anyone else, a well-capitalized firm could hire 20 of you and *that* is what you are competing against. What room is there for the small, individual trader to make profits in the market?

The answer, I think, is simple but profound: you can make money because you are not playing the same game as these other players. One reason the very large funds have trouble beating the market is that they are so large that they *are* the market. Many of these firms are happy to scrape out a few incremental basis points on a relative basis, and they do so through a number of specialized strategies. This is probably not how you intend to trade. You probably cannot compete with large institutions on fundamental work. You probably cannot compete with HFTs and automated trading programs on speed, nor can you compete with the quant firms that hire armies of PhDs to scour every conceivable relationship between markets.

This is all true, but you also do not have the same restrictions that many of these firms do: you are not mandated to have any specific exposures. In most markets, you will likely experience few, if any, liquidity or size issues; your orders will have a minimal (but still very real) impact on prices. Most small traders can be opportunistic. If you have the skills, you can move freely among currencies, equities, futures, and options, using outright or spread strategies as appropriate. Few institutional investors enjoy these freedoms. Last, and perhaps most significantly, you are free to target a time frame that is not interesting to many institutions and not accessible to some.

One solution is to focus on the three-day to two-week swings, as many swing traders do. First, this steps up out of the noise created by the HFTs and algos. Many large firms, particularly those that make decisions on fundamental criteria, avoid short time frames altogether. They may enter and exit positions over multiple days or weeks; your profits and losses over a few days are inconsequential to them. Rather than compete directly, play a different game and target a different time frame. As Sun Tzu wrote in the *Art of War*: "Tactics are like unto water; for water in its natural state runs away from high places and hastens downward … avoid what is strong and strike at what is weak."

GENERAL PRINCIPLES OF CHART READING

Charts are powerful tools for traders, but it is important to think deeply about what a chart is and what it represents. Though it is possible to trade by focusing on simple chart patterns, this approach also misses much of the richness and depth of analysis that are available to a skilled chart reader. Top-level trading combines traditional left brain skills of logic, math, and analytical thinking with the intuitive, inductive skills of right brain thinking. Charts speak directly to the right brain, whose native language is pictures and images. Part of your edge as a discretionary trader comes from integrating these two halves of your being; charts are a powerful tool that can facilitate this integration and foster the growth of intuition.

Modern software packages are a mixed blessing for traders. On one hand, they have greatly increased the scope and breadth of our vision. It is not unusual for a modern trader to examine 400 or 500 charts in the course of a trading day, sometimes more than once, quickly assessing the character of a market or a set of related markets. This would not have been possible in the precomputer era, when charts had to be laboriously drawn and updated by hand. However, charting software also encourages some potentially harmful habits. It is so easy to add various plots and indicators to charts and to tweak and change settings and time frames that some traders are forever experimenting and searching for the holy grail of technical indicators. Other traders bury price bars behind a barrage of moving averages and other indicators, thinking that complexity will lead to better trading results. Simplicity is often better than complexity. A chart is nothing more than a tool to display market data in a structured format. Once traders learn to read the message of the market, they can understand the psychological tone and the balance of buying and selling pressure at any point.

When it comes to chart setup, there is no one right way, but I will share my approach. Everything I do comes from an emphasis on clarity and consistency. Clean charts put the focus where it belongs: on the price bars and the developing market structure. Tools that highlight and emphasize the underlying market's structure are good; anything that detracts from that focus is bad. When you see a chart, you want the price bars (or candles) to be the first and most important thing your eye is drawn to; any calculated measure is only a supplement or an enhancement. Consistency is also very important, for two separate reasons. First, consistency reduces the time required to orient between charts. It is not unusual for me to scan 500 charts in a single sitting, and I can effectively do this by spending a little over a second on each chart. This is possible only because every one of my charts has the same layout and I can instantly orient and drill down to the relevant information. Consistency is also especially important for the developing trader because part of the learning process is training your eye to process data a certain way. If you are forever switching formats, this learning curve becomes much longer and steeper, and the development of intuition will be stymied. Keep the same format between all markets and time frames, and keep the setup of all of your charts as consistent as possible.

Chart Scaling: Linear versus Log

The one exception to the principle of keeping charts consistent might be in the case of very long-term charts spanning multiple years, or shorter-term charts in which an asset has greatly increased in value (by over 100 percent). In these cases, the vertical axis of the chart should be scaled logarithmically (called "semi-log" in some charting packages) to better reflect the growth rate of the market. The idea behind a *log scale chart* is that the same vertical distance always represents the same percentage growth regardless of location on the axis.

On a very long-term chart, *linearly scaled charts* will often make price changes at lower price levels so small that they disappear and they are completely dwarfed by price changes that happened at higher levels. The linear scale also magnifies the importance of those higher-level price changes, making them seem more violent and significant than they actually were. Compare Figure 1.1 and Figure 1.2, two charts of the long-term history of the Dow Jones Industrial Average (DJIA), especially noticing the differences between the two charts at the beginning and end of the series. They seem to tell completely different stories. The first chart shows a flat and uninteresting beginning followed by violent swings

(Continued)

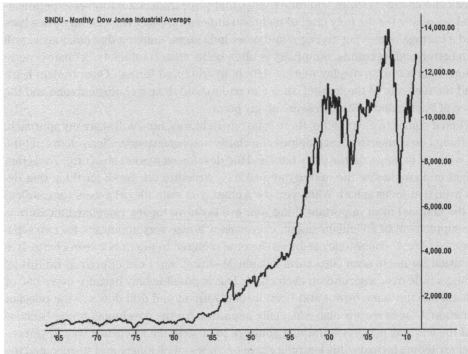

FIGURE 1.1 Nothing Seems to Matter Before 1985: DJIA on a Linear Scale

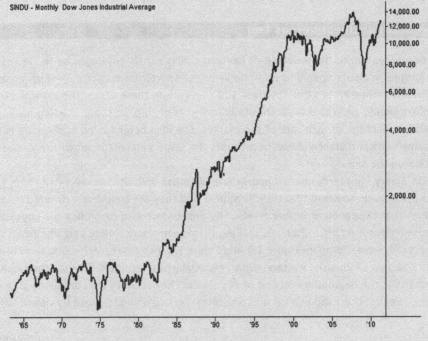

FIGURE 1.2 Investors' Actual Experiences: DJIA on a Log Scale

near the right edge of the chart, while the second, the log scale chart, shows more consistent swings throughout. Over this long history, the log scale chart is a much more accurate representation of what market participants would have experienced at any point on the chart. Remember, as a rule of thumb, there are two times when log scale charts should be used: any time you have greater than a 100 percent price increase on a chart, and for any chart showing more than two years of data, whether on daily, weekly, or monthly time frames.

Choosing Time Frames

Discretionary traders must clearly choose and define the time frame within which they will trade, and this choice of time frames is tied into deeper questions of personality and trading style. Most of the trading ideas and principles we examine in this book can be applied to all markets and all time frames, with some adjustments, but most traders will probably find themselves best suited to a specific set of markets and time frames. Traders switching time frames or asset classes will usually undergo a painful adjustment period while they figure out how to apply their tools in the new context. For now, let's leave these important considerations behind and focus on only the mechanical issues of setting up charts to cover multiple time frames. In the end, your charts must be a tool that serves your trading style, not the other way around.

Many authors have written about the advantages of combining multiple time frames. Multiple time frames can provide context for and inform patterns on a single time frame; skilled use of multiple time frames allows traders to better manage risk and to increase the expectancy of their trading plans. Nearly all technical traders consider action and structure in other time frames, though they do this in a variety of ways. Some traders are able to infer this information from a single chart, while many others prefer to actually look at multiple charts of the same market with each chart showing a different time frame. In a scheme like this, the primary time frame of focus is called the *trading time frame (TTF)*. A *higher time frame (HTF)* chart provides a bigger-picture perspective, while a *lower time frame (LTF)* chart is usually used to find precise entry points. Other variations, with up to five or six charts, are possible, and there are many traders who use only a pair of charts. Last, though the term *time frame* seems to imply that the x-axis of the chart will be a time scale (minutes, hours, days, etc.), the same proportional relationships can be applied to tick, volume, or any other activity-based axis scale on the x-axis.

In general, time frames should be related to each other by a factor of 3 to 5. There is no magic in these ratios, but the idea is that each time frame should provide new information without loss of resolution or unnecessary repetition. For instance, if a trader is watching a 30-minute chart, a 5- or 10-minute chart probably provides new information about what is going on inside each 30-minute bar, whereas a 1-minute chart would omit significant information. Using a 20-minute chart in conjunction with a 30-minute chart probably adds no new information, as the two charts will be very similar. One lesser-known relationship is that all vertical distances on charts scale with the square

root of the ratio of the time frames. This has implications for risk management, profit targets, stops, and volatility on each time frame. For instance, if a trader has been trading a system on 5-minute charts with $0.25 stops and wishes to transfer that to 30-minute charts, the stops will probably need to be adjusted to about $0.61 ($0.25 × $\sqrt{30/5}$). This relationship does not hold exactly in all markets and all time frames, but it is a good rule of thumb and can give some insight into the risks and rewards of other time frames.

The rule of consistency also applies to choice of time frames. Once you have settled on a trading style and time frame, be slow to modify it unless you have evidence that it is not working. This story will be told with the most clarity and power in a consistent time frame. In addition, if you catch yourself wanting to look at a time frame you never look at while you are in a losing trade, be very careful. This is often a warning of an impending break of discipline.

Bars, Candles, or Other Choices

Most traders today seem to be focused on using candlestick charts, but the more old-fashioned bar charts should not be overlooked. Both chart types display the same data points but in a slightly different format; they have the same information on them, so one is not better than the other. The main advantage of bar charts is that they can be cleaner visually and it is usually possible to fit more data in the same space because bars are thinner than candles. For many traders, the colors of candlestick charts make it easier to see the buying and selling pressure in the market, providing another important visual cue that helps the trader process the data faster.

Another issue to consider, particularly with intraday charts, is how much importance should be attached to the closing print of each period. Historically, this was *the* price in many markets, and it still has significance in some contexts. Profits and losses (P&Ls), margins, and various spreads are calculated off daily settlement prices; exchanges have complex procedures for calculating these prices, which are rarely simply the last print of the session. However, times are changing. In currencies, most domestic platforms report a closing price sometime in the New York afternoon, and we have to wonder just how important that price is for the Australian dollar or the yen, whose primary sessions ended many hours earlier. As more and more markets go to 24-hour sessions, the importance of this daily settlement price will continue to decline. The problem is even more significant on intraday bars, bar as closing prices on intraday bars are essentially random samples and may differ from platform to platform. If you are trading candlestick patterns, which attach great significance to the close, you are trading the patterns you see on your screen. If you switched to a different data provider, the data might be time-stamped differently, and you would see different patterns. How important can those patterns really be?

INDICATORS

Indicators are calculated measures that are plotted on price charts, either on top of the price bars or in panels above or below the bars. There are many different indicators in common usage, and traders have a wide range of approaches and applications for these tools. Some traders are minimalists, using few or no indicators at all, while others will use multiple indicators in complex relationships. In addition, some indicators are extremely simple calculations, while others are very complex, perhaps even using complex calculations borrowed from other applications such as radar or digital signal processing. There is certainly no one right way to set up or use indicators, but, here again, consistency is paramount. Few traders find success by constantly switching between indicators. There is no holy grail or combination of tools that will lead to easy trading profits.

One other important point is that you must intimately understand the tools you use. Know how they will react to all market conditions, and know what they are saying about the market structure and price action at any time. Focus on tools that highlight and emphasize important elements of market structure, because your main focus should be on the price bars themselves. Intuition comes from repeated exposure to structured data in well-planned and consistent contexts; make your chart setups serve this purpose. Much of this book—and Chapter 7 and Appendix B in particular—focuses on these ideas and reinforces the importance of fully understanding every tool you use.

THE TWO FORCES: TOWARD A NEW UNDERSTANDING OF MARKET ACTION

Price action is a complex and imperfectly defined subject. There are many traders who believe that price action is something nebulous that cannot be quantified. To other traders, trading price action means trading the patterns of price bars on charts, without the addition of indicators or other lines. In this book, price action simply means how markets usually move, which, frankly, is, usually randomly. Be clear on this point: markets are *usually* random and most of the patterns markets create are also random. However, we can sometimes identify spots where price movement is something less than random and is somewhat more predictable, and these less-than-random spots may offer profitable trading opportunities.

Price action is the term used to describe the market's movements in a dynamic state. Price action creates *market structure*, which is the static record of how prices moved in the past. Think about a finger tracing a line in the sand. Market structure is the line left in the sand; price action describes the actual movements of the finger as it drew the line. In the case of a finger, we would talk about smooth or jerky, fast or slow, and lightly or with deep pressure into the sand. In the case of actual price action, we would look at elements such as: How does the market react after a large movement in one direction? If aggressive sellers are pressing the market lower, what happens when they relax their selling pressure? Does the market bounce back quickly, indicating that buyers are potentially interested in these depressed prices, or does it sit quietly, resting at lower levels? How rapidly are new orders coming into the market? Is trading one-directional, or is there more two-way, back-and-forth trading? Are price levels reached through continuous motion, or do very large orders cause large jerks in prices? All of these elements, and many more, combine to describe how the market moves in response to order flow and a myriad of competing influences.

In the past, many authors have used a wide range of analogies to describe financial markets. Ideas and models have been borrowed from the physical and mathematical sciences, so terms like momentum, inertia, vectors, and trajectories have crept into the vocabulary. More recently, some thinkers have applied the tools of digital signal processing to market data, so we have a new vocabulary that includes cycles, transforms, and waves. Markets are confusing enough in their natural state; some of the analytical frameworks traders use add to the confusion. I propose a simpler model: that market action appears to be the result of two interacting forces: a *motive force* that attempts to move price from one level to another and a *resistive force* that opposes the motive force. These forces represent the sum of all analysis and decision making at any one time.

The normal state of existence in most markets most of the time is equilibrium. The two forces are in balance. Buyers and sellers have no sharp disagreement over price; the market may drift around a central value, but there are no large trends or price changes. Market action in this environment is highly random; if we were to analyze this type of action statistically, we would find that it conforms very closely to a random walk model. This is also precisely the type of environment that technically motivated traders must strive to avoid, as there can be no enduring statistical edge in a randomly driven market.

Markets in this state of equilibrium will have varying degrees of liquidity and ability to absorb large orders. Eventually, there is a failure of liquidity on one side, and the market makes a sudden, large movement in one direction. Perhaps this movement is in response to new information coming into the market, or it can simply be a result of a random price movement setting off further movement in the same direction. No matter the reason behind the movement, in theoretical terms, the motive force has, at least temporarily, overcome the resistive force. In the parlance of technical analysis, this type of sharp movement is called an *impulse move* or a *momentum move.*

From this point, there are basically two options. In many cases, the resistive force is quickly able to overcome the motive force, and the market finds balance again. This may be at a new level, or prices may immediately retrace their course and return to the preshock levels. Psychologically, market participants have chosen to view this large price movement as a temporary aberration, and new liquidity comes into the market that will dampen any future distortion. However, it is possible that the large price spike will lead to continued movement in the same direction. In this scenario, a feedback loop develops where the market makes a large movement, which, in turn, provokes another large price movement, and the market trends.

In most cases, the market structure of this trending movement will be a series of directional moves alternating with nondirectional periods in which the market essentially rests and absorbs the previous move. In the bigger picture, the motive force has overcome the resistive force, but there is still a subtle interplay of balance and imbalance on shorter time frames. Prices trend because of an imbalance of buying and selling pressure. (This is often, but not always, indicative of nonrandom action, as trends exist in completely random data.) Once prices are trending, at some point they will have moved far enough that the resistive force is once again able to balance the motive force, and the market again finds a new balance.

This interplay of motive and resistive forces, from a very high-level perspective, is the essence of price action and the root of technical analysis. The patterns we see in the market are only reflections of the convictions of buyers and sellers. They are useful because we can see them, trade them, and use them to define risk, but always remember that they are manifestations of deeper forces in the marketplace.

PRICE ACTION AND MARKET STRUCTURE ON CHARTS

Charts are a way to organize and to structure the flood of information the market generates and can reveal clues about the strength of the underlying forces. There is no one right way to read a chart, but I will share the basic elements of an approach that has been very useful to me over the years. These tools and this framework have shown themselves to be reliable time and time again, but these are *my* tools and *my* method. You must make them *your own* tools. Use everything here as a collection of ideas from which you can begin to build your own approach to the markets.

Market structure refers to the static structure visible on charts, made up of previous movements in the market and places where those movements stopped. The key elements of market structure are *pivot points* and the *swings* connecting them, both of which may be evaluated either in price (the vertical axis on a chart), in time (the horizontal axis), or in a combination of the two.

Price action is the dynamic process that creates market structure. Price action is also more subjective; in most cases, market structure is concrete. Market structure is static and is clearly visible on a chart, but price action usually must be inferred from market structure. Also, both are specific to time frames, though price action is often visible as the market structure of lower time frames. These definitions and their implications will become clear over the next chapters.

Pivot Points

The basic units of market structure on any time frame are pivot highs and lows (also called swing highs or lows). A *pivot high* is a bar that has a higher high than the bar that came before it and the bar that comes after it. At least in the very short term, the bar's high represents the high-water mark past which buyers were not able to push price, and can be considered a very minor source of potential resistance. A *pivot low* is the same concept inverted: a bar with a lower low relative to both the preceding and the following bars. Figure 1.3 shows a chart with every pivot high and pivot low marked. Note that it is possible for a bar to be both a pivot high and a pivot low at the same time, and that pivot highs and pivot lows are very common.

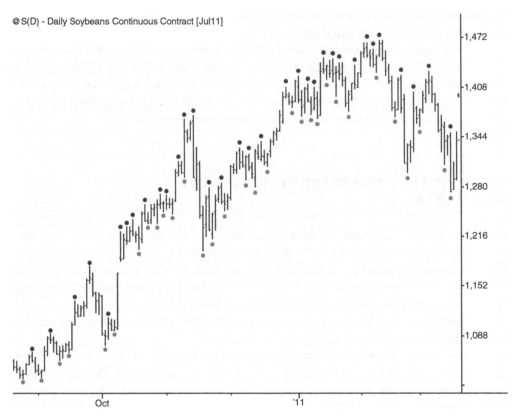

@ S(D) - Daily Soybeans Continuous Contract [Jul11]

FIGURE 1.3 Every Pivot High and Low

Another name for the type of pivot in Figure 1.3 is a *first-order pivot*. Though these first-order pivots do sometimes coincide with major turning points in the market, they are so common that they cannot be extremely significant. Every major turning point, by definition, comes at a pivot, so it is easy to overstate their importance; once you see a chart with every possible pivot marked, it becomes obvious that this structure is so common that it is nearly insignificant. It is also interesting to consider that most pivots on one time frame mark significant market structures on lower time frames, but this is a complication that we will save for later. As a stand-alone concept, first-order pivot highs and lows have limited utility; their power comes from their relationship to other pivots and their ability to define market structure. They are like a single brick in a building—not that interesting or useful by itself.

Second-order pivot highs (also called intermediate-term pivots) are first-order pivot highs that are preceded and followed by lower first-order pivot highs; again, this structure is inverted for second-order pivot lows. In Figure 1.4, notice that these second-order pivots begin to define some more significant structural points. It is much more likely that second-order pivots will come at important turning points, but remember that there is no predictive power because this is a pattern that is defined post hoc. They always look far

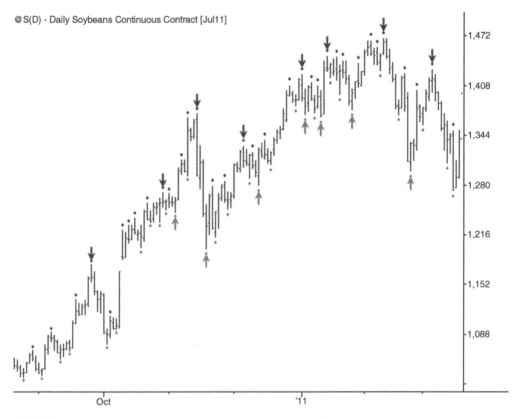

FIGURE 1.4 Second-Order Pivots (Marked with Arrows) Define More Important Market Structure

more significant in the middle of a chart than they do on the right edge. It is also worth noting that there is no law that says second-order pivot highs and lows have to alternate; it is possible to have three second-order pivot highs or lows in a row. If you are going to use this concept systematically, make sure your rules plan for this situation.

Predictably, this concept can be extended on many levels, but in actual practice, most of our focus is on third-order pivots, which usually mark major inflections (see Figure 1.5). Almost without exception, a trader who could identify these third-order pivots in advance would have nearly perfect entries on both sides of the market. This cannot be done, but it does point out that these third-order pivots delineate the market structure very clearly. It is worth your time to train your eye to see these pivots quickly; the value in this structure is in providing context for the market's movements. Once you understand the basic ideas behind this concept, it is probably a good idea to not be too rigid with these structures and definitions. If you see something on a chart that is fulfilling the basic role of one of these structures but for one reason or another does not exactly fit the criteria, it often makes sense to bend the rules for that case. The goal is to define meaningful market structure, not to blindly follow a set of rules.

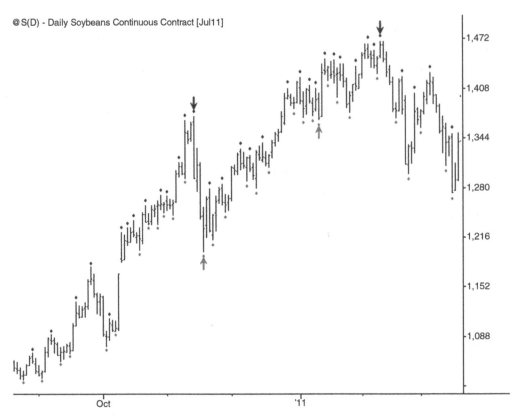

FIGURE 1.5 Third-Order Pivots Usually Define the Most Important Market Structure on Any Time Frame

It also should be obvious that this is a backward-looking analytical method. This is a problem with all swing or wave methods: they offer fantastic *explanations* of past market action, but have little or no predictive power at the right edge. This pivot structure is not intended to be a trading methodology; it is context. For instance, a sharp down move might be interpreted differently if it comes at a point where the market had been making consistently higher second-order pivot highs and lows compared to an environment where they were more randomly distributed. As another example, a movement that penetrates a significant third-order pivot high or low can sometimes significantly change the market environment. The purpose of this tool is to provide that structure and context, not actual trade entries.

Length of Swing

Once we have defined the second- or third-order pivot structure of the market, we can connect the pivot highs and lows with lines to outline the swing structure of the market. (In the spots where highs and lows do not alternate, take the lowest low of the series or the highest high of the series as the anchor point.) If this type of analysis is new to you, it is probably a good idea to draw the structure on a few hundred charts until it becomes somewhat intuitive; eventually you want to be able to glance at a chart and see this structure immediately. Like everything else, it gets easier only with continued practice and familiarity. It is impossible to overstate the importance of this skill.

Once the individual swings are delineated, we can start to consider what the market structure actually tells us about the balance of buying and selling pressure in the market. The core concepts are simple:

- When buyers are stronger than sellers, upswings will be longer, both in price and in time, than downswings.
- When sellers are in control, downswings will be longer than upswings.
- Significant support and resistance levels are visible as rough areas (not precise lines) beyond which pivots have been unable to penetrate.
- When there is relative equilibrium, there is no clear pattern to the swings.

There is nothing mysterious about market structure and price action. They grow from these simple patterns, which then combine in a nearly infinite number of variations. Focusing on the variations is difficult because they are legion—it is an exercise in futility to try to catalog all of the complexities and variations of patterns, though this attempt has been repeated many times throughout history. Understand the root. Understand the market structure. There are a handful of common patterns and templates that provide the foundation for most of the significant patterns in the market. We will spend much of the rest of this book refining these templates, looking at specific ways to trade around them, and considering how to manage the risk of those trades. Here is a brief introduction to a few of the most important of these patterns. Commit them to memory; you will be seeing them again.

Figure 1.6 shows the basic uptrend template: upswings are longer than the downswings, creating a consistent pattern of higher pivot lows and higher pivot highs. This pattern, inverted, would become a downtrend.

Figure 1.7 shows a market in a trading range. This is a random environment in which the conviction of buyers and sellers is relatively equal and there is no clear pattern to

FIGURE 1.6 An Uptrend

FIGURE 1.7   A Trading Range

FIGURE 1.8   A Break in the Uptrend Pattern

prices. There can be sudden, sharp moves within trading ranges, but they are often more or less unpredictable.

Figure 1.8 shows a pattern that gives a warning of a break in an uptrend's established pattern. This is often the first step of a trend change, but you cannot trade based only on this pattern; this is a warning sign to pay careful attention to what comes next. There is great value in knowing when patterns have broken, as this suggests a potential change in the balance of buyers and sellers in the market.

Figure 1.9 shows an example of a classic breakout above resistance. This suggests one of two things: On one hand, markets in trading ranges (see Figure 1.7) are highly random and this type of move may be nothing more than a random (and temporary) move beyond previous levels. On the other hand, it could be an early warning that buying

FIGURE 1.9   A Breakout of the Trading Range

FIGURE 1.10 A Breakout Preceded by Higher Lows into Resistance

pressure is now stronger than selling pressure in this market, and it is possible that prices could trend significantly higher from this point.

Figure 1.10 shows a particular pattern that often precedes the best breakouts. If buyers are able to hold the market higher on successive declines, a pattern of higher pivot lows pressing against the resistance area will result. This suggests real buying conviction supporting the move and the potential breakout.

This is certainly not a complete encyclopedia of swing patterns, but it does highlight the basic concept: the length of swings and the relative position of pivot points can give insight into the character of the market.

Market Structure versus Traditional Chart Patterns

There are two broad schools of thought in technical analysis. One approach is to catalog every possible chart pattern and variation of those patterns. A trader using this approach might look for wedges, pennants, flags, boxes, ledges, head and shoulders patterns, and double tops and bottoms—these are only a few of the traditional patterns, and many more have worked their way into modern practice. These traders spend a lot of time studying these patterns and variations, and they usually have specific trading plans for each pattern. Richard Schabacker was the first writer to codify this approach, in the late 1920s, and it was crystallized in his landmark 1932 *Technical Analysis and Stock Market Profits*.

Upon his early death in 1935, his brother-in-law, Robert Edwards, took over the company he had founded and continued his work of market analysis. Later, Edwards teamed up with John Magee, and the two wrote *Technical Analysis of Stock Trends* (1948; 4th ed., 1964), which is now considered to be the ultimate, authoritative source on chart patterns. The Schabacker approach (which is not known by that name because few people know the history behind Edwards and Magee) is the predominant school of modern technical analysis, but there is another path.

The second broad school of technical analysis is Richard Wyckoff's approach. The core concept here is that chart patterns have very limited utility, and what predictive power they do have is highly dependent on the context in which they appear. The only real purpose of

(Continued)

chart patterns is to quantify and to define the buying and selling pressure in the market. In many cases, traders using both approaches will arrive at similar conclusions. These are two different means to the same end, but many traders find a richness and depth in the Wyckoff approach that surpasses a simplistic focus on chart patterns. We trade the underlying buying and selling imbalance, which is what will move price in our favor if we are correct.

Reading Inside the Bars

One skill that is often overlooked in chart reading is the ability to look at a bar on a chart and to infer what price action might have created that bar. In practical terms, this means being able to look at a bar on one time frame and immediately understand the most likely lower time frame scenarios that could have created that bar. In almost every case, there are multiple possibilities, but some are much more likely than others. It is not necessary to be 100 percent correct on this; sometimes we will simply guess wrong, but working to develop this skill will greatly increase the trader's intuitive grasp of price charts. For instance, consider the single candle in Figure 1.11 with an empty body (meaning that the close was higher than the open) and with moderately small shadows on the top and bottom. There are three things we know with certainty about this candle: the close was higher than the open; at some point, the market traded lower than the open; and, at some point, it traded higher than the close.

Most people with a little bit of trading experience would assume the candle opened, traded down to put in the low, trended up to make a high, and backed off to close under

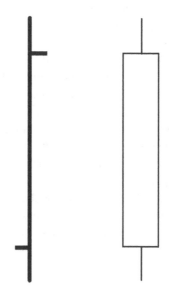

FIGURE 1.11 A Candle Is a Snapshot in Time—How Was This Candle Formed?

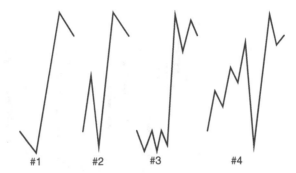

FIGURE 1.12 Some of the Many Possibilities of Lower Time Frame Action That Could Have Produced Figure 1.11

that high. This is the most obvious possibility (scenario #1 in Figure 1.12), but there are many others, some of which are also shown. Traders developing a sense for price action need to spend a lot of time contemplating all of the lower time frame scenarios that could produce each bar. Being locked into a single interpretation without considering the context can blind us to what might really be going on in the market.

Though charts contain a lot of noise and random action, there are points where structures within individual bars, or a small set of bars, are very important. One simple pattern to think about is that the location of the closing point relative to the high and the low of the bar may give some insight into the buying or selling conviction within that bar. For instance, a close near the high of the bar usually shows that buyers were in control going into the end of the time period. Yes, there are other possibilities and patterns that could have created the close near the high, but, more often than not, buyers were in control. Conversely, closes near the middle of the bar, visible as long shadows on candle charts, show a certain neutrality and lack of conviction. It is also worth considering the extreme case where several bars in a row close on their absolute highs. Many traders would assume that this is indicative of a very strong market, but, statistically, this condition more often indicates short-term exhaustion and at least a slight reversal—be careful of entering with the trend after several bars close on their highs.

Trend and Trading Range Bars Large bars relative to recent bars on one time frame most likely contain trends on the lower time frame, especially if the close and open are near opposite ends of the bars. Small bars on one time frame are probably trading ranges on lower time frames, and, in general, bars that have their opens and closes nearer to the center point of the bar are also more likely to have been trading ranges. This is a simple concept, but understanding this dynamic is a key to building intuition about price action and the interaction of time frames. There is much subtlety here, but these are the essential concepts. Figure 1.13 shows lower time frame trends and trading ranges within the three boxes in the left panel that correspond to the three higher time frame bars in the right panel. Do not accept price bars at face value. Always think deeply about what is going on behind the scenes, on lower time frames.

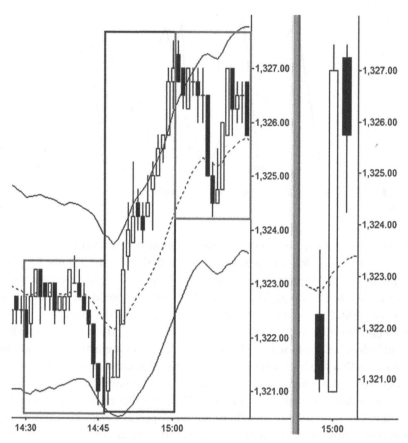

FIGURE 1.13 One- and 15-Minute S&P Bars, Showing Lower Time Frame Trading Range and Trend within Higher Time Frame Bars

The right panel of Figure 1.14 shows a daily chart of the E-mini S&P 500 futures at a time when the trend on that time frame was losing momentum. What are the signs on this time frame that suggest a loss of momentum? Each bar continues to make a higher high up into mid-April, but at a declining rate. We could characterize these as "reluctant highs," to indicate waning momentum. In addition, the bars are becoming smaller, indicating that trading interest is drying up, and there are no more large trend bars (that open near the lows and close near the highs) in April. On each of the multiple time frame charts in this book, the lower time frame in the left pane expands on the highlighted area of the higher time frame chart on the right. In this case, the lower time frame tells the same story of loss of momentum, but in much more vivid detail. There are multiple failure tests above the highs, as the market spikes to new extremes and is unable to find the buying pressure to support itself there. Note that this reversal on the lower time frame could simply be subsumed into a trading time frame consolidation, but the lower time frame clearly shows the change in the buyers' conviction.

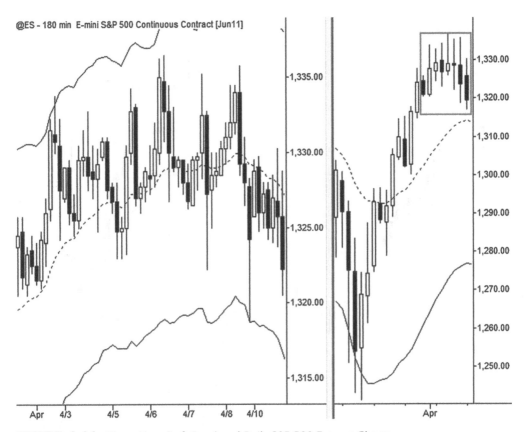

FIGURE 1.14 Three-Hour (Left Pane) and Daily S&P 500 Futures Charts

Notice that the lower time frame shows multiple tests and failures at the high. This level of resolution is lost on the higher time frame, which simply shows a gently rounding top.

Many traders focus on trading *pullbacks*. A pullback (also called a *flag* or *consolidation*) is a move against the prevailing trend. For instance, a pullback in a downtrend bounces against the trend and is an opportunity to enter a short position; a pullback in an uptrend is a decline. Most traders train themselves to see these structures easily, but pullbacks can also be hidden in higher time frames: one or two small bars that hold near the extreme of a trend leg (near the lows in a downtrend or the highs in an uptrend) are often a complete lower time frame pullback. As such, these simple one- or two-bar pullbacks (*high and tight flags*) are tradable structures in very strong trends, as in Figure 1.15. This is a common and important pattern.

Another important pullback pattern in an uptrend has several bars with downward closes separated by a single bar with an upward close. This pattern usually hides a complex pullback on the lower time frame, which is a three-legged structure consisting of an initial pullback followed by a small, failed attempt to resume the initial trend. From that second leg, the market turns down again to make another countertrend leg that is usually approximately as long as the first one. This is a very common pattern, especially

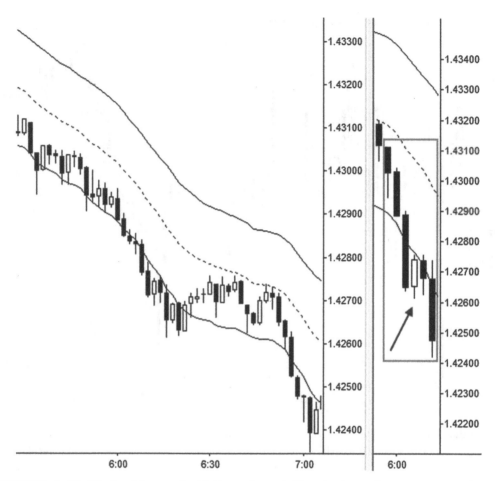

FIGURE 1.15 The Small Bars on the 15-Minute EURUSD Chart (Right Pane) Hide a More Significant Pullback on the 2-Minute Lower Time Frame

in extended trends, and will be explored in much more detail later. Figure 1.16 shows an example of a two-legged complex pullback. On the higher trading time frame, it is not so obvious and has to be inferred from the presence of one or two with-trend candles in the middle of the pullback, but the complete structure is clearly visible on the lower time frame.

One of the quantifiable tendencies of price motion is for markets to make directional moves out of periods of contracted volatility. Even if the normal expectation for a market is mean reversion and reversal (as it is in the short term for equities), there is usually at least a slight edge for continuation out of areas of volatility compression. One simple way to quantify volatility contraction is by looking for inside bars, which are bars whose entire range is enclosed within the range of the previous bar—in other words, a bar whose high is equal to or lower than the previous high and whose low is above or equal to the previous low. A series of multiple inside bars on one time frame usually contains a

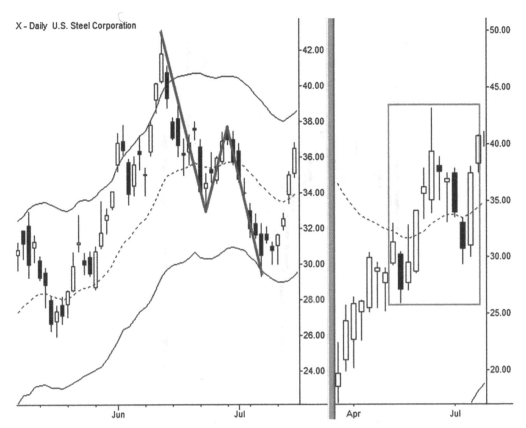

FIGURE 1.16 The Daily Chart of X (Left Pane) Shows a Clear Two-Legged Complex Pullback
The weekly chart hints at this structure, but it must be inferred from the single upward-closing candle in the middle of the pullback.

triangle on the lower time frame, which is a visual pattern that strongly suggests volatility contraction. Trading *within* triangles is usually a losing proposition, as the market is in equilibrium and the actual movement within the pattern is highly random. However, they can set up good breakouts with expectations for strong, extended moves away from the pattern. It is easy to overlook multiple inside bars (see Figure 1.17), but this is a powerful and subtle pattern that is worth some attention.

The examples in this section were deliberately chosen to be less than perfect because it is important to start thinking about these concepts in the context of actual market action, which is always less clear and noisier than we wish. Remember that charts are artificial structures that we impose on market data. They are useful because they organize the data, but we are always dealing with a trade-off between effective summarization and loss of detail. There is no perfect answer, but many of the limitations can be overcome if we work to constantly remember what the chart actually is, and to try to understand the buying and selling pressure that each bar represents. The chart is not the market; the chart is a *representation* of the market.

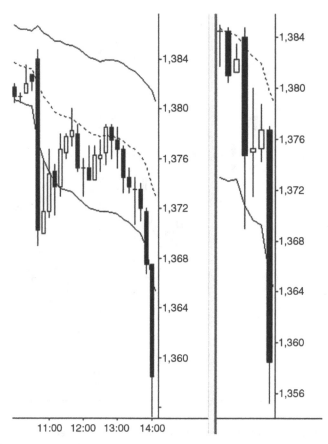

FIGURE 1.17 Multiple Inside Bars on the Hourly Chart of the E-mini S&P 500 Futures (Right Pane) Hide a Clear Lower Time Frame Triangle on the 10-Minute Chart

CHARTING BY HAND

I started trading in the 1990s, in the twilight years of the old, classic paper chart books. A book would come in the mail at the beginning of the week, printed on newsprint; each day it was up to the trader to track down prices for each of the markets and update the charts by drawing a new price bar. At the beginning of the next week, a new book would arrive with the past week's prices filled in, and the process would repeat. Actually, in my very early trading days I did not even have the chart book, but I bought a pad of graph paper, went to the library, and started building charts from histories I found in back issues of newspapers. I did not realize the value of what I was doing at the time, but this process immersed me in patterns as they were emerging. There is something about physically drawing lines that engages a different part of the brain than looking at a screen does. Because of this work, I assimilated patterns quickly and developed a sense of the forces at work behind the patterns early in my development. When you are drawing open, high, low, and close on each price bar, you will spend time during the day wondering what new configurations could appear at the end of the day, and thinking about how the day's trading might unfold to create those patterns.

Most readers are probably shaking their heads and laughing at this point, thinking that this is a quaint and hopelessly anachronistic practice, but I beg to differ. Modern computer charting has the advantage of breadth. It would simply not be possible to review a large number of charts every day without the aid of a computer to generate those charts; however, there is still great value in pencil and paper. This is not a practice that will reward you with immediate results and profits; it works on a much deeper and more profound level of perception, and it takes time. I would suggest that interested traders commit to doing this for a period of not less than two months, consistently, and then evaluate the impact of the exercise on your ability to read the market. I know of no better exercise to help a developing trader assimilate the patterns of the market and to begin building intuition. You will be amazed at the transformation in your vision.

There are two specific ways to do this exercise. One is to simply plot standard bar or candle charts, by hand, for whatever time period is under consideration. Every trader can at least do daily charts, but intraday traders might be able to do 15- to 30-minute time frames. Lower time frames will give much more exposure to patterns, but the time for contemplation is reduced. Above all, you want to pick a time frame that will allow you to make an unfailing commitment to this exercise. Doing it for a few days and then giving up will result in nothing but wasted time.

The other way is to construct a swing chart, which is also known as a *kagi* chart. In this type of chart, vertical lines indicate price movement (along the y-axis of the chart), while short horizontal lines illustrate the breaks between upswings and downswings. These breaks are defined according to some rule set, the specific choice of which is not that important. Traditionally, you may look for a specific dollar or point amount of a reversal off a high, and then flip direction, as in a standard point and figure chart. For instance, suppose a trader is working with a $1.00 reversal; if the stock trades up to

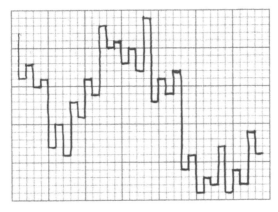

FIGURE 1.18 Example of Swing Charting (Kagi) by Hand

$60.00 and then backs off to $59.25, this is only a $0.75 reversal off the high, so the only line on the chart is currently a vertical line that stops at $60.00. If the market turns back up from $59.25 and trades up to $65.00, that original line is now extended to $65.00 on the chart. Assume now that the market falls back to $63.00, which exceeds the $1.00 reversal threshold, so now a short horizontal line is plotted at $65.00 (the high of the previous swing) to connect to the next downward vertical line, which now extends to $63.00. This process is repeated, so the x-axis is not scaled for time or activity, but rather for specific reversal amounts off previous swings. (Consider what this type of chart tells us in relation to the previous discussions on pivots and length of swings.) It is also possible to define the reversal with other tools, such as reversing a specific multiple of the average range off the previous swing, J. Welles Wilder Jr.'s Parabolic SAR (stop and reverse), moving average crossovers, or whatever trend indicator you find appropriate. Figure 1.18 shows an example of this type of chart, drawn by hand. Do not underestimate the power of this simple charting exercise.

CHAPTER 2

The Market Cycle and the Four Trades

To every thing there is a season, and a time to every purpose under the heaven.

—Ecclesiastes 3:1, KJV

The early twentieth century was a time of great progress in markets and in thinking about markets. There were giants on the earth in those days—legends like Jesse Livermore, old man J. P. Morgan, Bernard Baruch, and Charles Dow. In this fertile environment, Richard Wyckoff developed his understanding of markets and the trading process through conversations and interviews with these master traders. After amassing a sizable personal fortune in the markets, he laid out his system in a set of correspondence courses, as was the practice of the day, to educate the public and to help them avoid the scams and frauds that were so prevalent at the time. Referring to the Wyckoff method is a bit of a misnomer, for he offered no simple system or one way to trade. Rather, Wyckoff created a method for understanding the buying and selling convictions of very large traders and institutions through the patterns their activity left on prices. If the smaller trader could recognize the signs they left in the market, he could align his positions with their activity and interests; in the end, it is the buying and selling pressure of these large pools of money that actually moves the markets. This method is as powerful and as relevant today as it was a hundred years ago.

Wyckoff proposed a four-stage market cycle. His idea was that the cycle resulted from the actions of these large players who planned their operations in the market to take advantage of the uneducated public's inappropriate reactions to price movement, but we also see evidence of this cycle in the price patterns of assets such as medieval commodity prices; stocks in early, unsophisticated markets; or trading on very short time frames. It is unlikely that there is the same intervention and manipulation in all of these cases, so the Wyckoff cycle may simply be an expression of the normal ways in which human psychology expresses itself in the marketplace.

WYCKOFF'S MARKET CYCLE

In this brief introduction, we will consider three aspects of each phase of the cycle. First, we will try to understand the market using a simplified model focusing on the psychological perspective of two major groups: the smart money players who are assumed to be driving the market, and the general, uninformed public. Second, we will consider the crowd psychology of the public, and how individuals are naturally inclined to make mistakes that work in favor of the smart money. Last, we will begin to consider the distinctions and patterns of each part of the cycle from a pure price-pattern perspective; this analysis is important because it motivates and provides context for many trading patterns and methods.

Figure 2.1 presents this cycle in a simple, idealized format. The four phases are:

1. *Accumulation:* A sideways range in which large players buy carefully and skillfully, without moving the price. The public is unaware of what is going on; the market is off the radar and out of the public focus while under accumulation.

2. *Markup:* The classic uptrend. At this point, the public becomes aware of the price movement, and their buying serves to propel prices higher. Smart money players who bought in the accumulation phase may sell some of their holdings into the strength of the uptrend, or they may just hold and wait for higher prices.

3. *Distribution:* Eventually, the uptrend ends and the market enters a distribution phase in which the smart money players sell the remainder of their holdings to the public who are still generally anticipating higher prices. Really smart money players might even sell more than they own and go short in this range.

4. *Markdown:* The downtrend that follows distribution. Smart money players who are short will buy back some of their shorts into this weakness. Eventually, the public realizes that higher prices are not in their future, so they panic and sell their positions. This panic, more often than not, marks the end of the downtrend.

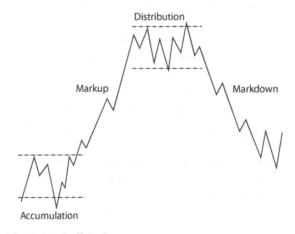

FIGURE 2.1 The Classic Wyckoff Cycle

Accumulation—Building a Base

Accumulation is the first stage of the cycle; large operators (funds, banks, other institutions, or even large individual traders) buy without alerting the public to their intentions. This is actually very difficult to do, as buying pressure will naturally support and even raise prices. These players must buy slowly and generally passively over a long period of time to build their positions. From a technical perspective, prices move sideways in a trading range bounded by rough areas of support and resistance, an intermediate-term moving average is flat, and price chops back and forth on both sides of that moving average. As we mentioned earlier, these conditions are indicative of a market in equilibrium, and most technical traders should avoid trading price action like this. However, Wyckoff argues that this is precisely the goal of the longer-term players. They are working very hard to make this look like a market in equilibrium, but it is not. There is a subtle imbalance as smart money is buying and accumulating positions in preparation for the coming uptrend.

There are a few important points to keep in mind about a market in accumulation. First, there is the obvious play of positioning in the accumulation area with the smart money; in most cases this is essentially a higher time frame play. The line between trading and investing can become somewhat blurred if the technical trader plays in these areas, but the key difference is that traders remain alert for signs that the accumulation has failed. If contradictory price action and market structure emerge, they will exit their positions, while investors will usually wait for lagging fundamentals to signify that something has changed. This leads to the second point, which is that accumulation areas are usually not simple plays in actual practice. It is difficult to time the precise beginning and end of these areas, and the limits of the range are often not cleanly defined. Traders paying breakouts above the range, or stopping out of their positions below the range, will often find themselves executing at exactly the wrong points as they react to price spikes in the noisy range. This is what the market action is designed to do in these areas, so do not play this game.

There are some price patterns and clues we typically see associated with classic accumulation. The most common of these is what Wyckoff called a *spring*, which is called a *failure test* at the bottom of the range in modern terminology. To understand this pattern, think of it from the perspective of the large players accumulating inventory in the range. If these large buyers were to go into the market and buy aggressively, that buying pressure would be a significant portion of the market activity. The market would almost certainly explode higher, which is not what the large players want at this point. It is critical that they measure their buying activity over a long period of time so that they do not lift prices; it is a game of deception. If these large players discover that they can consistently get filled near the bottom of the range (where the market is cheapest), they might buy even more slowly to see if the prices would decline even further. Low prices are *good* for these players, who are trying to accumulate large positions at the lowest possible price. What if they wanted to judge the other market participants' interest in the stock? Perhaps they might stop buying altogether and let the market fall under its own weight.

From this point, there are two different scenarios that they would be watching for. In one, the market drops and keeps dropping, and they see that the rest of the market really has no conviction or interest. Depending on their plan for the campaign, this might or might not affect their decision to continue buying. Perhaps they are very happy to buy the market even lower, or perhaps it is weaker than they expected and they might have to slowly unwind their positions. Large players like these do not take significant losses very often, but they are also not always right. The other possibility is that they stop buying and the market falls, but other buyers immediately step in and arrest the decline. In this case, the large players just got an important piece of information: there is underlying buying interest in the market.

Keep in mind that these types of buyers, and so this type of price action, tend to be very large and very slow moving. These are usually institutions that may buy many times the stock's average daily trading volume, so most of these plays develop on an almost glacial scale; but, even so, there are critical inflection points that can be defined in minutes or seconds. These drops below the bottom of the accumulation range are examples of specific points in time that require attention and focus.

The presence of other buyers just under the level where the institutions were buying telegraphs real interest. The large player would probably be compelled to immediately resume their buying plan, working very hard to not spook the market. Again, it is a game of deception. If enough players sense the buying pressure, the market will explode into an uptrend, and the large players do not want this until they have accumulated their full line. This type of activity leaves a distinctive and important pattern on a price chart: it will be clear that the market has defined a support area and that price has probed below that support, but that the market spent very little time there because buyers immediately stepped in and pressed the market higher. This is one pattern that candlestick charts can highlight well. Candles with long shadows extending below support but with few or no closes below that support are a sign of accumulation. If we were to look inside the candles on a lower time frame, we would see that most of those excursions below support lasted less than a quarter of the time frame of each candle (i.e., a daily chart spends at most a few hours below support, an hourly chart less than 15 minutes, etc.). Figure 2.2 shows an accumulation area in daily October 2010 Platinum futures. The dotted line is not an exact level, but notice that only candle shadows touch the area—the market is unable to close near the level. Also, the bar marked A is a classic Wyckoff spring, which is a bar that tests below a level and immediately finds buyers. In this case, the price movement off this day led to a multimonth rally.

This is an important lesson about putting chart patterns in context. A simple statistical test of candles with long lower shadows would find that there is no predictive power to that pattern, but when a market is potentially in accumulation, the presence of these springs can distinctly tilt the probabilities in favor of the upside. Everything we do as traders is a matter of shifting probabilities. We deal in probabilities, not certainties, but the position and context of the higher time frame can often provide warning that a market could be under accumulation, lending more importance to these lower time frame patterns. Notice also that this is a subtle pattern. Though these are not exciting patterns, they are important and contribute to a trader's overall read on the market's action. It is

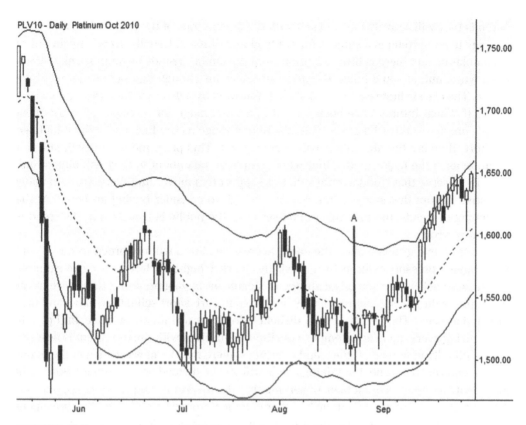

FIGURE 2.2 Accumulation in Daily Platinum Futures with a Classic Spring at A

also worth considering that what I am presenting here is an idealized and simplified perspective on a market in accumulation. In actual practice, these patterns are often much more complex and obscured by noise.

From a longer-term perspective, crowd psychology is simple and easy to understand while a market is in accumulation. If the smart money operators are accumulating well and doing their job right, the public simply does not care about the market. The distinguishing psychological feature of a market in accumulation is that it is off the public's radar; no one is thinking about it or talking about it. No journalist writes an article about a market in sideways consolidation, and no one talks about such markets on television. They are invisible and boring; only smart, professional traders know to watch for these formations. At some point, unobserved and unnoticed, the accumulation breaks to the upside and the stock moves into the next phase of the cycle.

Markup: The Classic Uptrend

The second part of the cycle is the uptrend (*markup*), and the action of the smart money is not as clearly defined here. Perhaps the institutions may simply hold their full line until the stock is marked up to prices at which they consider it advantageous to sell, or perhaps they will actively buy and sell with the fluctuations of the trend. The public psychology in an uptrend is a subject for study in and of itself. Usually, trends begin out of accumulation and there is little attention from the public. Trends begin in sneaky, unnoticed ways, but, at some point, the price advances far enough that people start to take notice. The classic first reaction is disbelief, followed by a desire to fade (go against) the move. If Wheat futures have been locked in a $1.00 range for a couple of years, most people are apt to regard a price $0.50 above that range as too high and will be inclined to short, thinking the aberration will correct itself. This price movement will still not be in focus in the major media, but, when people do talk about it, they will almost universally observe that "fundamentals do not support this move" and there are also many narrative factors that suggest "the risk is too high to consider buying up here." At the beginning of trends, the prevailing mind-set from the public is usually that the trend is somehow wrong.

As the trend grinds higher, the early, aggressive shorts will be forced to cover, and their buying pressure will, in turn, push the market higher. (Here is a clear example where short sellers are actually a source of significant buying pressure; things are never as simple as they seem, and regulatory pressures to curb short selling are naive and misdirected at best.) The public's initial disbelief slowly turns into acceptance, and people start buying every dip in an attempt to position themselves with the trend that is now obvious and fully underway. If the trend continues, there may be news stories in the major media featuring the trend, but talking heads will still be divided on the subject. Some will have switched their bearish bias, observing that the market is simply going up, perhaps "climbing the wall of worry" put up by other commentators who still insist the movement cannot be justified by the fundamentals. If you are positioned long in such a trend, this is good—the division of opinion is fuel for the fire. You *want* dissenting opinions at this point in the market cycle.

We will spend an entire chapter refining our understanding of the characteristic features of price action in trends, but the basic pattern is a series of with-trend legs interspersed with pullbacks, which are also called retracements. Trend traders usually focus a lot of attention on the relationship of each trend leg and pullback to previous legs, in terms of magnitude, length (time), and character (primarily referring to lower time frame price action). Trading plans in trends usually involve either buying into the pullbacks or buying breakouts to new highs as the trend continues higher.

Though there have been many attempts, no one has found a reliable way to judge the large-scale psychology of market participants; however, an understanding of the emotional cycle that drives trend moves is very important. Because market action is, at least to some degree, the sum of many traders' and investors' hopes and fears, many people observe that price action often encourages traders to make mistakes. Markets often present us with the temptation to do the wrong thing at the wrong time, and we will be lured into doing so if we do not understand the psychology of the crowd. Understand this so that you can stand apart from it. The emotional cycle of trends can be summarized as disbelief, acceptance, and, eventually, consensus. When everyone agrees, the trend is usually close to being over.

In some trends, mania sets in and things get a little crazy. Now, *everyone* will be talking about the movement. All the pundits will be in agreement. Even though the market may have appreciated several hundred percent in a year's time, it is now obvious to everyone that there is real demand and the situation is only going to get worse. There will be dire calls of shortages and claims that increased global demand cannot possibly be met by supply. Common sense goes out the window and people do not recognize the significance of the most basic fundamental factors, or, more accurately, they do not understand how fundamental factors change. For instance, in the case of an agricultural commodity, there will be news stories about how the world is running out of the commodity, probably a story here and there about some blight that will destroy the crop on one continent or another, and what are basically calls for the end of the world. For some reason, no one will notice that farmers just planted three times the acreage that was planted in the previous year—the invisible hand is funny like that. Though the manic uptrend seems like an unstoppable force, something very interesting is about to happen: this unstoppable force is about to meet the immovable object in the form of massive supply coming online.

Here is an important lesson for the objective trader: your clue to the fact that psychology has reached the mania stage is when stories begin to show up in the popular, nonfinancial media. At times like that you have one job and one job only—detach yourself from the mass psychology and begin to exit the market. At the very least, you must book partial profits and take steps to reduce the risk on your remaining line.

Distribution—The End?

Nothing goes on forever. At some point, higher prices will bring increased supply into the market, balance is achieved, and prices will stop rising. From a technical perspective, there are, broadly speaking, two ways this can happen. The manic blow-off end-of-trend pattern just discussed is unusual, but deserves attention because it presents dramatic opportunities and dangers. More common is that the uptrend just runs out of steam, and the market goes into another sideways trading range. The large operators who accumulated positions in the first stage and who held most of their line through the markup now begin quietly selling their inventory to the public (*distribution*). In the accumulation phase, it was important that they hide their buying so as to not cause the market to break into an uptrend too early. Similarly, they must now sell carefully because too much selling pressure could crack the market into a downtrend.

To the untrained eye, distribution areas are indistinguishable from accumulation areas—they are both large, sideways ranges. However, on a more subtle level, we will see that many of the classic signs of accumulation will not be present. When prices drop below support, the market will not rebid quite as quickly. In general, prices may spend more time hugging the bottom of the range; pressure against the top of the range is a bit more common in accumulation. There may even be false breakouts of the top of the range, leaving the candles with long shadows above the highs of the range. This pattern is the opposite of the Wyckoff spring, and is usually called an *upthrust*. Eventually, prices will drop below support at the bottom of the range and will fail to bounce. The market will roll over into the last phase, markdown.

Psychologically, the public is usually still hopeful when a market goes into distribution. They will seize every potential breakout as proof that a new uptrend is just around the corner, and will usually look for any excuse to keep buying. Keep in mind that this pattern occurs in markets that have just had substantial advances, so it is easy to say things like "Look, this thing is up 50 percent year over year, the fundamentals are great, and the Street obviously loves it." Every dip is an opportunity to pick up additional shares or contracts, which are now cheaper, so they are basically on sale. Who could pass up such a great opportunity? The public, however, is blind to the subtle differences in patterns that hint that another trend leg up might not be in the cards.

Trading real markets is not quite this simple. For one thing, markets in second-phase uptrends will frequently enter fairly extended sideways ranges in the middle of the trend. Should these be treated as further accumulation areas, in preparation for another markup, or is the trend over and these are distribution areas? There *are* subtle clues in market structure and price action, but it is not always possible to make an accurate judgment in real time. Looking back, or at the middle of a chart, the answer is obvious, but it will not be so obvious at the hard right edge. Even with the best analysis and trading plan, we will simply make the wrong decision sometimes, so any good trading plan will focus on risk management first.

Markdown: The Bear Market

The last stage is *markdown*, which, in many ways, is the inverse of the markup. Psychologically, if the market has been in a protracted distribution phase, the public will most likely have lost some interest. Some traders will be optimistic, and will plan to "get back in" whenever it moves, but, in general, the public focuses on the same things the major media do: hot markets that are moving. These traders will easily be able to justify buying new highs above the distribution area, as this is how another trend leg would begin. They also will be able to justify buying breakdowns below the distribution area, because the market would be cheaper (on sale?) at those levels. The level of interest will probably be relatively low because the public usually focuses on markets that move, but the general tone will likely be very positive. After all, everyone is now in agreement that the market is going higher, right?

Real downtrends begin out of this environment of optimism or complacency. Eventually, it becomes clear that the declines are a little steeper than expected, and some longs begin to unwind their positions, adding to the selling pressure. The mood of the market changes from optimism to disappointment, and aggressive shorts may even begin to show some teeth as they make larger profits on each successive decline. Bounces fall short of previous highs, and people begin to sell even more aggressively. At some point, everyone becomes convinced that the company is going out of business or that commodity is "done" or the currency will never rally, and that the correct play is to short it into oblivion. As you might expect by now, such an emotional extreme more often than not marks the very bottom, and the market stabilizes into accumulation in preparation for the next uptrend.

Market structure and price action in a downtrend are not a perfect mirror image of the first stage, but the differences are subtle and difficult to quantify. One of the major pieces of received wisdom from old-school traders is that markets tend to go down much faster than they go up. There is some truth to this, as volatility reliably expands on declines in many markets, and there is also a subjective side to the analysis, as there is a distinctly different feel to rallies in a bear market compared to sell-offs in a bull market. Both structures are pullbacks in established trends, but there is a special kind of franticness and volatility that seems to be a unique attribute of bear markets. Bear market rallies tend to be sharp and vicious, whereas pullbacks in bull markets are usually much more orderly. There is a surprising degree of symmetry—most elements of uptrends and downtrends are mirror images of each other (reflected around the y-axis), but most traders also find that a very different skill set is required to trade each environment. This may explain why some traders avoid bear markets whereas others specialize in them.

The Cycle in Action

The structure laid out here was originally conceived around the equity markets and on time frames ranging from months to years. It applies especially well there, but it also has relevance to other markets and shorter time frames. Commodity markets tend to follow a similar cycle, but the cycle in commodities is often driven by the production and consumption cycle. Commodities, in general, tend to be a little more cyclical and more prone to seasonal distortions, especially of volatility, than stock indexes are. Currency markets tend to be a little less cyclical and tend to trend better than most other asset classes over longer time frames. That said, there certainly are times when this cycle does apply to the currency markets—for instance, in extreme situations accompanied by emotional elation or stress.

The concept of fractal markets, as Mandelbrot and Hudson (2006) have written about, is especially important when considering the Wyckoff cycle. Simply put, this means that the same patterns appear in very long-term markets as in very short-term markets. However, much of the academic work supporting this concept does not recognize that patterns may not be *tradable* on all time frames. It is not always possible to trade 5-minute charts the same way as weekly charts, even though the patterns may superficially appear to be similar. In addition, not enough work has been done on the relationship of fractal markets and liquidity. In the shorter time frames, patterns are bounded by liquidity. For instance, very active stocks might show fractal patterns down to the 15-second time frame, while less liquid commodities or stocks might degenerate into noise anywhere below the daily level.

So, it should be easy to make money trading this cycle, right? Find accumulation on your chosen time frame. Buy. Wait for distribution. Sell and sell short. Cover shorts when the market goes back into accumulation. Repeat. Simple, right? Not so fast. Though this cycle provides a useful road map and large-scale framework, there are many nontrivial problems in actual application:

- Accumulation does lead to significant advances, but it is difficult to time entries out of accumulation areas. Buying breakouts results in a string of small (or, depending on your trade management discipline, not so small) losses that do add up.
- Buying within the accumulation area is not simple, as there are usually no clear risk points. Setting stops under accumulation areas is usually wrong, because you want to be buying those flushes, not selling into them.
- Sometimes what looks like accumulation turns out to not be accumulation, the bottom drops, and the market does not look back. Small losses can quickly become big problems in this environment.
- Trading bull and bear trends (markup and markdown) is also not as simple as might be expected. There are many tradable patterns in trends, as well as patterns that suggest the trend is coming to an end, but it takes real skill to identify and to trade these patterns.
- Markup periods often go into long, sideways ranges that may be either accumulation or distribution. The pattern is not always accumulation → uptrend → distribution; it is sometimes accumulation → uptrend → accumulation, or some other variation.

And perhaps most importantly, remember that no trader is correct 100 percent of the time, and being wrong means being on the wrong side of the market. Risk management is essential to limit the damage on the times you are wrong.

THE FOUR TRADES

Wyckoff's market cycle is a highly idealized view of market action, but it does lay the foundation for a simple categorization of technical trades into four categories. There are two trend trades: *trend continuation* and *trend termination*, and two support and resistance trades: *holding* and *failing*. Though this may seem like an arbitrary classification system, it is not. Every technical trade imaginable falls into one of these categories. Trades from certain categories are more appropriate at certain points in the market structure, so it is worthwhile to carefully consider your trades in this context.

The first question to consider is: Are all of your trade setups in one category? If so, this may not be a bad thing—a successful trading methodology must fit the trader's personality—but most traders will have the best results when they have at least two counterbalancing setups. For instance, a trader who focuses on breakout trades should probably understand the patterns of failed breakouts. A trader who trades pullbacks in trends should probably also be able to trade the patterns that occur at the ends of trends. There are two reasons behind this suggestion. First, you should become intimately familiar with the patterns associated with the failure of the patterns you trade. The second reason is related to self-control and psychology—there is an old saying: "If the only tool you have is a hammer, every problem you encounter will look like a nail." If you are only a skilled breakout trader, you may find it difficult to wait for the excellent breakout trades, and may try to force suboptimal patterns into this mold. If you have the freedom and the skills to switch to the setups that match the market conditions, you will be a able to adapt your trading skills to the market environment. There is certainly room for the specialist who does one trade and does it very well, but many traders find success with a broader approach.

Some market environments favor certain kinds of plays over others. If you are a trader who trades all categories, are you applying the right kind of plays to the right market environments? For instance, do you find yourself having many losing trades trying to short against resistance levels in uptrends because you feel they have gone too far? If so, your results might improve if you apply with-trend trades to those situations and more carefully define the market environments that will reward your *fading* (going against the trend) of strength into resistance. Those environments exist—you just aren't finding them with your plays. If you are a specialist who focuses on only one setup or pattern (and, to be clear, this is not a criticism if you are successful this way), then you need to realize that only a few specific market environments favor your play and wait for those environments. You can redefine your job description to include *not trading*. Wait on the sidelines, and wait for the environments in which you can excel. Again, those environments exist, but you probably are burning through a lot of mental and financial capital trying to find them. Clarify your setups. Categorize them, and then simplify, simplify, simplify.

Let's look briefly at each of the four broad categories and ask the following questions from a general, high-level perspective:

- Which trade setups fall into this category?
- What are the associated probabilities, reward/risk profiles, and overall expectancies of these trades?
- How do these trades fail?

Trend Continuation

Trend continuation plays are not simply trend plays or with-trend plays. The name implies that we find a market with a trend, whether a nascent trend or an already well-established trend, and then we seek to put on plays in the direction of that trend. Perhaps the most common trend continuation play is to use the pullbacks in a trend to position for further trend legs. It is also possible to structure breakout trades that would be with-trend plays, and there is at least one other category of trend continuation plays—trying to get involved in the very early structure of a new trend. In the context of our simplified stage model, trend continuation trades are most appropriate in markup or markdown, but these early trend trades may be attempted where accumulation breaks into the uptrend or where distribution breaks down into the new downtrend. If you are trading in these areas of uncertainty, it is important to not be stubborn. An aborted breakout of accumulation into an uptrend may well be an upthrust, which is a sign of potential *distribution*. Listen to the message of the market and adjust accordingly.

Trend continuation plays tend to be high-probability plays because there is a verifiable, statistical edge for trend continuation; these plays are aligned with one of the fundamental principles of price behavior. It is important to have both the risk and the expectation of the trade defined before entry; this is an absolute requirement of any specific trade setup, but it can be difficult with trend continuation trades. The key to defining risk is to define the points at which the trend trade is conclusively wrong, at which the trend is violated. Sometimes it is not possible to define nonarbitrary points at which the trend will be violated that are close enough to the entry point to still offer attractive reward/risk characteristics. On the upside, the best examples of these trades break into multileg trends that continue much further than anyone expected, but the most reliable profits are taken consistently at or just beyond the previous highs.

There are several common failure patterns associated with these types of trades. First, there may simply not be enough with-trend pressure to push the market into another trend leg, so previous resistance holds (in the case of an uptrend) and the market rolls over into a trading range (or distribution). Traders trading simple pullbacks need to be aware that many pullbacks in strong trends are complex, two-legged consolidations (see Chapter 3), so a good trading plan will plan for that possibility. Dramatic failures of these trades are somewhat uncommon, but they do happen. Most failed trend continuation trades tend to be rather polite affairs, usually giving the trader a chance to get out for a small loss. However, there is always danger when everyone is leaning the same way in a market, and, especially in well-established trends, there are places where many market participants have piled into a very obvious trend continuation play. In these situations, especially in extremely overextended markets, reversals can be dramatic as everyone scrambles for the exit at the same time.

Trend Termination

More than any other category, precise terminology is important here. If we were less careful, we might apply a label like "trend reversal" to most of the trades in this category, but this is counterproductive because it fails to precisely define the trader's expectations. If you think you are trading trend reversal trades, then you expect that a winning trade should roll over into a trend in the opposite direction. This is a true trend reversal, and these spots offer exceptional reward/risk profiles and near-perfect trade location. How many traders would like to sell the high tick or buy the very low at a reversal? However, true trend reversals are rare, and it is much more common to sell somewhere near the high and to then see the market stop trending. Be clear on this: This is a *win* for a trend termination trade—the trend stopped. Anything else is a bonus, so it is important to adjust your expectations accordingly.

The obvious spots in the cycle for trend termination trades are where the uptrend stops and moves into distribution, and vice versa on the downside, but there are other possibilities. Some traders specialize in finding overextended spots in established trends, and *fading* (going against the trend) these for a very quick and short reversal. For instance, a trader might find spots where the rallies in the uptrend have run up too far too fast, and take short positions against those rallies, planning to cover one to three bars later. These are trades for only the fastest and most nimble traders; developing traders are well advised to avoid these countertrend scalps because they remove focus from the big picture. Staying in a consistent time frame is important for these definitions; a trader might look for spots where the short-term downtrends (pullbacks) in the uptrend have overextended themselves, and then take long positions against those lower time frame downtrends. In this case, the trader is actually positioning countertrend on the lower time frame but with the trend on the trading time frame. Is this a trend continuation or trend termination trade? The answer depends on your perspective and your time frame, and it is only important to be consistent. Understand what you are trying to accomplish with the trade and how this best fits in the evolving market structure.

Trend termination plays are not usually high-probability plays, but the compensation is that winning trades tend to offer potential rewards much larger than the initial risk. If your patterns allow you to position short near the absolute high point of a trend leg with some degree of confidence, then you have a well-defined risk point and the potential for outsized profits on some subset of these trades. Over a large enough sample size, the risk/reward profile may be very good, leading to a solid positive expectancy even if most of these trades are losers.

Trend termination trades are countertrend (counter to the existing trend) trades, and trade management is an important issue. Most really dramatic trading losses, the kind that blow traders out of the water (and that don't involve options) come from traders fading trends and adding to those positions as the trend continues to move against them. If this is one of the situations where the trend turns into a manic, parabolic blow-off, there is a real possibility for a career-ending loss on a single trade. For swing traders, there will sometimes be dramatic gaps against positions held countertrend overnight, so this needs to be considered in the risk management and position sizing scheme. More than any other category of trade, iron discipline is required to trade these with any degree of consistency.

Support or Resistance Holding

There is some overlap between these categories, and it is possible to apply trades from these categories in more than one spot in the market structure. We might expect that most support/resistance trades will take place in accumulation or distribution areas while the market chops sideways, but a trader trading with-trend trades could initiate those trades by buying support in the trend. Are these trend continuation trades or support holding trades? The answer is both, so traders must build a well-thought-out classification system that reflects their approach to the market. Your trading patterns and rules are the tools through which you structure price action and market structure, and they must make sense *to you*. Take the time to define them clearly.

It is easy to find examples of well-defined trading ranges on historical charts where you could buy and risk a very small amount as the market bounces off the magic price at the bottom of the range. These trades do exist, but they are a small subset of support holding trades. Support, even when it holds, usually does not hold cleanly. The dropouts below support actually contribute to the strength of that support, as buyers are shaken out of their positions and are forced to reposition when it becomes obvious that the drop was a fake-out. For the shorter-term trader trading these patterns, there are some important issues to consider. If you know that support levels are not clean, how will you trade around them? Will you sell your position when the level drops, book many small losses, and reestablish when it holds again? Will you simply position small in the range, plan to buy more if it drops, and accept that you will occasionally take very large losses on your maximum size when the market does drop? If you are scaling in, how will you deal with the fact that your easy wins will not be on your full size, as you did not have the opportunity to buy your full line near the bottom of the range? By the time you see the support level is holding, the market will already be far from the level, increasing the size of the stop loss needed.

Because of these issues, support/resistance holding trades, as a group, tend to have the lowest reward/risk ratios. By definition, *at* support, there is an imbalance of buying pressure that creates the support, but the market is usually in relative equilibrium just above that support. Most traders will try to avoid trading in these equilibrium areas, so many support holding trades set up in suboptimal trading environments. It is worth mentioning that there is a special subset of support/resistance holding trades that actually are very high-probability trades: failed breakouts. Remember, when everyone is leaning the wrong way, the potential for dramatic moves increases greatly, and nowhere is that more true than in a failed breakout.

Support or Resistance Breaking or Failing

Support/resistance breaking trades are the classic breakout or breakout from channel trades and, ideally, would be located at the end of accumulation or distribution phases. In fact, these trades actually define the end of accumulation or distribution, as the support or resistance fails and the market breaks into a trend phase. Another place for support/resistance breaking trades is in trends, but many of these are lower time frame breakout entries into the trading time frame trending pattern. Many traders, especially daytraders, find themselves drawn to these patterns because of the many examples where they work dramatically well. Many trading books show example after example of dramatic breakouts, but there is one small problem with breakout trades—most breakouts fail.

In addition, the actual breakout areas tend to be high-volatility and low-liquidity areas, which can increase the risk in these trades. They occur at very visible chart points, and so they are often very crowded trades. The presence of unusual volume and volatility can create opportunities, but it also creates dangers. Execution skills probably matter more here than in any other category of trade, as slippage and thin markets can significantly erode a trader's edge. These trades can offer outstanding reward/risk profiles, but, especially in short-term trades, it is important to remember that realized losses can sometimes be many multiples of the intended risk, significantly complicating the position sizing problem. This is not a fatal flaw, but it must be considered in your risk management scheme.

Depending on the time frame and intended holding period for the trade, it may be possible to find that there are patterns that precede and set up the best examples of these trades. The best resistance breaking trades will be driven by large-scale buying imbalances, and these imbalances usually show, for instance, as the market holds higher lows into the resistance level before the actual breakout. Breakouts driven by small traders who are simply trying to scalp small profits in the increased volatility are less reliable and are usually not set up by these larger-scale patterns. In the very best examples of these trades, buyers who are trapped out of the market by the suddenness of the breakout will be compelled to buy into the market over coming days or weeks, and this buying pressure will provide favorable tailwinds for the trade. Traders specializing in breakout trades usually spend a lot of time studying the patterns that set up the best trades, and maintain a watch list of potential candidates for trades at any time. Executing unplanned breakout trades in a reactive mode is unlikely to be a formula for long-term success.

SUMMARY

These four categories of trades provide an excellent framework for thinking about technical trades. This is a simple, valid, and consistent labeling scheme, and it is nearly impossible to find a technical trade that does not fit within these categories. Many trades may fit into more than one, especially when the complexities of multiple time frames are considered, but this does not compromise the utility of the system. This is not intended to be a rigid, artificial classification system, but rather a dynamic framework that can grow and evolve with your trading style and your understanding of market behavior.

Not to wax too philosophical, but there is another way to think about this cycle. Some branches of Eastern philosophy believe that every manifest thing we see, feel, or experience in any way comes from the interaction of two opposing, primordial forces. These philosophies tell us that one force can never fully overcome the other, and, when one seems to predominate, it contains within itself the seed of the other. In the market, buying and selling pressure are these twin opposing forces. When buying pressure seems to be strongest, the end of the uptrend trend is often near. When the sellers seem to be decisively winning the battle, the stage is set for a reversal into an uptrend. This is why it is so important for traders to learn to stand apart from the crowd, and the only way to do this is to understand the actions and the emotions of that market crowd.

PART II

Market Structure

CHAPTER 3

On Trends

Don't fight forces, use them.

—R. Buckminster Fuller

Market movements can create a bewildering number of patterns and variations of patterns. Simple structures take on different meanings depending on context, and patterns sometimes develop and resolve in unexpected ways. Add to this the complexities of the interactions of multiple time frames and related markets, and we end up with a seemingly infinite number of possibilities. The human mind needs some kind of structure to help process information, so various solutions have been proposed by different schools of technical analysis. The classic chart patterns (head and shoulders, double top, pennant, flag, wedge, etc.) are one attempt at providing structure. Other solutions have been proposed, ranging from in-depth quantitative analysis to the various schools of wave and cycle analysis; these, and many other approaches, work for some traders. All of these offer valuable perspectives, but let us turn our attention to a simple, robust framework that focuses on the fundamental price structures created by price trends.

THE FUNDAMENTAL PATTERN

What I am presenting here is not new; I owe a tremendous debt to the authors and traders who have come before me. No significant intellectual construct emerges ex nihilo—anything of value rests on a foundation built by someone else. In the case of trend structure, Tony Plummer (2010) has written about the basic trend pattern, which he calls the "price pulse," with clarity and in-depth. This simple, fundamental trend pattern is found at the core of even elaborate methodologies, like Gann or Elliott, when they are stripped to bare essentials. This pattern, very simply, is *how markets move*, and

49

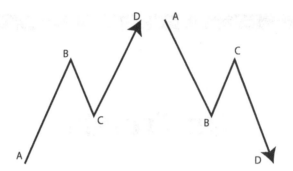

FIGURE 3.1 The Fundamental Trend Pattern: Impulse, Retracement, Impulse in an Uptrend and a Downtrend

it is a profoundly powerful concept. The fundamental pattern of market movement on all time frames is this: a movement in one direction, a countertrend *retracement* in the other direction, and another leg in the original direction. Visually, these movements are often labeled with letters, as in Figure 3.1.

This is a very rough schematic structure, but it is a powerful pattern that repeats on all time frames. Whether we look at trends spanning decades or seconds, we will find this same impulse, retracement, impulse structure, though the psychological significance of the pattern will vary depending on the time frame. It is also reasonable to ask why this structure should exist at all, and there are several possible answers. Put yourself in the shoes of a trader who has to buy a significant amount of an asset in a very short time. Your primary objective is to get the order done without having a large impact on prices. How might this best be done?

The best option in most cases is to buy a little bit, wait so that you don't move the market too much, then buy some more, and repeat until the order is completely filled. This is how good execution traders work large orders. Smart traders (or smart algorithms) will judge how to plan their buying by the market's response to their orders. In this way, they are judging the supply or the selling conviction hanging over the market. A single trader executing an order in a market otherwise composed of pure noise traders would create some variation of this price pattern by trying to fill a buy order through this natural process.

There must be a firm theoretical foundation for anything in the market; you should be able to clearly articulate why something should be the way it is. Market prices are the result of buyers and sellers negotiating for prices, nothing more and nothing less. We do not need to invoke some mystical force to create the patterns we see in the markets; they are simply the result of buyers and sellers finding prices in a competitive environment. This is also why the fundamental structures in the markets have not changed since antiquity. Some of the earliest written records we have are price records from Phoenician merchants, which paint a story of price movements very similar to those we see today, albeit on a much slower scale.

FIGURE 3.2 Each Trend Leg Breaks Down into a Three-Legged Structure on the Next Lower Time Frame

Fractal Markets

A fractal is a type of pattern in which the parts resemble the whole (see Mandelbrot and Hudson 2006). Markets are fractal in nature, meaning that essentially the same patterns appear on all time frames: Patterns on single-tick charts combine to form 1-minute bars. The patterns on the 1-minute bars are the same as those on the single-tick bars, and they combine to form the patterns on 5-minute bars. (The time frames are a convenient but unavoidably arbitrary structure.) This pattern building continues all the way to daily, weekly, monthly, and yearly patterns, which all contain essentially the same patterns.

Figure 3.2 shows a schematic example of how this might play out in the market. Each trend leg is an impulse, retracement, impulse pattern, and each of those legs also breaks down into the same pattern on the lower time frame. Though only three levels are shown on the diagram, this structure theoretically extends down to the one-tick level. Furthermore, the entire large structure in Figure 3.2 could be a setup leg for a trend on the next higher time frame.

This is not an abstract concept, but an important tool to understand market structure. No pattern exists in the vacuum of a single time frame. The market is like a set of Russian nesting *matryoshka* dolls—digging into one time frame will reveal similar structures nested on lower time frames, all the way down to the tick level. Understanding this structure is a key component of building intuition about markets. Traders usually focus on one specific time frame, but it is important to understand that the patterns of the lower time frame actually create the patterns on the trading time frame, and that the patterns on the trading time frame are influenced by evolving patterns on the next higher time frame. In practice, the interactions of structures on lower time frames are usually components of price action, while higher time frames are more likely to provide context or motivation for market structure patterns within the trading time frame.

TREND STRUCTURE

We now turn to the structure of trends in a little more depth: how they start, how they unfold, and how they come to an end. The presence of a trend suggests an imbalance of buying and selling pressure; it is this imbalance that actually drives the price change of the trend, and the trend will eventually end when the market finds equilibrium at a new price level. It is extremely important to be able to read the trend structure and to know what patterns support a continued imbalance or what patterns indicate that the trend might be coming to an end.

Impulse and Momentum

The first leg (AB) of the basic structure is often called a *momentum move* or an *impulse move*. In an uptrend, this is a relatively sharp advance driven by buying pressure (demand) overcoming existing selling pressure (supply) and creating a lack of liquidity on one side of the market. After a market has been locked in an extended trading range with no clear momentum, the emergence of a sharp momentum move penetrating one side of the range is often a sign that there is a new imbalance of buying or selling pressure. Figure 3.3 shows an example of a new trend emerging in the 30-year Treasury bond futures. Notice a few things about this pattern: first, it is not subtle. Even someone with no chart-reading experience would recognize that the right side of the chart shows a break in the existing pattern. Next, notice that prices were able to penetrate through the upper channel, though the last bar of the chart is somewhat suggestive of a short-term climax. Last, the fast line of the MACD registered a new momentum high. (This idea will be explored in Chapter 7, but essentially, the MACD made a new high reading relative to its recent values.)

Figure 3.4 shows an example of a downtrend emerging in the intraday Standard & Poor's (S&P) 500 futures. In this case, a large downward-closing 5-minute bar penetrates the lower channel, and spikes the MACD to a significant new low. This brings up an important idiosyncrasy of the MACD: the indicator is calculated from moving averages, which smooth and lag prices, so the indicator also lags price movements. It is important to understand this and to understand the picture you would have seen at the time. (Lay a piece of paper over the chart to hide everything to the right of the price spike, and

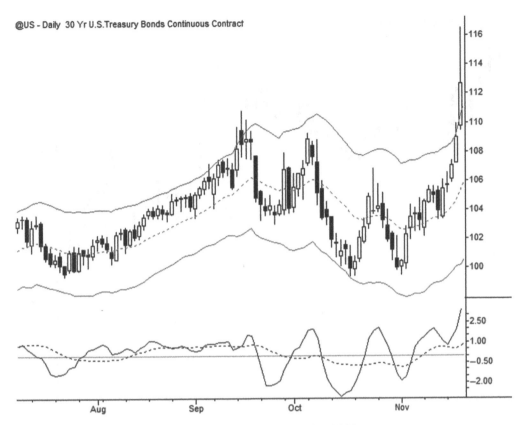

FIGURE 3.3 Thirty-Year Treasury Bond Futures, November 2008
Strong momentum emerges at the right side of the chart, penetrating the upper channel and spiking the MACD to a new high.

then slide it to the right to reveal one bar at a time to see the response of the indicator.) Also, notice that both of these cases are very clear, and that the indicator is somewhat redundant because the information is already clearly visible in the price structure.

Impulse moves drive trends. As long as each trend leg extends in a momentum move approximately consistent with previous moves, the probabilities favor buying the next pullback for another trend high, or, in the case of a downtrend, shorting the pullbacks for another run at the lows. What you do *not* want to see in a trend is the emergence of sharp *contratrend* momentum on one of the pullbacks. Figure 3.5 shows an example in which very sharp downward momentum emerged on a pullback in Sugar futures. Notice that this pullback completely broke the established trend pattern, and spiked the MACD to a sharp new low, which is not consistent with an intact uptrend. Though it is important to understand the subtle clues the market gives us, sometimes the most important ones are very obvious. There is no point trying to trade with the uptrend after an event like this; it is safe to assume the trend is broken until further notice.

Remember, the normal pattern in an established trend is that each setup leg is a momentum move, and the subsequent extensions also function as momentum moves setting

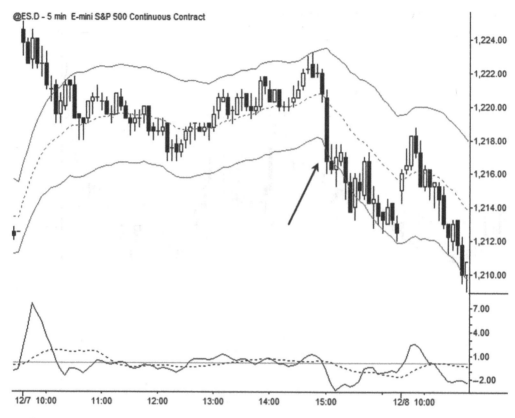

FIGURE 3.4   Five-Minute S&P 500 Futures, December 7, 2010
A large downward price spike (marked with an arrow on the chart) sets off an extended downtrend.

up the next trend leg. Economics 101 tells us that increased demand in a market will lift
prices as the market tries to find a new market-clearing price; this description of trend
movement is one of the mechanisms through which that adjustment happens. Eventually,
higher prices will bring enough sellers into the market that a new, perhaps temporary,
equilibrium is achieved. Astute technical traders can usually see clues to this process
in the market tape. The most important patterns are: new momentum highs or lows,
subsequent trend legs making similar new impulse moves, and the absence of strong
countertrend momentum on pullbacks.

Climaxes

Buy pullbacks following an upward impulse move, or short bounces after strong selling
impulse moves. That, in a nutshell, is a very effective plan for trading trends. Simple,
right? Not so fast—there is a potential complication, and it is one of the most significant
problems in technical analysis. It is true that there should be follow-through (range expansion) in the direction of previous impulse moves; however, *extremely* strong impulse

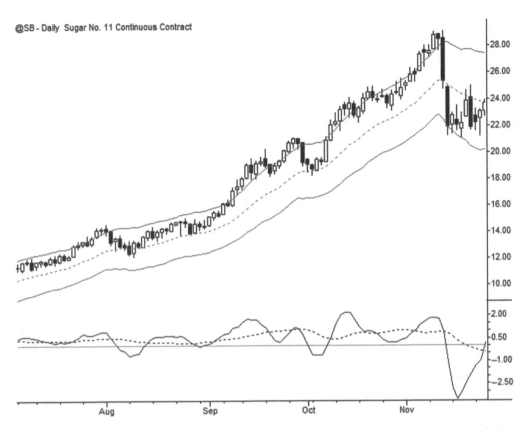

@SB - Daily Sugar No. 11 Continuous Contract

FIGURE 3.5 Sugar Futures, November 2010—Two Large Downward Closing Days Break the Trend Pattern

moves are more indicative of *climax* or *exhaustion*. This is one of the common ways that trends end, so it is important to fully understand these patterns.

Figure 3.6 shows a classic example of a buying climax that ended a trend in silver futures. A naive trader might have noticed this action and read it as extreme strength. However, in these types of formations a type of short-term mania sets in as emotional buyers chase the market higher and higher. At some point, the last buyer who wants to buy has bought, and the market becomes extremely vulnerable to a sell-off. The slightest pause or speed bump will send a market like this crashing back into the vacuum on the other side, as there is no more natural buying pressure underneath the market. In addition, there may even be traders who bought into the last trend leg, and they are now the ultimate weak-hand longs. As soon as the pattern changes and real momentum emerges to the downside, they will run for the exits en masse, and their selling pressure will add fuel to the fire. Note the classic signs of a buying climax in this example: an accelerated trend rate, large range bars, many *free bars* (bars with a low above the upper channel), and a subsequent collapse.

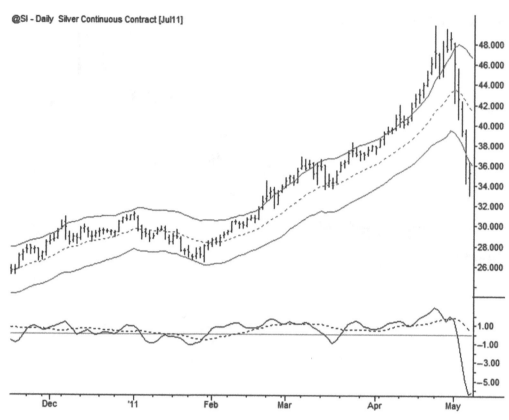

@SI - Daily Silver Continuous Contract [Jul11]

FIGURE 3.6 Daily Silver Futures, May 2011—A Near-Perfect Example of a Buying Climax

This type of structure is often called a parabolic move or a blow-off. Notice also that the range of the bars in the blow-off becomes much larger than previous bars as the trend steepens and the bars pull away from the average; this is a reflection of expanded volatility, specifically intraday volatility. There will also often be a very large volume spike near the extreme of the climax move. It is not uncommon to see bars that trade four or five times the average volume for the instrument, but this information is also mirrored in lower time frame price action and volatility. Yet another common characteristic is that many more bars close at or near their high in a buying climax and on their low in a selling climax. This shows that the climactic conditions extend to the intraday (or intrabar if a weekly or monthly chart) time frame as well, which are probably showing exhaustion or climaxes on their own time frames. Last, it is extremely unusual to see bars that are completely outside the Keltner channels, called *free bars*; the presence of these bars is another sign of potential climax.

The same pattern works symmetrically to the downside, as in Figure 3.7. In this particular example, the panic was not quite as extreme as the mania in Figure 3.6, and traders might not have known until several weeks afterward that the market had bottomed. However, the message to *not* short into the pullback following the climax selling

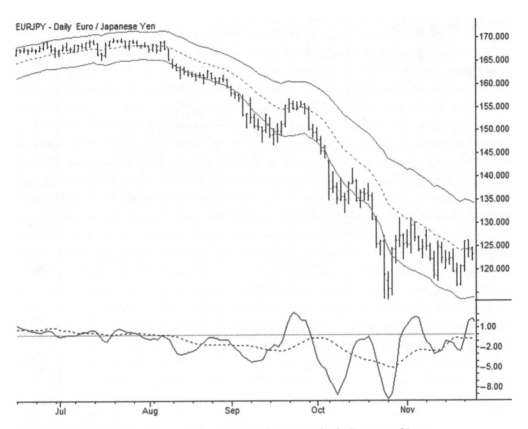

FIGURE 3.7 A Selling Climax in the EURJPY Following Multiple Downtrend Legs

was clear. A climax, by itself, is probably not enough information to justify assuming a countertrend position (though it does have the advantage of defining a clear risk point), but it should at least put trend traders on notice. Do not enter pullbacks following potential climaxes.

Notice that these examples have come after extended, mature trend runs; a potential climax out of a trading range is much more problematic. Climactic conditions can be defined only by their proportional relationship to recent market history. Volatility contracts greatly in ranges, so any indicators measuring range expansion will also be skewed—in other words, it takes a much smaller movement to make a climax pattern on a breakout of a range. Furthermore, strong breakouts of ranges, even if they are apparently climactic, usually see continuation, so these are difficult trades, and it is probably best to look for climaxes only after extended trends.

Figure 3.8 shows the Dow Jones Industrial Average (cash index) in the days following the terrorist attacks on the World Trade Center on September 11, 2001. Even in this exceptional example, with several days on which the stock market did not trade due to the uncertainty following the attacks, the patterns of climax and exhaustion are consistent. Markets move in response to emotion; robust technical tools quantify

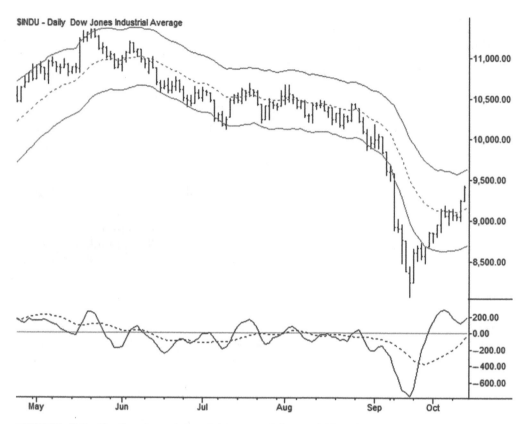

FIGURE 3.8 The Dow Jones Industrial Average Before and After the Terrorist Attacks of September 11, 2001

those movements and underlying emotions in ways that make them consistently readable, even in extreme examples. This chart captured a time of great turmoil, but even so, the climax pattern is familiar: large ranges, parabolic expansion outside the bands, many free bars (highs below the lower band), and many large bars that close on their low. In this case, there was no clear upside momentum following the climax, but the selling climax should at least have been a warning to traders not to short into the following pullback. In this case, the extreme reached in mid-September held as the low for over a year.

Speaking of extreme situations, Figure 3.9 shows the Dow Jones Industrial Average as it behaved during the crash of 1929. The patterns are essentially the same as we see in any other climax situation, and the geometric relationships of the market to the moving average and the channels are consistent with anything we would see in modern markets. One of the challenges thrown up against technical analysis is that many authors claim it is a self-fulfilling prophecy, as many traders are using the same tools and making the same decisions. While this is completely rational, it is a flimsy argument because many technical tools and patterns work on periods of market history where no one was using

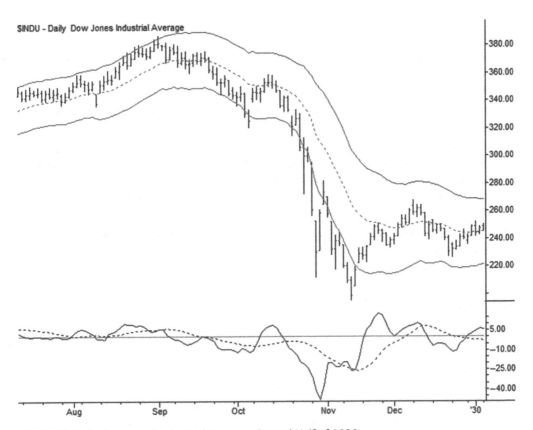

FIGURE 3.9 Dow Jones Industrial Average, Second Half of 1929
Note the same selling climax pattern.

them. No one in 1929 was using exponential moving averages or Keltner channels, yet they would have been reliable tools. This is food for thought.

There is another point here, concerning expectations from technical patterns. Neither this 1929 climax low nor the 2001 climax low marked the ultimate low for the market. In both cases the low was retested several times and failed to hold, albeit after the market put in a substantial bounce. Do not assume that these climax patterns are necessarily justification to assume a countertrend position, but *do* use them as warnings to lighten up or exit existing with-trend positions.

Climax patterns are important and can be extremely dangerous to traders who do not understand how they work. We will revisit this structure several times and consider specific trading patterns that can set up around them, but the key, for now, is that you can identify the characteristic patterns of climaxes on charts and know to avoid getting caught in the mania or the panic of the crowd. It is not possible to identify these areas with 100 percent accuracy, and it is not always possible to separate climactic moves from simple strength or weakness that should see continuation. Sometimes you will misjudge and make the wrong decision; this is unavoidable, but be sensitive and responsive to this potential error and make adjustments as soon as possible. Do not trade in the direction of blow-off climaxes.

To review, some of the most important characteristics of these areas are that they:

- Usually come after two or more trend legs in the same direction.
- Show an acceleration in the direction of the previous trend. Many analysts and traders describe this as a market that has gone parabolic.
- Are relatively infrequent.
- Usually come at a significant new high or low for the time frame being considered. It is unusual to see climax moves in the middle of a range.
- Are confirmed by the emergence of sharp contratrend momentum. If this does not happen, the trend might simply be very strong.
- Vary in significance. Small exhaustions into previous support and resistance are common, especially on lower time frames, and may not define important structural points for the market on higher time frames.

Pullbacks

After a normal (nonclimactic) impulse move, the market will usually go into a *pullback* or *retracement*. A pullback is a countertrend movement (i.e., it is against the direction of the trend that set up the pullback) in a trend that usually leads to another price movement in the direction of the original trend. In other words, after an impulse move up, the pullback will be a downward movement against that initial impulse; pullbacks in downtrends are bounces against the preceding downward impulse move. Conceptually, the pullback is a natural consequence and reaction to the impulse move. Volume is typically lighter in pullbacks, which is to be expected since impulse moves are driven by active buying, but many of the traditional volume relationships of technical analysis are not as reliable as many people believe.

Other terms for pullbacks are *consolidations* or consolidation patterns. These are functional labels—they explain what pullbacks do, which is to pause and to consolidate the energy of the previous trend leg, usually in preparation for another trend leg in the same direction. These are not always easy to trade, as it can be difficult to define precise entry and risk points in these patterns. However, working to overcome those challenges is worthwhile, because some of the most reliable statistical tendencies in the market are for continuation out of these formations. Figure 3.10 shows an example of standard pullback patterns in the S&P 500 futures.

The character and extent of the pullback can give some insight into the buying pressure behind the market. In fact, judging the commitment behind pullbacks is a key component, perhaps *the* key component, of reading the market tape. If buyers are aggressively accumulating positions, then they will not let the market come in as much on the retracements; they will step up and buy aggressively at higher prices. This will result in shallower, smaller pullbacks compared to a situation in which buyers are relatively more

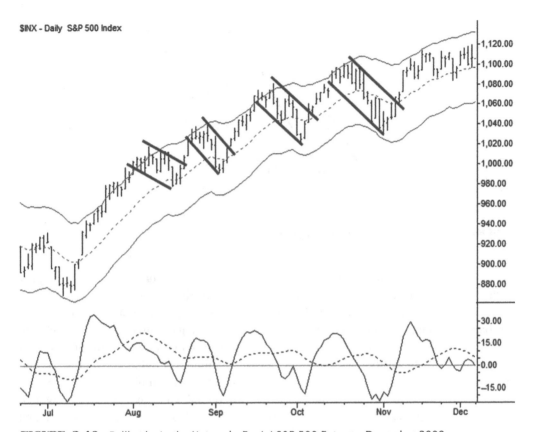

FIGURE 3.10 Pullbacks in the Uptrend—E-mini S&P 500 Futures, December 2009

complacent. If buyers are more uncertain, they will demand lower prices as protection and will not be willing to bid the market aggressively higher. The end result will be deeper pullbacks, perhaps with a more complex structure.

So far, all of the pullbacks examined have been simple pullbacks or consolidations, meaning that they are composed of one contratrend movement. The trend leg ends, the pullback begins, and, at the bottom of the pullback, buyers push the market to new highs. It is not always this simple. Another common pattern is the *complex pullback*, which is a standard pullback followed by a failed attempt to resume the original trend. When this attempt fails and rolls over, the pullback puts in a second leg against the larger trend. A complex pullback is actually a complete trend leg (impulse, pullback, impulse) structure on the lower time frame, and we also commonly refer to them as two-legged pullbacks. Figure 3.11 shows a schematic example of simple and complex pullbacks. Commit these patterns to memory; they are the fundamental patterns of with-trend trading.

It is important to understand these complex pullbacks for several reasons. First, they are common. Trend traders will make the bulk of their profits in trends that extend for several legs, and pullbacks in trends tend to alternate between simple and complex.

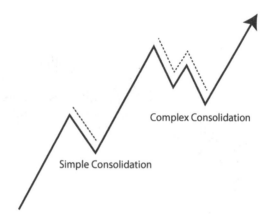

FIGURE 3.11 Simple and Complex Pullbacks

(This *rule of alternation*, which describes this alternation between simple and complex pullbacks, is one of the useful rules from Elliott wave theory.) For instance, it is extremely unusual to find a trend that has five large trend legs interrupted by four simple pullbacks; far more common would be five large trend legs interrupted by two simple and two complex pullbacks. Traders cannot negotiate the market structure of extended trends successfully without a good understanding of complex pullbacks. Another reason to understand these patterns is that many traders will execute a plan that is some variation of entering into a pullback and exiting if the pullback continues to move against them. Complex pullbacks will stop these traders out of their positions as the pullback makes new countertrend extremes on the second leg. Any successful trend trading strategy has to account for the possibility of complex pullbacks. With this in mind, return to Figure 3.10 and examine the third pullback in the sequence, which is a good example of a complex pullback in a real market situation.

Measured Move Objective

This combination of impulse/retracement/impulse pattern leads to a three-legged structure that should be considered the standard trend structure. A rough profit target for the follow-through leg, the trend leg following the pullback, is the so-called *measured move objective (MMO)*, which assumes that the CD leg in Figure 3.12 will approximately equal the length of the AB leg.

Treat this relationship as a rough guideline; all proportions and ratios work in markets simply because they express the magnitude of fluctuations that are normal for any particular market. For instance, if a stock has been fluctuating intraday in swings of 0.40 on average, it would not be realistic to expect a 4.00 profit on a single swing. Conversely, looking for a profit of 0.04 in that same stock would probably be too conservative, and it might be difficult to justify the necessary risk for such a small target. Certainly, there are

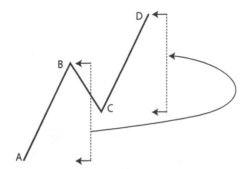

FIGURE 3.12 Measured Move Objective: Add Distance AB to Point C to Predict Approximate Location of D

examples where markets reach this measured move objective exactly, but it is best to be prepared to be flexible: If the swing seems to be falling short, perhaps be willing to take a slightly smaller profit. If the market is driving into the measured move objective with good momentum, it may often be possible to take profit *beyond* the level. Do not expect markets to precisely conform to any set of ratios and relationships.

Another way to use a measured move objective is as a potential entry spot. A common area where this may occur is in a complex pullback, when it makes sense to look for the second leg of the pullback to terminate in the area of the measured move objective. Last, remember that this measured move objective, if used as a price target, provides a target for only a *single* swing. It is entirely possible to establish a position in a trend and hold it through multiple pullbacks and multiple trend leg extensions, in which case the measured move is valid only for each of the individual swings.

Three Pushes

The parabolic expansion into climax pattern is a dramatic but rare pattern. There are a number of other more common and subtle patterns that can also indicate climax. One of the most important of these is *three pushes*, which appears on a price chart as three drives to a new high or low after a somewhat extended trend. The pushes are usually symmetrical in time (meaning that they are more or less evenly spaced horizontally on the chart) and in price. In the best examples, the third push breaks a trend line drawn across pushes one and two, indicating a short-term climax on a lower time frame. The three pushes that make up this pattern are also usually spaced more closely than most of the other highs in the trend, indicating that the pace of trading activity (not necessarily volume) has accelerated. For instance, if a market has been making new highs on the trend every 15 bars, the three pushes pattern might occur with highs spaced five bars apart. This is only a guideline, but the more frequent drives to new highs suggest a certain franticness on the part of buyers. Figure 3.13 shows a classic example of this pattern, which ended a trend in Wheat futures in early 2011.

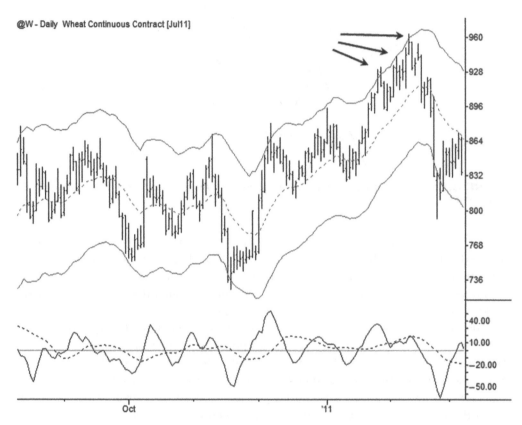

FIGURE 3.13   Daily Wheat Futures, Showing Three Drives to End a Trend

If you have not seen this pattern before, you are probably thinking that it sounds very strange. What is magical about three pushes? Why not four or five? To be sure, nothing works all the time, but this pattern is reliable enough that it demands attention when it occurs. As with all other potential trend termination patterns, it may not justify a countertrend position, but it should at least be a warning to tighten stops and perhaps to reduce exposure in the direction of the prevailing trend. At the very least, do not greatly increase risk into the next pullback, because that pullback now has a higher probability of failure.

As with all patterns, you should be asking, "Why should this pattern exist? What makes it work?" In this case, it is most likely an outgrowth of the fundamental impulse/ retracement/impulse pattern that drives all trends. Figure 3.14 shows a schematic of the pattern, which also breaks out the three-legged structure that might not be obvious at first glance. This is an important pattern to commit to memory; it occurs in all markets and on all time frames, and is subtle enough that many market participants miss it when it happens.

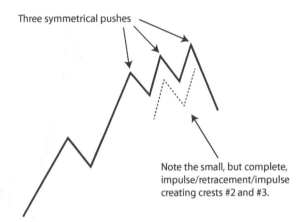

Three symmetrical pushes

Note the small, but complete, impulse/retracement/impulse creating crests #2 and #3.

FIGURE 3.14 Schematic of the Three Pushes Pattern Showing Underlying Structure

A DEEPER LOOK AT PULLBACKS: THE QUINTESSENTIAL TREND TRADING PATTERN

Imagine that you wanted to trade a trend in the most efficient manner possible. If you knew the future—when and where the trend would begin and end—it would be simple: buy at the beginning of the uptrend and sell at the end; short at the beginning of a downtrend and cover at the end. Since working time machines are hard to come by, we have to find another plan. The next best solution might be to use the pullbacks to position for the next trend leg. In other words, buy into the pullbacks in uptrends and short into the pullbacks (bounces) in downtrends. Even if we are buying in an uptrend, we would still prefer to buy at relatively low prices; using the pullbacks allows us to do this. Furthermore, it is possible to monitor some of the characteristics of the developing pullbacks to get some clues as to where the trend might end. Chapter 6 demonstrates several specific patterns and plans for trading pullbacks, but let's begin here by considering some of the important points that all pullbacks, and trades around them, have in common.

Characteristics of Winning Pullbacks

Pullbacks are contratrend movements, meaning that, in an uptrend, the pullbacks are actually lower time frame downtrends and, in the case of pullbacks in downtrends, the lower time frame will be in an uptrend. One important principle of market behavior is that trends that run counter to the higher time frame trend tend to be weaker and tend to abort suddenly as the higher time frame trend reasserts itself. This is useful from two perspectives: First, trading pullbacks makes sense because they offer excellent trade locations (i.e., buying relatively cheap in an uptrend or selling relatively high in a downtrend) with a good probability of success. Second, understanding this principle is important because it can filter out low-probability trades—if you enter a pullback on your trading time

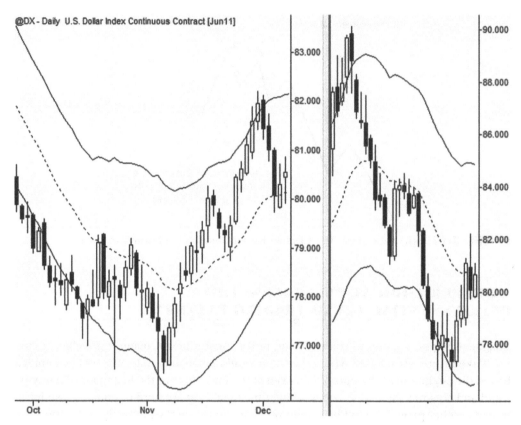

FIGURE 3.15 Conflicting Information from the Daily and Weekly Chart of the U.S. Dollar Index Futures

frame that is actually contratrend to the higher time frame market structure, this trade will have a much lower probability of success.

An example will help to clarify this. Figure 3.15 shows what appears to be a pullback in a good uptrend on the daily U.S. Dollar Index futures chart in the left pane. This is the second pullback off a potential trend change in early November; the market has rallied to the upper Keltner channel, and has pulled back approximately to the moving average. All other things being equal, this would normally be a good potential long trade. However, a look at the weekly chart (right pane) shows that this time frame is actually in a strong downtrend, and has only pulled back to its moving average. Seen in this context, the uptrend on the daily chart is likely to terminate suddenly as the weekly chart reasserts control and the downtrend on that time frame resumes.

Follows Good Momentum or Impulse   When trading pullbacks in a trend, it is helpful to make sure the market is actually trending. One of the best ways to separate out the suboptimal trading environments is to trade only pullbacks that are preceded by significant momentum in the direction of the trend. There are many ways to quantify this, but simple, visual chart analysis can be very useful. The highest-probability trades will follow large moves relative to previous swings on the chart. Again, we are into the territory of subjective analysis, but this is a legitimate skill that can be developed with experience and exposure to many patterns. The question the trader needs to ask is: "Am I seeing a move here that should have continuation?" The most important thing to keep in mind is that we are looking for sharp impulse moves and for significant momentum moves that indicate there is an imbalance in the market that should resolve with another move in the same direction. It is also possible to quantify this condition with the MACD or another momentum indicator—look for the indicator to register a significant new high or low (relative to its recent history), and trade only pullbacks following that condition.

Figure 3.16 shows an example of this kind of trading in action. For each of the points marked on the chart, compare the price action of the market to the action of the fast line (the solid line) of the modified MACD. At the point marked A on the chart, the MACD has registered a significant new high relative to its recent history (not visible to the left of the chart). This would suggest that a trader could look to buy any weakness to position long for another drive to the upside; the small pullback beginning six bars after A offered

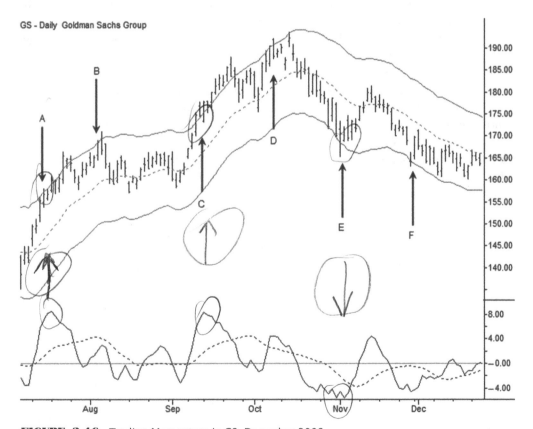

FIGURE 3.16 Trading Momentum in GS, December 2009

just such an opportunity. At the point marked B, the market made a new high but the momentum indicator did not. This is a *momentum divergence* (more on that in the next subsection) and suggests that long trades should not be entered on the next pullback. In this case, the market did go to new highs, but only after chopping sideways for nearly a month; being tied up in this trade for that length of time would not have been a productive use of financial or mental capital. At C, the market makes a new high, as does the MACD—buy the next pullback. At D, the new high in the market is accompanied by a momentum divergence, so a trader would be well advised to avoid buying the following pullback. In this case, the sell-off marked E spiked the MACD to a new extreme low reading, now suggesting that the next bounce would be a good shorting opportunity. This was true, and the higher MACD reading relative to the new price low at F would have been a warning to not short into the next bounce.

Does Not Follow a Momentum Divergence   A corollary to the preceding is that the best pullback trades will not come after a *momentum divergence*. There are both objective and subjective elements to this evaluation, but the simple MACD analysis in the preceding example is a good place to start. If we precisely define the ways in which we will measure momentum, it is possible to define some clear guidelines for trades to be taken and avoided based on the existing momentum conditions. Length of swing analysis provides some additional insight into the momentum behind each leg of the trend: Larger swings (vertical distance on chart) have stronger momentum than smaller swings, but the rate of the trend (price/time, visible as slope on the chart) is also important.

It is also possible that managing existing positions may require a slightly different mind-set than initiating new positions. For instance, a strong enough divergence could warn you not to increase risk or not to initiate new positions into the next pullback, but you might still be justified in holding a partial position that was initiated earlier at better prices. This is the kind of question that must be decided in advance, and your trading plan should encompass all the possibilities for managing existing positions as well as initiating new exposures.

Location in Trend   It is an axiom in technical analysis that the first entry in a trend is the best entry, but this is an example of the kind of hindsight analysis that must be avoided. All this really says is that if a market goes up, the best place to get in was at the beginning of the move—not a particularly helpful piece of knowledge. However, this concept *is* useful from a slightly different perspective; with each successive trend leg we should be slightly more suspicious of the move. It is hard to justify assuming the same kind of risk on the fourth or fifth legs as on the first or second, but it is also important to remember that markets *do* have outsized trend moves, and some trends go on far longer than anyone would have thought possible. It is rare, but a market can have 10 trend legs in the same direction without a significant pullback; most of these later legs will be generating momentum divergences and then rolling over those divergences. This is also a good reminder why you do not want to add to losing countertrend trades. Even if an extended trend move is a one in a thousand event, if it happens the one time you are being stubborn and adding to a trade as it grinds against you, that one time can put you out of business. Competent traders manage risks so that no single trade can ever take them out of the game.

Retracement Percentage   There is valuable information in the character and size of the pullbacks in a trend; a strong trend will tend to generate smaller pullbacks, relative to the with-trend legs, than a weaker trend. While we can measure and quantify these pull-backs in various ways, there is enough noise in the market that exact measurements and ratios are not particularly useful. This is another tool that that may be best synthesized into a quasi-discretionary framework.

A good rule of thumb is to expect retracements to terminate at about 50 percent of the preceding setup leg, plus or minus a very large margin of error. In practice, one good rule might be to look for terminations somewhere in the 25 to 75 percent range, but not to be surprised to see terminations either shallower or deeper. You basically have two broad choices for trading pullbacks: either enter at predetermined retracement levels with very large stops (which will mandate relatively small position sizes and has bad implications for reward/risk ratios) or wait for lower time frame and/or price action confirmation that the pullback has reached a termination. We will explore the second option in considerable depth in Chapters 6 through 10.

One special case of shallow retracements is more common on intraday charts than on higher time frames: sometimes an extremely strong trend is unable to pull back at all; the absence of any clear trend pattern is a pattern in itself. Prices may either move higher in a series of tight, stair-step trading ranges, or they will press against the upper channel and slide along that band as the market grinds higher. These can be treacherous patterns to trade. While these patterns do point to exceptionally strong imbalances and also to very strong trends, the lack of significant pullbacks makes it difficult to position in the trend at advantageous prices. In addition, these types of trends often feature the occasional large spike against the trend, most likely driven by anxious traders exiting trades near the edge of shallow pullbacks. These spikes can make it difficult to precisely define risk in with-trend entries. Figure 3.17 shows an example of this trending pattern in Baidu.com (Nasdaq: BIDU) in February through April 2010. Notice that a trader wait-ing for a pullback would have been frustrated, as none materialized; the market simply continued higher.

Symmetry and Lower Time Frame Considerations   A pullback is usually a pe-riod of lower volatility and action in which the market pauses and consolidates the strength (or weakness, in the case of a downtrend) of the trend legs. This is one of the characteristics of good pullbacks: they are generally periods of lower activity compared to trend legs. One of the most reliable tools for defining lower activity is to monitor price action on lower time frames, where we would expect to see less conviction in the direction of the trend on that time frame. Remember, the lower time frame trend is

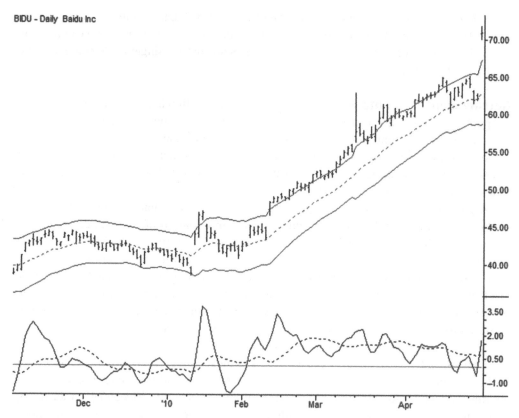

FIGURE 3.17 A Strong Trend in BIDU Holds the Stock Tight against the Upper Keltner Channel

countertrend to the prevailing trend on the trading time frame, so we should be on guard for that lower time frame trend to abort in the direction of the trading time frame's trend. Lower time frame ranges should be smaller in most pullbacks, and there should not be as much conviction in taking liquidity from the book. In addition, the best pullbacks are often more or less symmetrical on the trading time frame, though it is not unusual to see the occasional spike outside the confines of the pattern. These spikes can, in fact, offer attractive entry points for trades, but the majority of the action should be confined within clearly defined boundaries.

Compare Figure 3.18, which shows retracements in JPMorgan Chase & Company (NYSE: JPM) during the latter half of 2009, with Figure 3.19, which highlights retracements in U.S. Steel Corporation (NYSE: X) during the spring of the same year. Notice that the retracements in X are much more consistent: they are at approximately the same angle and the same depth, and they are generally clean, symmetrical geometric patterns. In contrast, the retracements in JPM are much more erratic. They cover very different angles, are less predictable in depth, and one, into early October, features a dramatic drop that would have shaken most longs out of the market. You would be correct in

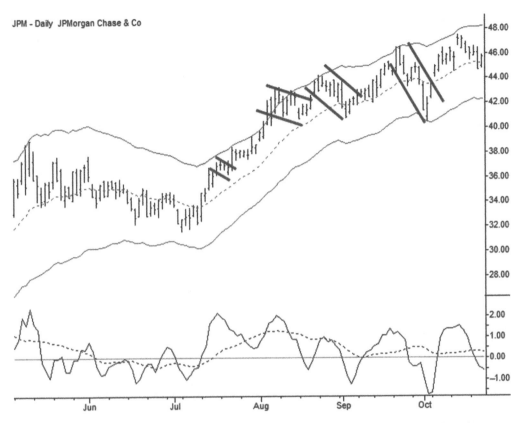

FIGURE 3.18 Erratic Pullbacks in JPM, Late 2009

surmising that the patterns in X would have been much more tradable, and that they probably offered better opportunity for most trend traders.

Common Characteristics of Failed Pullbacks

As important as it is to understand the patterns associated with successful pullbacks, it is probably equally important to understand the patterns that hint at impending failure. Understanding how patterns fail lets traders look for warning signs to exit losing trades, sometimes taking a smaller than expected loss. In addition, some very good trades are driven by traders trapped in failed patterns. This is especially common with failed breakouts, which will be covered in the next chapter, but some traders look for trades to set up around failed pullbacks as well. In general, pullback trades fail in one of three ways:

1. There is *no momentum* out of the pullback, and the market goes into a more or less flat trading range somewhere in the level of the pullback.

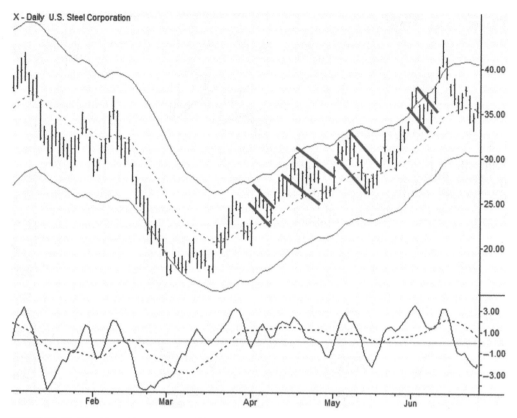

FIGURE 3.19 More Consistent Pullbacks in X, Mid-2009

2. The pullback *fails dramatically* as sharp, countertrend momentum emerges. The challenge is to distinguish between this scenario and the more common complex consolidation.

3. The next trend leg emerges out of the pullback, but it *fails in the neighborhood of the previous swing* (i.e., the high of the setup leg in an uptrend or the low of the setup leg in a downtrend).

Flat Pullback   One of the most common pullback failure patterns occurs when the market begins what looks like a good pullback but then there is simply no move out of that pullback. Instead, the market goes into a flat range, indicating that buyers and sellers are in relative balance. Trading in this new range is usually a bad idea since price action will be random and not driven by any real order flow. Also, breakouts from this new range are treacherous, with the potential for fake-outs in either direction. In most cases, the best course of action is to recognize the pattern once it has developed, book a small loss or gain on the trade, and move on to other opportunities. Figure 3.20 shows an example of a pullback in AAPL that failed to continue the trend and instead transitioned

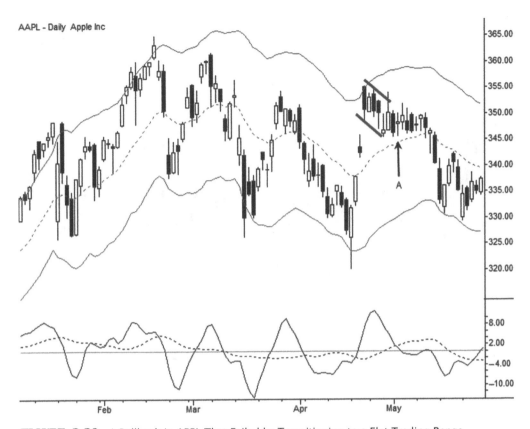

FIGURE 3.20 A Pullback in APPL That Failed by Transitioning to a Flat Trading Range

into a sideways range. Though it is difficult to set a precise point at which a trader should have recognized that the pullback was not working as expected, it should have been obvious no later than four or five bars after the point marked A on the chart. In this case, the pullback eventually failed dramatically as sharp downside momentum came into the market, but it could just as easily have resolved to the upside. The point is that this pattern indicates that whatever edge existed in the pullback is now gone.

Sharp Countertrend Momentum as Pullback Is Violated   The previous example showed a case where a pullback failed via sharp contratrend momentum after first going into a sideways range. However, the market is not always so polite. Some of the most dangerous pullback failures, at least in terms of the possibility of creating large losses, occur when the pullback simply fails sharply by breaking to the "wrong side." Pullbacks that were anticipated to have been continuation patterns in uptrends may fail through sharp breakdowns, and vice versa. These are the patterns that make risk management based solely on pattern geometry difficult—how far away do you put the stop? No matter where you might think it should go, there will, in some subset of these patterns, be spikes to that level and beyond. Figure 3.21 shows an example of a continuation

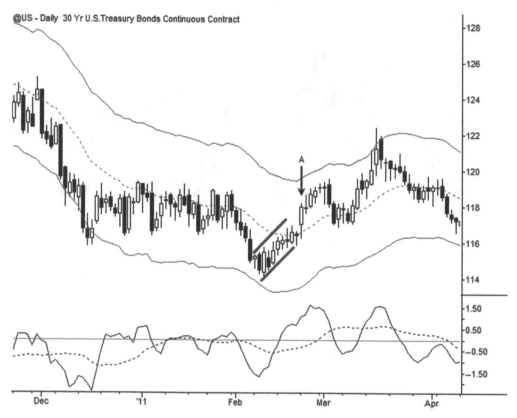

FIGURE 3.21 A Pullback in 30-Year Treasury Bond Futures That Failed via Sharp Momentum

pattern in the 30-year Treasury bond futures that seemed to have everything going for it: the market had consolidated on support for two months, the breakdown of that support was fairly clean and had good momentum, and the market started to consolidate under that previous support. This is an excellent pattern on which to base a short trade, but in this case it was not to be. At the point marked A, buyers swept the market up through the top of the pullback, back above support, and it did not look back.

It absolutely is necessary to limit your risk on these patterns, because many of them will not return to your entry price after they fail. In fact, if the pattern was a truly excellent setup, there may be many traders trapped on the wrong side of the market, and this pressure can sometimes create a long-term inflection point in a trend. Imagine shorting at the very bottom of a turn into an uptrend, and shorting more as the market rallies, only to see a full-fledged uptrend emerge. Traders will inevitably be caught in situations like this; it is the task of risk management to make sure that they become normal, planned-for losses and not outright disasters.

However, there is another important pattern to be aware of. It is sometimes possible to turn trapped traders to our advantage, as many excellent trades are driven by traders trapped either into or out of the market. In the aforementioned example, if you

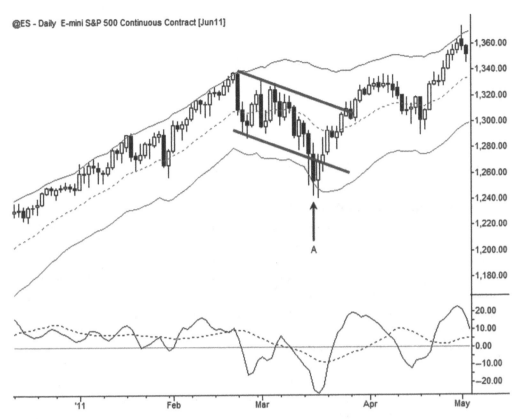

FIGURE 3.22 A Failure to Break Down Out of a Pullback in the S&P Futures Sets Up a Good With-Trend Entry

have continued shorting into the new uptrend, eventually you would have been trapped on the wrong side of the market with an outsized loss and forced to throw in the towel. This, obviously, is not good. However, take a look at Figure 3.22, which shows a complex consolidation in an uptrend in the E-mini S&P 500 Futures. At the point marked A, the consolidation had failed: the pattern was broken by two large candles under the bottom of the pattern, with a close far underneath at A. If you were an aggressive short, it might even have been reasonable to initiate a short on this bar, but look carefully at what happened next. There was no momentum and no selling conviction below the level. Within two days, the market was solidly back above the consolidation, went on to take out the highs, and put in another trend leg over the next several weeks. This is an extremely important pattern for pullback traders, who are always trying to find the ideal combination of trade location and probability. Usually, buying as low as possible means buying when prices are declining, but this type of failure at the bottom of the consolidation allows an entry at low prices that is also aligned with short-term momentum. This is an outstanding entry pattern for pullback traders.

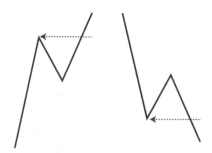

FIGURE 3.23 Profit Targets for Pullbacks In Uptrends and Downtrends

Failure around Previous Pivot   When trading pullbacks, it is unrealistic to assume that every pullback will result in a new trend leg equal to the setup leg or that they will give rise to trends that continue for many more legs. This, of course, is the best-case outcome, but it is far more common to find pullback trades that give opportunities for smaller profits. More consistent results will come from taking at least partial profits at a more conservative profit target; the pivot high or low (in an uptrend or a downtrend, respectively) of the setup leg is an ideal target and should be considered the first, most conservative profit target for any pullback trade. Figure 3.23 shows this pullback target schematically for both uptrends and downtrends.

The third pullback failure occurs around this profit target—either before, at, or just beyond it. It is not necessary to examine each possibility in detail, because they are all conceptually the same. The market reaches the neighborhood of the first profit target and simply is not able to trade very far beyond that target. For traders taking partial profits here, these patterns are not even actually failures; the first target was reached. The important point is that traders should always be on guard for potential failure at this area, particularly in the area of previous pivots (e.g., the high of the setup trend leg preceding the pullback).

There are many possibilities for trade management, depending on the trader's personality and the details of the exact trading plan. Many traders prefer to exit some portion of their pullback trades at these targets, with the idea that they will be able to endure a failure at the target without a substantial loss. In fact, by booking partial profits and reducing the position size, many times it is possible to walk away from this kind of failure with a profit on the overall trade. Figure 3.24 shows an example of a failure at the first profit target in the GBPUSD. A sustained downtrend made a complex pullback (note also the failure entry at the top of the pullback, similar to Figure 3.22 inverted), which broke down and failed to extend beyond the previous swing low. A trader on guard for this failure could certainly have booked a profit on the trade, even though the actual downswing was much smaller than previous downswings.

There are several issues to consider here. First, of the three possibilities (failure inside, precisely at, or beyond the setup leg's extreme), the one that actually trades beyond the previous pivot to make a marginal new high or low before failing is the most treacherous. The reason is that there are likely to be more trapped trend traders, and more traders

FIGURE 3.24 A Pullback in the GBPUSD Fails Near the Trend Extreme

who will be aggressive about adjusting their positions as the market retreats from that extreme; this can lead to very sharp countertrend momentum on these failures. The second issue is a mechanical one. If you intend to take profits around these previous swings, spend some time considering how you will do this. What percentage of the position will you exit? Will you do it by bidding or offering at the previous extreme, or will you wait to see the market fail? (Note that waiting for the failure can result in substantial slippage at times.) If you do exit part of the position, will you ever add it back? As you consider the theory and structure of markets, also begin to consider them within the framework of an applied trading plan.

TREND ANALYSIS

There are many tools in technical analysis for identifying and analyzing trends. The choice of which to use will depend on many factors: your personality, your trading style, what kind of trend you want to identify, where (in terms of the age of the trend) you want

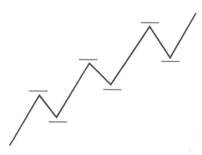

FIGURE 3.25   Higher Highs and Higher Lows in an Idealized Dow Theory Uptrend

to identify it, and how you want to trade it. A trader looking for mature trends in markets that trend well might simply look for charts that "begin at one corner of the chart and travel to the other." This might seem to be an overly simplistic approach to finding trending markets, but it works for certain kinds of traders. Other traders might look for subtle patterns and momentum shifts that suggest a trend might be turning, with the idea that they will aggressively pursue entries at those spots so that they have bought the low or sold the high if a new trend develops. All of these approaches are valid, but let's begin with a broad, structural approach to trend identification. This is pure market structure approach based largely on the work of the early authors who laid out the principles of what became known as the Dow Theory.

Dow Theory Trend Patterns

An uptrend is a pattern of successively higher pivot highs (HHs) and higher pivot lows (HLs) (see Figure 3.25). Both are important. Most people readily accept a definition of an uptrend that requires higher highs; this is intuitive, but it is easy to overlook the importance of accompanying higher lows; if a market is only making higher highs, but is not also clearly holding higher lows, the buyers are not solidly in control of that market. Conversely, a downtrend is a series of both lower lows (LLs) and lower highs (LHs) (see Figure 3.26). This is perhaps the most elementary definition of trend possible on any time frame.

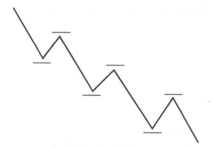

FIGURE 3.26   Dow Theory Downtrend with Lower Lows and Lower Highs

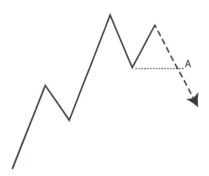

FIGURE 3.27 Dow Theory Trend Change #1

Under this system, there are three possible trend states: up, down, or uncertain; many people incorrectly assume that a market is either in an uptrend or in a downtrend, but the third possibility is important. There are several reasons that a trend could be identified as uncertain. For example, perhaps the pattern in the market actually *is* unclear and more or less random; we can usually force any structure into some pattern, but such a Procrustean approach is rarely constructive. It is far better to have tools that respect the realities of the market, and at times the market is simply uncertain. The best trend identification tools will respect the potential for ambiguity.

One of the most important aspects of the study of trends is the study of how they end. Under this idealized Dow Theory structure, there are two categories of trend changes. In the first, the market fails to make a new extreme on a with-trend leg. In an uptrend, if the market falls short of the previous pivot high, the trend status becomes uncertain. Note that it is not yet in a downtrend, because the downtrend requires both lower highs *and* lower lows. Conceptually, buyers failed to push the market to new highs; this is a warning shot across the bow, but not a confirmation of a trend change. It is not uncommon to see a market fail to make a new high, consolidate a bit, and then continue the uptrend unabated. The trend change is actually confirmed only when price trades through the last pivot low, marking a lower low (see Figure 3.27). Once that previous pivot low has been violated, any upswing will now begin from a lower low. Since the market has put in both a lower high and a lower low, the technical requirement for a trend change to downtrend is satisfied.

The second trend change occurs when prices retreat so aggressively from the highs that they take out the previous pivot low; at this point, the trend pattern is broken because the market shows a higher high and a lower low. (See point A in Figure 3.28.) This pattern is less common, because it requires significant volatility off the high to take out the pivot low in one swing. It is, however, an important pattern because it often suggests trapped trend traders and can set up very attractive countertrend trades, or a sharp trend change with potential for continuation in the new trend. The actual trend change is more complicated in this case, requiring two more steps. The next rally must fall short of the previous high (point B in Figure 3.28), but the trend change is not confirmed until the market again takes out the previous low. Why? Because it would be possible for the

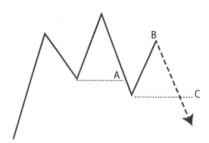

FIGURE 3.28   Dow Theory Trend Change #2

market to put in a lower high at B, hold a higher low than C, and then continue in an uptrend by trading through B. The only way to be certain that the market will show the lower high and lower low is for the previous low to fail to hold as support.

It goes without saying that these patterns are simply inverted for a downtrend changing to an uptrend. In the first case, a downtrend fails to make a lower low, and then the trend change is confirmed when the previous pivot high is violated. In the second case, a sharp rally takes out the previous pivot high, the subsequent decline falls short of new lows, and then the next rally makes a new high.

An Important Complication: The Complex Consolidation   Figure 3.29 shows an uptrending market with a complex consolidation, which is a powerful continuation pattern. Note that a naive application of the previous change-of-trend rules would have flagged a downtrend at precisely the point you should have been *buying* this market. This complex consolidation pattern is very common, and it often leads to exceptional trade opportunities in the direction of the existing trend. If you were to use this structure in a vacuum, you would frequently find yourself positioning short at precisely the point you should be buying in these complex consolidations.

This does not compromise the validity of this simple labeling system, which does what it is designed to do very well: it identifies breaks in the pattern of trends, and marks

Trend change?

FIGURE 3.29   A Complex Consolidation Will Flag a Trend Change According to a Strict Interpretation of Dow Theory Rules

those areas for further attention. Also, in any trading tool there is always a trade-off between being early with many false alerts and being late while waiting for confirmation. Next, we examine a few other methods of identifying trends, all of which lag this swing analysis and all of which also have their own false signals.

Indicators

It is possible to use information from indicators to quantify the direction, strength, and potential of trends. These tools may be applied in a strict, quantitative manner, either singly or in combination with other indicators, or they may be used as discretionary inputs into a more extensive process. In the case of trends, indicators and other tools can be useful because they are sometimes able to filter out noise and to reveal the deeper market structure. An experienced trader can do this based on the raw patterns of price, but newer traders will often find that an indicator simplifies their task considerably. In addition, experienced traders may still want to use some combination of these tools to aid in scanning many markets quickly for specific trade conditions.

Slope of a Single Moving Average   Moving average models are used in econometrics to analyze and forecast trends. One of the simplest trend indicators used by traders is the slope of a single moving average. The length of the moving average will determine the sensitivity of the average, or, more accurately, the time frame on which it will evaluate trends. For instance, a 10-period moving average will have a lot to say about the trend over the past 10 bars, but is not likely to be relevant to the trend over the past 100 bars.

Figure 3.30 shows trend changes marked by the slope of a 50-period simple moving average. Notice that the average lags the actual trend change in the market, but that many false signals come when the average is flat. Those trades could be eliminated by the creation of an "undefined" zone around the average, but this would also come at the expense of later signals for many valid trend changes.

Other Indicators   There are many trend indicators derived from crossovers of one or more moving averages, and a number of more complex tools are also in common use. The Directional Movement Index (DMI) and the Average Directional Index (ADX) were created by Welles Wilder (1978) to quantify trend direction and strength. Linda Raschke and Laurence Conners (1996) advocate usage of the ADX without the DMI to define the strength of the trend while gauging trend direction from other indicators, and they introduce a number of other refinements to the use of this tool. Other traders will use tools such as the MACD histogram or other momentum indicators to provide indications and warnings of trend change. Last, a number of indicators exist that use more sophisticated math, such as linear regression lines, or that apply digital signal processing tools to price data in order to expose the underlying cycles.

Each of these approaches has its merits, but they also bring dangers. Traders can be seduced by the siren song of finding the perfect indicator, and can spend years searching for the best settings or the best combinations of tools. Many traders will find better

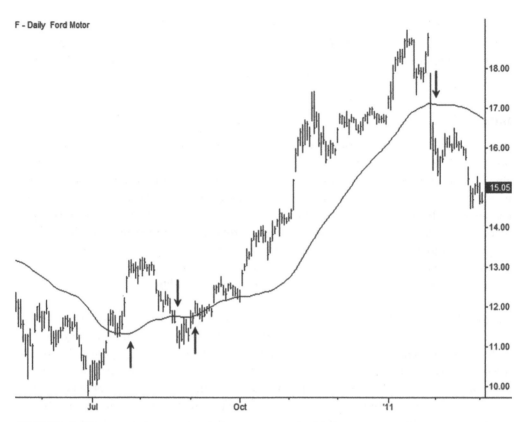

FIGURE 3.30 Trend Changes Flagged by the Slope of a 50-Period Moving Average

results by learning to read price action and market structure, using simple tools to constrain their actions to the realities of the marketplace, and always remembering that our tools are only tools. Go back through the last several charts, and notice how the trend changes given by each of the following tools usually lags the trend changes that you would have identified by simply reading the emerging price structure in each chart. There is no right or wrong here, but there is also no holy grail.

Understanding Trend Integrity

For most traders, the question of trend integrity is paramount. How strong is the trend? Are there any warning signs that suggest it could turn? How far might it go? What should our expectations be when it does turn? How can we monitor the strength of the trend as it waxes and wanes, and gain some more insight into the relative buying and selling pressure behind the trend? These are all important questions, and they all can be addressed by some very simple analyses. There are three primary points to consider: length of swings, rate of trend, and the character of each trend leg.

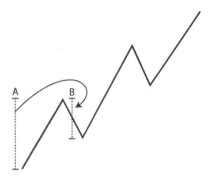

FIGURE 3.31 In an Uptrend, Upswings Are Larger than Downswings

Length of Swing Analysis

Simple math tells us that in an uptrend the upswings must be longer than the downswings, and the reverse is true in downtrends. If a market is gaining more on the upswings than it is losing on the pullbacks, the net effect will be to move to a higher price level—this is a very elementary definition of a trend and is also consistent with the Dow Theory trend construct. One very simple way we can look at trends is to draw lines connecting the pivot lows to the pivot highs in each of the major swings, and then simply compare the lengths of those lines to previous swings in terms of both vertical distance (price) and horizontal distance (time). Some examples will help to clarify. In a strong uptrend, the upswings are larger than the downswings, usually both in price and in time (see Figure 3.31).

Any break or change in this pattern should be a warning that something is changing and that the trend integrity could be weakening. For instance, a common pattern that suggests the trend is running out of steam occurs when successive upswings are shorter relative to previous upswings, as in Figure 3.32. It is also interesting to consider the overlap between this length of swing analysis and traditional chart patterns. For instance, Figure 3.32 might also be read as a "gently rounding top" by chart pattern–oriented traders. With some slight adjustments, the same pattern of smaller upswings might

FIGURE 3.32 Shorter Upswings Can Be a Warning of Impending Trend Failure

FIGURE 3.33 The First Downswing That Is Larger than the Preceding Upswing, in Time or Price, Is a Warning to Pay Attention

generate a double top, a triple top, or a head and shoulders pattern. This is a good lesson—all of these patterns are *essentially the same pattern.*

A very important structural element in swing analysis is the first downswing in an uptrend that is longer than the preceding upswing (see Figure 3.33). Vertically, this swing will make a lower low, setting up a potential trend change condition, but it is even more important to realize that this swing can indicate a distinct change of character in the market. It usually shows a failure on the part of the buyers to support the market, and, depending on the strength of the selling pressure in the swing (which must be judged from price action or lower time frame market structure), it may even set up a potential countertrend short on the next bounce. This is perhaps the single most important pattern in length of swing analysis.

Of course, it is not always so simple. Though we might expect a shortable bounce following the pattern in Figure 3.33, it is also possible that this type of downswing may simply set up a complex consolidation. Furthermore, though a complex consolidation is usually a trend continuation pattern, there are other possible resolutions that may follow that pattern. Any of the possible pullback failure patterns apply equally well to complex consolidations because they are simple pullbacks on the higher time frame.

These examples have dealt exclusively with uptrends, but they are simply reflected and reversed for downtrends. These patterns can form a foundation for a robust understanding of trend analysis. Do not be put off by the simplicity of this analysis. In the right context, simple tools work very well.

Using Trend Lines to Define Rate of Trend

Trend lines are one of the most used and abused tools in modern technical analysis. One good working definition of a trend line is a line drawn between two points on a chart, but then there are the internal trend lines, which can be drawn anywhere through the middle of price bars. There are many possible variations of these lines, but the one rule is that however the trader chooses to define trend lines, they should be used and applied consistently.

The Standard Trend Line   Standard uptrend lines are drawn between higher lows in an uptrend; the standard downtrend line is a line drawn between lower highs in a downtrend. The uptrend line shows where buyers have stepped in on the declines with additional demand and have bid the market higher, which is why Wyckoff called this line the *demand line*. In a downtrend, the downtrend line, or the *supply line*, shows where additional sellers have come into the market to arrest the bounces. If you are drawing standard trend lines, be certain of these points:

- They slope *with* the trend. Uptrend lines are upward sloping, and downtrend lines slope downward.
- Uptrend lines are *underneath* prices, marking areas of potential support. Downtrend lines are possible resistance areas, and must be drawn *above* prices.

Figure 3.34 shows examples of correctly drawn standard trend lines in the XLF.

FIGURE 3.34   Standard Trend Lines in the SPDR Select Sector Fund for the Financial Sector (NYSE: XLF)

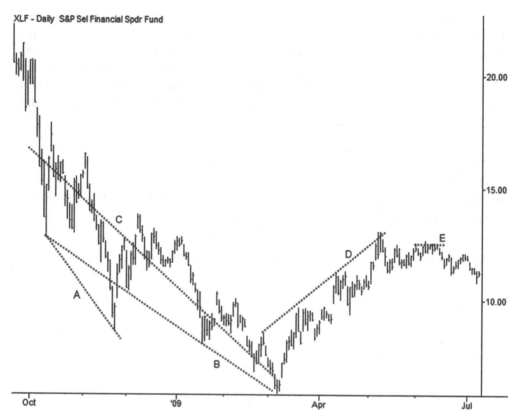

FIGURE 3.35 Nonstandard Trend Lines in XLF

Figure 3.35 shows examples of nonstandard trend lines:

- A is drawn between *lows* in a downtrend instead of between highs in a downtrend.
- B is also drawn between lows in a downtrend. Furthermore, it ignores a large price spike in an effort to fit the line to later data.
- C is more of a best-fit line drawn through the center of a price area. These may be drawn freehand or via a procedure like linear regression.
- D is drawn between highs in an uptrend.
- E raises a critical point about trend lines: They are lines drawn between successive *swings* in the market. If there are no swings, there should be no trend line. It would be hard to argue that the market was showing any swings at E, at least on this time frame. This trend line may be valid on a lower time frame, but it is nonstandard on this time frame.

In general, trend lines are tools to define the relationship between swings, and are a complement to the simple length of swing analysis. As such, one of the requirements for drawing trend lines is that there *must actually be swings* in the market. We see many cases where markets are flat, and it is possible to draw trend lines that touch the tops or bottoms of many consecutive price bars. With one important exception later in this chapter, these types of trend lines do not tend to be very significant. They are penetrated easily by the smallest motions in the market, and there is no reliable price action after the penetration. Avoid drawing these trend lines in flat markets with no definable swings.

The Parallel Trend Line   This useful tool is built in three steps:

1. Draw a correct, standard trend line.
2. Create a parallel line. (Most charting packages will allow you to clone the line, but you can accomplish the same thing by drawing the trend line, dragging it away while preserving the angle, and then redrawing the original line.)
3. Anchor the parallel line to the opposite side of the trend. (In an uptrend, it should be attached to pivot highs, and to pivot lows in a downtrend.) It is very important that it is anchored to the most extreme point *between the two initial anchor points for the standard trend line.* The parallel line must not cut prices between those two initial points.

The purpose of the parallel trend line is to create a trend channel that shows the range of fluctuations that the market has accepted as normal. In general, if you are long in an uptrend and prices rise to the upper parallel trend line, it probably makes sense to be slightly defensive and to take some profits. The same idea applies, inverted, to down-trending markets. Of course, the market can take out the parallel channel and continue, but this is frequently an area where there is additional volatility and heightened potential for reversal.

Figure 3.36 shows an example of a parallel trend line on weekly bars of the S&P 500 Cash index. A few points to consider: The long dotted line is the parallel trend channel, which was drawn at point A on the chart. This is important; the line was in place in mid-2010, so it provided an already-established reference going into 2011. Note that the partial line marked B is *not* correct because it cuts through prices between the two attachment points for the standard trend line. Most importantly, notice the price action at the points marked C, which provided clear reference points to reduce long positions or even to initiate aggressive shorts.

There are, broadly speaking, two expectations for price action near this line. In the first case, prices reach the top of the channel and pause or back off, as in Figure 3.36. Depending on your style, you may or may not want to attempt to fade the trend at the line, but this is difficult because there are usually no logical and clearly defined risk points. Trades like this may be overly aggressive, but it should at least be a reasonable spot to reduce exposure and to book partial profits. It is important to monitor price action around these levels carefully, because there is the chance that the market will pause, consolidate, and then press through the channel. When this happens, it is a strong vote of confidence from the dominant group in the market (buyers in uptrends, sellers in

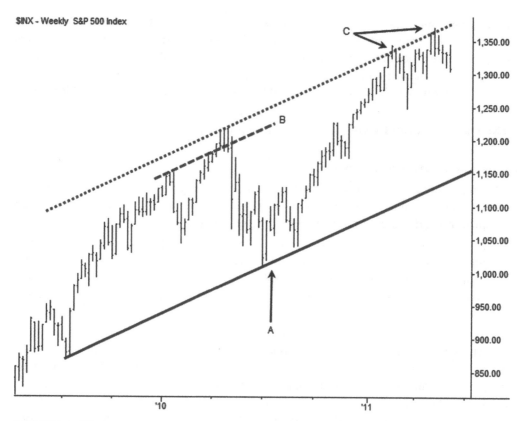

FIGURE 3.36 A Parallel Trend Line on the Weekly S&P 500 Cash Index

downtrends) and often leads to a new trend that proceeds at a faster rate. Figure 3.37 shows an example of this phenomenon in silver futures.

This is a good example of what people mean when they say "reading the market tape," which is, in part, judging how the market acts around critical levels. A key component of this is price action on lower time frames, which can only partially be inferred from the trading time frame. A complete understanding requires inspection of several lower time frame charts, and, ideally, monitoring in real time as the action develops. If you found yourself short after point A in Figure 3.37, it would have been relatively easy to see that you were on the wrong side of the market. What should have happened, if your short was correct, was a fairly immediate meltdown. Being responsive to information often allows a trader to reduce losses on losing trades, and, ideally, to position on the correct side of the trade.

One- to Three-Bar Trend Lines   In general, the significance of a trend line depends on the significance of the points used to define the line. However, there are some special cases where very short-term trend lines may give good trading signals. Charles Drummond (1980) has used these short-term trend lines as the foundation for his Drummond

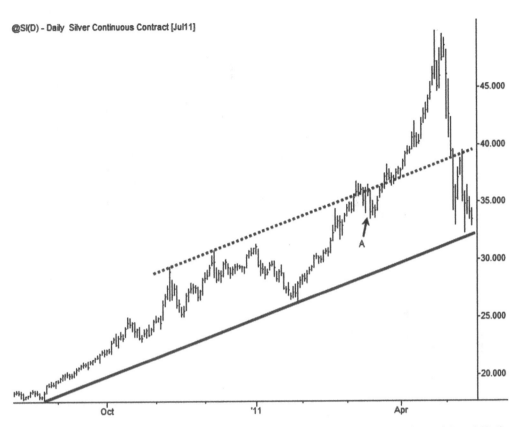

FIGURE 3.37 A Break of the Parallel Trend Line Can Often Lead to an Accelerated Trend (Daily Silver Futures)

Geometry, a unique and interesting perspective on the traditional concepts of support and resistance. In addition, Al Brooks (2009) writes about similar usage of short-term trend lines primarily applied to intraday trading, which he calls *Micro Trendlines*. Newer traders might be best off avoiding these lines, as there is the temptation to simply connect *any* two points on a chart to see what happens. It is easy to become sidetracked and spend much time drawing, erasing, and redrawing trend lines, when they should be focusing on the bigger-picture trend structure as it develops. At some point in their development as traders, they may find that these small trend lines offer some interesting opportunities for precisely timing entries.

The two-day line drawn from the day before yesterday's low to yesterday's high, and extended into today's space on the chart will often define areas where the market is likely to exhaust itself in an overextended condition. (The corresponding downtrend line can be drawn from the day before yesterday's high to yesterday's low, and into today's price range.) This line is not even a trend line proper, in that we do not look for the slope of the line to contain prices or to define the trend. Rather, the point where the line intersects today's prices is a potential reversal or inflection point. As with all trend

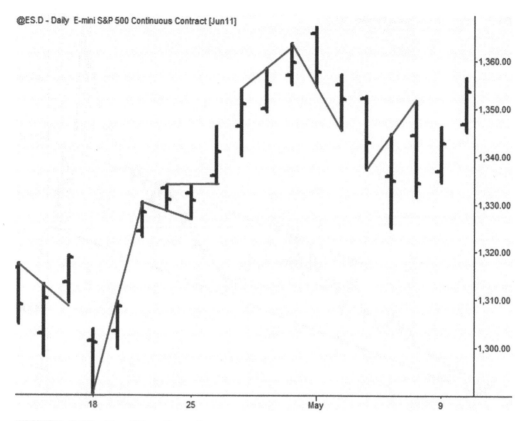

FIGURE 3.38　Trend Lines Drawn between Two Bars Can Provide Good Inflections on the Next Bar

lines, there is no magic here; it works because markets tend to oscillate within certain volatility levels that can be geometrically defined by the previous movements of that market. Figure 3.38 shows examples of these very short trend lines, but these are only a few isolated examples.

One good application for these short-term trend lines occurs frequently in pullbacks. These pullback patterns often have fairly clean boundaries of support and resistance, and small trend lines can be drawn over, under, or touching multiple bars in a row. (This is an exception to the rule earlier that trend lines should define relationships between real swings in the market.) A very common pattern is to see these short-term trend lines violated for short periods of time, and for the recovery from that break to actually be the catalyst for a move in the opposite direction of the break. For instance, Figure 3.39 shows a clean buy off a (nonstandard) trend line at the bottom of a pullback in an uptrend. Normally, this would probably not be an attractive spot to initiate a long, as we try to avoid buying after a buying climax, but the duration of the consolidation was sufficient to work off the climax condition. The market consolidated long enough that it was reasonable to attempt a long trade. If you had been looking for a spot to buy this market, note how

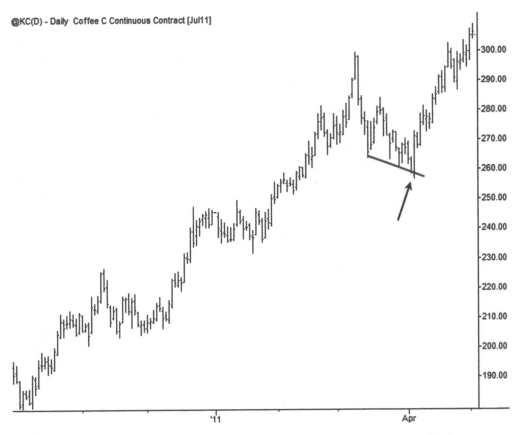

@KC(D) - Daily Coffee C Continuous Contract [Jul11]

FIGURE 3.39 The Break of the Trend Line under the Pullback Was the Catalyst for the Move

the break of the very small trend line actually provides the entry point. You will have to decide how you want to manage the risk in these trades, but one simple way might be to wait for the market to recover back above the trend line, and then to buy with a stop just under the low of the bar that broke the trend line.

It is always important to ask why a pattern should work. In this case, there is a good explanation. The little spike beyond the short-term trend line is a buying or selling climax on lower time frames, so it is a natural exhaustion point for the countertrend move. Furthermore, there will be traders who exit their positions when those trend lines are broken, and they will be forced to chase the market to get back in. Remember that trapped traders drive some of the best trades, and that traders can be as effectively trapped out of positions as in. The key to the success of this pattern is that the market should not spend much time outside the trend line. (The definition of "much time" depends on the time frame—if weekly bars, probably not more than two days. If daily bars, then probably not more than a few hours. But on a 1-minute chart, we would want to see prices back above the trend line in less than 30 seconds.)

Rate of Trend

Markets rarely trend at one simple, consistent rate. It is very common to see a trend line broken and for the original trend to hold, albeit at a more shallow slope. This is one reason why naively trading on breaks of trend lines can be frustrating; these breaks are often simply moves into another degree, level, or rate of trend. Figure 3.40 shows trend lines redrawn to define the new rate of trend. This often has to be done many times in extended trends, leaving a characteristic fan of trend lines.

It is also possible for a market to define a new, steeper trend. A common spot where this can occur is on a break beyond a parallel trend line, but this can also happen at any point in a trend if a catalyst further tips the supply/demand imbalance. In Figure 3.41, Cotton futures slowly ramp into a trend that eventually ends in a parabolic climax, and ever-steeper trend lines must be drawn to contain the new trend. These greatly accelerated trends will eventually reach rates that are unsustainable, as they often end in minor climax moves. At some point, trend lines will be more or less vertical, and it is important to avoid attaching too much significance to a break of a nearly vertical trend

FIGURE 3.40 A Fan of Trend Lines as the Intraday Russell 2000 Exchange-Traded Fund (ETF) (IWM) Finds New Rates of Trend on Small Breaks of the Trend Line

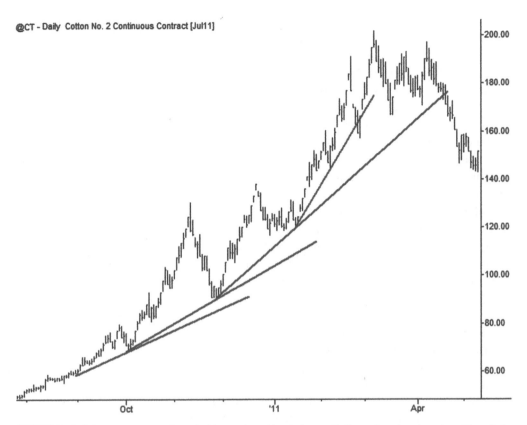

@CT - Daily Cotton No. 2 Continuous Contract [Jul11]

FIGURE 3.41 Steepening Trend Lines Are Needed to Define the Accelerating Trend in Cotton Futures

line. They are still useful from the standpoint that they do define the rate of the trend, but they are also broken easily and with impunity. However, if these trend lines are marking parabolic markets, it is important to be responsive to the possibility of a dramatic collapse. Trend lines may not be the ideal tools to trade in these areas, but they can point out important structures and areas to watch.

Character of Trend Legs

One important question for discretionary traders to consider is how to weigh objective and subjective elements in technical analysis. Some things are simple and clear, which is one reason that many traders focus on indicators: Price is above the moving average, or it is not. The MACD histogram is higher than it was yesterday, or it is not. In each of these cases, there could not be much room for debate. However, when we start talking about things like character of moves or judging the conviction behind such moves, we are on shakier ground. Two analysts could look at the same chart and the same set of data, and come to different conclusions, and the same analyst might even make a different call looking at the same data on a different day. To some critics, this invalidates the discipline of technical analysis, or forces them to focus on only the objective elements. This is a mistake, because some of the most powerful tools of technical analysis are at least partially subjective. The question should be: How can we build, refine, and verify the validity of our subjective analyses?

This is a good question. Part of the answer is to remember that the beginner has not seen enough market data to start to develop this subjective sense. For this reason, beginners are probably better advised to stick with more concrete elements, and to take careful notes of their impressions and subjective judgments as intuition starts to develop. Intuition, the classic "market feel," is based on a combination of a number of elements, most of which in themselves are fairly objective. Where the subjective element comes into play is in the synthesis of many individual factors, and it can be difficult to articulate precise rules for this part of the process. This is what good traders do: they are synthesizers, taking many disparate elements and combining them into a whole that is much greater than the sum of the parts. As an example, in considering the character of trend legs, the following elements might be important:

- Length of swing on the trading time frame. Longer swings usually mean more conviction, with the exception of potential exhaustion if a market is overextended. As a rule of thumb, if, after several swings in the same direction, a swing emerges that is two to three times the length of the average swing, this may indicate an overextended market and a possible climax.
- Number of bars in each leg. This is a measure of time, and is usually redundant because we can perceive the same information via the slope of the trend on the chart. There is almost never any need to count bars.
- Height of bars near the beginning and end of the legs. Larger bars (relative to the average bar size) usually indicate increased conviction, but very large bars near the end of a swing can indicate exhaustion or climax, which will usually be obvious on the lower time frame.
- The position of the closes in the trading time frame bars. In general, closes below the midpoint of the bar in an uptrend probably indicate some disagreement on a lower time frame. Conversely, closes right at the extreme high of the bar, especially for multiple bars in a row, can indicate exhaustion. This is counterintuitive, but it is a statistically verifiable principle of price behavior.
- Presence or lack of significant price action around previous resistance levels.
- Presence or absence of lower time frame pullbacks within each trend leg. Trend legs can be clean one-directional moves on the lower time frame, or they can hide ABC structures on the lower time frame. Complex consolidations can work off overextended conditions, setting the market up for another trend thrust.
- Higher time frame considerations. For instance, if a trend on the trading time frame is exhausting into a higher time frame resistance, this might be something to pay attention to. In contrast, if a strong uptrend develops on the trading time frame at

the same point where a higher time frame bull flag breaks out, this is a pattern that is likely to see some continuation.

- Volume and trading activity matter. How easily does the market go up? Are there gaps up that do not fill on a daily chart? Intraday, are price levels skipped because large orders clear many levels in the book?

SUMMARY

Many traders focus their trading activity exclusively on trending environments; there is certainly some justification for this because many outstanding trades come in trending environments. Market structure in trends is often driven by a strong imbalance of buying and selling pressure, it is relatively easy to define risk points for trades, and some of the cleanest, easiest trades come from trends. However, markets do not always trend. We do not always know when markets are trending, how long the trend will last, or what potential our trend trades may have. A complete understanding of market structure also includes a good grasp of the trading ranges, and the common patterns by which markets transition between the two.

CHAPTER 4

On Trading Ranges

The heavy is the root of the light.
The unmoved is the source of all movement.

—Daodejing (ca. 6 BCE)

P rice action in trends is often not that difficult to read, as there are a number of patterns that give insight into the integrity of the trend at any moment; trading ranges are more complicated because price action in those ranges is much more random. The defining patterns of trading ranges are the tests of support and resistance near the confines of the range, but price action around support and resistance is complex. Much of the conventional wisdom about support and resistance is not correct, and many support or resistance levels used by traders are probably no better than any random level in the market. The study of trading ranges must begin with a careful look at support and resistance, with a willingness to question some long-held beliefs about these levels.

SUPPORT AND RESISTANCE

In their venerable bible of technical analysis, Edwards and Magee (1948; 4th ed., 1964) define *support* as "the price level at which a sufficient amount of demand is forthcoming to stop, and possibly turn higher for a time, a downtrend"; they give the inverse definition for *resistance*. The idea is that, as price declines, lower prices will naturally find more willing buyers. At some point, price declines far enough that buyers are willing to soak up all the sell orders in the market, and the market will stop going down. This theoretical concept is sound, but there is another important point to consider: real markets have so many competing influences and so much noise that prices frequently stop at random levels. That, coupled with our innate tendency to find patterns in random data, can cause support and resistance areas to appear on charts for no significant reason.

Potential Support/Resistance

To start, consider an important refinement to the concept of support and resistance. This may seem like a subtle and insignificant point, but it is important. Anytime you think, speak, or write about a support area, attach the word *potential* to that definition. Prices are not coming down to a support area; they are coming down to a *potential* support area. Too many times, traders think that these areas are magic lines on the chart, and that price will bounce there. This may be as much a function of language as anything else, but this change in thinking will remind you that the best we can say about a support area is that it is an area where price may have a higher probability of pausing. It is easy to point to these areas in the middle of charts and to say how well they worked, but dealing with decision making under the uncertainty of the hard right edge is quite a different matter. Be flexible and open to the message of developing price action; always attach the qualifier *potential* when considering any support or resistance level.

In addition, support and resistance should properly be thought of as zones or areas rather than exact lines. If you were drawing them on paper charts, just like trend lines, a crayon might be the appropriate tool, not a drafting pen. It is unrealistic to expect prices to come to a potential resistance level and to stop precisely at the level. It is far more likely to see prices stop at some point in front of the level, or for the level to be violated. If the level is significant and closely watched by many market participants, it is not uncommon to see large spikes through the level, followed quickly by renewed selling at the resistance level. Consider this action in the context of the classic Wyckoff springs and upthrusts discussed earlier; traders need to consider this point in their process of risk and trade management.

Broken Support Becomes Resistance

One of the classic rules of support and resistance is that support, once violated, becomes resistance. Conversely, resistance, once violated, becomes support. (You already should be thinking, "Wait a minute—support, once violated, becomes *potential* resistance.") The reason given for this is that traders made a stand at a previous resistance level by attempting to sell enough to hold down prices. They failed when price traded through that resistance, and those traders incurred losses on their short positions that were entered at the level. If price returns to the same level after trading higher, they will be at breakeven on their shorts and will cover them (buy them back) in an attempt to reduce further losses, or so the theory goes. Their previous selling efforts at a level now turn into buying pressure at the same level, which may be able to at least temporarily halt a rally. Schematically, this pattern looks something like Figure 4.1; after resistance breaks (A), we can anticipate possible support when price trades back to the level that was formerly resistance.

The Dark Secret of Support and Resistance

We can find many examples of this principle in real market action. Consider the following examples where a support level, once violated, becomes resistance and vice versa, on

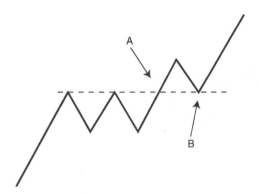

FIGURE 4.1 Resistance Becomes Support

intraday charts of Baidu, Inc. (Nasdaq: BIDU), a fairly volatile and active stock at the time. Notice how well these levels are defined, and how well they hold on the retests. Figure 4.2 shows a classic example where a resistance level held at A, was broken at B, and then held cleanly as support on a retest at C.

Figure 4.3 shows another example where previous support was broken, but then held as resistance on three successive retests. Note in particular that the last retest saw

FIGURE 4.2 Resistance Breaks (B) and Holds as Support on the Retest

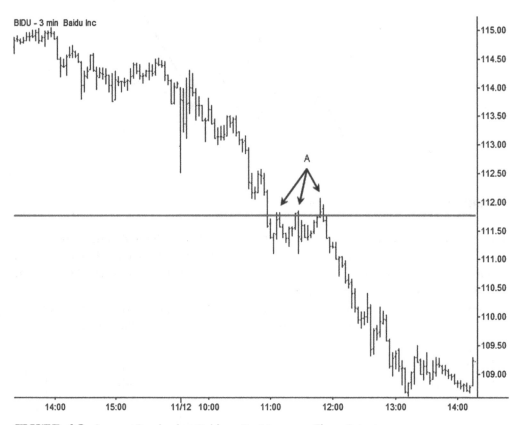

FIGURE 4.3 Support Breaks, but Holds as Resistance on Three Retests

price trade well through the level, but sellers quickly won and drove the market lower. It is common to see price penetrate a level just enough to lure traders into making the wrong decisions at these points. In this case, shorts using the level to manage their risk would have likely bought to cover, as it seemed resistance was failing; this type of action and reversal is often a catalyst for a strong move when the trapped traders panic out of their positions.

Last, Figure 4.4 shows an example in which a level was engaged nine times in the space of two trading days, holding cleanly on all but two of the tests.

These are textbook examples of price action around support and resistance levels, but there is one small problem: the levels in these examples are random price levels! These are not actual support and resistance levels; they were drawn by hiding the price bars and randomly drawing lines on the chart without regard to prices or market structure. (This was done on a live video available at http://adamhgrimes.com/blog/2011/12/04/randomsrlevels/) You can, and should, reproduce this experiment yourself. This is an experiential process—you must actually *do* this yourself, ideally several times. You may be very surprised to see that many of the standard patterns around support and resistance

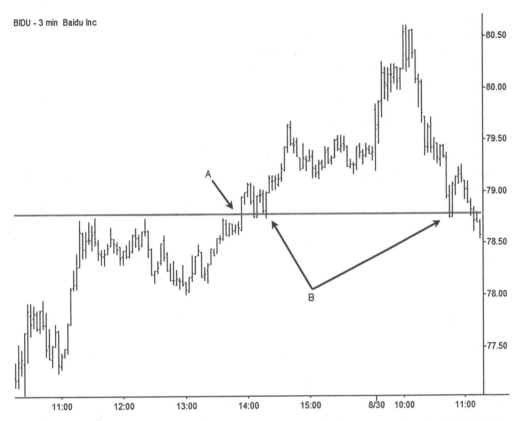

FIGURE 4.4 Clear Resistance Is Tested Multiple Times, Breaks (A), and Then Holds Cleanly as Support When Retested (B)

occur around these random levels in just the same way. Almost any random line drawn in the market will function as believable support or resistance.

Create Your Own Support and Resistance Levels

1. Take a price chart of any market and hide the bars. Depending on your charting package, there are many ways to do this, but the easiest is probably to set the color of the bars the same as the background of the chart.
2. Draw random lines on the chart. They may slant as trend lines, be horizontal, or even be curves. When you draw them, you will be drawing on a blank chart space, so many of the lines will not touch prices. This is fine—they *are* random lines, after all.
3. Restore the price bars and then look at each point where price touches your random lines. Imagine that these are important levels, generated by whatever process you use to find your support and resistance levels.

(Continued)

4. Another refinement, if your charting package will allow it, is to draw lines on higher time frames (weekly or monthly) and then switch the price chart to intraday (5- to 30-minute), preserving the same lines on the chart. Again, examine with fresh eyes each spot where price touches the level.
5. Now, ask yourself if the support and resistance levels you are using are better than these lines. Are you sure?

In almost all cases, when you ask traders how they know that the levels they are using are actually valid, the answer is something like, "Well, look at how it works. Can't you just see that these are good levels from the way the market trades around them?" The answer is, "No, you can't." Your eye will be fooled by the presence of a line on the chart, and you cannot trust your subjective evaluation of levels. Remember, if something is random, we cannot use it to make money; so the question you really need to ask yourself is: how do you know the levels you are using are any better than random levels? This is a question of profound importance that few traders consider deeply.

Support and Resistance in Action

Leaving aside for now this critical concern about the validity of levels, let's consider some practical issues of trading support and resistance. In most cases, the most significant support and resistance levels, the ones that are more likely to have an actual impact on prices, are levels that are very obvious on a chart. When these levels do work in a clearly nonrandom fashion, it is usually because many market participants are watching them, and they are obvious to everyone. Visible pivots (especially on higher time frames), levels that have been tested several times, extremes of large spikes, and the highs and lows of the previous day are examples of areas that may attract unusual attention and interest from market participants.

Expected Value around Support and Resistance   Figure 4.5 illustrates a common fallacy about trading around support and resistance. Imagine you are contemplating buying the market at the point marked "??" and you broadly reason that there are only two possible price paths. If price goes down a small amount, the support level will be violated, so you can justify a very tight stop. On the other hand, there seems to be virtually unlimited upside potential. Many traders make the mistake of thinking that they can buy very close to support with tight stops because the potential reward is much greater. They reason that if the reward is 10 times larger than their risk, they can be wrong many times and still make money.

To see the problem with this plan, assume for a moment that the market in Figure 4.5 is a random walk market, and you will have a reward of 10 units for a risk of 1 unit if you buy the market at the point marked with the question marks. If the random walk describes the price path, then over a large set of trades, you will discover that your win ratio is a little over 9 percent, leaving an expected value of zero. If you try some other strategy—taking smaller profits, for instance—your win ratio will increase, but now the

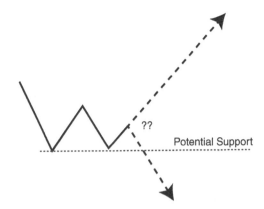

FIGURE 4.5 If Reward Is Much Greater Than Risk, Is It Always a Good Idea to Buy Here?

reward/risk ratio will also shift, again resulting in an expected value of zero. There is no possible way to profit in a random walk market—*this is absolutely axiomatic*. If it is not intuitive, you must work with these concepts until it is; without that understanding, it is very difficult to trade profitably.

So there is no escaping this truth—if you are buying in front of support or shorting in front of resistance, you must have an edge beyond just having a much larger profit target than stop loss. You must have a reason for expecting nonrandom price action off the level.

Clean or Sloppy Tests Support and resistance often do not hold perfectly clean tests. Allowing for these sloppy tests may sometimes lure us into seeing levels where none actually exist, but they actually *are* a reality of market action. There is no perfect solution here, but one thing to consider is the past history of price action around a level. If it has been violated many times with sloppy tests, it is reasonable to assume that future tests will also be sloppy. Figure 4.6 shows examples of several sloppy support tests in Netflix, Inc. (Nasdaq: NFLX) on a daily chart. Just by looking at the chart, you can see this stock has not held clean levels in the past, so it would be unrealistic to expect it to start doing so in the future.

However, even if a market does tend to hold levels cleanly, this does not mean that these levels are easy to trade. It might seem as though a good plan would be to get a position as close to a level as possible, and to stop out a tick on the other side of the level. In many cases, the catalyst for an up move may be a drop of clean support, which will generate volatile selling as stop orders are triggered, followed by strong buying that pushes the market back above the level. (Obviously, the reverse applies for resistance.) The market essentially knows where stop orders are likely to cluster, and those stops will often be targeted. Figure 4.7 shows some examples of very clean support and resistance on an intraday chart of Freeport-McMoRan Copper & Gold Inc. (NYSE: FCX). (Note that the lines have been offset from prices to highlight the clean tests.) Though the eye is drawn to these clean levels, notice that this same chart has other points with sloppier tests of levels.

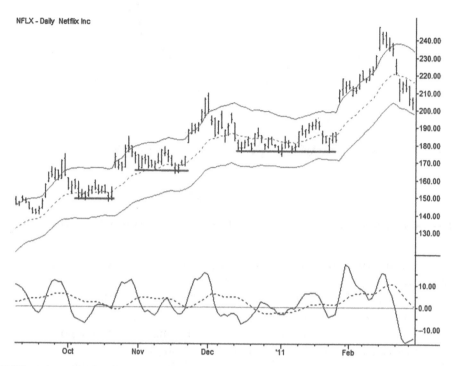

FIGURE 4.6 Sloppy Tests of Support in NFLX

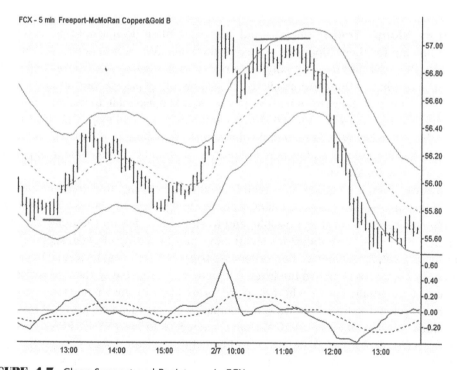

FIGURE 4.7 Clean Support and Resistance in FCX

Stop Placement for Support and Resistance In considering stop placement, there is a trade-off between close stops that allow tight risk points with lower probability and wider stops that result in larger, infrequent losses. At first glance, it would seem like further stops are always preferable since they give the market more room to fluctuate and a higher probability of the trade being profitable, but there is another factor to consider: many traders will size positions based on the risk in the trade. (See Chapters 8 and 9.) Tighter stops allow larger position sizes and potentially better reward/risk ratios, so there is good reason to use stops that are as tight as is reasonably possible. The right answer depends on a combination of your style and personality, and the reality of the specific market you are trading.

In general, there are three specific areas where you might consider placing stops against support levels. In Figure 4.8, imagine that you have established a long position in Natural Gas futures somewhere near the right edge of the chart. The three possible stop areas are marked on this chart.

Stop B is probably the most logical stop, a tick beyond the most extreme level reached in the support area. This stop has the benefit of respecting the geometry of the

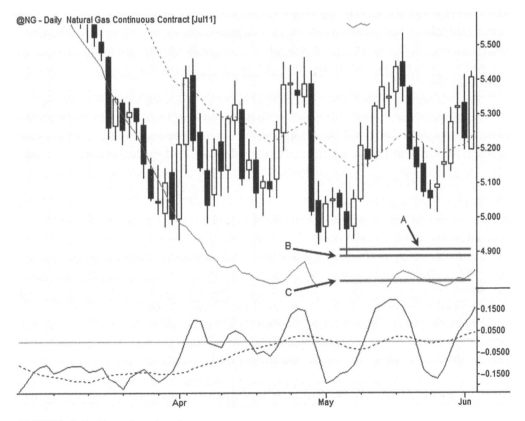

FIGURE 4.8 Three Stop Levels

pattern as faithfully as possible, but a violation of this level does not necessarily mean that the range has broken. It is entirely possible that your stop will be hit, and then the range will hold against the new, lower support level, or that this level will drop and be immediately rebid in the classic Wyckoff spring. The danger with this stop is that the level is visible to everyone. It is an obvious point in the market and you can sometimes incur severe slippage due to many orders being clustered at the same price. Another option, but a bad one, is to put a stop two or three ticks beyond the level. In almost all cases, if the market trades to the low of that bar, it will trade below it. By placing your stop a few ticks out, all you are doing is increasing the chance that your stop will be hit while prices are moving with strong momentum, which will increase the potential for slippage. Do not place stops in areas that are likely to suffer from poor liquidity and adverse order flow.

There is also good justification for stop C, which is a more or less random distance below the low point of the range. The question is how far is far enough, and there is no good answer. It is entirely possible that you could put your stop some distance below the B stop, only to have it hit by the momentum below the bottom of the range. This is ideally where you would like to be *buying* to initiate a position if supported by other factors, so this is almost the worst exit possible. To some extent, it is possible to judge the required distance by the character of the market, as some markets tend to be more vulnerable to spikes than others, but surprises will happen. You will sometimes see very thin, volatile markets put in polite drops below the bottom of the range, and you will also see completely unprecedented slippage in nonvolatile markets. There is no perfect answer.

The stop marked A, actually *inside* the support level, seems to make little sense at first. At this point, support is still holding and the trade is still valid, so why does it make sense to stop out of the trade here? This stop will seem very foreign, and perhaps silly, to many traders, but give it some careful consideration. It has the benefit of virtually eliminating slippage even in thin markets because you are exiting long before the mass of other stop orders is hit. Ideally, put the A stop somewhere you can be reasonably certain that, if the market goes there, it will also drop below the B stop level. Again, it is not possible to do this every time perfectly, but many traders will find that the A stop is a valuable addition to their tool set.

The most important thing here is that *you must have a stop at the time the trade is initiated.* Stop placement can be so complicated that it may seem like you should just buy and get out when the market *really* drops below the level without having a clearly defined plan. The problem is that sometimes the market drops below the level and it is the beginning of an extended trend—it drops and never looks back. Being caught in a single trade like this can do significant damage to your account; your first job is to manage the risk of any trade, and to limit the damage from losing trades.

Special Dangers of Clean Support/Resistance   Levels that have shown multiple clean tests are potentially dangerous because many traders may be lulled into establishing very large positions with stops just on the other side of the level. When these levels are violated, the triggering of these stops can lead to extreme slippage beyond the level, sometimes resulting in a loss that is several times your intended risk. Couple this with the possibility that you may be holding a very large position due to the anticipated small risk, and this is a recipe for disaster. If trading against a clean level, keep the following points in mind:

- Clean levels actually tend to set up good breakout trades beyond the level.
- Expect additional volatility and slippage. Your risk is probably at least twice what you think it is. In intraday trading with very tight stops, losses of 5 to 10 times your intended risk are possible.
- Do not give your trade "a little more room" beyond the level. Think about what will happen if it is a good breakout trade against your position and turns out to be the beginning of a substantial trend run.
- If holding overnight, these levels are prone to large overnight gap risk, and, furthermore, these tend to be opening gaps that do not reverse.
- Even with these complications, it is possible to trade against these levels if you do it correctly and respect the additional risk they bring to the trade.

Classic Accumulation/Distribution   Some of the most important information we can get within trading ranges comes from the presence of price structures that suggest large interests are accumulating or distributing the stock. It is also worth mentioning that analysts and traders have considered the volume and changes in volume to be extremely important around these areas, but I have been unable to substantiate those claims in my own work. I realize that this will strike many technical traders as heresy, and there are many obvious examples of patterns with strong volume confirmation or support. (This is not the same as saying that volume is unimportant. I have not found volume to be important and have found my trading signals to be as reliable as those generated by traders who focus on volume, but there may well be aspects of volume analysis that I am missing.) However, closer inspection of a large number of chart patterns will find that volume helps as much as it hurts, that good signals occur as often with or without volume confirmation, and, in the end, it is simply another degree of freedom to deal with. Simplify, simplify, simplify.

Wyckoff terminology for these patterns, *springs* and *upthrusts*, can be confusing at first glance. A spring is a quick drop below support, which immediately finds enough demand to push prices back above support. An upthrust is a push above resistance, followed by an immediate failure as the market meets sufficient supply to push it back down. Both of these are essentially fake-outs, which do nothing more than run stops outside of support and resistance. We do not need to create elaborate structures or patterns; sometimes simple is better, and these two simple price patterns, taken in context of the bigger picture, are among the best tools to identify accumulation or distribution.

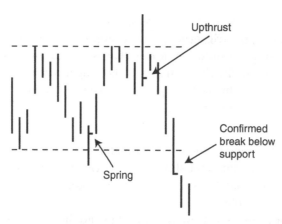

FIGURE 4.9 A Spring and an Upthrust in an Idealized Trading Range

Figure 4.9 shows examples of both springs and upthrusts, with a confirmed break below support at the end of the chart.

The key to both of these patterns is that they are quick probes beyond support and resistance. A trader watching the market around these areas would probably comment that there was "no conviction" beyond the level, or that prices did not want to "hang out" at the new extremes. Psychologically, these formations usually suggest that there are a number of traders who are afraid of being trapped out of the market. Imagine you are a large buyer looking to buy as close to a specific price (the bottom of the range) as possible; your goal is to get the best price you can by buying as low as you can. If the market trades down to that price, you may buy a little, but if it is weak you might hold off a bit to see if it will fall even lower. If the market then trades through your buy point, you may buy a little more, but you might also be willing to let the market continue to fall. Why hold it up with your own buying if you can buy lower? However, if the market drops below your target price and other traders buy aggressively, you may now be concerned about having to chase prices higher. In this case, you would be forced to buy very aggressively, quickly driving prices back above support. This type of thought process, in the aggregate from thousands of traders, drives much of the price action around these levels.

There are always two sides to every trade, and it is a good mental exercise to cultivate the practice of trying to see price action from as many different perspectives as possible. Imagine that you are a trader shorting the market into the same level where the previous buyer was willing to buy. You are looking for weakness and further extension below the level, so what do you do in the same scenario? Once price drops below the level and now is back above, you realize that the breakdown has failed. Rather than hold a failed trade, most traders would elect to buy back the short. Your covering is buying pressure; it makes no difference whether traders are buying to establish positions or to cover shorts. Buying is buying, and, all other things being equal, it will push prices higher.

Price Action around Support/Resistance One of the reasons for attaching the qualifier *potential* to support and resistance is to remind us that these levels do not always hold. When traders are first introduced to these concepts, they expect that support and resistance areas will be lines that will contain price movements on charts and that trades can be easily set up on these levels. This is the most basic entry-level knowledge, and the problem with it is that it is not true. It is much more difficult to identify true levels than many traders think (i.e., they are much more rare than much of the trading literature suggests), and, in actual practice, these levels break just about as often as they hold. For instance, one definition of a trend is that it is a type of price movement or price action that breaks support or resistance—the repeated failure of support or resistance is what actually drives trends. When resistance eventually is able to hold against an uptrend, the trend will pause and the market will enter consolidation. Fortunately, there are some characteristic patterns associated with levels holding or breaking that can inform our analysis around these levels. Time spent studying these patterns and considering the variations that can occur in all time frames is time well spent. A good understanding of how levels hold or break will do much to enhance your ability to read the market.

The archetypical pattern of a level holding is *price rejection*. This is an objective feature of price action, but it is also appropriate to talk about subjective elements because the market is responding to the psychology of decision makers in these areas. Ideally, when price reaches a support area that will hold, there is an immediate (in the context of the time frame) and sharp movement away from the level. It feels like price simply does not want to be there at all, and the market immediately moves away from the level. Figure 4.10 shows a particularly dramatic example of price rejection in the AUDJPY, which came into a potential support area and was strongly rejected in a single session. These tests are rarely as dramatic as this one, but successful tests of support and resistance will always have some element of price rejection.

This AUDJPY level illustrates another important point about support and resistance. In general, most traders find that the difficult trades to execute are often the best trades. It is very easy to buy a market as it grinds down into a support level, but it would have been much harder to buy the AUDJPY near that extreme support level. The best tests of support and resistance usually combine an objective, clear level with some form of overextension. In other words, a large price spike down to support is likely to set up a better bounce from that level than would a slow trend down into support. In fact, a market trending down into support is not showing price rejection, and this type of pressure often presages a significant break of support. The quick spike test, or a test of an oversold market coming into support, requires real execution skills, as prices will be moving quickly, spreads will be wide, and there may be an extreme lack of liquidity in the book. In addition, there is the chance of a large loss if prices continue to drop or drop even faster. But skilled traders find that they are compensated for these risks by quick profits and a good expected value over a large set of these trades. If you are uncomfortable buying spikes to support or shorting spikes to resistance, consider adding these to your trading plan. At the very least, it may make sense to

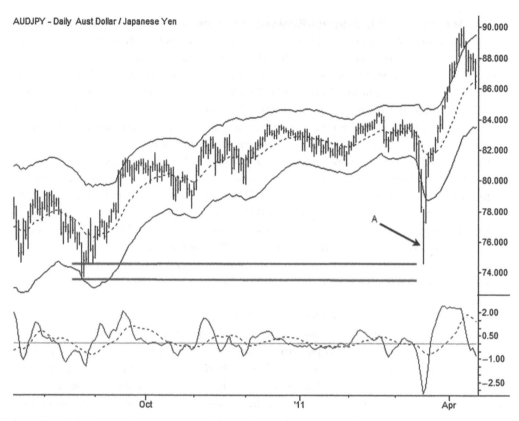

FIGURE 4.10 Price Rejection in the AUDJPY

watch for trend termination patterns on lower time frames when one of these patterns is underway.

Multiple Tests   This is not to say that price will touch the level once, never to return. It is certainly possible for a level to have multiple tests, and it can be difficult to read the balance of buying and selling conviction on these subsequent tests. Each test actually weakens the level because price should not be able to return to the level if it is going to hold. If there is genuine demand at a level, why did buyers not chase prices higher? Why are we back here? Those are the questions you need to ask. Traditional technical analysis tells us that a level is more valid the more times it is tested, but I believe that this is one of those pieces of the conventional wisdom that is absolutely wrong. If a level is going to hold, it should be tested once, twice, or maybe three times, and then there should be a move away from the level backed by strong conviction. If price is able to return to the level three or more times, probabilities begin to shift in favor of the level breaking. Traders make a critical mistake when they buy in front of the same support level multiple times, because the confidence that comes

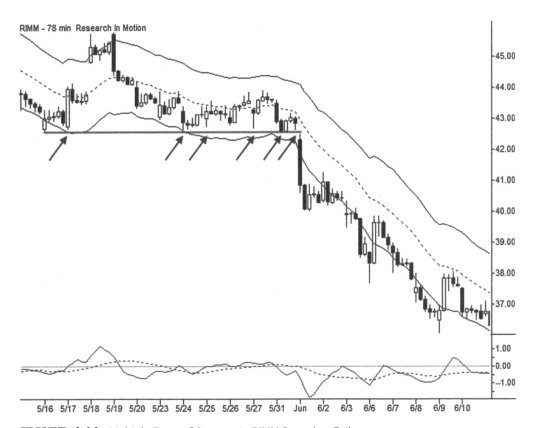

FIGURE 4.11 Multiple Tests of Support in RIMM Precede a Failure

with earlier successes leads to the temptation to increase position size. This is a recipe for disaster.

Levels can be tested multiple times and still hold, but you should be very suspicious of them after two tests. Ideally, the key is that we need to see renewed price rejection on each of the tests. If we do not see this, if price returns to the level and there is not enough conviction to push price away from the level, this is much more indicative of the level failing. If the market is able to go quiet and dull at or near the level, this is often a harbinger of impending failure. Figure 4.11 shows a 78-minute chart of Research in Motion Limited (Nasdaq: RIMM). (78-minute charts divide the U.S. trading session for equities into five equal periods. Traders using hourly charts will always have a bar that is longer or shorter than the others.) Traders buying support should have been suspicious on the third test of the level; there was no justification for holding or initiating positions on any subsequent tests of this level. The selling began in earnest once the level was decisively violated.

A useful tool for traders developing a sense of price action around support and resistance levels is a very short-term (2- or 3-period) lower time frame moving average. The only purpose of the moving average in this case is to smooth out the smallest fluctuations

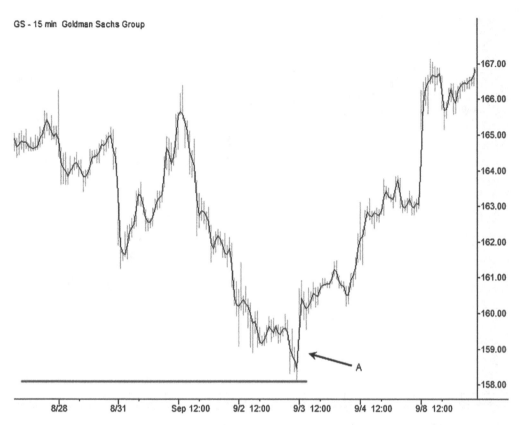

FIGURE 4.12 Price Rejection at Support

in prices in order to highlight the overall intent behind the moves. Though it is possible to use a similar technique on the trading time frame, dropping down to the lower time frame, at least for the purposes of study and learning, will help to build intuition about what kind of price action can generate structures seen on the trading time frame. Figure 4.12 shows a 2-period moving average on 15-minute price bars of Goldman Sachs Group, Inc. (NYSE: GS). The price bars have been ghosted to better highlight the action of the moving average as the market comes into a potential support area marked near the bottom of the chart. (This level is based on price structure not visible off the left edge of the chart.) Note that the moving average comes near the level and is violently turned away at A.

Figure 4.13 shows another example, in this case where GS came up against a resistance level. Note that the initial price rejection, at A, was weak and had no conviction. Price quickly found itself back up against the level, and consolidated there for many bars at B. This is *not* what we should see if a level is going to hold, and price did eventually break through at C. Study these patterns well, at first with the aid of a moving average as in Figures 4.12 and 4.13, and then without. If a support or resistance will hold or fail, price rejection will usually tell the tale.

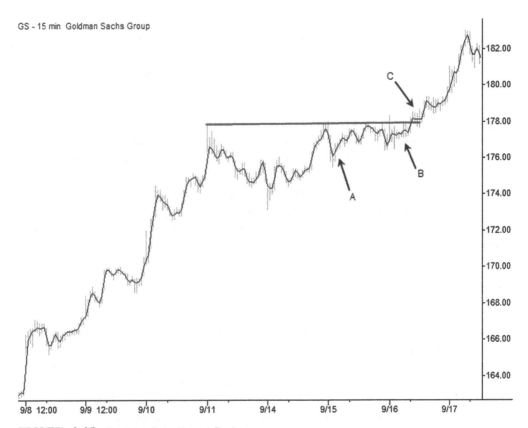

FIGURE 4.13 No Price Rejection at Resistance
Consolidation leads to a break of the level.

Last, it is worth mentioning that there is a third possibility for price action around potential support and resistance areas, which is *no action at all*. The market may approach a level and trade through it with no pause or unusual price action; the anticipated level simply was not there, and, if we have not planned for the possibility that the level simply does not exist, it is easy to be taken by surprise. Plan for every possibility and actively work to reduce potential surprises that can unbalance you and lead to poor decisions.

TRADING RANGES AS FUNCTIONAL STRUCTURES

Markets tend to alternate between trending periods and trading ranges. In trends, prices continue moving in the same direction. Because these trends are driven by an imbalance of buying or selling pressure, price movements are somewhat persistent and more predictable in terms of direction, magnitude, and timing. Trading ranges are directionless areas where the market is in relative equilibrium. In these spots, price action is much more random; price action within the range, timing of the exit from the range, and the direction of that eventual exit are all much less predictable than corresponding points in trending markets. Because markets in trading ranges tend to approximate random walks, most traders are well advised to avoid trading within the randomness of these structures and to limit any involvement to the margins, near support or resistance.

In context, trading ranges generally have one of two structural functions relative to the previous trend: they can be large-scale continuation patterns, or they can function as reversal patterns. Traders who are aware of these different functions, and of some of the distinguishing factors that may tilt the odds in favor of one resolution over the other, can often position for the next major trend move within the trading range. Note that this is not the same as trading within the range itself; a trader following this plan is essentially positioning within a higher time frame structure and ignoring minute details on the trading time frame. This is potentially confusing, so some examples will help to clarify this concept.

Continuation Ranges

Traditional technical analysis tells us that, all other things being equal, trading ranges are usually consolidations in the trend that preceded them, and are usually continuation patterns. In my experience, this is one of the pieces of conventional wisdom that is correct; it makes sense to approach most ranges with the idea that they will be continuation patterns, that the trend will continue and is "innocent until proven guilty." It is also often helpful to consider these formations on higher time frames. After an extended trend run on the trading time frame, the market may be essentially unreadable on that time frame as it enters into a large trading range with many unpredictable movements. However, the higher time frame will often tell a simple story: the trading time frame trend may have pushed the higher time frame into an overbought or overextended condition, and the unreadable range on the trading time frame is actually just a simple pullback on the higher time frame. This is a case of a higher time frame providing clarity by pulling us up out of the noise on the focus time frame.

Consider Figure 4.14, which shows daily and weekly charts of the S&P 500 Cash index in late 2008. The daily chart in the left pane is a mess; it is very hard to suss out any useful information from this chart—there are many competing and conflicting technical factors, and the best we can do is to label it some kind of trading range. However, the weekly chart tells a very different story, and shows a clear pullback in a downtrend. This is a case where the longer range on the daily chart resolves into a simple continuation pattern on the higher time frame.

Reversal Ranges

The other possibility is that the range can be a reversal of the higher time frame trend. Any of the factors that can suggest an end of a trend on one time frame (overextension, momentum divergence, specific terminating formations, etc.) apply to all time frames.

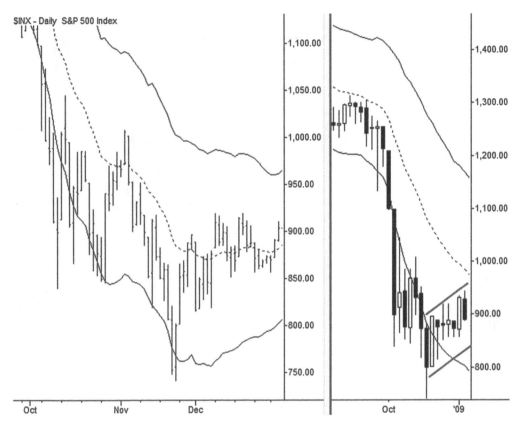

FIGURE 4.14 The Weekly Chart (Right) Clarifies an Otherwise Unreadable Situation on the Daily Chart (Left)

Figure 4.15 shows the S&P 500 Cash index again, this time at the highs in early 2010. The weekly was overextended, and daily price action suggested a certain lack of conviction at the highs. Again, to show that this isn't hindsight analysis, here is what I wrote in my morning report on April 26, 2010, the point marked A on the daily chart: "The market [may be] vulnerable so that when a shock finally does hit, the effect may be out of all reasonable proportion. This is why we are focusing attention on finding a good spot to enter a countertrend trade.... Today, we have a potential trade setup in the S&P 500 index. If the index closes below the previous YTD high . . . we will be short." This turned out to be the exact high of the market for many months, and we were fortunate to cover the last of that short a few days later, near the lows on the day of the Flash Crash.

It is also worth mentioning that there are many cases in which it is not so simple to make a directional call. Though we have just looked at several good examples, realize that they are best-case situations. Sometimes it is not possible to make any kind of directional call, and traders have no justification for taking a position. In these cases it is appropriate to stay flat (to have no position) and to wait for further clarification before making a trade.

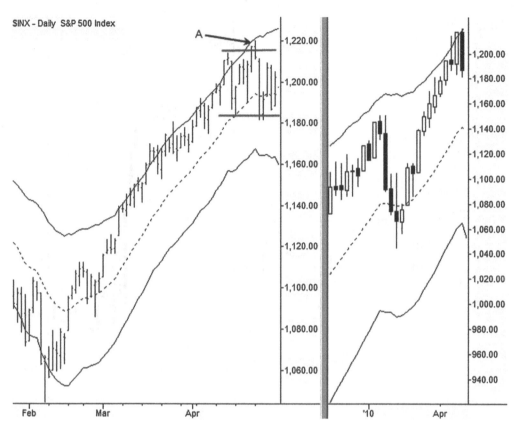

FIGURE 4.15 A Potential Reversal on the Weekly Gives a Downward Bias to the Trading Range on the Daily

Volatility Conditions in Trading Ranges

I believe it is counterproductive to catalog too many variations of patterns within trading ranges, due to the random nature of price action within these ranges. The Edwards and Magee crowd will recognize more than a dozen variations of trading ranges, but, to me, they are all the same. They all fulfill one of two functions in the higher time frame, and they are all noisy patterns roughly bounded by support and resistance. Why clutter a simple model with unnecessary variations, qualifications, and conditions? Visually, the most important factor in distinguishing between different types of ranges is what is happening with the edges of the range. Is the range contained by parallel lines, are the edges converging, or are they expanding? Each of these may have some subtle differences, with some effect on the expected resolution of the patterns.

Parallel Ranges: The Box The simplest range is one that trades between parallel prices in a box formation; volatility is relatively constant for the duration of the range. On the lower time frame, we will see trends (it is a little-known fact that many of the best

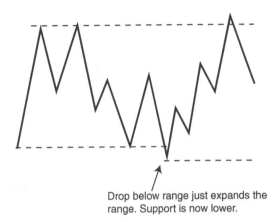

Drop below range just expands the range. Support is now lower.

FIGURE 4.16 A Simple Parallel Range

trends occur within higher time frame consolidations) that terminate in the trading time frame support and resistance. The confines of the range may be violated, but violations will usually be short-lived. It is also possible to see prices probe to a level and hold slightly beyond the range, and for the range to now trade between these expanded price levels. Do not naively assume that every break of a range will lead to an actual breakout. Many times, the range is simply expanded, as in Figure 4.16.

A common variation of this box pattern is the diagonal trading range, which is a box with sloping sides. This is a very common structure as a retracement in the higher time frame trend, and, in fact, the diagonal range sloping against the higher time frame trend (see Figure 4.17) could be considered the most common pullback pattern. Again, there may be lower time frame trends within this trading time frame trading range, and there may be temporary violations of the edges of the range—do not expect perfect, clean tests. This pattern is especially important because it often defines a complex pullback. Be on guard for springs near support in larger-scale uptrends, and for upthrusts near the highs of these patterns in downtrends. These offer *exceptional* entries into higher time frame trends.

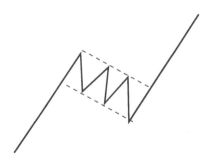

FIGURE 4.17 A Sloping Parallel Range Is a Very Common Continuation Pattern

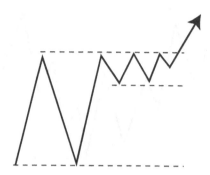

FIGURE 4.18 A Tighter Consolidation Against Resistance Often Leads to a Break of That Resistance

One final structure to be aware of is a tight consolidation near the edge of one side of the range, as in Figure 4.18. Remember, if the edges of the range are going to hold as support or resistance, the pattern we expect to see is price rejection near the level. If, instead, prices are able to consolidate and hold near one side of the range, this is more indicative of pressure building against that side of the range. This is a classic precursor of breakout, and many chartists would read this as a smaller range inside a bigger range, a not incorrect definition. Furthermore, this pattern is also the basis for the classic cup and handle chart pattern, but reading the simple dynamics of emerging market structure will usually give a better read on the market than any chart pattern.

Converging Ranges   Trading ranges are periods of relative consensus, where the market tends to trade around a price level in equilibrium. One common variation of the trading range idea sees the market making successively smaller swings, as if zeroing in on a target price level. The edges of this range appear to converge at some point in the future, and this pattern often appears to be a triangle on price charts, as in Figure 4.19. Traditionally, the assumption is that these triangles set up good breakout trades, and there are many rules regarding direction and price targets for these breakouts. I have not found any of these traditional rules to be effective or reliable; sometimes they work

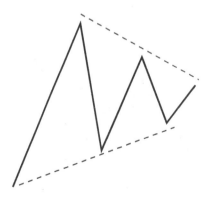

FIGURE 4.19 A Converging Range

FIGURE 4.20 An Ascending Triangle. Holding Higher Lows into Resistance Is a Sign of Increasing Buying Pressure

well, but just as often they do not. My trading rules for triangles are simple and reduce to one principle: do not fade the first breakout from one of these formations. Though these breakouts may not be reliable or consistent enough to build a trading program on, you certainly do not want to be caught on the wrong side of a strong move out of any kind of consolidation.

There are many variations of these converging ranges, which chartists describe as symmetrical triangles, ascending or descending triangles, wedges, pennants, and so on, usually with the qualification that "volume is very important in these formations." (How do they know that?) Most of these are traditionally taken to be continuation patterns, but, for me, it is simple: they are all basically the same pattern. They clearly show volatility compression, which puts us on guard and in breakout mode, looking for continuation of any breakout from these ranges. There is one exception that might be slightly more significant: the ascending triangle (see Figure 4.20), where price holds successively smaller declines (higher lows) into a clearly defined resistance level (or the same formation, inverted, to the downside). This type of pattern typically shows strengthening conviction on the part of buyers, reflected in weakening price rejection from resistance, and usually leading to a breakout above that resistance. This is another pattern that sets up good breakout trades.

Whenever a market makes a very large, sharp movement in one direction, followed by a similar move in the other direction, this suggests confusion on the part of market participants as they try to process whatever information caused the price shock. The normal expectation, following this kind of price movement, is for the market to spend a period of time consolidating, most likely in some kind of converging triangle formation. It is very common to see traders incur multiple losses in these areas because they are first drawn to the market by the large price movements, and then they get caught in the random oscillations of the triangle. Simply by recognizing that a large spike followed by a quick reverse spike usually leads to a triangle and a very suboptimal trading environment, many of these losses can be avoided.

Expanding Ranges Chartists also recognize a number of formations relating to widening triangles where each swing, both up and down, is bigger than the preceding swings. There are also a number of diamond-shaped formations where price first

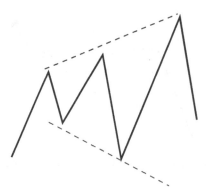

FIGURE 4.21 An Expanding Range

expands and then contracts in a classic triangle, and, of course, there are associated trading rules and targets for each formation. My rule for these is simple: the market is confused (as evidenced by the price action) and I do not have to have a position. I find it difficult to define my risk or to control my positions when volatility is expanding in an unpredictable (nondirectional) fashion. Furthermore, these areas tend to expend a lot of stored-up energy and we do not often see strong moves out of these patterns. More often than not, they resolve into random, directionless, low-volatility ranges. As much as possible, I avoid these types of environments or at least significantly reduce risk in them, but this may not be the right answer for all traders. Figure 4.21 shows a schematic example of a widening range.

SUMMARY

Compared to trends, trading ranges are more complicated, and present more challenges and dangers to traders who would trade within these structures. The highly random nature of price action in these ranges often creates illusions of patterns that do not exist. In addition, lower volume and potential liquidity problems create a real danger of large adverse price spikes which result in much larger than expected losing trades. However, market structure rests on an alternation of trending and trading range patterns; it is not possible to truly understand the story of how supply and demand plays out in the market without a thorough understanding of trading ranges, and of price action around support and resistance.

So far, we have looked at both trends and trading ranges in some depth, but our study is still missing an important element. Many of the best opportunities come at those points where trends become trading ranges and vice versa. Many of the largest losses and greatest dangers also come in these areas, so it is important that we spend some time studying price action and market structure in these transition areas.

CHAPTER 5

Interfaces between Trends and Ranges

What we call the beginning is often the end. And to make an end is to make a beginning.

—T.S. Eliot

Even the most powerful market trends eventually come to an end, and they can do so in several ways. Traders riding trends need to understand the patterns of trend termination, but it is also equally important to consider what follows the end of a trend. At best, these *interfaces* between trends and trading ranges are periods of great uncertainty and potential volatility. At worst, many traders will find that these are the most difficult areas of market structure to read reliably, and that they are the source of consistent losses. These areas also offer the greatest opportunity for many traders, but this opportunity is accompanied by risks and uncertainty. Using a simplified model of market structure where markets are always either trending or in trading ranges, there are only three possible transitions:

1. *Breakout:* A market breaks out of a trading range, and enters a trend.
2. *Trend termination into trading range:* An established trend ends, and the market enters a trading range.
3. *Trend reversal:* An established trend ends, and reverses into a trend in the opposite direction.

To this list we must add a few failures that may complicate issues. After the fact, we might miss these areas as they will simply be continuations of previous conditions, but a trader making decisions at the hard right edge of the chart would likely have placed trades based on information available at the time. This difference between "middle of the chart" (i.e., after the fact) analysis and trading at the right edge is poorly understood

121

by many traders, and is a key reason why trading results often diverge from backtest and study results. If we are going to do analysis that mirrors what a trader experiences as the chart unfolds in real time, we must consider the new information provided by every bar on the chart. To complete our analysis of possible scenarios, we need to also consider these failure patterns:

- A market breaks out of a trading range, a new trend does not develop, and the market remains locked in a larger trading range.
- An established trend appears to end, but the trend termination fails and the market continues in the established trend.

Let's consider some of the patterns, opportunities, and dangers associated with each of these scenarios.

BREAKOUT TRADE: TRADING RANGE TO TREND

The term *breakout trade* is applied to a class of trades where the trader attempts to enter in the direction the market is already moving, usually when a support or resistance level is broken. Many breakout trades come at points where the market has pressed against the same support or resistance level several times, but has been unable to break (or hold) beyond that price level. Once the level is actually broken, pent-up buying or selling pressure may drive the market into a sharp, dramatic trend. It is easy to find examples of good breakout trades on charts (see Figure 5.1) where a trader could have realized an extremely high reward/risk ratio by taking a position on the breakout. There are a number of profitable trading systems that rely on breakout entries, and anecdotal evidence suggests that this trade entry was one of the main concepts behind the Turtles' success in the 1980s and 1990s. There is also good, simple logic for focusing on these types of trades: if a market is going to go higher, it has to take out previous price highs. If a market is going lower, it must take out previous lows in the process. Traders focusing on breakout trades will naturally catch all the big trend moves.

There is a significant problem—the majority of breakout trades fail. In most cases, excursions beyond support or resistance are usually short-lived, as they are quickly met by offsetting pressure that pushes the market back into the range. Traders indiscriminately entering breakouts would find that any profits they make would be eaten away by transaction costs and by failed breakouts. In many cases, volatility is high and liquidity is low at these points. Even in the best cases, with the best possible risk control, the small losses will quickly add up. In the end, it is a case of death by a thousand cuts that will slowly grind a trading account down to nothing.

There is a slight division in the trading world between equity traders and futures traders regarding terminology for these trades. To most stock traders, a breakout is specifically a break *above* resistance, while a breakdown is a break *below* support; in other words, a breakout is a long trade, while a breakdown is a short. Futures traders,

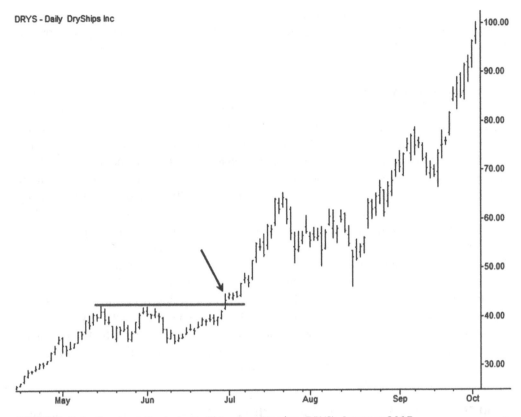

FIGURE 5.1 Breakout Trade in DryShips Inc. (Nasdaq: DRYS), Summer 2007

however, tend to use the term *breakout* without distinction for both cases. In general, most stock traders, especially nonprofessionals, view shorting in a different light than going long, and futures traders are much less likely to have this bias. In this book, I use breakout for both trades as well, since there is really no quantifiable difference between the two.

Patterns Preceding Good Breakouts

The best breakout trades are driven by high institutional interest and involvement. Markets, especially deep, liquid ones, do not make large moves without the commitment of large pools of money. In general, these large traders are usually trading positions that are so large they could not enter them on the actual breakout. Small traders—the public who, on balance, tend to lose money—focus a lot of attention on entering at the actual breakout points. In many cases, the larger traders who are already positioned will take advantage of the volatility and sell a portion of their positions to the small traders rushing to buy the breakouts. Think about this if you trade breakouts; this is the pressure that often results in failed breakouts. How smart is it for you to be buying where very large traders are selling, or vice versa? Since these large traders have often positioned themselves before the breakout, they often create telltale patterns that help us separate the best breakouts, driven by large-scale interest, from those that are more likely to fail.

Higher Lows into Resistance   One of the classic patterns sees prices holding higher lows into a more or less clearly defined resistance level. To understand the significance of this ascending triangle pattern, imagine that a market is oscillating randomly in a trading range, but then some large buyers become interested in accumulating a position. They would naturally want to buy at as low a price as possible, so they would use the declines to begin buying. Eventually their buying pressure will arrest the decline and the market will resume its upward movement, at which point they will likely turn off their buying to avoid paying elevated prices. Skilled operators could even offer some of their line out, with the dual intent of booking a small profit and of actually holding prices down by their selling pressure. If several large buyers recognize this activity in the market, they will become more aggressive in their buying, while still attempting to measure and control it so as not to force prices higher. As competition in the market intensifies and buying interest builds, the declines will become shallower simply because more people are buying them; this will force large traders to become even more aggressive in buying at higher prices. A mild feedback loop develops within the trading range that often leaves the patterns shown in Figure 5.2. This is often a setup for an excellent breakout trade, and applies equally well, inverted, to the downside.

Tight Range Near Extreme of Larger Range   Another pattern, conceptually similar to the previous one, is a tight range near the edge of a larger, established trading range. This tight range is often less than 25 percent of the height of the larger range, and shows that large traders have become interested enough in the market to hold it near the edge of the larger range. Why are they now willing to pay higher prices (or to short at lower prices), rather than letting the market naturally drift back into the middle of the range? This pattern suggests more urgency to their actions and more conviction, and also frequently supports exceptional breakout trades. Figure 5.3 shows a schematic representation of this pattern, which was mentioned in Chapter 4 as one of the classic signs that support or resistance is likely to fail. Remember, a failure of support or resistance is often a successful breakout trade.

FIGURE 5.2   Shorter Swings into Support or Resistance Often Set Up Good Breakouts

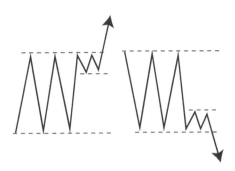

FIGURE 5.3 A Tighter Range Near the Edge of a Larger Range Often Precedes a Good Breakout of That Edge

Prebreakout Accumulation At this point, you should realize that we are starting to see the same patterns over and over. This is not rocket science; the patterns of the market are subtle, but they are also logical and, at their core, they are simple. Earlier, we looked at the classic Wyckoff springs and upthrusts as signs of accumulation and distribution. If large players are positioning themselves in the range in anticipation of a breakout, it is very likely that we will see these springs and upthrusts in the prebreakout ranges. Much accumulation and distribution is invisible; institutions spend a lot of money on salaries for skilled execution traders and in the development of execution algorithms. All of this subterfuge is designed to hide the execution of these large orders. However, there are points in the market where they cannot really hide their hands, and, if we know exactly what to look for, we can sometimes get clues as to their intentions. Violations of support and resistance in well-defined ranges are important areas to watch. If excursions beyond the range are short-lived, printing springs and upthrusts at the edges of the range, this becomes strong evidence that large traders are positioning in the market, and often sets up good breakout trades.

Characteristic Patterns at Good Breakouts

Again, a good breakout is driven by institutional interest that eventually garners the interest of the public and results in a feedback loop that propels the market far from the breakout point. It is overly optimistic to assume that prices will trade cleanly through the breakout level and never come back. (This, incidentally, is the absolute best-case scenario for breakout traders, and trades like this are rare.) However, there are some common patterns at the actual breakout point that can separate the best breakout trades from the rest.

High Volatility A breakout should be a clearly visible event. If a market approaches a breakout point, trades tightly below the point with significant signs of accumulation, and then very politely and gently lifts through resistance to trade higher, this is probably not a good sign. Good breakouts are driven by unusual order flow, so we need to see increased volume, activity, and interest associated with the actual breakout. In general, the ranges of individual bars should expand, and they almost always will expand on lower time frames. Breakouts from less significant levels may not always see this increased volatility, but a good breakout that marks a transition to an extended trend is almost always a volatile event. Note that it may be difficult to measure this volatility with traditional measures, but the quantitative measures that will be most useful will be instantaneous measures of volatility such as the ratio of the current bar's range to a window of previous bars.

Slippage Is Good   The difference between the intended and actual execution prices in a trade is called *slippage*. If a trader is planning on paying a breakout above $20.00 and receives fills at $20.20, this is 20 cents of slippage and can be a significant cost of trading. Most traders think of slippage as only that: a bad thing, a cost to be avoided. However, around breakout points, slippage is actually desirable. It should be difficult to buy a market making a good breakout. You should *have* to pay higher prices to get in if the market is really moving.

Many traders panic when they receive significant slippage. A bad fill is seen as increasing risk and cutting into profits, and it is hard to argue with this logic, at least on the surface. Think deeper, though, and consider the possible reasons for the bad fill. Sometimes it may be the trader's fault, in which case it should probably be treated as an error and is subject to the *error rule* (i.e., fix it immediately). However, slippage is a fact of life in breakout trades. In fact, *positive* slippage, where you receive a better than expected price, is often the killer here. Imagine you are looking to pay a breakout above $50.00 in a fairly volatile market, expecting that you will be slipped and have to pay $50.05, $50.10, or even $50.20. What if you execute your order and discover that you are filled for your full size at $49.98? This is *not* a good thing. Someone was willing to sell this market to you at a great price, and caveat emptor—the selling pressure, against your potential breakout, was stronger than expected. Positive slippage is often a sign of an impending failed breakout trade.

Immediate Satisfaction   The logical extension of all of these factors, and one of the reasons that certain personality types are drawn to this kind of trading, is that the breakout trader should receive immediate feedback on whether the trade is right or wrong. As always, *immediate* must be taken in context. If trading intraday, then confirmation should come within seconds, but a trader trading on the weekly time frame might demand some confirmation of the trade within a few days. Immediate satisfaction does not mean an instant win, and it does not mean an easy trade. A very short-term trader might pay $20.15 for a breakout, only to see the stock trade to $20.30 in the next few seconds and immediately be offered at $20.10. This is nothing more than extra volatility and order flow around the breakout level, which is to be expected, and the trader can now begin the process of managing the trade. On the other hand, a breakout trade that is paid for at $20.15 and then immediately begins to slowly grind lower is no breakout at all.

Especially for short-term traders, breakout trading can be exciting, and the immediate feedback allows for rapid learning and skill development.

Patterns Following Good Breakouts

In a good breakout, the extra volatility and one-sided liquidity lead to a sharp move above the breakout level. Nothing in the market continues indefinitely, though, and eventually this initial thrust gives way to a pause and a pullback. This is a critical point because, if the breakout is the beginning of a new trend, this first pullback after the breakout is the optimal time to establish positions for the new trend. If the breakout is going to fail, it is going to fail at this first pullback. In addition, the character of the price action in this first pullback can communicate a lot of information about the conviction behind the move and the character of the market.

Pullback Holds Outside the Breakout Level This is probably the most intuitive example, and the one that many traders focus most of their efforts on. The market breaks through the level, trades sharply beyond the level, and then makes a clean pullback that holds outside the breakout level. This makes sense because there should be urgency and real order flow following the breakout. Large players should be interested in defending the breakout level, and small players should be willing—perhaps stupidly, but still willing—to chase the market. All of this should logically result in the market being unable to come back to the breakout level. It is easy to find examples of these patterns, and also very easy to manage these trades that never come back to the entry price. Figure 5.4 shows schematic examples of this pattern.

Pullback Violates the Level It is certainly easiest to manage trades when the pullback holds outside the breakout level, because it is simple to put a breakeven stop at your entry price and never be at a loss on the trade. For the trader, this is the ideal situation, but think about it for a moment; ask yourself why the market should work this way. Why should the large players who positioned inside the range, and maybe even provided some liquidity at the breakout point, defend the level precisely or aggressively? It is safe to assume that many of them are working from a hybrid approach that combines valuation with at least a quasi-technical approach. Though they may recognize the validity of

FIGURE 5.4 First Pullback Holds Outside Breakout Level

the breakout as a price structure, many of them would also be perfectly happy to add to their positions at lower prices.

There is an important lesson here for smaller traders: we would like clean, perfect trades where the market almost magically respects lines we draw on our charts, but there is no reason for the world to work like this. There is no logical reason for the market to have to hold outside the breakout level. If you are a breakout trader, an interesting exercise is to take a reasonable sample of trades in your time frames (perhaps 500 trades), go through them methodically, and categorize them into ones that held cleanly beyond the breakout level and those that did not. Then ask yourself, objectively, if those that conformed to the ideal pattern of holding outside the level performed better after the breakout (in terms of trend extension) than those that did not.

There is also probably another dynamic at work here in many of these situations. Imagine for a minute a simplified market model with only three groups of participants: strong-hand large players who are trading on a mixture of technical and fundamental concepts; small, nimble, but naive short-term traders who trade only off price levels; and noise traders whose random trades obscure what would otherwise be very clear in the price action. Furthermore, imagine that a breakout has just occurred, in which the large players accumulated before the breakout, the small traders entered on the breakout, but, after the breakout, the large players were not willing to commit enough capital to propel the trend higher. Perhaps they had not yet accumulated their full line in the prebreakout level, perhaps they sold enough at the level that they wanted to buy more at lower prices, or perhaps they were uncertain in front of some economic report. The point is that we do not know and can never understand the real motivations of these large players, especially since we are presenting a composite model of what would actually be thousands of competing interests in the actual market. Regardless, the key point is that they choose, for whatever reasons, not to support the market and it drops back through the prebreakout level.

What do the naive short-term traders do at this point? They recognize the failed breakout pattern and sell their positions en masse just below the breakout level. Who is buying from them? You got it—the large players are more than happy to pick up some extra inventory from the nervous short-term players, who are taking small losses on positions they just bought at slightly higher prices. (And who, by the way, just sold them those positions at those slightly higher prices?) The large traders will certainly be willing to soak up this extra inventory. Once they see the selling dry up as the short-term traders have fully exited their positions (or, in some cases, actually established short positions), the large players only then will resume buying aggressively. At this point, the short-term traders recognize the error of their ways, see that the breakout was valid after all, and rush to get back into the market, but now they are entering a moving market in the direction it is already moving. Their buying action will remove enough liquidity that the market begins to trend in earnest.

There are a few valuable lessons here: Do not expect levels to hold cleanly. The initial breakout level failed to hold on the pullback, which triggered the short-term traders to exit their positions. This, in turn, was actually the catalyst for the real move. Make

FIGURE 5.5 The Breakout Level Can Also Be Violated on the Pullback

sure your trading plan respects the realities of the market; any other plan is a recipe for disaster. Figure 5.5 shows schematic examples of breakout trades violating the breakout level on the pullback. Remember, this is not necessarily a sign of a failed breakout.

Patterns of Failed Breakouts

The preceding example is not meant to imply that every breakout trade works, nor that short-term traders were necessarily stupid to exit their trades on a failed breakout. Breakouts do fail, they fail frequently, and price movements following these failures can be violent. One of the characteristics of market action is that markets will probe levels for resting orders, seeking out levels where that will create trading volume. It is not that difficult to figure out where these orders might be placed, since traders use previous pivots and visible support and resistance levels to define risk points for trades. Stop orders tend to cluster just outside the day's range, or at more or less predictable chart levels.

This may not be completely intuitive at first, but here is one way this could work. Imagine that you are a large player who would like to sell some of your inventory in a futures market. You can see that the market has held a resistance level cleanly (let's say $80.00 for this example) on several tests, and it is reasonable to assume that many traders are short against this visible level. If so, where will those traders probably put their stops? There is no exact level, but we can assume that they will be clustered just beyond the resistance, probably in the range from $80.01 to $80.20. What do you do the next time the market trades up to $79.98? Remember, you actually are holding more of a long position than you are comfortable with and you want to sell some, but you want to sell as high as possible. Paradoxically, one good way to accomplish that goal might be to actually buy *more* at $79.98, $79.99, and eventually to try to buy enough that your buying pushes the market to $80.01. Even though you need to sell, the most effective way for you to sell actually begins with you *buying more*.

If you are correct and shorts have their stop orders clustered there, those stops will trigger and a rush of additional buying will come into the market. As soon as those stops fire off, you can stop your buying (which is a good thing, because now you are even more long than you were before), and you will be more than happy to sell some of your position to those stop orders. If this campaign is successful, you will be able to sell a significant portion of your position into the volatility resulting from those orders, and, if you continue selling the rest of your inventory after the burst of stop orders is completed, you will most likely roll the market over into a strong sell-off. This is a highly simplified model, but this type of action happens constantly in all markets and all time frames. It is relatively easy for even moderately sized players to probe most markets, and thin markets can be probed with very small size. There are plenty of inactive stocks in which a few hundred shares could push prices through support and resistance at critical points, so the capital and risk required to execute these campaigns is often much smaller than you might expect. Failed breakouts like this are very common. Fortunately, they set up some exceptional trading opportunities for the traders who know the patterns and who are prepared to trade them.

Failure Test of Breakout Level   Again, we encounter inconsistent terminology, as different traders will call this trade by different names. What I call a *failure test* is the simple case just described, where a market trades beyond a significant level just far enough to trigger stops without any significant follow-through beyond the level. As a pure price pattern, a failure test is a brief excursion beyond a level, followed by an immediate reversal. "Immediate" in this case is dependent on time frame; intraday traders might be looking for a reversal within seconds to minutes while very long-term traders might consider any action reversed within a few weeks to be a failure test. As a working definition, a rule of thumb might be that you want to see no more than two or three bars on your time frame outside the breakout level and then strong momentum reversing the move. This is one case where the close of the bar on your time frame can be very important.

The reason for this is that lower time frame price action is the key to judging the probabilities around this trade. Conceptually, in the case of an upside breakout, buyers are swept into the market by the breakout, and then they will sell their positions if the breakout fails. These exits are usually accompanied by some degree of urgency, ranging from mild to outright panic, and this order flow creates downside momentum. It is extremely unlikely to have this kind of action and *not* to have a close back below the breakout level. Old-school chartists sometimes referred to this kind of action as a "turkey shoot"—the turkey would poke its head above the level (perhaps a fencerow), and would immediately have its head shot off. This actually describes the price action in the best examples of these failures very well.

In Figure 5.6, compare the price action on the two or three bars following the two points marked A to the same time period following B. In the first two cases, once a bar closes back on the other side of the breakout level, strong momentum steps in and we see good price rejection from the breakout level. Remember, this price rejection is the fundamental pattern of support or resistance holding; in this case the level is holding after being broken, but the same concepts still apply. Even though the trade marked B would have also been a successful fade of the breakout level, the action following B is *not* typical of the action following the best trades. The market spent too much time consolidating too closely to the level.

At the risk of confusing the issue slightly, it is important to consider that there is another variation on this pattern in which the reversal bar actually does not show strong reversal momentum. In this case, the close of that bar may occur very close to the level,

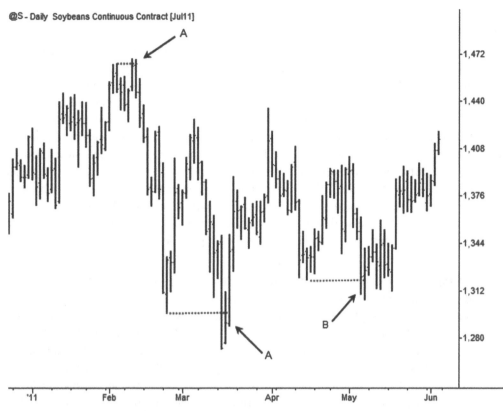

FIGURE 5.6 Points A Show Good Examples of Breakout Failures; B is More Typical of Continuation Below the Level

either inside, outside, or perhaps right at the breakout level. However, lower time frame price action shows a lack of conviction beyond the breakout level. For instance, in the case of an upside breakout, bounces would be slow and reluctant on the lower time frame, and the market might be seen to move down with much less resistance than when it moves up; we would say that such a market "goes down a lot easier than it goes up"—this is typical of a market that may be holding at higher levels without strong underlying conviction. If this type of action is seen, sharp failure momentum back inside the level is likely to emerge within the next several bars.

If this does not happen, then it is more likely that a simple pullback after the breakout is underway, which, remember, does not need to hold outside the breakout level. This is one of the most complex and subtle areas of chart analysis; there is much more art than science involved in discerning the difference between these failed and successful breakouts. In all cases, the distinguishing feature is the lack of conviction and momentum beyond the level, both of which can be read in price action and in the chart of lower time frames. Even so, traders who focus on these trades must be prepared to be wrong many times and perhaps to make multiple adjustments to positions as the market structure unfolds. These are areas of great uncertainty where the market is in a state of flux; extreme flexibility is required to successfully navigate these waters.

While there have been constant reminders that nearly everything in technical analysis is time frame dependent, one important element is not: When significant price action is anticipated at a specific price level, it should occur at that level. Whether the trader is watching tick charts or monthly charts, the presence or absence of action at a level is an objective criterion that cannot be ignored. For instance, imagine that a long-term investor, perhaps trading weekly or monthly bars, is expecting significant action as a market breaks to a multiyear high. If this does not happen, if the market simply trades beyond that new high without any increase in activity, range, or volume, then this is more suggestive of a failed breakout and the investor might choose to adjust her position within her risk management framework. You can think that she used lower time frame price action to inform this decision, but, in reality, she simply did not see activity that supported the idea of an imbalance at a specific price level.

Failed Pullback Following a Breakout   The pullback following a breakout is potentially the first pullback in a new trend, so any of the common trend failure patterns associated with other pullbacks apply to this pullback—with one small exception. If the breakout level was truly an important level, there should have been a high level of activity on the breakout and it is relatively uncommon to see breakout pullbacks fail by going into flat ranges. It is far more common to see these pullbacks fail with very strong momentum out of the pattern or fail on a second test of the extreme reached after the pullback. There are usually too many competing influences and too much order flow for the market to just go dead after a breakout, and this type of consolidation, when it does happen, is usually indicative of a successful breakout. The fact that the market is able to hold outside the level shows that there is real conviction behind the move, and can often set up a sustained move in the direction of the breakout (see Figure 5.7).

For the trader looking to trade failed breakouts, the best pullback failures will see a sharp reversal and failure out of the wrong side of the pullback formation, indicating a complete failure of conviction outside the breakout level. For instance, assume that

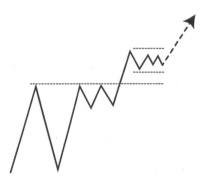

FIGURE 5.7 Consolidation Outside the Prebreakout Range Is Usually Constructive

sellers are able to force a breakout below an important support level and hold the market in a consolidation below that level. If they give up or fail, buyers will step in aggressively and bid the market back above support, which will show on price charts as a few large bars with good momentum breaking out of the top of the smaller consolidation. This is not what we should have seen if the sellers had enough strength to push the market lower. The presence of sharp momentum against the direction of the pullback is a reality that all market participants will be forced to acknowledge, and can often lead to a sizable move back below the breakout level.

Failure Pullback If sharp momentum emerges against the breakout, confirming the breakout failure, the first pullback is probably tradable against the direction of the breakout. As this pattern describes what comes *after* the best failure patterns, it is not actually useful in making decisions at the time of the breakout. However, if you find yourself holding a position against this pattern as it develops, a large loss is probably looming around the corner. If you have no position, this pattern may offer a reasonable spot for a scalp or a short-term trade against the breakout, but it certainly should be a warning to get out of Dodge if you are holding on to a losing breakout trade.

This may be slightly confusing, so see Figure 5.8 for clarification. Point A shows a typical breakout, and at point B the market is consolidating in a standard breakout pullback. At this point, you would be fully justified in holding a long position as long as the lower time frame price action is judged to be favorable. However, C marks a classic breakout pullback failure, as sharp downside momentum breaks out of the bottom of the pullback. Now, think back to trading pullback trades—one of the strongest conditions setting up good pullback trades is that they are preceded by good momentum. In this case, the move following point C is on very strong downward momentum (against the direction of the breakout), and the ensuing trend leg is longer and steeper than previous downtrends. Shorting into the pullback at D is a good trade based just on that criterion, but, in this case, it is further motivated by the failure of the breakout level at A. When price turns down after this pullback at D, there may be some panic as the last trapped longs scramble for the exits.

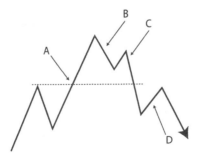

FIGURE 5.8 The Pullback Marked D Often Offers an Excellent Trade Following a Breakout Pullback Failure at C

Consider what this pattern would look like on the higher time frame—it would probably simply show strong momentum away from the breakout level, or price rejection at
the breakout level. Even though there are many potential variations, the fundamental
price patterns are relatively simple and consistent.

TREND TO TRADING RANGE

Structurally, trends that terminate into a trading range will always do so through a failed
pullback, but this may not be extremely useful information in real time. To some extent,
this labeling system is mostly a semantic argument, saying little more than if a trend fails
to continue then it will go into a trading range, which, by definition, is a price area that
does not continue in either direction, up or down. The value comes from three factors:
understanding the patterns that can precede a failure of trend continuation, differentiating between those failures that are likely to lead to a dramatic reversal and those that
are more likely to transition into a sideways range, and finding specific risk management
points for trades that set up around these patterns.

We have already examined the patterns associated with failed pullbacks in some detail in Chapter 3, and we will look at further refinements in Chapter 6, but, in most cases,
failed pullbacks are preceded by some form of a momentum divergence. This momentum
divergence, by itself, is not sufficient reason to take a position against the trend, but it is
an initial warning that the trend is losing some conviction. Once this condition appears,
countertrend positions are justified if supported by other factors, the most important of
which are lower time frame price action and the emerging market structure on the trading time frame. Other common conditions preceding failed pullbacks are extremely high
volatility, indicating possible climax or exhaustion, and/or the presence of multiple trend
legs in the same direction. After many directional pushes (more than three), it is likely
that the market needs further consolidation before continuing the trend; the probability
of pullback failure becomes higher with each subsequent trend leg.

For both with-trend and countertrend traders, the key moment to watch in pullbacks
is the inflection point where the pullback begins to move back in the direction of the
trend. It is important to be alert here and on guard for some sort of a failure as the market attempts to begin a new trend leg. Trends always end with some form of a failed
pullback pattern, which takes one of three broad forms: First, pullbacks may fail by transitioning directly into a trading range, as in Figure 5.9. There is simply no move out of the
pullback as prices stabilize around a price level in the pullback itself. The initial range is
likely to be small, and may be expanded through a series of excursions above and below
the confines of the range, each of which could tempt unwitting traders into attempting
breakout trades at these spots. Buyers and sellers have reached equilibrium, and there is
no imbalance to propel to trend higher—there is also usually no reason to be trading in
these formations.

Pullbacks may also fail on a test of the pivot that defines the previous trend extreme.
There is not much difference between tests that are precisely at the level, those that
fall short, or those that slightly penetrate the old trend extreme, though the last case may

FIGURE 5.9 Trends May Terminate into Trading Ranges When Pullbacks Become Ranges

lead to sharper countertrend momentum due to trapped traders who entered on the false breakout. Again, the common thread tying these scenarios together is that there is a lack of conviction beyond the previous trend extreme, the market finds equilibrium as supply and demand balance, and a period of sideways trading activity follows. Figure 5.10 shows an example of a failure test at the previous high in an uptrend that ended the trend.

Last, pullbacks may fail via the failure pullback sequence: sharp countertrend momentum; a small pullback, which often sets up a good trade; and then another strong counter (the original trend) thrust. In this case, the move out of the failure pullback often exhausts itself somewhere close to the measured move objective (MMO), thus defining the initial extreme of the new trading range. Figure 5.11 shows a road map for this type of action. The swing marked A is the confirmation that the trend had decisively ended, at least for the time being.

The common pattern tying all of these transitions from trend to trading range is a failed pullback, and this point is important: trends fail when pullbacks fail. This is why it is so critical for all technical traders, whether they trade with the trend, countertrend, in ranges, or on breakouts of those ranges, to be familiar with the patterns associated with pullbacks and their failure. The point of a trading methodology is not to predict the future, but to understand the forces at work in the market at any time, their relative balance, and the most likely resolution of emerging price structures. When something changes, and this happens frequently, a good trading methodology will embrace

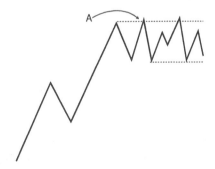

FIGURE 5.10 A Failure Test at the Previous Pivot Extreme May Be a Catalyst for the Market to Transition to a Trading Range

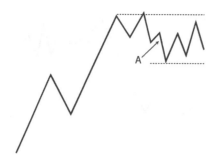

FIGURE 5.11   Sharp Countertrend Momentum May Exhaust into a Trading Range

this change and make adjustments to trades. Exactly how you choose to implement this will depend on your personality and your chosen methodology, but the key is that you understand the ebb and flow of market dynamics. Managing trades in this fluid environment is the next challenge to consider.

Trade Management Issues

Beginning traders assume that catching the end of a trend is a profitable trade because the market will reverse into a trend in the opposite direction. This is the classic "buy the low or sell the high," which, though emotionally gratifying when it works out, can be very challenging to execute. First, this outcome is fairly rare; many trends end by transitioning into trading ranges. As the market chops sideways in the ensuing range, there are no outsized profits, and aggressive traders may even find themselves taking multiple small losses as they continue to try to position for the major trend change that never comes. In addition, most of these ranges, especially if they are able to hold and consolidate somewhere in the neighborhood of the previous trend extreme, are more likely to be trend continuation than reversal patterns on the higher time frame. It certainly is possible to trade these trend terminations into trading ranges profitably, but doing so demands lower expectations; sometimes small trades within the range may be all the market offers.

Once a position has been established in a suspected trend termination, the first thing to look for is confirmation that the trend has indeed terminated. Usually, this is not difficult: if an uptrend terminates, the market will stop going up, and vice versa for a downtrend. However, this somewhat tongue-in-cheek observation ignores the cases where the trend extreme is retested or perhaps even slightly exceeded in the developing trading range. It is important to monitor price action in order to separate trend continuation from these brief tests of trading ranges; in general, failure patterns such as springs and upthrusts mark the tests in successful trend terminations. The presence of strong momentum beyond the previous trend extreme is an undeniable sign that the trend is continuing.

Once the trend termination has been successfully identified, it is important to take higher time frame market structure into consideration. The trading time frame trading range will eventually terminate, but is an exit from one direction more likely than the other? On the trading time frame and lower time frames, the range will probably be volatile, noisy, and more or less random—extremely difficult to read. On a higher time frame, structures like this usually resolve into either continuation or reversal patterns in that higher time frame trend, so it is sometimes possible to tilt the odds in favor of one resolution or the other. For instance, imagine that a trading time frame trend terminates into a trading range, the higher time frame has shown multiple trend legs in the same direction, and the higher time frame is now overextended and is showing a momentum divergence. These higher time frame factors would suggest that the trading time frame range is more likely to be a reversal pattern, and this has obvious implications for how a trade in should be managed.

However, a trend on the trading time frame may terminate into a range that is a simple with-trend consolidation on the higher time frame. Pressing trades *against* that higher time frame trend is usually a bad idea, as that trend is very likely to reassert itself and at least make an attempt at another trend leg. A very common pattern here is to see the trading time frame range create a complex, two-legged pullback on the higher time frame. For instance, if the higher time frame is in an uptrend and the trading time frame rolls over into a range that holds near the extreme of that trend, shorting below the bottom of such a range is exactly the *wrong* trade on the higher time frame. The only reasonable trade is buying the bottom of the complex pullback, whether establishing longs or covering countertrend shorts. If a successful short in this range is not covered at the lows in an attempt to allow for more market volatility in a potential breakdown, this is fine, but once the market turns higher and the higher time frame trend seems to be regaining control, any remaining profits must be protected aggressively. There is nothing worse than correctly identifying a trend termination, correctly executing countertrend trades at exactly the right time, watching them grow to nice profits, and then aggressively adding to those positions at the point you should be taking profits. Errors like this can make the difference between a successful and a failed trading career.

TREND TO OPPOSITE TREND (TREND REVERSAL)

The most likely outcome following a trend termination is a trading range, but there is another possibility: a dramatic transition from a trend in one direction to a trend in the other direction without an intervening range. The reason this scenario is uncommon is that an established trend is a powerful force, and it usually takes a lot of work, a lot of time, and a lot of contrary pressure to end that trend. Without these factors and the accompanying price action, the best bet at any point is for trend continuation. Having said that, there are two specific scenarios in which a sudden reversal is somewhat more likely than usual: following a parabolic climax or on a "last gasp" test of a previous trend extreme.

Parabolic Blow-Off into Climax

Trends end in one of two ways. The most common is for the trend to simply run out of steam and roll over, as momentum divergences develop against the trend and the market eventually finds balance at a new price level. This type of trend ending is more likely to be followed by an extended trading range, which itself may be a consolidation for another leg in the direction of the original trend. The other classic trend-ending pattern occurs when a trend ends in a parabolic range expansion that culminates in a buying (or selling) climax. These moves are dramatic and powerful, often exceeding any reasonable limits that could have been imagined. They seem to be the ultimate expression of a strong trend, but they carry within themselves the seeds of a dramatic trend reversal.

In the case of a buying climax, every buyer who wants to buy does so into the climax, spurred by the powerful emotions that accompany such a move. When the buying stops and the market pauses for even a moment (again, dependent on the time frame), it becomes obvious that the last willing buyer just bought and there is no one left to buy. The market then collapses into that vacuum; sharp countertrend momentum emerges that usually extends into multiple trend legs. This pattern is not common, but it is very powerful. Trapped traders can drive markets much farther, much faster than anyone would have expected, and this problem is magnified by the already elevated volatility levels around these spots in the market.

Every trend that eventually ends in a parabolic expansion begins life as a normal trend. It goes through the same normal stages of evolution as any other trend, and it is usually impossible to identify good candidates for parabolic expansion early in the life cycle of the trend. (If it were possible, then it would be worthwhile to do nothing other than to trade these trends, which might offer 10 or 20 times the profit potential of any normal scenario.) Typically, trends that end this way develop two characteristics: they last a long time and they accelerate into a steeper trend before the actual expansion. This acceleration can either be a series of ever-steeping trend legs or occur at a single inflection, as in Figure 5.12. In this example, Wheat futures in mid-1996, the market lifted above a recent trend channel at point A and began a new, steeper trend. At B, it engaged a multiyear trend channel and traded cleanly through it as momentum continued to increase. At C, it showed many bars trading completely outside the Keltner channels (multiple *free bars*), a most unusual event. This type of price action is unsustainable, and the market collapsed back into the vacuum at D. The price extreme reached in this parabolic move was a high-water mark that would remain unchallenged for more than a decade; it is common for the extreme points marked by these parabolic moves to represent long-lasting and significant elements of market structure.

Psychologically, one of the keys to this type of action is the acceleration of the normal trend preceding the parabolic expansion. It is unusual to see a trend that is simply trading with a normal trending pattern break into this kind of expansion without first having an inflection or a series of accelerating trend legs. In the section on trend lines in Chapter 3, we looked at how a set of steeper trend lines was needed to contain a trend that increases in strength; seeing many of these steeper, short trend lines is one warning that a market could be primed for a blow-off. If you are ever on the wrong side of one of these moves, remember than they can go much further than anyone would ever think possible—there is great danger of a career-ending loss at these points. This should be a hard-and-fast trading rule: if you are ever on the wrong side of a parabolic expansion,

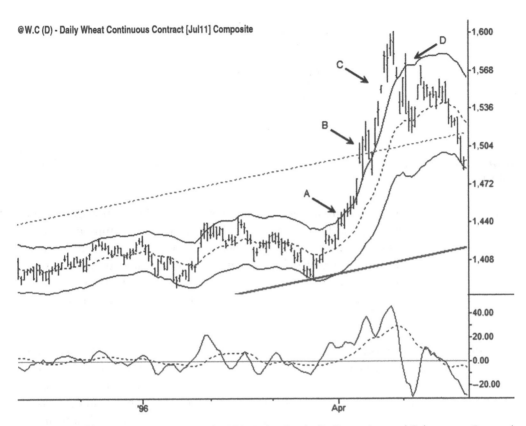

FIGURE 5.12 Wheat Futures in Mid-1996 Had a Parabolic Expansion and Subsequent Reversal into a Downtrend

limit risk with iron discipline. Do not hold on hoping the market will come back, and do not add to your position hoping to average out of your loss. At some point the market will reverse, but you may have been margin called and taken out of business long before that happens.

Like most things in technical analysis, we see similar patterns on all time frames— intraday, daily, and all the way out to monthly and beyond, but the pattern varies in significance depending on the time frame. A parabolic exhaustion on a 1-minute chart might mark a high that lasts for several hours, whereas the corresponding pattern on a daily chart could set a high that would hold for many years. It is also fairly common to see lower time frame moves that are counter to a higher time frame exhaust themselves in a small climax into ideal entry points on the higher time frame. For instance, if you are watching a potential complex pullback in an uptrend on the daily chart, watch intraday time frames carefully as the market comes near the measured move objective for the complex pullback (see Figure 5.13). If you see a selling climax and a parabolic exhaustion on the intraday time frame, entering long in the reversal is an excellent trade because it plays to both the intraday selling climax and the market structure of the higher time

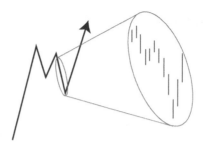

FIGURE 5.13 Watch for Parabolic Expansion and Exhaustion into Ideal Higher Time Frame Entry Points

frame. Though slightly more complex because it depends on the interaction of two time frames, this is actually one of the best and most reliable trend reversal setups: positioning with a higher time frame pattern against a parabolic exhaustion on a lower time frame. Position sizing and risk points may be different depending on whether you want to trade it as a stand-alone reversal on the shorter time frame or want to focus on the entry on the higher time frame pattern, but this is a powerful pattern that should be in every technical trader's arsenal.

Expectations Following Parabolic Exhaustion   Once the entry in the parabolic expansion has been identified, it is important to start considering reasonable expectations for the trade. There is, of course, the possibility that the exhaustion will be absorbed and the market will continue in the direction of the original trend. In the case of large-scale exhaustions, this is very unlikely as they tend to cause structural shifts in the psychology of market participants, but there are also many smaller climaxes, especially on shorter time frames, that do often result in continuation after further consolidation. One classic example is a small climax that caps a trend, resulting in a two-legged complex consolidation. After this structure, the extreme condition created by the climax may be worked off, and it is quite likely the market can continue the original trend. Again, this is extremely unusual after larger climaxes as in Figure 5.12, but, even then, it is possible.

More common is the sequence of a sharp countertrend move, consolidation, and then another sharp break in the direction of the countertrend move. This technically completes a two-legged complex consolidation, but the distinguishing factor is that the countertrend momentum is much sharper than in a standard pullback. The easy trade is usually playing for this second countertrend leg, but this is also the point where the market may extend into a new trend. The key will be judging the bounces that are in the direction of the original (preclimax) trend. If they are reluctant and are smaller, ideally both in price and in time, than the legs in the direction of the new trend, there is a good chance that a trend change has taken place. It is also not unusual to see a market spend an extended period of time consolidating before making another move.

Last, another pattern to be aware of is the triangle consolidation that is set up by two back-to-back impulse moves in opposite directions. If a market makes a sharp move, followed by an almost equally sharp move in the opposite direction, there is a very high probability of an extended consolidation. One of the most common areas to find this

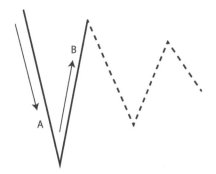

FIGURE 5.14 Two Sharp Moves in Opposite Directions Usually Lead to a Triangle

formation is following these parabolic climaxes. If the first, very strong countertrend move is immediately reversed by another movement in the direction of the original trend, there is a good chance of a protracted consolidation following. For most traders, these are not profitable areas in which to tie up mental or financial capital. Learn to read this pattern, pictured in Figure 5.14, as a warning sign, and simply avoid trading in these areas.

Last Gasp

There is a trading rule that says, only half in jest, that the market will always do whatever will hurt the greatest number of traders. Part of this is subjective—we all use humor to deal with losses at times—but there also is a reality here, driven by that core tendency of markets to seek volume and activity. After an extended run-up followed by a well-recognized topping formation (e.g., head and shoulders or double top), there will likely be many traders who short in anticipation of a trend reversal with stops just beyond the recent highs. In addition, there will be traders who think they are smarter than the market, and who will be playing for trend *continuation* at these points. They too will buy, either on stops or with contingent orders when the market violates the previous high. Regardless of the reason behind the buying, there is almost always a lot of latent buying pressure waiting just beyond the previous highs.

The moment of truth comes as soon as the market probes that area, stops are elected, and the initial buying dries up. Are there larger buyers there, waiting to bid the market higher with commitment, or was the whole move a fake-out? If the latter, this will be obvious as prices fall back below the previous highs and many of the shorts who were stopped out will reestablish (selling pressure). Trapped longs will eventually have to sell as well, whether they were holding established positions or entered on the breakout. The result of all of this selling pressure is that the market finally reverses and downside momentum develops as selling leads to more selling.

This is a special case of a *failure test* at the highs of an old trend, and, in the right context, is an extremely reliable trend termination pattern. The actual "last gasp" pattern is nothing more than a Wyckoff upthrust, but the key is that it is preceded by sufficient consolidation to set up the potential for another trend leg up; the pattern draws its power

FIGURE 5.15   Two Upthrusts in Disney Cap an Uptrend

from the failure of that potential. (It is exactly reversed for a downtrend—i.e., a spring after a long-enough consolidation that the market appeared to be primed to break down.) Traders who recognize this pattern early can establish short positions at advantageous prices or at least can aggressively limit damage on long positions. Figure 5.15 shows a fairly brutal example in Walt Disney Company (NYSE: DIS): after a gap up and a short consolidation, the stock put in an upthrust at the highs. After consolidating again for nearly a quarter, another upthrust back above the level decisively ended any hopes for another easy trend leg up and the market gapped open lower the next day.

Trend Change Without Warning

Sometimes the absence of a pattern is a pattern in itself. Trends are powerful forces in markets, and it is very rare to see one stop and turn with no warning. Strong trends usually require time and substantial price action to reverse, so with-trend traders are usually rewarded for being somewhat stubborn in their exits. With a winning trend trade, it often pays to give it a little more room, or even to add to the position as it fluctuates against the trend. This is normal, but there are cases in which a market makes a stunning reversal into a trend in the opposite direction without any warning.

This is very rare, but that is precisely why it deserves attention. Trends do not normally stop and turn on a dime. When they do, it is usually driven by some new piece of information or a major catalyst. Whether it is company-specific news, a crop report, or a large-scale economic report, fresh information causes market participants to immediately and dramatically reassess their commitment to the market. As traders scramble to adjust positions in the new environment of heightened uncertainty, volatility increases and a feedback loop develops in which large price movements trigger further price movements. The large price movements eventually provoke a reaction from traders who would not have reacted to the news alone as they are forced to make a decision about existing positions or potential entries. Markets can make breathtaking moves under these conditions, so be on guard for these large-scale reversals with no warning.

Change of Character

In all of these cases of a trend reversing into the opposite trend, the common ground is that the market displays a distinct change of character. The pattern of the established trend is first broken, and then a new movement emerges that shows strong momentum counter to the established trend. Traders who are actually watching the price bars develop will see that price is moving differently; this is a form of tape reading. Traders who are only looking at static price bars, for instance, examining charts at the end of the day, will still be able to infer price action to some extent by carefully examining lower time frames.

Though this is a very important point, do not overcomplicate it. Working with the traders I have trained, I sometimes refer to a trading skill I (half) jokingly call "Hey, that's different." Sometimes it really is that simple—sometimes it is enough to notice a break in the established pattern. Intuition is useful here, as it can often alert the trader that *something* has changed, even if it is stubbornly nebulous at first. Once you know that the pattern has been broken, you can dig deeper and attempt to better quantify the break. For instance, if a market has been uptrending for quite a while, a change of character could be as simple as a downswing that is bigger than the preceding upswing. If this is the first time this has happened in many swings, it is time to carefully monitor the market over the next few swings to see if something crucial has changed. Confirmation can come from a number of other factors, indicators, or market relationships, but be open to a hint from your intuition that the pattern has somehow shifted.

TREND TO SAME TREND (FAILURE OF TREND REVERSAL)

A successful trend reversal is a trend failure: the trend fails to continue. A failed trend reversal, then, could be described as a failed failure pattern. This may seem like an unnecessary complication; it is certainly important to keep our labeling system as clean and simple as possible, but there is a distinction between simple trend continuations and failed trend reversals. In both cases, prices continue to move in the direction of the trend, but the difference is that, in a failed trend reversal, traders may have been encouraged to enter countertrend positions in anticipation of the trend change. An example of this might be if a well-watched index or commodity puts in a large-scale head and shoulders pattern. The media will be discussing the obvious pattern for weeks, some large traders and funds will establish countertrend positions, and many small traders will join the party. If this trend does not reverse, if the trend reversal fails, these traders will be forced to adjust their positions, and their activity will add fuel to the fire as the original trend continues on. Another much more common example is the complex pullback. The second countertrend leg of this pullback will be viewed by some market participants as a legitimate trend reversal. When it becomes obvious they are wrong, their efforts to adjust their positions add momentum to the other side.

It is probably not necessary to study these failed trend reversals in detail, because, at some level, they are just a type of trend continuation. Realize that they derive their power from potentially trapped traders who were aggressively anticipating trend reversal (see Figure 5.16). Anytime too many people are leaning in the same direction, the market is vulnerable to an outsized move in the opposite direction.

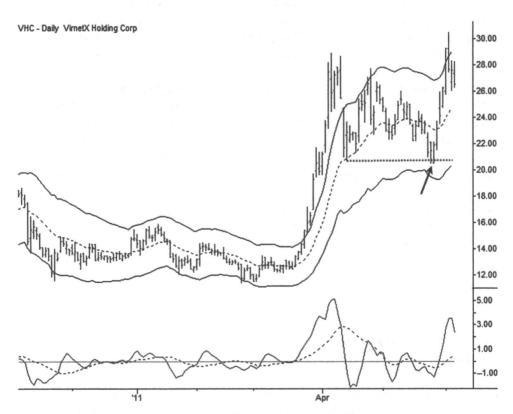

FIGURE 5.16 Failed Breakdown (Arrow) Leads to a Retest of Highs with the Possibility of Continuation into Another Trend Leg

SUMMARY

Part One of this book laid a solid foundation for the need to have a verifiable edge in the market. Part Two has taken the basic forces driving price movements—mean reversion and range expansion—and has begun to put them in the context of actual, practical market structure. All of this has still been more or less theoretical, with no attempt being made to delineate precise entry and exit points in patterns. Before moving on to examine actual trading patterns, this is a good time to review what we have learned so far, and to put it all in context.

First Principles

- Markets are highly random and are very, very close to being efficient.
- It is impossible to make money trading without an edge.
- Every edge we have is driven by an imbalance of buying and selling pressure.
- The job of traders is to identify those points of imbalance and to restrict their activities in the markets to those times.
- There are two competing forces at work in the market: mean reversion and range expansion. These two forces express themselves in the market through the alternation of trends and trading ranges.

The Four Trades

- Traders usually view market action through charts, which are useful tools, but are only tools.
- Trades broadly fall into with-trend and countertrend trades. These two categories require significantly different mind-sets and approaches to trade management.
- There are only four technical trades. Some trades are blends of more than one trade, or an application of one trade to a structure in another time frame, but these are just refinements. At their root, all technical trades fall into one of these categories:
  - Trend continuation.
  - Trend termination.
  - Support and resistance holding.
  - Support and resistance failing.
- Each of these trades is more appropriate at one phase of the market cycle than another. If you apply the wrong trade to current market conditions, you will lose.

Market Structure and Price Action

- Market structure refers to the pattern of relative highs and lows and the momentum behind the moves that created that pattern. Market structure is a more or less static element.
- Price action refers to the actual movements of price within market structure. Price action is dynamic and ephemeral and must sometimes be inferred from market structure.

- There are three critical areas of market structure to consider: trends, trading ranges, and the interfaces between the two.

Trends and Retracements
- Trends move in a series of with-trend impulse moves separated by retracements.
- Retracements often contain lower time frame trends that run counter to the trading time frame trend.
- Trends that run counter to the higher time frame trends tend to reverse.
- Complex consolidations in trends are a reflection of the lower time frame trend structure and are common.

Trend Terminations into Trading Ranges or Reversals
- Trend terminations are usually set up by momentum divergences, and are confirmed by market structure. Do not attempt trend termination trades without clear evidence of a change of character.
- Trends may terminate either into trading ranges or into trend reversals.
- Trends end in one of two ways: by rolling over as the trend loses momentum, or in parabolic climaxes.

Trading Ranges
- Trading ranges are defined by support and resistance zones, which may or may not be clean, exact levels.
- Classic accumulation/distribution patterns are recognizable at the extremes of ranges.
- Violation of support and resistance does not necessarily invalidate the trading range. It is possible that the range has simply expanded or moved to a new level.
- Trading ranges serve a structural function in the higher time frame; higher time frame market structure can give a bias to the direction of the break from a trading range. In the absence of contradictory information, assume that any trading range is a continuation pattern.

Breakouts
- Breakouts from trading ranges are volatile and are driven by disagreement over price.
- The first pullback after a breakout is critical for assessing the strength of the nascent trend.
- Breakout failures are far more common than successful breakouts.

PART III

Trading Strategies

CHAPTER 6

Practical Trading Templates

Do not [just blindly] repeat the tactics which have gained you one victory, but let your methods be regulated by the infinite variety of circumstances.

—Sun Tzu, *The Art of War* (ca. 210 CE)

This chapter presents eight specific trading patterns that should be seen as guidelines for actual trades. They are also concrete expressions of quantifiable, directional edges in the market; they highlight points in market structure around which there are sometimes imbalances of buying and selling pressure that can set up profitable trading opportunities. These are not a simple set of patterns to be memorized, found in the market, and then traded profitably. We do not trade these patterns; we trade the underlying buying and selling pressure that sometimes creates these patterns. This is an important and subtle distinction that sets my approach apart from that of many other traders. There are reliable, repeatable patterns in the markets, but these patterns are useful only inasmuch as they reveal the buying and selling pressure that shapes evolving market structure. The true value in these patterns is that they define precise points for your entries and exits and give you tools to manage the risk in each trade, but enduring success will follow only if these are part of a larger analytical framework that encompasses a complete understanding of market structure, price action, and the psychological dynamics that create them.

These patterns are introduced in order of complexity: *Failure tests*, though they are aggressive countertrend trades, are clearly defined with relatively few subjective elements. The next three patterns are variations of *pullbacks*; the first two are distinguished by whether they enter with or against the direction of the short-term trend. The last pullback pattern is the *complex pullback*, which is often the source of consistent losses for ill-prepared trend traders. The fifth pattern in this chapter is the *Anti*, which offers a rigidly disciplined entry at a potential trend change. Last, three variations of *breakout trades* bring up the rear and close out the chapter.

149

FAILURE TEST

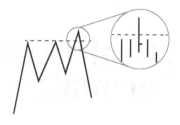

Trade Type

Support/resistance holding or trend termination.

Concept   Markets probe for stop orders and activity beyond significant price levels. Many times, there is no real conviction behind these moves, and the moves fail and reverse quickly once the stop orders are triggered. Entering after such a move allows for excellent reward/risk potential with a clearly defined risk point.

Setup   The market must be overextended or in some way primed for reversal. The best examples of this trade occur in mature, extended trends, and will usually be accompanied by momentum divergence on the trading time frame. Another common variation occurs in an extended consolidation just under resistance. This type of consolidation would normally have a high expectation of producing another trend leg above that resistance, so many traders are monitoring the area and will enter on a potential breakout. If this breakout occurs and fails, there will be many trapped traders, which can add momentum to a downside trade off that level.

Trigger   For a short entry, the market trades above a clearly defined resistance area, but immediately reverses on the same or the following bar and closes back under the resistance. There can be significant volatility, volume, and activity on the breakout, but there should be no real conviction beyond the level. Enter short on the close of the bar that closes back below resistance. The buy setup is exactly symmetrical. Figure 6.1 shows examples of long and short failure test entries in Fossil, Inc. (Nasdaq: FOSL). Point A marks a brief probe below support, but the same day immediately closed back above the support level. At B, the stock attempted to break to new highs, but there was not enough buying pressure to hold it above the resistance level and it failed on the same day. A long entry would have been justified on the close of A, and a short on the close of B.

Figure 6.2 shows another classic example of this trade, in the EURUSD. In the bar preceding A, all systems seemed to be "go" for a continued trend run above the previous highs, and the market actually closed solidly above the resistance level. However, at A

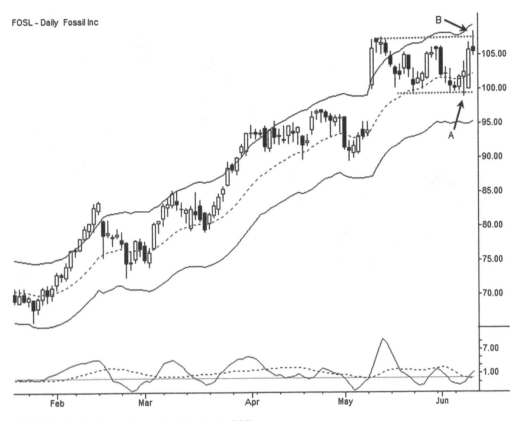

FIGURE 6.1 Two Failure Test Entries in FOSL

the market failed dramatically, and the subsequent sharp selling shows that this point did in fact mark a major structural inflection in this currency.

Stop The stop for this trade is clearly defined: a hard stop must be entered just beyond the extreme of the test beyond the level. For instance, the stops on the two trades in Figure 6.1 would have been placed below the low of the bar marked A and above the high of B. The EURUSD trade in Figure 6.2 is only slightly more complicated; the failure occurred on the close of the day marked A, but the previous day set the high-water mark for the excursion above resistance. Therefore, you would have had to place the stop above the high of the bar *preceding* the entry bar. In all cases, the stop goes just outside the most extreme test beyond the triggering support or resistance level.

Because this is an aggressive countertrend trade, it is important to not add to losing trades. Respect the stop level without question. In addition, there is significant gap risk with trades held overnight. On losing trades, there is sometimes enough pent-up pressure to cause gap opens beyond the stop, so it may make sense to trade these on smaller size and risk compared to other setups.

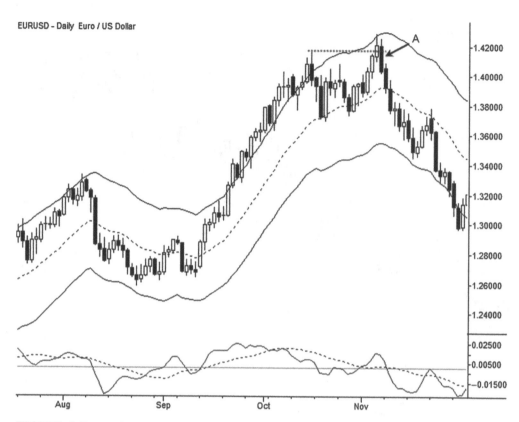

FIGURE 6.2 A Failure Test Short in the EURUSD

Profit Target   Most traders find best success with a plan that allows for taking partial profits as the market makes them available. For instance, one plan would be to take profit on the first part when the profit equals the initial risk on the trade. The profit target on the second portion is discretionary, but consider the possibility of a longer, complex correction that leads to continuation of the original trend. Some of these trades will turn into dramatic trend reversals, but this should not be your baseline expectation. In general, consolidation near the level, particularly if the first profit target is not reached, is a bad sign. For instance, if you enter short on B in Figure 6.1 and the market spends two to three days trading above 105, this is most likely a precursor of a losing trade. Reduce exposure or close out these trades if they do not work quickly in your favor.

Failure Patterns   While it is certainly important to know what the pattern should look like if it's working, from a pedagogical standpoint it probably makes more sense to focus energy and attention on what should *not* happen. If these early signs of failure can be recognized, it is often possible to reduce position sizes and to reduce the size of the ultimate loss. In addition, careful study of the typical patterns associated with failure can lead to a deeper understanding of the dynamics behind the trade. The key to most failure patterns is to understand what should *not* happen if the trade is good—to look for price action and emerging market structure that contradict the reasons for being in the trade.

In this case, what we do not want to see after trade entry is simple: the market should not be able to consolidate near the level, nor should it exceed the stop-loss point. Consolidation near the level is more consistent with an impending breakout and continuation of the existing trend. If the failure test trade is successful, price should move sharply away from the level, and the trade should be immediately profitable (within one to three bars on the trading time frame). This is another expression of the classic price rejection, a further confirmation of the validity of the failure beyond the level.

One last point to consider is that some of these trades will hit the stop point and, on the same or the next bar following the stop-out bar, will once again fall back inside the level. Though it can be psychologically challenging to reenter immediately after a loss, this second trade, taken on the second failure, is also an excellent entry. This is another reason for trading both entries on smaller risk—this second entry sets up often enough (and is virtually obligatory) that the sum of the risk on both trades should not be significantly larger than the maximum risk taken on other types of trades.

Comments   This is the simplest and most clearly defined of all the patterns in this chapter. There is no subjectivity in stop location and little subjectivity in managing losing trades—if the market makes a new extreme, then you are wrong and must exit the trade. There are only two potential complications with this trade. The first is the reentry following a stop-out, which is usually a simple failure on the higher time frame. Traders must be aware of this possibility and must plan for this in their risk management and position sizing.

The second potential issue deals with managing winning trades; it is important to consider the trade-off between high probability of a smaller profit and the lesser probability of a large payout. Some percentage of these trades will evolve into major trend reversals; however gratifying that is, it is not the most common outcome and should not be your expectation when trading this pattern. Many winning trades will give the trader the opportunity to take some profits around the first profit target, at which point the market begins consolidating or turns around and hits the stop. It is important to strike a balance between taking sufficient early profits that the entire set of trades will be profitable, while maintaining enough exposure that the much less common home runs make a significant contribution to the bottom line. There is no easy answer to this, and the choice will depend on a large degree on the personality and inclination of the individual trader.

The failure test pattern is the classic Wyckoff spring and upthrust; the only adaptation is the addition of a firm stop level and a concrete trading plan. The basis of this pattern was first written about nearly 100 years ago, and it works just as well today. More recently, Victor Sperandeo (1993) has written about this pattern, which he calls the "2B" trade. His books include many valuable ideas and perspectives on this pattern and other trading-related issues.

PULLBACK, BUYING SUPPORT OR SHORTING RESISTANCE

Trade Type

Trend continuation.

Concept   Pullbacks are probably the most important structural feature of trends. For many traders, pullbacks are the quintessential with-trend trade, using the countertrend pullback to position in the larger trend at an advantageous price. The broad term *pullback* encompasses a large number of specific patterns: flags, pennants, wedges, continuation triangles, and many others, but the exact shape of the pattern is not that important. In reality, these are all functionally the same—they are continuation patterns in trends. It is not necessary, nor is it constructive, to have separate trading plans for each of these patterns. Understand what the pattern is and what it does, and trade it accordingly.

Setup   The most important condition for this trade is that the market must be trending. Though it is not always possible to separate trending from nontrending environments with precision, many losing trades are the result of attempting pullbacks in nontrending environments. Objective tools to identify trends have been discussed in Chapter 3, but the problem can be reduced to whether the setup leg preceding the pullback shows good momentum—it must be a move that should see continuation after consolidation.

At the risk of oversimplifying, if the market is in an established trend, the preceding setup leg should be at least as strong as previous trend legs in the same direction. In other words, it should not break the pattern of the trend and should not show momentum divergence. Pullback trades are also possible on trend changes or following breakouts of trading ranges, though this more properly falls under the Anti trade category. In these cases, there will be no established trend, but the setup leg should show a distinct change of character compared to the preceding environment. Whether in an established trend or at the beginning of a new potential trend, the same condition applies: the setup leg should suggest momentum in the market that must be resolved through an attempted third leg (impulse-retracement-impulse) continuation.

One useful way to approach trend trades is to consider conditions that would contradict this trade, which are the standard preconditions for countertrend trades. In the absence of any of these (e.g., momentum divergence, overextension on higher time frames, etc.), with-trend trades are fully justified.

Different markets have different characters with respect to the integrity, length, and strength of trends—some markets trend better than others. For instance, it is somewhat unusual for most intraday index products to have trends that extend more than three legs, but individual equities, especially if they have had unusual news that day, may trend much further. Some commodities, such as meat products, do not tend to trend well, but petroleum products and grains are capable of significant, extended trends with many clean trend legs. On longer time frames, interest rate products, and currency rates often show multiyear trends. In general, there is an old rule of thumb that says that larger markets (in terms of nominal value) trend better; though this is difficult to prove quantitatively, it is a useful guideline to keep in mind. Certainly, extraordinary conditions do occur where a market makes a move that is out of all proportion to historical precedents. Your trading plan should allow you to participate in those moves with at least partial positions, but these unusual moves should not be the main focus of your plan.

Once the main prerequisites of a trending market with no contradictory conditions are satisfied, we turn to the geometry of the pullback pattern itself. Good pullbacks almost always show reduced activity (smaller ranges for individual bars) and the absence of strong countertrend momentum. This is why traditional technical analysis suggests that volume should be lighter in pullbacks—they are zeroing in on the (valid) fact that trading activity should be less on the pullbacks. In many cases, pullbacks *will* have lighter volume, but this is not the distinguishing feature. In all cases the best pullbacks have reduced activity, which is visible on the lower time frame, in price action, and in the lack of strong countertrend momentum on the trading time frame—but necessarily lower volume per se.

Last, it also makes sense to be responsive to developing market structure, even after the trade is initiated. A pullback may emerge at a spot where the trade was justified, but developing price action may suggest that the trend is losing integrity. If this happens, it is not necessary to hold the trade to the original stop-loss level. It is often advisable to scratch the trade, exiting for a small win or loss, and to wait for better opportunities. A good trading plan will allow flexibility and will encourage the trader to be responsive to developing market conditions.

Trigger The actual entry for this trade is buying against the support level near the bottom or selling short against the resistance near the top of the pullback. There is an important trade management issue to consider, as Figure 6.3 shows: support and resistance levels usually *slope* in these patterns. One of the advantages of buying against support is that, usually, your risk is fairly clearly defined, but, in the case of buying into pullbacks, price can decline (or rally, in a pullback against a downtrend) much further than expected while the pattern remains valid. It can be difficult to define the risk on a position entered against a sloping support or resistance level, but it does not make sense

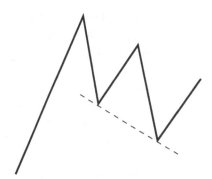

FIGURE 6.3 Support in a Pullback Is Usually Sloping, Not Flat

to exit a trade that is still within the sloping level. Having the level itself is not enough; it is also important to have a clear trigger against that level to support the actual entry.

There are two ideal triggers. In the first, the market has defined a clean pullback. Sometimes it is possible to draw a trendline on both sides of the pullback, but, barring that, a parallel trend channel (see Chapter 3) can be used. The entry trigger is a failure of this trend line or channel, followed by an immediate reversal; that is, the line is penetrated, but prices recover back above the trend line within a few bars. Conceptually, what has happened is that traders buying into the pullback against the support level have been washed out of the market by the drop below that support. Note that this will often coincide with a lower time frame climax, though this is usually clear from the trading time frame and it is not necessary to explicitly examine lower time frames in most cases. The bar marked A in Figure 6.4 shows an example of this entry in Caterpillar, Inc. (NYSE: CAT). The single candle with a long shadow below the support at the bottom of the flag is indicative of a small climax move on the lower time frame. This entry has the advantage of excellent trade location; some of these will actually be very near the low tick of the pullback. The only real disadvantage of this entry is that considerable experience may be required to read the market correctly at these spots, and, even on relatively long time frames, you have to pay attention because the exhaustion below support will happen on a single bar. This is a skilled trader's tool, not a buy-and-forget entry.

The second entry trigger is actually buying against the support at the bottom of the pullback, for example, at point B in Figure 6.4. It is always possible to find examples of this entry on historical charts, but it can be considerably more difficult to make this trade in real time. Stop placement is problematic because the support can drop, washing weak-hand longs out of the market; the recovery from this fakeout is actually the previously discussed entry. Why put yourself in the position of being the weak trader who is washed out of the market? However, if you are executing some variation of this buying against support plan (or shorting against resistance), it *is* essential to limit your loss and your risk on these trades; some of them will drop support and trade lower with a vengeance. Note also that this entry has much in common with the tools and techniques

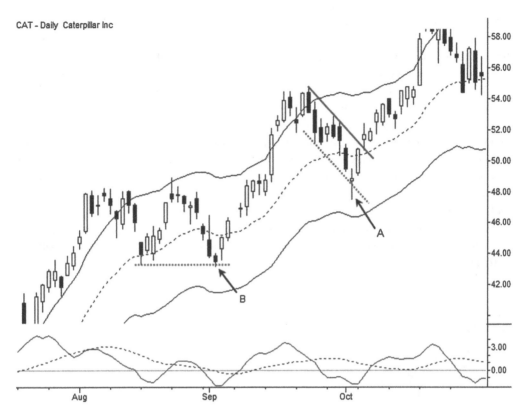

CAT - Daily Caterpillar Inc

FIGURE 6.4 Two Entries in Pullbacks in an Uptrend

for simply trading against any support and resistance level—the same ideas, risks, and caveats apply.

One pattern to avoid is buying against multiple (three or more) tests of support in a pullback, as this pattern is often more indicative of an impending failure. The operative concept here is usually lower highs into support, as successive bounces find fewer willing buyers. This is not to say that retracement patterns that show this characteristic never work out, but, on balance, they are lower-probability plays. Most traders will have the most success if they restrict their operations to the best possible trades. The best pullbacks are pauses in strong trends; there should be enough interest in the market that the pullback does not languish too long near support or resistance.

Stop   There are basically two schools of thought on stop placement in general. Many traders want to put the stop as close to the pattern as possible, with the idea that doing so minimizes the size of losing trades. This is correct as far as the magnitude of the losses goes, but there are two other points to consider: First, trades should be sized so that every loss is equivalent; there is no such thing as a "low risk" trade. (Some types of trades may be traded with different levels of risk, but, even then, risk levels should be consistent for all trades of that type.) Second, and more importantly, very close stops have a higher probability of being hit. When the probability of the loss is considered, a very tight stop often is a much larger loss in terms of expected value than a farther stop.

My preference is to put stops farther away from the pattern, and to introduce a small random "jitter" element to stop placement. One common mistake is to put your stop where everyone else puts theirs, because markets tend to seek out those stop levels. If you put yours a few ticks or cents beyond the obvious levels, you may still be swept out if there is extra volatility beyond the level, but this is an unavoidable risk of trading. The best we can do is to minimize it with intelligent stop placement. Figures 6.5 and 6.6 show several pullback trades with both near and far stop levels marked; realize that these are well-chosen examples of perfect entries, and perfect entries will rarely occur in actual trading. Again, these are only guidelines, and active management is important. Stops may be tightened dramatically a few bars into the trade, and the trade may also be managed with a time stop.

FIGURE 6.5 Three Idealized Pullback Entries in the EURGBP (One Long and Two Short) with Near and Far Stop Levels

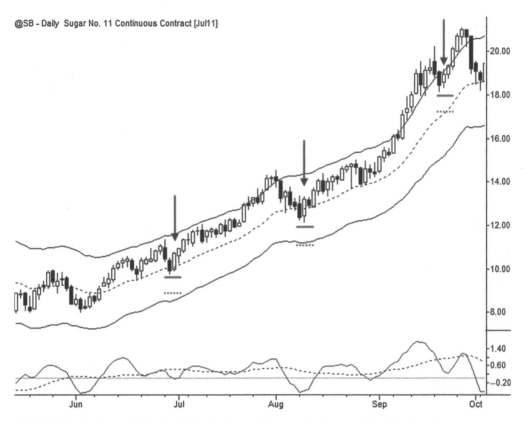

@SB - Daily Sugar No. 11 Continuous Contract [Jul11]

FIGURE 6.6 Three Pullback Entries in Sugar Futures with Near and Far Stop Levels

Profit Target   The most conservative profit target is at the previous pivot high of the setup leg for long traders, or at the low of the setup leg for shorts. (See Figure 6.7.) Many traders who focus on pullbacks will bid or offer (for short or long trades) part of their positions at the level, and are prepared to exit more of the position if the market runs into trouble there. These levels are often cleared easily, but there can be considerable volatility as some traders exit positions and others look to enter on breakouts beyond the level. The difference of opinion and two-sided trading in these spots can lead to unusual activity, but the strongest trends will continue past this level, extending into another leg. A good exit plan will allow for the possibility of taking partial profits while holding on to part of the position for a possible extension into further trend legs.

Another common target is the *measured move objective (MMO)*, which is calculated by taking the length of the setup leg (AB in Figure 6.8), adding that number to the pivot point marked C, and expecting the CD leg to be approximately the same length as the AB leg. There is no magic to this method. There is no mystical force at work here; the operative concept is that markets tend to trade with a fairly consistent level of volatility, and the MMO simply targets the approximate level at which we could expect the next

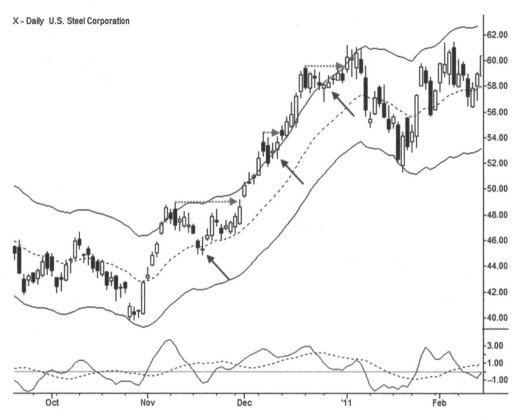

FIGURE 6.7 Three Idealized Entries in U.S. Steel Corporation (NYSE: X) with Conservative Profit Targets Marked

swing to terminate based on the prevailing volatility levels and the average swing sizes of the market. Rather than treating this as an exact level, consider it a zone and give some consideration to what the correct course of action would be if the market stalls somewhere near this area. In general, the correct plan would be to take partial or complete profits even though the trade had not quite reached the target.

Last, it is also possible to manage pullback trades using risk multiples as profit targets, for instance, taking partial profits at one or two times ($1\times$ or $2\times$) the initial risk on the trade. This is a solid plan, but it probably also makes sense to incorporate information from the conservative and MMO profit targets, as they are based on the reality of market structure and volatility-driven relationships. For instance, if the first $1\times$ risk profit target is a little beyond the conservative previous swing target, it might be a good idea to move the target to the conservative target. However, if you are trading the $1\times$ plan and find that your first target is significantly beyond the conservative target, an adjustment might skew the reward/risk ratio significantly. These are the types of issues that must be considered within a comprehensive trading plan.

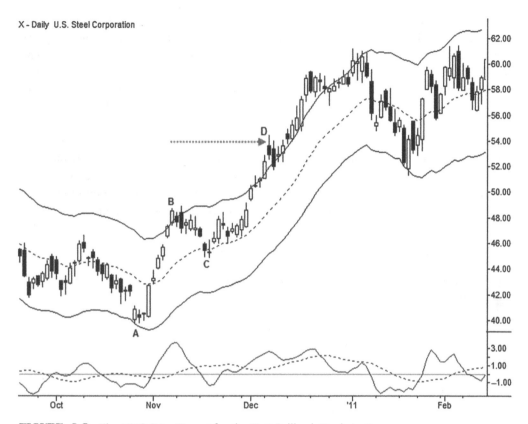

X - Daily U.S. Steel Corporation

FIGURE 6.8 The MMO Price Target for the First Pullback Trade in X

Comments We will look at several variations of this trade, but the concept of using pullbacks in trending markets is one of the most robust discretionary trading techniques. It uses the normal pattern of a trending market (impulse-retracement-impulse) to position at attractive prices in the trend. Trading these patterns successfully is not as easy as might be expected. One challenge is assessing the strength of the trend while looking for that fine line between a very strong market and one that is overextended, perhaps primed for reversal. Trades in the latter market are much more likely to fail and result in losses, so being able to discriminate between the two environments is an essential trading skill. All of the information in the sections on trend structure must eventually be considered in trading these patterns and incorporated into your trading plan. Much of this can be quantified, but some traders will be more comfortable using much of this information on a subjective, almost subconscious, level.

Another potential challenge is in the timing of the entry. Because pullbacks often have many of the characteristics of small trading ranges, price action within pullbacks tends to be more random and it can be difficult to time the entry point with confidence. In addition, pullbacks are actually contratrend lower time frame trends, so early entries can result in losses if the lower time frame trend is still in control. The third challenge is stop placement. The general idea with stop placement is to avoid the noise and to place stops at a level that would prove the trade incorrect. Finding this point in pullbacks can be a little more difficult; the lower time frame trends sometimes continue further than expected, and conservative stops can be hit at exactly the wrong point. In fact, one of these failures is so common that it deserves separate consideration under the category of complex pullbacks.

Despite all of these potential issues, many traders will find that pullbacks offer some of the most attractive and consistent trading opportunities. A profitable trading plan can be built around this one trade, though an awareness of trend termination patterns will inform your perspective and help you manage losing trades. The next setup looks at an entry that combines the power of the pullback with the direction of momentum on the shortest time frames.

PULLBACK, ENTERING LOWER TIME FRAME BREAKOUT

Trade Type

Trend continuation and breakout blend.

Concept   This trade setup times the entry into the pullback by using the momentum of a lower time frame breakout so that the trade will be entered when the market is moving in the intended direction of the trade. This entry has the advantage of offering the confirmation of momentum with the trade-off that trade location will not be as good. This entry will require larger initial stops compared to entering near support or resistance, and have correspondingly lower reward/risk ratios.

Setup   This is another variation on the pullback concept; the same setup conditions as in the previous trade apply here.

Trigger   The difference is the actual entry trigger, which, in this case, is on a breakout of some structure within the pullback itself, usually visible most clearly on a lower

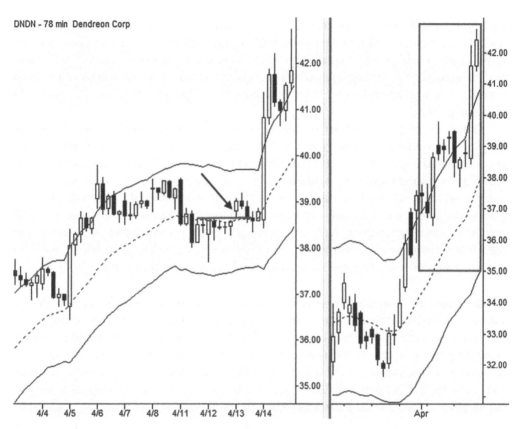

DNDN - 78 min Dendreon Corp

FIGURE 6.9 A Breakout on the Intraday (Left Pane) Serves as an Entry into the Higher Time Frame Pattern

time frame. Figure 6.9 shows an example in Dendreon Corporation (Nasdaq: DNDN) in which a breakout of resistance on the 78-minute time frame provided a good entry into the pullback on the daily chart. Taken by itself, the breakout on the 78-minute is not a compelling entry—it *is* a valid breakout, but it does not have any supporting factors that make it an exceptional trade. The daily chart provides context for this otherwise unimpressive breakout, and the upward momentum from the intraday time frame transitioned into a larger move on the daily time frame. This is a single example, but the same concept can be applied to any set of properly related time frames: 1-minute/5-minute, 10-minute/30-minute, daily/weekly, or weekly/monthly.

Some traders simplify this approach to merely trading breakouts of the previous bar on the trading time frame. Over a large set of trades, this approach is hit or miss because the high of the trading time frame bar may or may not actually be an important point in the market or on the lower time frame. There is no magic to a breakout of the bar on any time frame, because the chart is simply a representation of the underlying market. In most cases, paying attention to lower time frame price action will allow for cleaner entries, but it is sometimes possible to identify clear support and resistance on the trading time frame. For instance, if a series of two to three bars all have the same high and all of the other conditions for a good pullback are fulfilled, paying a breakout through those highs is often a good entry. This is perhaps more common intraday, but it also occurs on higher time frames, particularly in liquid markets. It is not, however, common enough to be a bread-and-butter trade; it is more properly understood as a variation of a common pattern.

One other issue to consider on higher time frames is that markets will frequently gap open beyond intended entry points. This happens in all setups, but is particularly common and the gaps may be unusually large in these pullback breakouts. Consider this carefully in your trading plan. Will you skip these entries altogether, wait for a better entry, or enter at whatever price you have to? If you do enter on the gap, will you enter your entire position or perhaps only a partial and look to add the rest at a later point? If you do enter on the opening, will you enter right *on* the opening print, or will you wait for a few minutes' price action to define the opening range? There may not be one right or wrong answer to each question, but some are surely better than others.

Stop There are basically two schools of thought on stop placement in these trades. In the case of the lower time frame breakout trigger, many traders will want to use a very tight stop, operating under the assumption that if the breakout is truly a critical tipping point, they can simply exit the market for a very small loss if the anticipated move fails to develop. Furthermore, after booking this very small loss, they will have the freedom to reenter the market multiple times until they finally catch the move they were looking for all along. Traders taking this approach will argue that they are trading a higher time frame pattern with potential reward proportional to the swings on that time frame while using much smaller risk levels from the lower time frame.

Though this is potentially a valid approach in some contexts, it is not usually the best practice. The small losses do add up, and these very tight stops do not respect the reality of the noise level in the market. My preference is to use a larger stop that is true to the geometry of the trading time frame pattern. Yes, there is motivation to have the stop as tight as reasonably possible (because the trade will then support a larger position size, *not* because it is a lower-risk trade), but there is an unavoidable trade-off between reward/risk ratio and probability. Assuming both traders trade consistently, the trader using a tight stop and the trader using the wider stop will have approximately the same expected payoff over a large number of trades. (There is an important lesson there.) In addition, the trader using the very tight stop with the plan to reenter will incur multiple transaction costs (including paying the spread, which is not trivial in some markets or time frames) and runs the ultimate risk of not having the position on when the market finally does make the move.

For traders using very tight stops, position sizing is a serious problem. How many entries will it take until they finally catch the trade? Two? Five? More? Each one of these attempts will incur a loss. If they trade small enough that the losses are insignificant, the winning trades will also be insignificant. If they trade with meaningful size, they will not be able to enter the same trade very many times. Why play these games when a proper stop can be set that involves less work, lower transaction costs, and better payout?

Profit Target   The same profit targets apply to all pullback trades.

Comments   This trade setup addresses the key issue of precisely timing the entry into the pullback pattern. In the best cases, the market will never return to the entry price and the trade will be easy and painless from that point. These cases where the trade works perfectly are a minority, but, even in other cases, the character of the move after the pullback often gives good information about the balance of buying and selling pressure in the market. This combination of a breakout trade nested within a pullback is a powerful tool for discretionary traders on all time frames.

TRADING COMPLEX PULLBACKS

Trade Type

Trend continuation.

Concept   Complex pullbacks, which are pullbacks composed of two distinct countertrend legs, are very common, especially in mature trends. A good understanding of these structures is important, because they will often result in losses for traders who are trading simple pullbacks. Furthermore, many of the best pullbacks—those followed by the strongest, cleanest moves—are complex pullbacks, so a comprehensive trading plan must embrace this pattern.

Setup   A complex pullback is a complete ABCD trend structure itself: the first countertrend leg is a lower time frame trend (counter to the higher time frame trend), followed by a retracement against the lower time frame trend (i.e., in the direction of the higher time frame trend), which is then followed by another countertrend leg. To actually trade these patterns, traders need to be aware of two distinct forms: one that shows the

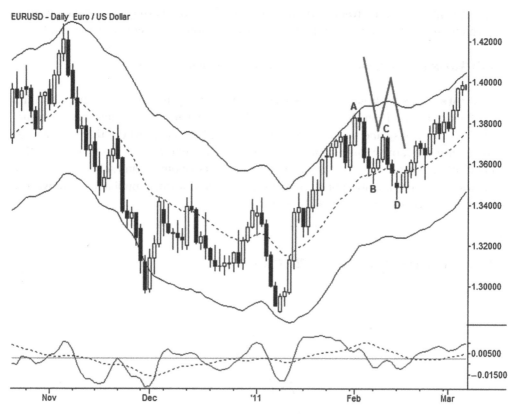

FIGURE 6.10 A Complex Pullback in the EURUSD
Note two clearly visible countertrend legs (AB and CD).

three legs clearly and one that hides them, buried within the lower time frame structure. Figure 6.10 shows a near-perfect example of the first type of complex consolidation that clearly shows three separate legs with an ABCD structure.

There are other cases in which the structure of the complex consolidation is not as clearly visible on the trading time frame. The lower time frame will usually show the distinct trend legs, but they may not be visible on the trading time frame. For experienced traders, it is usually not necessary to explicitly examine the lower time frame, as the structure can usually be inferred from the trading time frame. At first, it may be easiest to recognize this structure on candlestick charts because they better highlight the open-to-close direction within each period. Most candles in pullbacks will be colored against the trend that set up the pullback; that is, pullbacks in uptrends will consist of full candles (red on modern charting packages) and pullbacks in downtrends will usually be empty (green) candles. This second complex pullback pattern is one or two with-trend candles in the middle of what otherwise looks like a simple pullback. The with-trend candle or candles usually represent(s) an aborted attempt to resume the primary trend, and this

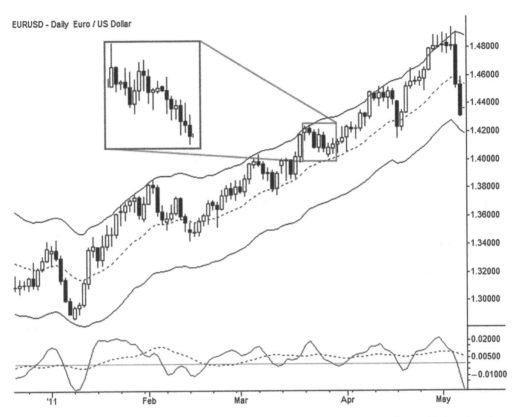

FIGURE 6.11 What Appears to Be a Simple Pullback on the Daily Chart of EURUSD Resolves into a Complex Consolidation on the 120-Minute Time Frame (Inset)

usually hints at a complex pullback hiding under the trading time frame structure. Since some traders will treat moves out of complex pullbacks differently than those out of simple pullbacks, it is important to be able to discern this subtle cue. Figures 6.11 and 6.12 show examples of hidden complex pullbacks.

In a sense, complex pullbacks are nothing more than a category of pullbacks, so all of the conditions for other pullback trades apply here, with one modification. It is usually a good idea to avoid pullbacks after conditions that could indicate a buying or selling climax. We have looked at these parabolic expansions and have seen that they frequently cap trends, so it does not make sense to enter with-trend pullbacks after such a move. Confirmation of the end of the trend is very strong countertrend momentum following such a condition, but market structure can unfold in another way: Rather than shifting into an immediate change of trend, the market can also consolidate and work off the overextension through a more extended consolidation. Normal (simple) pullbacks do this, as they give the market time to pause and digest each trend leg. In the case of a more serious overextension, a larger consolidation is usually required if the trend

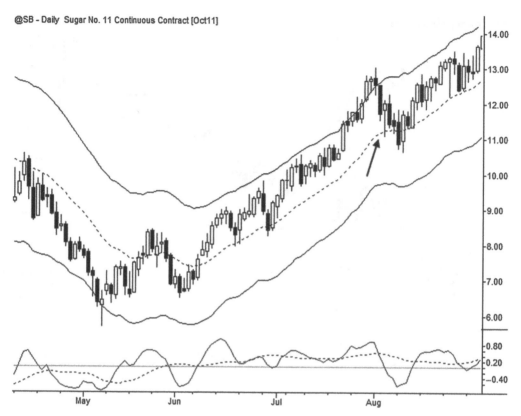

FIGURE 6.12 A Hidden Complex Pullback in Sugar Futures
This would be a clear complex pullback on an intraday time frame.

is going to continue, and these longer consolidations often take the form of complex consolidations.

If you see a condition that would normally eliminate the possibility of a pullback (e.g., a buying or selling climax), a with-trend trade may still be possible following a complex consolidation in that same area. It is often easier to evaluate the integrity of the trend on the higher time frame, as the trading time frame complex consolidation will usually be a simple consolidation on the higher time frame. Figure 6.13 shows one way a complex consolidation can provide a potential entry after a small buying climax.

Trigger   Either of the two triggers already discussed for pullbacks—entering at support or on a breakout—are valid for complex consolidations. The support play, especially if backed up by a momentum shift on the lower time frame, is easier in complex consolidations than in simple consolidations because the stop is more clearly established due to the termination of the second pullback leg. In addition, both countertrend legs of the pullback tend to be similar lengths, so it is often possible to predict the general area where the second leg will stop using a measured move objective (AB = CD). (This is a

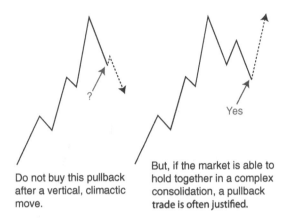

?

Yes

Do not buy this pullback
after a vertical, climactic
move.

But, if the market is able to
hold together in a complex
consolidation, a pullback
trade is often justified.

FIGURE 6.13 Complex Pullbacks Can Provide Entries Where Simple Pullbacks Should Be Avoided

guideline for trends in general, but the market tends to respect this principle even more strongly in pullbacks.)

Stop Another advantage of complex consolidations is that the stop level is more clearly defined. In simple consolidations, it is usually a bad idea to set a stop just underneath (for a long position) the consolidation area, but in complex pullbacks this is often an excellent risk point. There certainly are variations of complex pullbacks that have three or more pullbacks, each of which would result in another stop-out, but they are uncommon. The movements out of those also tend to be less reliable, so it does not make sense to make these a focus in the trading plan.

Profit Target The same profit targets apply to complex as to simple pullbacks, perhaps with the expectation that a stronger move could develop from a complex consolidation. You might be justified in taking less of your position off at your first profit target, and trying to press more size for a larger move compared to a simple pullback. If you decide to do this, weigh the benefits of having simple rules (e.g., take one-third of your position off at the previous swing) that enforce discipline and consistency against any incremental gains from a more complex approach.

Comments One important issue not yet considered is that these complex pullbacks often come following losing trades in simple pullbacks. This creates a risk management question that must be considered. Assume you want to risk $10,000 on each trade, and you just booked a $10,000 loss on a simple pullback, which, a few days later, is clearly developing into a complex pullback. What now? There are many possible answers, but it is important to have a clear plan before this situation is encountered. Risk management scenarios deserve careful consideration, planning, and maybe even quantitative modeling—these are not decisions to be made on the fly.

THE ANTI

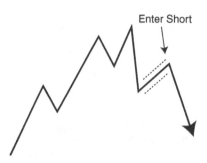

Trade Type

Trend termination.

Concept   This trade is a very specific pullback variation that attempts to enter the first pullback after a potential trend change.

Setup   There are two setup conditions for this trade. The first is that the market must have made a pattern that suggests the current trend could be terminating. Many of these patterns were discussed in Chapters 3 and 5: loss of momentum on successive thrusts, an extremely overextended market on the higher time frame, some type of double top or bottom formation where the market is unable to make a continuation, or perhaps a failure test. The second requirement is that the market then makes a move that shows a distinct change of character, such as a shift of momentum against the old trend. In the case of an uptrend, a downswing would emerge that was much stronger than previous downswings. This move would likely register a new momentum low on momentum indicators, suggesting further that the integrity of the uptrend had been challenged. This is the setup sequence, and both parts are important: the *initial market structure* that provides justification for potential countertrend trades, followed by a *shift of momentum* that shows that the dominant trend players have lost control of the market.

Trigger   The actual entry for this trade is in the first pullback following the strong countertrend price movement. For example, imagine a market that has been in an uptrend and then puts in a sharp downward spike (countertrend to the uptrend). The next bounce following that spike is potentially the first pullback in a new *downtrend*; this trade represents an attempt to reverse, or at least to create a significant pause in the preexisting uptrend. Price action and evolving market structure must be carefully monitored in the pullback for warning signs that the pullback could fail and that the original trend may still be intact. This structure is a pullback and, to a great extent, can be traded like any other pullback. What distinguishes this pullback is its position in the evolving market structure as the first pullback following a potential trend change; normal pullbacks are continuation patterns in established trends.

The Anti pullback may be entered via either of the two pullback entries already explored. The breakout entry may actually have a slightly better edge in this context than in a normal pullback, but it is also possible to position within the pullback using the support/resistance of the pattern itself. This is also a good example of how trading skills can be modular; the skills of trading pullbacks are applied here in another context. The third entry for this trade is probably not ideal. Because this is a countertrend trade, your risk point is clearly defined so you can simply enter anywhere into that first pullback with a stop outside the existing trend extreme (i.e., shorting into the first bounce following a strong down spike with a stop above recent highs). This is a sloppy entry in most cases, but there are times and time frames when we may not want to micromanage and fight over every tick.

Stop The general rule of stops in countertrend trades applies here: these stops must be respected without exception. There are two reasonable stops for this pattern. One choice is to simply put the stop beyond the trend extreme. Any price action inside that level (below it for an uptrend, above it for a downtrend) is consolidation and may still be supportive of trend change. If the level is violated, we know the countertrend attempt has failed and the probabilities favor trend continuation. This is the most conservative stop: farthest away from the market and at a level where the trend reversal has decisively failed.

More aggressive stops, corresponding to larger position sizes, can be placed closer to the market, using any of the guidelines for stops in pullbacks. As usual, there are at least two arguments to consider: One, these areas tend to be more volatile, so closer stops may be more likely to get hit in the noise. Two, there can be a lot of pent-up countertrend pressure at these inflections, and the move, once it starts to develop, is often very clean. The most important thing is to have a plan and to execute it consistently so you are not making emotionally driven decisions in the heat of battle.

Profit Target The question of where to take profits is tied in to the expectations for countertrend trades in general. In some sense, the term *countertrend* is a misnomer, because the ideal outcome is for a new trend to begin from the point the trade was initiated; the trade would then be a with-trend trade in this new trend. Countertrend trades demand closer profit targets and tighter risk management than with-trend trades because of the danger of exceptional volatility if the trend change fails and the old trend reasserts itself. One good profit-taking plan splits the difference, taking off a significant amount of the exposure (33 to 66 percent) at the first profit target and holding the rest for a possible extension into a new trend.

The MMO is an important factor in this trade. It is very common to see the first thrust after the initial pullback exhaust itself at the MMO, and then to see the market turn back down and eventually violate the previous trend extreme. Why? Because, at this point, the pattern has evolved into a complex consolidation, and trend continuation (of the original trend) is more likely. Monitor the market carefully for action in the neighborhood of the MMO. If it breaks, there is the possibility that you have just caught a major trend reversal. If, however, it holds and there is no continued countertrend momentum (and the pattern suggests a complex consolidation), be very protective of any remaining profits in the position.

Figure 6.14 shows an example of a sell Anti on the 30-minute chart of SPY. Consider every element of this trade carefully: The market had been in an extended uptrend and gapped above the upper channel at A, indicating a potential climax and overextension. This was the first warning of a potential trend change. At B, a strong countertrend leg developed, longer in both price and time than previous upswings. This down leg showed a distinct change of character and suggested that the bulls might have lost control, at least for a moment. The momentum indicator confirmed, marking a significant new low (relative to its recent history) at B1. Point C marked a controlled pullback, and it is at this point we can begin to assess the balance of buyers and sellers in this market. It is entirely possible that the drop at B will be erased and the market will explode to new highs, but the clue will be price action at point C. If, as in this case, the upward movement is weak, the probabilities favor another leg down as a natural reaction to B. This is a

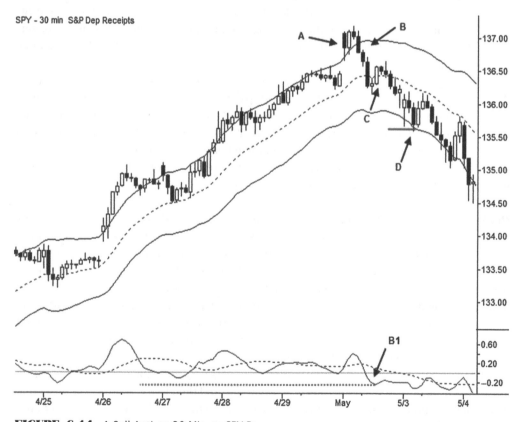

FIGURE 6.14 A Sell Anti on 30-Minute SPY Bars

subtle way to read the market, but these are important principles. Furthermore, there is no magic here and even beginning traders can quickly assimilate this type of thinking into their repertoires. The measured move objective (marked D in Figure 6.14) provided some minor support, and would have been a reasonable spot to take initial profits. Once those profits are booked, it also makes sense to tighten the stop so that the worst possible outcome is a breakeven trade.

Comments This is a powerful trade, and the sequence should be internalized: there must be, first, a reason for even contemplating the possibility of a countertrend trade; second, an initial impulse to confirm that the trend pattern is broken, that the dominant group has lost control of the market; and third, the actual entry in the pullback. This is a reliable pattern on all time frames, and is especially powerful for intraday traders when combined with time-of-day influences.

The name *Anti* is borrowed from Linda Raschke. In *Street Smarts: High Probability Short-Term Trading Strategies* (1996) she gives a specific definition of this trade in that it quantifies the momentums on two time frames using the stochastic indicator. The pattern essentially is that the fast and slow lines of the indicator are sloping against each other. Look at Figure 6.14 again and notice that the slow line (dotted) of the moving average convergence/divergence (MACD) has just rolled over, and the fast line hooks up after B1. This shows that the shorter-term momentum is against (hence the term *Anti*) the longer-term momentum following a shift of that longer-term direction. There is validity in that approach and screening tools can be developed off similar indicator patterns, but my preference is to focus on the price structure. The indicator will sometimes highlight structures that are not clearly visible on the price bars, but it will also give false positives at times. The core concept of this trade is captured more cleanly in the pure market structure approach.

BREAKOUTS, ENTERING IN THE PRECEDING BASE

Trade Type

Support/resistance breaking.

Concept   Breakouts are an important class of trades and can give rise to strong price moves beyond the breakout point. Schematically, there are three places to enter breakout trades: before, after, or on the breakout. Trades entered on the breakout can incur high slippage and poor trade location due to the high volatility and low liquidity that accompany many of these trades; many traders find better success with executing either before or after the actual breakout. We will first look at some characteristic patterns preceding good breakouts in which the market tips its hand and shows that energy is being built up to support the breakout. (Think classic accumulation.) It is possible to enter in these formations preceding the breakout in order to have better trade location and to sidestep the potential slippage.

Setup   Unfolding price action creates many potential support and resistance levels in the market. Most of these are insignificant—most support and resistance levels are nothing more than mirages. However, a very small set of these levels become extremely important, and, when violated, the pressure gives rise to a strong move beyond the level. For breakout trades, this is the first and most important condition: you must identify one of these significant levels that is likely to give good action when broken. If you are working with these levels and their accompanying formations, entering the trades properly, and managing them appropriately, breakout trades can be relatively easy. If you attempt breakout trades at insignificant levels and without a good plan, consistent losses will erode your trading account.

Good breakout levels are usually levels that are clearly visible to all market participants. For instance, there are levels that have been tested cleanly multiple times, and it is obvious to even a casual chart reader that price has been unable to penetrate the level. This creates trading opportunities because some traders will make decisions when price eventually does get through the level. Whether they are stopping out of existing positions, taking profits, or entering on the breakouts does not matter; what does matter is that there will be additional volume and order flow when this important price level is

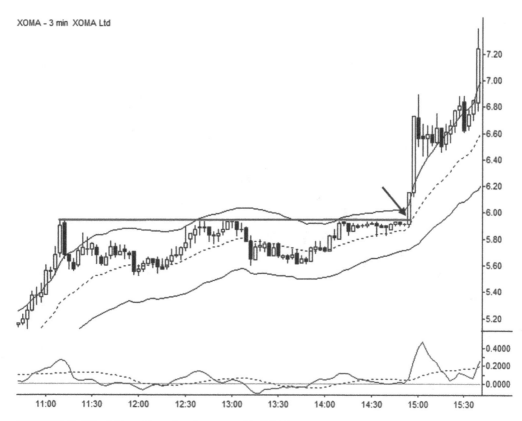

XOMA - 3 min XOMA Ltd

FIGURE 6.15 A Very Clean Breakout Level in XOMA

violated. Figure 6.15 shows an example of a very clean level that set up a good intraday breakout in XOMA Ltd (Nasdaq: XOMA).

On daily and higher time frames, it is unusual to see perfectly clear levels, but significant and visible support or resistance can still set up good breakout trades. Figure 6.16 shows an example of a typical breakout level on a daily chart, here illustrated in the stock of Cree, Inc. (Nasdaq: CREE). There are two other points to consider on this chart: First, penetrations of levels before the breakout usually seem to expend some of the energy behind the breakout, and often lead to poor trades. The key question is how long and how significant these penetrations through the level were. In Figure 6.16, the level was not perfectly clean, but there was no significant price action above the level preceding the breakout, only small and short-lived failure tests. Second, the actual breakout entry was a gap through the resistance level, which brings some execution challenges to the table. Many traders will be tempted to skip these trades, as they will be forced to enter at significantly higher prices than they had planned, and will be exposed to the danger of a gap failure. This is a mistake because a gap through an important level usually hints at a powerful shift in market dynamics. Some of the best breakouts are "gap and go" trades that open beyond the level and never look back.

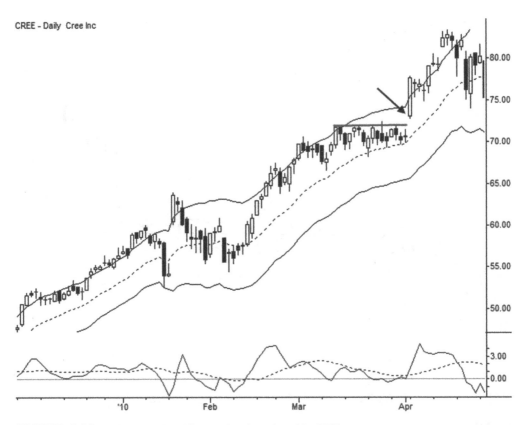

FIGURE 6.16 A Gap Opening Above a Breakout Level in CREE

The best and strongest breakouts will usually be preceded by a formation that indicates buying pressure may be building against the resistance level. (Though this discussion focuses on buying breakouts, the exact patterns apply, inverted, for breakdowns below support.) One common form of this pattern is a tight range near the top of a larger range, as in Figure 6.17. This is another form of accumulation in which the pressure from buyers has pinned the market at a relatively high price. This small range near a resistance level, usually inside of a larger range, is referred to as a breakout base.

Another variation of this same idea has a market holding successively higher highs into the resistance level, as in Figure 6.18. This is yet another variation on the accumulation theme, as buyers have been willing to buy the market at higher prices on each decline. Though not a bidding war, this pattern does suggest that large buying interests are watching this market and may be building substantial positions. In these cases, the base is not as clearly defined by a chart pattern, which can make stop location more challenging, but the important factor is still the coiling of buying pressure against resistance. Also, the classic cup and handle formation is a variation on this same idea. This is also an illustration of the principle that most classic chart patterns can be better understood in the context of simple length of swing analysis.

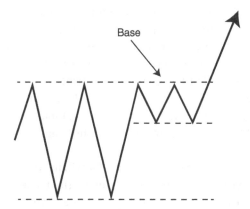

FIGURE 6.17 Schematic of a Breakout Base

Trigger The actual entry is in the consolidation preceding the breakout. Positioning in this prebreakout base allows us to avoid having to play in the extreme volatility of the breakout itself. As a rule of thumb, entries in consolidations are usually less precise than entries in trends. Conceptually, we would like to buy as close to the bottom of the base as possible, but the most important thing is to get the position on. There are at least three logical entry triggers, each with some potential drawbacks. (These examples are for long trades, but apply, reversed, to shorts as well.)

- Once the base establishes itself, bid near the bottom of the smaller range. One potential drawback is that this order will be filled only in a declining market, meaning that you are buying against the short-term momentum. Another drawback is that the order may not be filled at all, so it may not be possible to get the position. Sometimes you will identify the range, bid near the bottom, and then watch the breakout as the market never returns to the bottom of the base. In these cases, you will miss the trade. However, the times that the order is filled will result in the best possible trade location, at or very near the bottom of the range.
- Once the base establishes itself, wait for springs (i.e., drops below the support at the bottom of the base that immediately recover back above the support level) and enter on the close of those bars. Though you will now probably be entering with the short-term momentum due to the recovery back above support, not every range features

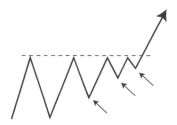

FIGURE 6.18 Higher Lows into a Resistance Level: Another Form of Prebreakout Accumulation

springs or upthrusts. In addition, this is a high-maintenance execution technique that requires good focus on subtle details of price action.

- Just get the position on, anywhere in the range. This one isn't pretty, but the reality of trading is that our executions are not always at perfect, ideal points. Imagine we identify a breakout trade that has 10 points of upside potential out of a 5-point large range, with a 1.5-point base near the top of the larger range. If we can buy in that base and give it a 2-point stop, then maybe it doesn't make sense to try to squeeze an extra half point out by bidding near the low of the range.

There is no right or wrong here, and each trader will have to make the decision based on his personality and on how he intends to manage the trade. A trader who takes the proverbial 30,000-foot view and wants to manage things from a big-picture perspective might establish anywhere in the range and just not care about pennies. Another trader might intend to actively trade around and manage the position on the actual breakout; for this trader, pennies might be very significant indeed.

This is also a good place to consider the adverse selection effect of entering on limit orders. Assume that trader A and trader B both identify the same set of 10 potential breakout trades and are buying bases before those breakouts. Also assume, though they would not know it in advance, that five of the trades will be losers. Trader A indiscriminately buys in the base and manages the trades, exiting his losers if they drop decisively below the bottom of the range. Trader B is much more precise with his entries and always bids at the bottom of the range. He is also disciplined about his exits from losing trades, and exits at the same points trader A exits his losing trades. Trader A and B both book their disciplined losers, though trader B's total loss is slightly smaller because of his consistently better trade location. Of the five winning trades, perhaps three went to the bottom of the range where trader B was filled on his position before the breakout. Trader A and B both booked winners, though, again, trader B's winners were slightly bigger, due to better trade location. Assume that the two remaining winning trades never went to the bottom of the base, so trader B was not filled on his entries, while trader A participated fully.

This is a truism of using limit orders, and one that most people choose to ignore: if you enter on limit orders, you will price yourself out of some set of winning trades that never trade to (or, more realistically, through) your limit price *while you will always participate fully in all losing trades*. This is important—traders entering on limits will not be filled on some winners but will be filled on *every* losing trade. In our hypothetical example, we know trader B will miss some of trader A's winning trades. We also know that he will have a small advantage, compared to trader A, on every trade because of better trade location, and the key question is whether that incremental gain is enough to more than compensate for the missed profits from the remaining two trades. This trade-off between market order and limit order entry styles is an important issue to consider, and one that is sorely neglected in the trading literature.

Stop   There are two separate parts in the life cycle of this trade, requiring two separate approaches to trade management. The trade entry, by definition, is early. We are

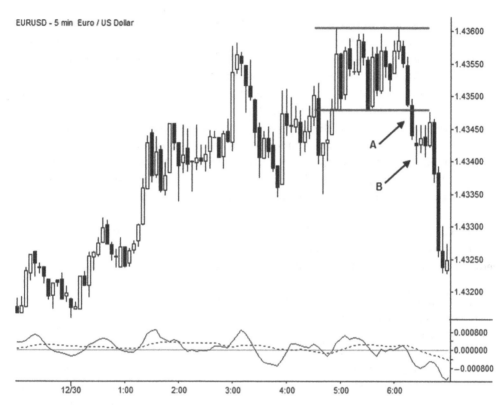

FIGURE 6.19 A Failure below the Bottom of a Range in 5-Minute EURUSD

anticipating a breakout that may or may not happen, so when do we exit if the planned-for breakout does not develop? One simple strategy might be to put a stop below the lowest point reached while the market was in the base, with the plan that if you are stopped out on a temporary drop you probably must reenter the trade. Another approach is to set a much wider stop for the purposes of position sizing and risk management (see Chapter 8), with the idea to stop out before the level is reached if developing price action contradicts the trade. For instance, in Figure 6.19, a trader using the second plan would not have been stopped out when the bottom of the range dropped at A. Quick drops below previous support are to be expected, and rapid recoveries are actually ideal buying opportunities. However, once the market consolidated below that support level at B, the probabilities began to favor a breakdown and another trend leg down, so there was no sense in riding the trade to the initial stop level.

The second issue to consider is how you will manage the trade after the breakout occurs. Here, knowledge of the pullback patterns that occur after breakouts is essential. There are many possible choices, but the plan must be consistent with the realities of market action. If watching $50.00 as a potential breakout level, many traders would move their stop up to $50.00 or right under that level once the breakout actually happens. Their logic is that, if the breakout was actually valid, price should not come back below $50.00. This would seem to make sense, but the market does not work like this. Many excellent breakouts come back to retest or to exceed the breakout level in an effort to shake out weak-hand players; a good trading plan will not put you in this position of weakness.

My approach to stops is so consistent that it is boring—I always set stops at places where the market should not go if my trade is correct. If I set a stop there and the market reaches the stop, the trade is wrong and I must exit. Setting a stop somewhere that it can be hit without my trade thesis being violated is anathema to me—why incur additional risk and transaction costs in the normal volatility of the market? Furthermore, it also usually does not make sense to dramatically tighten the stops once the breakout actually occurs, though it is also important to be sensitive to the patterns that suggest a breakout is failing. Distinguishing between these failures and the standard pullbacks of successful breakouts is a key skill for breakout traders to develop.

Profit Target   Some traders will set ratio-based targets for breakout trades. Common examples use, for instance, measured move objectives based on the width of the preceding range or the base. These make sense for the same reason that all measured move objectives do—they simply define the magnitude of swings that are average for any given market, though it is important to realize that prebreakout conditions often feature abnormally contracted volatility. Ratio-based targets are apt to be unnecessarily conservative in these cases.

In general, I do not favor setting profit targets for breakout trades, because, in the best cases, you just entered a new trend at its inception, and it does not make sense to give up that trade location as long as the trade is working well. Consider all of the possibilities, ranging from outright failure to a single extension above the level to a completely new trend. Just like with all my trades, I will take partial profits at a level approximately equal to my initial risk in the trade, and then will usually hold the remainder as long as the new trend appears to be intact, perhaps taking partial profits at other inflection points as the trade develops. Once you have a breakout trade that has gone through one successful, confirming pullback, it is simply a trend trade and can be treated as such, managing the pullbacks as in any other trend.

Comments   We should also take a minute to consider simple channel breakout systems. It is well known by now that the core entry technique of the system the Turtles were taught was a breakout of a 20-day or 55-day channel. If you examine these levels carefully, you will see that most of them violate the rule I gave that good breakout levels have to be very real, visible levels in the market. In fact, most of these 20-day or 55-day highs/lows are not points that your eye would be drawn to on a chart. The success of some of the Turtles has grown into the stuff of legend and myth, but the breakouts were not the important part of that system. The general trading public has the idea that the Turtles traded breakouts of 20-day highs, but, in reality, much of their success was due to systematic approaches that were designed to capture every trend in markets that trended well at the time. The trade-off was that they had to accept many small losses on entries that did not develop into good trends, but, for their system to work, they *had* to be involved at the start of every potential trend. Our work in this book is focused on shorter-term swing trades around breakout levels, which is a completely different kind of trading.

BREAKOUTS, ENTERING ON FIRST PULLBACK FOLLOWING

Trade Type

Support/resistance breaking.

Concept　The first pullback after a breakout offers a spot to initiate a position in the direction of the new trend supported by the confirmation of a successful breakout. This entry also avoids the volatility of the actual breakout area, and the uncertainty inherent in positions established in the prebreakout base.

Setup　The market has made a successful breakout of an important level. Furthermore, there is good activity (volume, volatility, and price action) beyond the level, proving that it was a valid breakout. The initial upthrust exhausts itself, the market rolls over, and a pullback begins.

Trigger　This pullback can be treated as a standard pullback, with any of the standard pullback trigger entries.

Stop　If the pullback is treated like any other pullback, the logical choice is to use the same stops you would apply to any pullback trade. There are two other levels worth considering here: the actual breakout level itself and any prebreakout reference level (e.g., support in the base, or the highest low preceding the breakout). Many traders will work with the idea that the breakout level should be a good price for stops, but it is not. Some of the strongest continuations will drop back below the level, stopping out naive weak-hand short-term traders, and then turn to trade much higher. These traders, now trapped out of the market, will have to chase it higher, adding additional impetus to the move.

However, a good prebreakout level usually is a serviceable reference, and it is usually possible to tighten stops enough that a loss does not have to be taken to this level. (This level may still serve a useful purpose as a last-ditch exit and as a reference for position sizing.) It is very hard to justify holding a simple breakout pullback that drops below the pivot low of the prebreakout base, as this type of action is much more indicative of a failed breakout. However, it is not uncommon to see failed breakouts spend more time consolidating before breaking out and working on a second breakout attempt. These are certainly not the cleanest and easiest trades, and most traders will find that they enjoy the best success restricting their involvement to first breakout attempts.

It is easy to overcomplicate these trades and to try to factor too many additional levels and patterns into the trading plan. At the end of the day, the first pullback following a breakout is nothing more than a pullback; there is no need for a complicated trade management plan if you already have the skills to trade pullbacks on other contexts.

Profit Target   These are standard pullbacks, so standard pullback profit targets apply with one caveat: trends from good breakout levels tend to be exceptional trends. There is a better than average chance that any ensuing trend will extend for several legs with strong impulse moves. It still makes sense to maintain the discipline of taking partial profits, but it also makes sense to allow yourself the opportunity to participate in the potentially outsized trend run. This is another place where as a trader you will need to tailor the plan to fit your personality, but, of course, the key is to actually have a plan. Do not put yourself in a situation in which you have to make reactive decisions on the fly.

Comments   In some sense, this is a hybrid trade, combining characteristics of both breakout and pullback trades, but it can be simplified further: it is really nothing more than a simple pullback trade.

One last thought on breakout trades: we have not considered the higher time frame in these trade setups, and it often does not matter. A clear breakout level on the trading time frame will usually be an even clearer resistance level on the higher time frame, but there are cases where the breakout is further supported by the higher time frame structure. For instance, if an upside breakout on the trading time frame comes near the bottom of a higher time frame pullback in an uptrend, then the trading time frame breakout is essentially a breakout entry into the higher time frame pattern. Time frames often have complex interactions with influences flowing in both directions, but these considerations can sometimes add significant support to individual trade setups.

Al Brooks, in *Reading Price Charts Bar by Bar: The Technical Analysis of Price Action for the Serious Trader* (2009), discusses many variations of breakout trades. Though many of his comments and trading ideas are specific to intraday index futures, most of them can be applied with some modification to other markets and time frames. Brooks's approach is different from mine in that he focuses much more on the minute details of each individual price bar and its relationship to previous bars, while I tend to think there is much more noise and randomness in the market at most times. Regardless, his book offers a valuable perspective and good food for thought.

FAILED BREAKOUTS

Trade Type

Support/resistance holding.

Concept   Most breakouts fail.

Setup   When most traders think of breakout trades, they think of big, dramatic winning trades, and it is not hard to find examples like this. However, the trader actually trading breakouts quickly comes face-to-face with a harsh reality: failed breakouts are more common than winning breakouts. This is not an indictment of the breakout trading concept, because exceptional reward/risk ratios can compensate for lower probability. Furthermore, good breakout traders know how to prequalify their trades by focusing on the patterns that tend to support successful breakouts and may have a higher winning percentage than might be expected. There certainly is money to be made trading breakouts, but it is also worthwhile to spend some time thinking about the patterns associated with breakout failures.

It is difficult to nail these patterns down because it is not uncommon for good breakouts to have reactions that violate the breakout level. Imagine the frustration of the trader working with this flawed plan: pay into the actual breakout, and flip the position short if the breakout level does not hold. In the very common case of a volatile breakout with a pullback that violates the breakout level, this trader will first take a loss on the long position, and will now be positioned short as the pullback in the new uptrend begins its advance. This is a futile plan, but many developing traders fall into this trap because they attach too much importance to the retest of the actual breakout level. It is important to understand how the market really moves, rather than clinging to some idea of how the market logically *should* work.

There are two setup conditions to consider: the strength of the move beyond the breakout level, and the character of the first reaction after the breakout. Good breakouts should have strong momentum, volume, and interest beyond the level. If this does not happen, it is more likely that the breakout will fail, perhaps painting a spring or upthrust outside the previous support or resistance level. In successful breakouts, the first reaction should be controlled and in proportion to this breakout thrust. It should look like a good pullback in the new trend, for that is exactly what it is. If the breakout fails, it

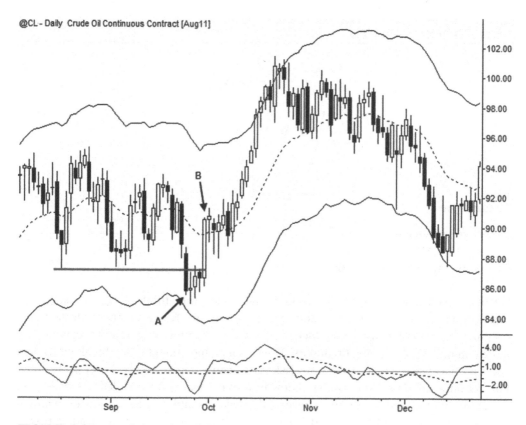

FIGURE 6.20 A Failed Breakout Below Support in Crude Oil

will be through a failure of this first pullback; this is a critical point in breakout trading. If the first reaction is very strong (i.e., the first downswing after an upside breakout or vice versa for a breakdown through support), it suggests a failure of the break interest and greatly increased probability of trade failure. This is potentially confusing, so some examples may help to clarify.

Figure 6.20 shows a failed breakdown attempt below support. The actual bar of the breakout was a good entry, showing strong momentum through support, and the subsequent consolidation was also consistent with the breakout play. Most traders trading this pattern should have been short, and should have been holding through the three small bars following the point marked A. Though not a large pattern, these bars were a pullback or consolidation near the extreme of the previous downthrust and below previous support. However, even with this generally constructive setup, the trade failed as buyers stepped in and swept the market back above support at B, possibly fueled by additional short-covering volatility. This is nothing more than a classic pullback failure via strong countertrend momentum emerging in the pullback.

Figure 6.21 shows another example of a failed breakout, this time an upside breakout in Goldman Sachs (NYSE: GS). There were several elements that should have put

FIGURE 6.21 A Failed Upside Breakout Attempt in GS

the long pullback trader on warning: the actual breakout at A was not on good momentum and did not show strong conviction. The pullback (four black candles beginning two bars after A) retraced most of the breakout thrust. Though the penetration back through the breakout level is not in itself cause for concern, it is not good to see so much of the breakout retraced so easily. The actual failure came at point B, as the stock put in a failure test at the previous high. This is one of the standard ways in which pullbacks fail and a good opportunity to use another trading pattern (the failure test from the beginning of this chapter) in a supporting context. Good trading is nothing more than the disciplined application of a few relatively simple fundamental building blocks.

Trigger Conceptually, this is the most problematic of the trade setups because we have to strike a balance between waiting for confirmation that the breakout has failed while still getting a good trade location. In terms of actual execution, *the breakout failure is nothing more than a failed pullback.* Breakout traders need to understand that the pullback pattern is a critical building block for these trades, and it is important to understand the patterns that suggest pullbacks failing and continuing.

Stop   Saying most breakouts fail trivializes many of the issues we face trading these patterns because of the extreme volatility associated with breakouts and their failures. Being caught on the wrong side of a breakout trade (whether a successful or a failed breakout) is bad news. Stop placement is fairly simple, as the ultimate stop is above the extreme of the initial pullback thrust, but in this trade you must respect your stop fully and without question. If the stop is hit, get out of the trade. Do not try to trade around it; do not try to average your price. Just get out. You may play these games and get away with it 30 times in a row, but the 31st trade could wipe out many months' profits. There is danger here—real tail risk—that is hard to comprehend and impossible to quantify.

Profit Target   There are two likely resolutions to these trades. In some markets (for instance, longer-term commodities) failed breakouts can be absorbed into a large-scale consolidation. After spending some time working off the failure, the market may make another breakout attempt and continue to grind higher. The second possibility is that the market may truly melt down and collapse after a failed breakout. This outcome is slightly more likely in shorter time frames, but what we are looking for here is a violation of the base before the breakout and wholesale panic as trapped traders scramble to adjust positions. A good trading plan will consider both possibilities, with a provision to take partial profits at a relatively close target while holding a portion for a larger swing.

From a practical standpoint, it probably makes sense to use the same profit targets on all trades, taking first partial profits at a point equal to the risk on the trade. In my own trading plan, I tend to be be aggressive in taking those profits on failed breakout trades, perhaps even exiting more than half of my position at the first target. As in all other trades, I will adjust that target to respect the geometry of the pattern. If a target is beyond a clear and significant level, adjust it by moving it slightly inside the level. This is nothing more than trading common sense.

Comments   This is the most complex and least well defined of the major trade setups. Newer traders are probably best advised to not focus on this trade until some success is achieved with the other setups, but it is important to study these failure patterns even if you only intend to trade breakouts in the direction of the initial breakout. Awareness of how patterns fail and how trades fail can help you limit your losses and manage losing trades with equanimity. After you have traded many breakouts and internalized many variations of these patterns, you will begin to develop some intuition about them. Until then, the guidelines in this chapter will help you avoid some of the more serious and more obvious mistakes in trading these patterns.

SUMMARY

This has been a fairly long list of potential trading patterns, presented in the order in which I believe most traders should learn them. We started with the simplicity of the failure test, progressing to more complex pullbacks, then to the special situation of pull-backs after trend changes. Last, the volatile set of breakouts were added, and failed breakouts, which can be touchy, subjective, and dangerous, bring up the rear, so the progression is from simple and well-defined to complex and potentially confusing. There are only three core concepts here, which express the tendency of the trend to continue and the tendency of support and resistance to both hold and break. The other trade se-tups are derived from combinations of these core trading concepts. If this chapter has been confusing, consider this alternate classification.

Primary Trades
- Pullback: The sine qua non of trend trading patterns (trend continuation).
- Failure test: A quick-and-dirty countertrend entry with a well-defined risk point (support/resistance holding).
- Breakout: The ultimate expression of support/resistance failing.

Derived Trades
- Anti: A trend termination pattern that uses the pullback pattern as an entry and for confirmation.
- Buying support in a pullback: Basically a failure test entry into the pullback pattern.
- Paying a breakout of a pullback: A combination of a lower time frame breakout with a trading time frame pullback.
- Breakout, entering in base before: Anticipatory entry into a breakout trade; may use support at the bottom of the base as an entry trigger, so the trade is actually a support holding trade.
- Breakout, entering on first pullback following: Puts a simple pullback entry and prob-ability in the context of a breakout trade.
- Breakouts, failed: A more complex version of the failure test; many of these are sim-ple higher time frame failure test trades, but the motivating patterns are the failure patterns of pullbacks.

This is not an exhaustive list of the trade entries I have used successfully, but it is a list of the most important ones. Notice the trades that are *not* here: no trades in ranges unless the range is a more significant structure in another time frame, no simple buying or selling at support levels, and no fading overextended markets. I have not found these to be reliable trades, nor have they been profitable for me over a very large sample size. If I have a burning desire to execute one of these trades, I can usually accomplish it within one of the trade structures I have already set out. For instance, rather than simply shorting into a runaway bull market that I feel has gone too far, I can wait for the market to make a buying climax and then enter on the Anti. The trade may still fail, but it is at least supported by a real pattern with a defined risk point.

It is also interesting to consider where these trading patterns fall in the course of the idealized market structure outlined in Chapter 2. In accumulation, we can buy failure tests of the low of the range, especially if the higher time frame supports an advance. The breakout trades naturally belong at the transition between accumulation and markup. The pullback variations are, of course, the ideal tools for trading both the markup and markdown periods. The transitions from markup to distribution (and from markdown to accumulation) are a bit more problematic. For example, we actively try to *avoid* having positions within those areas until they are set to break out, and even catching the exact end of the trending period may result in meager profits as the market simply chops sideways. Regardless, the Anti pattern is the ideal tool to catch these turns, and it is also common for trends to end with a final failure test at the highs.

The patterns in this chapter are more than a menu of trade setups to be used à la carte according to the trader's whim. Rather, this simple set of trading patterns offers a comprehensive tool kit for approaching market structure and price action in any market and any time frame. Consider the cycle:

- Buying support in a range via failure tests (springs) near the bottom of the range.
- Entering in a base preceding a breakout.
- The actual breakout.
- The first pullback following a breakout.
- Pullbacks as the new trend gains steam.
- The possibility for complex pullbacks as the trend matures. Monitoring the strength of pullbacks gives insight into trend integrity.
- A possible failure test at the eventual high of the trend.
- An Anti at the high of the trend.
- Selling resistance near the previous trend extreme via failure tests (upthrusts).
- Entering early in anticipation of a breakdown through support.

A trader can trade this entire cycle, or can use these trades as signposts to monitor the health of the market and its transition from one regime to another. Within this relatively simple set of patterns lies the key to all price action and market structure. Properly applied, this sequence is nothing less than a complete analytical methodology.

CHAPTER 7

Tools for Confirmation

There are in fact four very significant stumbling blocks in the way of grasping the truth . . . namely, the example of weak and unworthy authority, longstanding custom, the feeling of the ignorant crowd, and the hiding of our own ignorance while making a display of our apparent knowledge.

—Roger Bacon

I s more information always better? Some traders, when they are considering a trade, will use multiple indicators and analytical tools, solicit opinions from other traders, and even consider elements such as fundamentals that do not really have a bearing on their time frame. This approach can lead to "paralysis by analysis" as so many factors are considered, with so many conflicting points of view, that the trader simply does not know what to do. The justification offered for this approach is that an officer on a battlefield would want every possible piece of information, wouldn't he? Perhaps not. It might be better for the decision maker to have processed intelligence from verified and trusted sources that has already been filtered from the massive flow of raw information. In trading, the equivalent is to focus on a few simple tools that are completely understood—depth of information, rather than breadth.

It is critical that traders understand the subtleties of every tool they use. They should know how they react in every possible market environment, and furthermore, must understand the complex interactions between multiple tools. This may lead to an approach that disregards a lot of information that many traders assume to be useful, but, for instance, why would you use indicators that do not add to your analysis? Why would you listen to news that is old news and is already fully priced into the market? Why would you try to guess how complex fundamental factors might influence the price if you do not have the skills to fully understand those fundamentals? Why would you solicit opinions from traders who may trade with completely different styles and may be less competent and knowledgeable than you are? Traders do all of these things, but most of them do not make sense. Limit your scope to tools that truly add value.

So far, we have looked at a number of trading patterns and templates that allow the trader to trade in alignment with the dominant forces in the market and to take advantage of the slight statistical edge that exists around some specific market structures. These patterns are tradable on their own, in isolation, but they become more powerful when placed in the context of the higher time frame and supported by price action on the lower time frame. Though we have touched on this idea in other places, this chapter now offers some concrete examples and suggestions for maximizing the power of the interaction of these multiple time frames. It will also cover the use of a few specific indicators in considerable detail; use this as a departure for your own work with your preferred tools and indicators.

Next, we consider tools to quantify relationships between markets; a good understanding of the connections and interactions between various markets can be a powerful tool for teasing out nonrandom price action from the random noise. This is not a subject to be approached lightly, as it is possible to spend many years digging deeply into the connections between various asset classes and individual markets. We will begin this work by looking at some tools to quantify these relationships and some potential issues that may arise when contemplating these cross-market relationships. Again, everything in this chapter should be taken as a template and a suggestion for your own work and exploration—adapt these ideas and make them your own.

THE MOVING AVERAGE—THE STILL CENTER

Many trading books will tell you to use a specific moving average like a 21-period exponential or a 50-period simple moving average. Anytime anyone tells you to use a certain average length, the logical question is: "Why that one and not another?" There is no magic to any moving average—they are all pretty much created equal, which is to say that all work sometimes and do not work other times. If you are viewing moving averages as support or resistance, or price crossing a moving average as a significant signal, you might want to reconsider your approach to these tools. There is great value in reducing everything to simple elements, to first principles, and then building the analytical structure up from that foundation. To that end, Appendix B takes a deep look at the differences between two commonly used moving average types and examines how they behave in different market environments. Though this understanding might not be useful for all traders, mastery rests on a *perfect* grasp of basic elements.

Ideas for Using Moving Averages

Traders have many ideas and approaches to using moving averages, but many of the things that are supposed to happen around moving averages are based on market lore and do not pass simple statistical tests. People will claim that certain averages are important because "hedge funds buy there," "everyone watches those averages," or "it becomes a self-fulfilling prophecy," but it is extremely difficult to support these claims with quantitative tests. Tests of statistical tendencies around moving averages fail to find that any average is objectively better than another, or in fact, that there is any verifiable edge around these averages at all. Regardless, there are practical ways to use these tools in trading.

As a Trend Indicator   One potentially useful application of moving averages is to use them as confirming trend indicators. For instance, when scanning many charts, a quick glance at a moving average—which summarizes the price structure, smoothes out the bumps, and highlights the overall trend—can give a quick read on the overall market structure.

There are two broad ways to use moving averages as trend indicators, which can be used separately or combined. The first is very simple: when price spends a lot of time on one side of a moving average, this suggests the market is trending in that direction; see Figure 7.1 for an example. Note that price may occasionally dip to the average, or even cross a bit to the other side, but it remains mostly above the average.

The second idea, which is closely related, is that a moving average will slope in the direction of the trend. A flat moving average is more indicative of a trading range, while up-sloping and down-sloping averages suggest uptrends and downtrends. As Figure 7.2

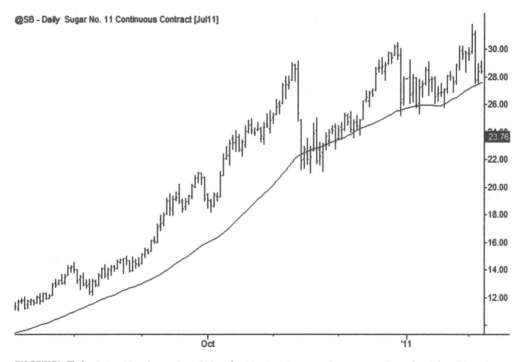

FIGURE 7.1   Price Mostly on One Side of a Moving Average Suggests a Trend in That Direction

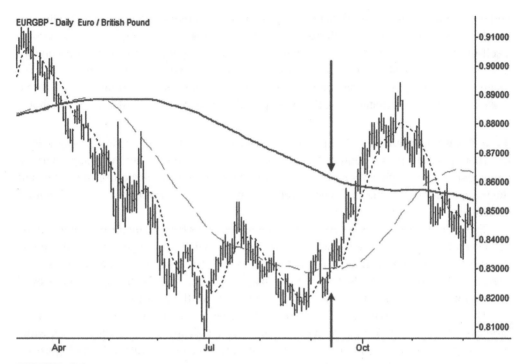

EURGBP - Daily Euro / British Pound

FIGURE 7.2 The Three Moving Averages Indicate Three Different Trends at This Spot

shows, this tool is very dependent on the length of the moving average chosen; in this diagram, the three averages each suggest different trends at the same spot. This is not a problem, for the market can actually be in an uptrend, downtrend, and trading range at the same time—it depends on what time frame is being considered—but the trader must understand these issues. Again, it is not necessary to use this as a mechanical tool—for instance, by executing only at the precise points where the line shifts slopes. A trader making decisions based off price structure will almost always find entries before they are confirmed by a moving average.

Avoid Markets in Equilibrium Markets are usually in equilibrium, and at those times markets are efficient in the academic sense—random walks prevail. There is no consistent edge possible in such an environment; it is not an exaggeration to say that *the essence of technical analysis is to identify markets that have a temporary imbalance of buying and selling pressure, and to limit our trading to those environments*. One way to identify markets in equilibrium is that they tend to stay close to an average price (moving average), which represents a rough area of consensus. If the market continues to trade around that average, chopping back and forth on both sides of it, it is probably best to move on and to look for better trading opportunities. This might seem like common sense, but a rule like this can keep traders from making multiple attempts at trading a flat market.

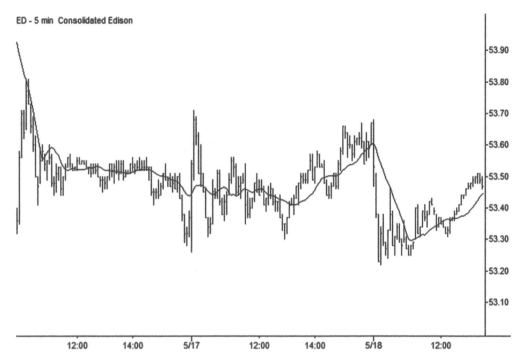

FIGURE 7.3 Avoid Trading Markets That Chop Back and Forth on Both Sides of an Intermediate-Term Moving Average

To be sure, nothing works all the time. Even random walk markets will show significant departures from moving averages; a significant move away from a moving average is not, in itself, sufficient evidence to declare that a tradable buying and selling imbalance exists. However, the absence of that condition virtually guarantees that an imbalance does *not* exist, and markets that remain close to intermediate-term moving averages almost always present challenging trading environments with no significant edge. Figure 7.3 shows a period where Consolidated Edison, Inc. (NYSE: ED) traded back and forth around a moving average with no clear trades to either direction. For most traders, simply avoiding this type of price action can add to the bottom line, as many small losing trades will be eliminated.

As a Reference for Trading Pullbacks Expecting a moving average to truly provide support and resistance is probably misguided, but there *is* a valid way to use moving averages as a crutch for trading pullbacks. Markets typically move by an alternation of momentum moves and consolidations, and it is usually a bad idea to initiate a trade when the market is overextended either to the upside or the downside in a momentum move. In almost all cases, it is better to wait for the market to work off this condition and to return to a short-term state of balance before entering in the pullback. It might seem to be a joke, but using a moving average like this "keeps you from doing something stupid"

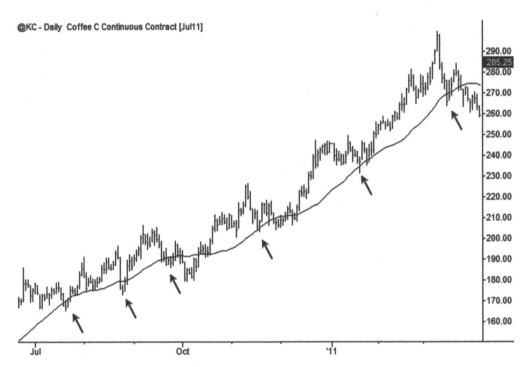

FIGURE 7.4 Using a Moving Average as a Reference for Buying Pullbacks
Do not buy when price is far away from the average.

(i.e., buying or shorting an overextended market). A simple but effective trading rule could be instituted that simply prevents you from buying or selling pullbacks that are far away from a moving average, assuming that *far away* has been precisely defined. It is also worth considering that a moving average is a good reference in a *normal* trend; very strong trends may not pull back as much. In general, it makes sense to build a trading plan that first addresses the most common situations that will be encountered, dealing with more extraordinary trending environments later. Figure 7.4 shows an example of some possible pullback entries at a moving average. Trade management and context are important, as there is no inherent edge to simply executing a trade at the moving average.

Slope of a Moving Average as a Trend Indicator   The slope of a moving average is another subjective application that does not test out well in quantitative testing, but it can be useful as a scanning tool or as a cue for the developing discretionary trader. The concept is that the moving average's slope can give confirmation of trend direction, with the time frame of the trend roughly corresponding to the time frame of the moving average. Longer-term (100-period or more) moving averages will address longer-term trends, while very short-term (less than 10-period) moving averages will give indications for the shortest intervals on the chart. An important point is that an attentive trader will almost always be able to identify inflection points based on price structure long before

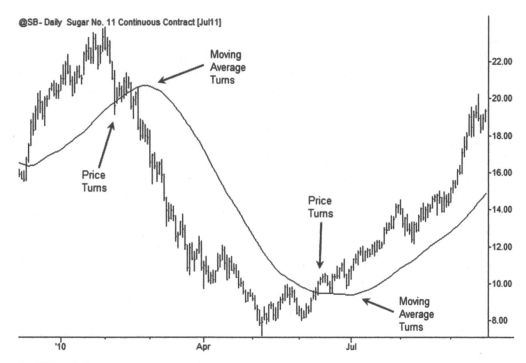

@SB- Daily Sugar No. 11 Continuous Contract [Jul11]

FIGURE 7.5 Though the Slope of the Moving Average Does Capture the Trend, the Trend Change Is Visible in Price Structure First

the moving average changes slope, as in Figure 7.5. It is probably a bad idea to filter trades based on this criterion—for instance, taking long trades only when the average slopes up—because the lag effect will cause you to miss many good trades at the beginning, but you will be green-lighted to take all the losers at the end of a trend. Focus on learning to read the price structure, but the slope of a moving average can be a useful aid, especially when scanning many charts rapidly.

CHANNELS: EMOTIONAL EXTREMES

A moving average may give some idea of consensus, value, and relative rest. Properly drawn channels define excursions from that area of consensus and may give some insight into where the crowd's emotional extremes lie. In most applications, this is the one and only purpose of channels: to define meaningful extensions. In order to do this well and consistently, the channels must be able to flex and to adapt to the changing volatility conditions of the underlying market. It should be obvious, but channels do not provide any kind of actual barrier to prices. The idea of buying at a band or selling at a band, with a few exceptions in highly mean-reverting instruments, is conceptually flawed. A better way for discretionary traders to use bands is to look for touches of or excursions outside the bands, and then to carefully monitor price action following those events, treating the band as an alert level.

Probably the most commonly used channels are Bollinger bands, which are set at a multiple of the standard deviation of price around an average of price. (Default settings are usually two standard deviations around a 20-period SMA). As the market becomes more volatile (as measured by standard deviation of price), the bands automatically widen to accommodate the larger swings. Most books on Bollinger bands (for instance, Kirkpatrick, 2006) claim that 68 percent of the values should fall within one standard deviation of the average, about 96 percent within two standard deviations, and that virtually all prices should fall within three standard deviations. Though this claim has been repeated in book after book, simple empirical observation shows that this is not true. First, prices are nowhere near normally distributed, so the rule of thumb for standard deviations does not apply; over a large sample of markets, approximately 88 percent (not 96 percent) of closes are within two Bollinger standard deviations of a 20-period average. Second, standard deviation of *price* is not a meaningful measure, so the width of the Bollinger bands does not track most accepted measures of volatility well.

Keltner channels were created by Chester Keltner, a grain trader in Chicago, but most traders today use a modification that is actually much closer to the *Stoller Average Range Channels (STARC)*. Regardless of terminology, the advantage of these channels is that they respond to a simpler and more consistent measure of volatility: the range of each bar. Also, since these channels use true range rather than simple range, they can also be applied to data that are close-only (e.g., economic data, funds, or some calculated indexes). They are simple, robust, and consistent: big bars = more volatility = wider bands, avoiding many of the potential issues with Bollinger bands. Figures 7.6 and 7.7 show Bollinger bands and Keltner channels applied to the same weekly chart of Wheat futures. Notice the typical "Bollinger balloon" effect of a large price change on the Bollinger bands; the Keltner channels also respond to the increasing volatility, but they do it in a much more measured and controlled way. As volatility contracts, Bollinger bands tend to tighten very aggressively, and so they will give alerts on small price movements out of these environments. This may or may not be desirable behavior, and traders who use these bands must know how to adjust for these quirks.

Whichever type of channel is used, the critical behavior occurs when the price bars engage the bands. It is important, then, that the bands be set at a level that is meaningful—too close and they will give insignificant signals, but too far and they are never touched. The Keltner channels that I use are set at a level that contains between 85 and 90 percent of all trading activity (the range of the bar, not just the close) across a wide range of markets. Table 7.1 verifies this claim empirically with an analysis of every bar from a large test universe. For each of the 2,403,774 bars in that universe, two statistics were recorded: "Inside" measures the percentage of the total range of all bars that was inside the bands. "Free bars" are bars that are pushed to such a dramatic extreme that the low of the bar is above the upper band, or the high of the bar is below the bottom channel—the entire bar is outside the channel. These are rare, but potentially significant, events that can indicate a condition of extreme imbalance in the market.

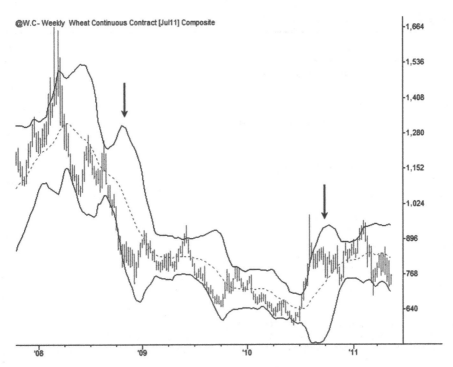

FIGURE 7.6 Bollinger Bands on Weekly Wheat: Notice How Bands Expand and Contract Very Quickly

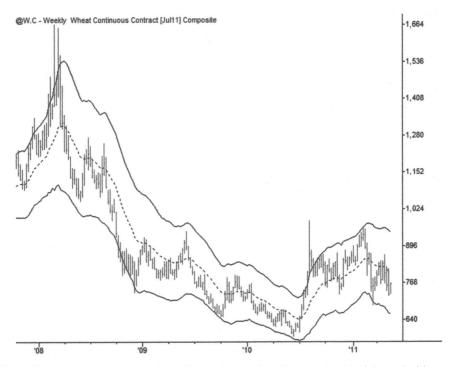

FIGURE 7.7 By Comparison, Keltner Channels on Wheat Futures Are Much More Stable

TABLE 7.1 Excursion Stats for 2.25 ATR Modified Keltner Channels

	Mean	Min	Max
	Large-Cap Stocks (496 stocks)		
Inside	87.7%	67.0%	100.0%
Free bars	3.4%	0.0%	11.7%
	Small-Cap Stocks (500 stocks)		
Inside	85.4%	36.0%	96.2%
Free bars	4.3%	0.2%	21.2%
	Futures (16 contracts)		
Inside	85.9%	77.8%	92.5%
Free bars	3.8%	0.7%	6.4%
	Forex (9 pairs)		
Inside	89.8%	87.8%	92.0%
Free bars	2.3%	1.5%	3.7%
	Randomly Generated Data (7 series)		
Inside	86.8%	85.8%	87.7%
Free bars	3.8%	3.3%	4.4%

"Inside" records the percentage of the total trading range that is inside the bands.
"Free bars" are the percentage of all bars that are completely outside the bands.
Min and Max show the lowest and highest stat for individual instruments (i.e., individual stocks, futures markets, etc.) in the sample classes.

Ideas for Using Channels

As with most technical tools, traders have developed many nuances and techniques for using bands or channels. Some traders use points where price engages the bands as decision points, either in a quasi or a purely systematic form with other supporting factors. In some markets and time frames, some bands do show a strong enough statistical tendency to support such a plan, but other traders use them as inputs into a broad, discretionary process. Regardless, it is always helpful to know that you have a head start and are placing trades aligned with an underlying tendency in the market.

Fade Move Outside the Channels   Some traders love to fade markets, specializing in buying weakness or shorting into strength. Bands or channels can be a vital criterion in such a plan. In many markets, there actually is a slight statistical edge to fading moves to the upper or lower Keltner channel, and it is possible to replicate this tendency with Bollinger bands if some adjustments are made. Fading makes sense only if the market is truly extended, if the rubber band is stretched and could be ready to snap back. Traders who fade markets that are in relative equilibrium will accumulate a steady stream of losses. A good rule of thumb is to not consider any fade trade unless the market is extended beyond the bands on whichever time frame you are trading. Remember, risk management is essential in this kind of trade, as the band does not present any kind of actual barrier. There is always the psychological tendency to attach too much meaning to any line on a chart; this is why traders focus on moving averages, bands, or even whole numbers (e.g., where grid lines fall on charts). The market can do anything, however, and there are no lines on charts that provide any firm barriers to price. Blindly fading bands with no risk management plan could easily result in staggering losses.

Enter on a Pullback from the Bands   A market overextended outside the band will, eventually, reverse back inside the bands. At this point, it is often possible to initiate a trade in the direction of the original band touch. Buying somewhere near the middle of the bands after the market touches the upper bands or shorting after it touches the bottom is often a good trade. This trade could potentially be executed mechanically, but many traders will find best results using this condition to identify markets primed to move and then executing those trades with discretion. For a discretionary trader, this is a useful illustration of quantifying a fundamental principle of price behavior through the structure of an indicator. Figure 7.8 shows examples of both fading moves to the band (marked A) and entering pullbacks on the moving average after the band has been touched (B). (In this case, the entry condition for pullbacks required a close outside the band, rather than a simple touch.)

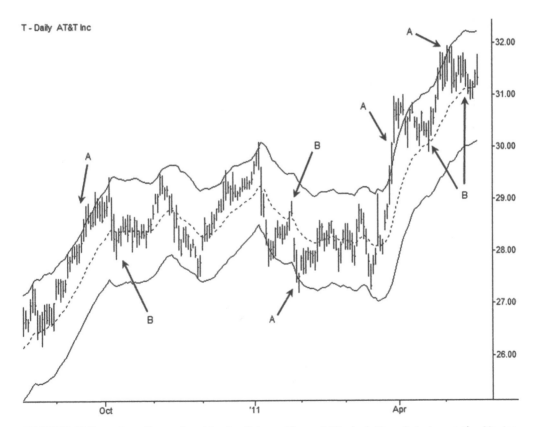

FIGURE 7.8   Fading Closes Outside the Keltner Channel (Marked A) or Entering at the Moving Average (Marked B)

Both of these are reliable trades that capitalize on basic elements of price behavior.

Slide Outside the Bands Markets normally move in alternating patterns of impulse and consolidation; the opposing trades of fading at the band and reentering in the middle of the bands capture this principle well. This is the pattern when the market machinery is operating normally. Strong buying (demand) eventually raises prices to a level where supply is adequate to overcome that buying pressure and the market drifts down. After a period of rest, buyers reassert themselves and push the market into another leg. However, this cycle can and does short-circuit, and it is also important to be aware of the patterns that occur in the distortions: normal strength results in a buyable pullback, or normal weakness results in a shortable pullback, but *extreme* strength or weakness usually indicates exhaustion. This is something to be aware of because amateurs often see the strongest moves and want to enter into the next pullbacks. Professionals realize that a very strong move often means the party is over and it is time to take profits and stand aside.

One pattern that indicates an exceptionally weak or strong market is shown in Figure 7.9. When a market presses into the upper or lower band and stays there, this is indicative of a one-sided market with extreme pressure. The absence of any real

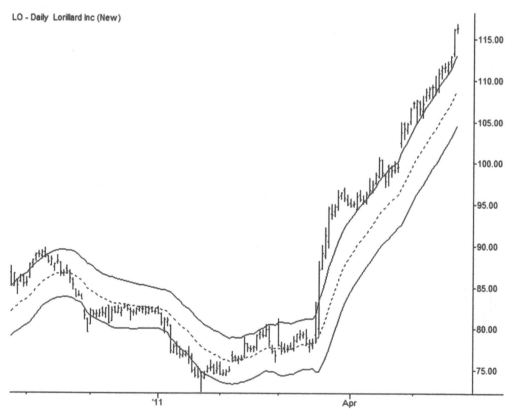

LO - Daily Lorillard Inc (New)

FIGURE 7.9 A Market Pressing into One of the Channels Is Indicative of a very Strong Imbalance This is also usually a difficult trading environment.

pattern makes it very difficult to trade this type of market. There are no pullbacks, and this structure is often a potential climax pattern on the higher time frame, so there is the ever-present possibility of a severe snapback. Many traders will be inclined to continually fade such a move because it is very difficult to find with-trend entries, but this is usually the wrong plan. The best course of action is almost always to have no position unless you are managing risk and profits in preexisting positions.

Spike through Both Bands Well-trending markets tend to be controlled, with more or less proportional actions and reactions. Another way this standard pattern can break down is for a market to make an extremely sharp move through one side of the band that is immediately reversed and then spikes clear through the other band. (See Figure 7.10.) As a general rule of thumb, whenever a market makes a sharp move in one direction immediately followed by an equally sharp move in the other direction, the normal expectation should be for that market to spend some time consolidating and oscillating in a series of smaller swings around a central price. This will usually result in a chart pattern that looks something like the classic triangle pattern. Remember that a big move

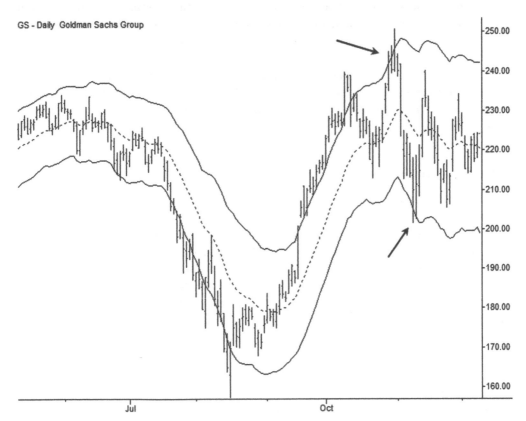

FIGURE 7.10 A Spike through the Upper Band Immediately Followed by a Spike through the Lower Band Usually Leads to a Triangle-Type Consolidation—Avoid This Environment

up followed by a big move down usually leads to a triangle, and this is a difficult trading environment that is best avoided.

INDICATORS: MACD

One of the recurring themes of this book is that traders must have a complete understanding of any tool they use. It is not constructive to use a tool that is simply a mysterious wiggly line without really understanding what it is saying about price action. With this in mind, Appendix B takes a deep look at how the *modified MACD indicator* is constructed, and how it reacts to specific price patterns. If you have background and experience with this or a similar tool, this material may offer a new perspective on the use of this indicator.

Though I have found this tool useful, many traders will have other favorite indicators that they will prefer to use. This is fine, and many of the applications of the modified MACD I discuss can be applied to other momentum indicators. However, be sure you understand what your indicator is really measuring. In general, most indicators fall into two broad categories: momentum indicators such as MACD, rate of change (ROC), and Momentum, or *overbought/oversold indicators* such as the Stochastic oscillator and the Relative Strength Index (RSI). The MACD is a momentum indicator and these techniques can be adapted for other momentum indicators, but do not try to apply them to overbought/oversold indicators. Many people do not think beyond the fact that their indicator has two moving lines. As always, think deeply and understand the nuances of the tools you are using.

Basic Interpretation of the MACD

Let's turn our attention to some practical applications of the MACD, and how it might be used in actual trading. Formally and precisely, the MACD measures the *changes in momentum* of prices, but there tends to be some persistence in momentum, so it is acceptable to treat the MACD as a proxy measure of momentum. (That is to say, an increase in the rate of change of momentum will likely lead to higher momentum and vice versa.) Most of the benefit from using this tool comes from its ability to pick out inflections that might not be clearly visible on price charts, to identify swings that are more or less likely to have continuation after consolidation, and to mark overextended points where the momentum is potentially exhausted. There are a few specific applications and patterns that can be applied to this tool or most other momentum indicators.

Fast Line Pop   One of the core ideas of technical analysis, and indeed of fundamental analysis, is that markets move to new prices in response to new information. This movement usually takes the form of a series of alternating waves and retracements. Simply put, a strong momentum move will usually result in another move in the same direction following a period of consolidation. This pattern is the foundation of market structure, but it is also possible to use a momentum indicator to define these conditions precisely. The most important concept here is that *momentum precedes price*, meaning that a sharp momentum move in a market pressing to new highs will usually be followed by higher prices after a consolidation, and the reverse is true to the downside. Be clear on this point: a momentum indicator will not somehow lead prices—this is not possible because the indicators are calculated from *past* prices. There are no true leading indicators in technical analysis; what *does* lead price is a strong move in the market itself, not the reading on an indicator.

One of the simplest ways to use a momentum indicator is to look for it to make a significant new high or low, and then to enter the pullback following that new momentum extreme. One complication is that the MACD is an unbounded indicator, so it is not possible to set fixed reference levels. In practice, it is enough to use rough intuitive guidelines created by comparing the indicator to its own recent history. A more systematic approach could, for instance, express the indicator's value as a percentile of a look-back window, and perhaps enter retracements following an excursion into either the top or the bottom decile. If you are just starting to look at this indicator, use the 40-bar history as a starting point, but you should be able to read the indicator without precise reference to this history very quickly. Again, the momentum pop on the MACD is just a visual representation of information that is already in the price bars, but it can be a useful confirmation in some situations.

Figure 7.11 shows the MACD applied to weekly bars of the Financial Sector SPDR (NYSE: XLF). At point A the market had made a strong down move, which also pushed the MACD line to a significant new low relative to its recent history. (Do not focus too much attention on the fact that it is a new low on this particular chart. The chart boundaries are arbitrary.) After an extended consolidation, the market made new lows into the point marked B, at which time the MACD again made a lower low. Following more consolidation, the market traded lower until the sharp reversal pushed the MACD to significant new highs (C). This upside momentum should have been a warning to shorts to not look to add short exposure into the next pullback. In this case, the market staged a substantial multiyear rally from this point.

This is an important concept, so let's review a more complex example, this time using a 5-minute chart of the E-mini S&P 500 futures. At the point marked A in Figure 7.12, the MACD confirmed the price weakness by making a significant new low, and prices slid lower with scarcely any consolidation. The action into 11:00 AM was perhaps slightly suggestive of a selling climax, so very short-term shorts would have been well advised to take profits into the small flush. Point B raises an important issue: is this a significant new high on the MACD? Perhaps so, as this is the highest reading that has been seen so far in this trading day, but there were other considerations (on the higher time frame) that suggested continued weakness. What if a trader has misread this MACD line and had entered a long trade? A losing trade would have been the result, but losing trades are a normal part of any trading plan. If the risk on this trade had been managed appropriately, the loss would have been small. Points C and D both show new price lows on the day,

FIGURE 7.11 New Extremes on the MACD Precede New Price Extremes

FIGURE 7.12 The MACD In a More Complex Environment

accompanied by at least marginal new lows on the MACD, but it is clear that the character of the market has changed somewhat. Though there may have been money shorting into retracements following these two points, they are not examples of the best possible trades.

Fast Line Behavior in Climax Consolidations or pullbacks following climaxes are not high-probability trades for trend continuation. Reversals or long, extended consolidations are more likely following these points. Though it is not always possible to distinguish a climax from good strength or weakness, it is important to keep this consideration in mind. If an extremely large momentum move emerges that is out of all proportion to the recent history of the market, be very careful of entering retracements. This is a case where the details of the mathematical construction of the MACD become significant. It is an unbounded indicator, so extreme market conditions can push it to theoretically infinite levels. In these extreme situations, the indicator will rescale so that recent history is highly compressed in a tight wiggly line. Rather than trying to read any significance into that line, accept that it shows that the market has made such an extreme move that the indicator should be disregarded.

Figure 7.13 shows this principle in action on a daily chart of Silver futures. After pressing to new highs, the market collapsed in a very sharp sell-off at point A. Note

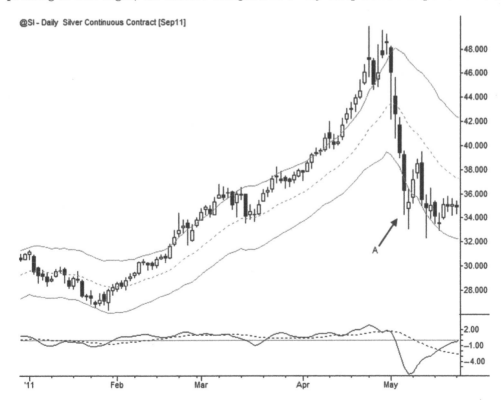

FIGURE 7.13 It Is Important to Understand the MACD's Reaction to a Climax

that the MACD fast line definitely made a significant new low, but this was clearly a climactic condition. Naive application of the MACD might have had a trader entering short in the first bounce off those lows, and a disciplined profit-taking plan would actually have locked in some profits in this case. The point is clear: this is not a reliable pattern to short. Consider also that a bounded indicator (e.g., stochastics) would simply have gone to the boundary and stayed there, rather than making this dramatic pop. Traders who use the MACD on intraday charts will see these types of distortions frequently if the markets they trade have large overnight gaps. It is usually best to disregard the indicator until the market has settled down and more normal momentum conditions emerge.

Fast Line Divergence   If the best pullbacks are preceded by the MACD fast line making a significant new high (or low in the case of a downtrend), then it follows logically that pullbacks that are not set up by a new high or low on the MACD are less likely to have good continuation. This is the concept of momentum divergence: a market makes a new high in prices that is not accompanied by a new high on the indicator, and vice versa to the downside. Figure 7.14 shows clean momentum divergences in Wheat futures. At A, price pushes to a new high, but the MACD fast line is clearly lower. At point B, prices

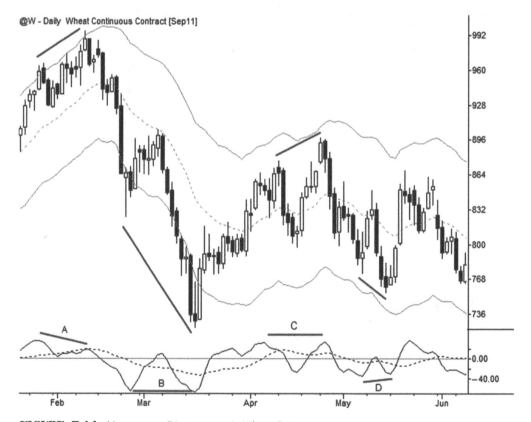

FIGURE 7.14   Momentum Divergences in Wheat Futures

drive to a dramatic new low (selling climax?), and the MACD barely moves below the previous low. C sets up yet another example of a divergence, as price makes a new high unaccompanied by a new high on the MACD. Last, D shows a new price low against a higher low on the MACD. In all of these cases, the momentum divergence would suggest that the dominant group in the market may be losing their hold and that a reversal is more likely than continuation. Any book on technical analysis will show you that this is the way divergence is supposed to work. There is only one small problem: divergences fail about as often as they work.

Figure 7.15 shows a darker side of momentum divergence. At least four momentum divergences set up against this trend, all of which failed. Any extended trend will set up multiple momentum divergences, most of which will fail. This is, in fact, one working definition of a trend: just as a trend breaks support or resistance, trends will also roll over momentum divergences. Traders using these divergences to set up countertrend trades will incur steady losses, but paying attention to these divergences can be equally damaging to traders who are only trading with the trend if they use them as warning signs to exit their positions prematurely. This does not invalidate the concept of momentum divergence, but it does highlight the importance of having a trading plan that respects

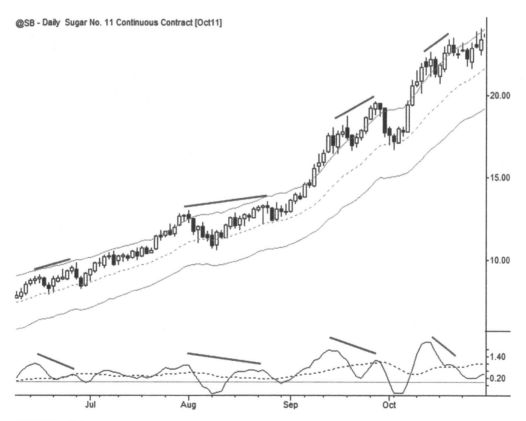

FIGURE 7.15 Strong Trends Result in Failed Momentum Divergences

the reality of market action. Clearly define how and when you will use momentum divergences, and, if you will actually set up trades using them, have precise plans for managing those trades. A skilled countertrend trader could likely have executed shorts on each of the momentum divergences in Figure 7.15 and emerged at the right edge of the chart with only small losses, but this is a difficult way to make a living.

This tool, like any other momentum indicator, measures potential divergences between subsequent *swings* in the market. If there are no swings, there is nothing to measure so we cannot have divergence. Many times, markets will set up patterns that resemble valid divergences, but there is no retracement in between the two points being measured. Consider the divergences marked in Figure 7.16. Though the indicator shows the classic patterns of divergence, at the corresponding points on the price bars the market was simply sliding higher.

A few further refinements will wrap up our consideration of divergences. It is possible to see momentum divergences without referring to the indicator, especially after the trader internalizes many patterns and variations of charts. There are subtle relationships between the length of swings, angle of swings (a visual indication of rate of change, assuming that vertical scaling is consistent), and the specific formations at the turn of

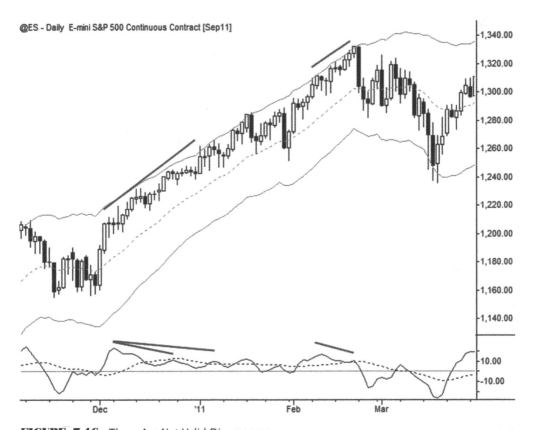

FIGURE 7.16 These Are Not Valid Divergences

swings that can reveal momentum conditions to the trained eye. The MACD fast line divergence is a crutch, but it is a useful crutch, especially for new and developing traders. Also, divergence is often a temporary and fleeting condition. A divergence obviously does not mean the market will never make another move in the same direction, so give some consideration to the timing and duration of divergences, which will vary depending on the specific indicator used to define them. With this MACD, a divergence can usually be assumed to have reset or to have fulfilled its expectation when one of three conditions occurs: price returns to an intermediate-term (e.g., 20-period) moving average, the MACD fast line crosses the zero line from the divergent state, or an extended period of time (10+ bars) elapses. If you have executed a countertrend trade based on a divergence, be protective of any open profits once any of these conditions emerges.

Last, there are a few logical inconsistencies to consider when trading divergences. One of the most important is that since pivot highs are matched to indicator values in an uptrend, we are comparing the *highs* of the bars to the indicator value; in a downtrend, the *lows* of the price bars are compared to the indicator value. This problem is that *highs and lows* of price bars are being compared to an indicator that is calculated from the *closes* of the price bars; the indicator is completely blind to any information encoded in the extreme points of the bars. There are a number of potential solutions to address this problem. A simple one would be to calculate the indicator off the midpoint of the bar (average of high and low of the bar), or off the average of the high, low, and close (this is called the *typical price* in some analytical systems). As a much more extreme solution, you could calculate separate indicators for bullish and bearish divergence, basing the tool for bearish divergence off the highs of the price bars and the other off the lows. A word of warning is in order, too: if you do something like this, make sure the extra information gained from the tool compensates for the additional complications—simplicity is greatly to be desired.

Beware of Overextended Fast Line Entries   Most people are familiar with the story that old man J. P. Morgan, when asked about the stock market, sagely replied, "It will fluctuate." Though probably said tongue-in-cheek, truer words have never been spoken. This should be your baseline expectation for any market: it will fluctuate. Extreme highs will be followed by sell-offs and vice versa. A trading strategy that consistently buys at extreme highs and sells at extreme lows is likely to be painful; a simple MACD-based rule can help us avoid many of these situations.

The rule is, very simply, to try to avoid buying when the fast line is extended into highs and try to avoid selling when it is extended into low territory. Though not strictly correct, many traders find it useful to think of the fast line as showing potential or stored energy that can be used to power the market's next move. When the line is dramatically extended to the upside, it could indicate that the move is already overdone and potentially primed for a small reversal. Though it is difficult to quantify this tendency into a precise rule set, many traders find that their results improve with the addition of a rule that prevents them from buying when the line is extended to the upside or shorting when it is extended to the downside.

Fast Line Drive and Hold   Probably no writer has done as much as Tom DeMark to foster an objective, scientific approach to trading with indicators. His work demands careful study; interested readers could start with his 1997 *New Market Timing Techniques*. One very important point he makes that is often overlooked by many traders is that an indicator's ability to go into overbought territory is often evidence of real strength in the market, and the reverse is true for oversold readings. Though the MACD does not have overbought/oversold levels and is not even properly an overbought/oversold indicator, many traders will initially be inclined to fade extreme moves on the indicator. This is natural, especially for traders who have some familiarity with stochastics, RSI, or a handful of other common indicators, but it is important to realize that one of the common patterns of the MACD is that the fast line will go into overbought territory in a strong trend and stay there for an extended period of time. The inability of the fast line to back off is a reflection of the conviction behind the price movement and should not be taken as an indication to start looking for countertrend trades. Figure 7.17 shows yet another example from Silver futures. In this case, a very strong uptrend pegs the MACD fast line in potentially overextended territory, and it stays there for much of the move.

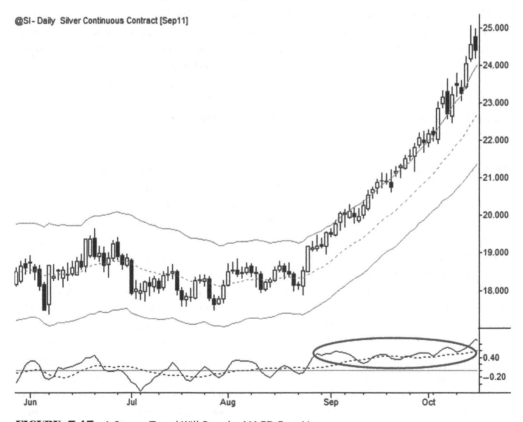

FIGURE 7.17   A Strong Trend Will Peg the MACD Fast Line

One easy way to avoid fading markets in situations like this is to look for divergence only after the fast line touches or comes very near to the zero line. This criterion is another expression of a point made earlier, which is that divergences can be valid only between different swings in the market. If there are no swings and the market is simply in a strong, extended push (as in Figure 7.17), then there really can be no valid information from the fast line of the MACD. In nearly all cases, the fast line will retreat to the zero line in the presence of an accompanying countertrend swing in price, and these are precisely the types of structures that can set up valid divergences.

Fast Line Hook   A turn in the fast line can often be the first indication of emerging momentum, especially when the market is poised at an inflection point. This is a case where a very sensitive indicator can sometimes seem to lead price because it is able to filter out the most important aspects of the price action. Figure 7.18 shows short entries in Freeport-McMoRan (NYSE: FCX) that were generated according to the following rule set: enter short on the first bar whose close causes the MACD fast line to turn down after prices have penetrated below the lower band and assuming there is no momentum divergence. (The inverse of this rule set could be applied to generate longs, but there are

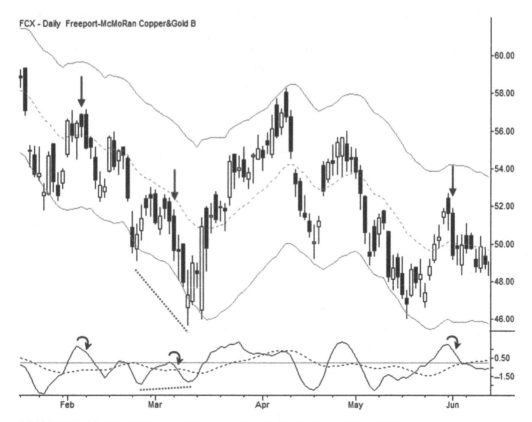

FIGURE 7.18   Shorts Generated by a Systematic Application of the MACD

no penetrations of the upper channel on this chart.) Though every trade on this chart would have resulted in a win, there are a few points to consider: First, and obviously, you should be inherently suspicious of any carefully chosen example in a book. Second, these entries would have been on the *close* of the bars, so, while still profitable, they may not be as good as they look at first glance. It is very easy to see a short entry on a large down bar and fail to realize that the entry was actually made near the low of that bar. (Also, depending on how you define divergence, the last trade on the chart may or may not have been permitted.) Regardless, this example shows how we can start to put some of these ideas together into simple rule sets, and how the turn of the fast line can provide precise entry points.

Slope of the Slow Line   So far, our attention has focused on the fast line of the MACD, and for good reason. Most traders find that nearly all of the value of the indicator is in the fast line, but the slow line can also provide another useful layer of information. The slow line is nothing more than a 16-period simple moving average of the fast line, so it has all of the quirks and idiosyncrasies of any moving average. In the MACD, the slope of the slow line is a good proxy for intermediate-term momentum, perhaps over 10 to 20 bars. At first glance, the slow line appears to have less noise and fewer false moves than the fast line, but this is just a reflection of the smoothing and lag of the slow line, which also will miss many signals that appear on the fast line.

In general, it is probably best to be suspicious of trades that set up against the slope of the slow line if the slow line has been extended and has turned back toward the zero line. Figure 7.19 shows two examples in Macy's Inc. (NYSE: M): traders initiating longs after the slow line turned down would have been frustrated as the market entered a more extended period of consolidation. Consider this to be, for practical purposes, a form of momentum divergence. After a period of time, the divergence works itself off and the trend is free to continue in the original direction. This commonly occurs later in an extended trend, and is often accompanied by a complex consolidation on the chart.

Position of the Slow Line   The position of the slow line relative to the zero reference line is also significant. On one hand, it is nothing more than a type of trend indicator. Since the slow line is an average of the fast line, for the slow line to be far above zero, the fast line must have spent a longer time above the zero line. The only way for the fast line to get far above zero and to stay there is for the market to have made an extended move to the upside. In this context, the position of the slow line is not incredibly useful because it is simply another confirming trend indicator that suffers from the typical problems that plague any quantitative measure of trend.

On the other hand, disagreement between the fast and slow lines can highlight or confirm pullbacks in prices. For instance, if the slow line is extended above zero but the fast line pulls back below the zero line, it often makes sense to be on the lookout for long entries. The reverse setup applies for shorting, of course. This is, to some extent, an arbitrary setup and condition, as changing the indicator parameters would give significantly different signal points on the market, but there is real value here. This condition

FIGURE 7.19 Avoid Buying When the Slow Line Has Been Extended Upward and Has Now Turned Down

often highlights a structural tension in the market where the short-term momentum, as measured by the fast line, is in conflict with the longer-term momentum measured by the slow line. Figure 7.20 shows the results of combining the fast line hook entry with this condition on a daily chart of Lean Hog futures. This is not intended to be a complete mechanical trading system, though a system could be built on this concept. Also consider, in Figure 7.20, the fast line hook entries (not marked) that were skipped. At the very least, the MACD provides some powerful clues about market structure, momentum, and price action.

MULTIPLE TIME FRAME ANALYSIS

Multiple time frame analysis provides another layer of depth and richness to market analysis. It can place patterns in one time frame in the context of other time frames to better identify those spots where the patterns are more likely to have arisen due to an actual imbalance in the market rather than as a result of random chance. Many traders

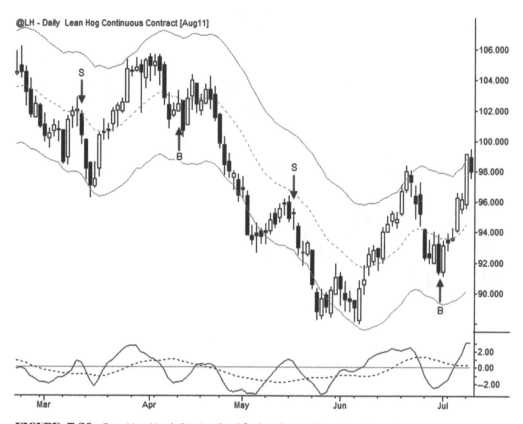

FIGURE 7.20 Fast Line Hook Entries Qualified with Fast/Slow Line Spread

assume that higher time frames are more significant; for instance, that patterns on the weekly chart are more important than patterns on 5-minute charts. This is not exactly true—structures on different time frames can take control at any time, and one of the major tasks of analysis is to identify what time frame and what structure are the dominant factors in a particular market at any point in time.

There are spots where price action may be completely dictated by what happens on a very short time frame, for instance, 1- or 3-minute charts, and other times when the most important factor might be a level that is visible on weekly or monthly charts. We can usually identify a dominant structure or set of structures on one time frame, and can often watch as control is essentially passed from one time frame to another. For instance, perhaps a resistance level is tested multiple times on the 1-minute chart, and then is broken cleanly with a clear consolidation just below the level. At this moment, the 1-minute chart would be in control, but perhaps this breakout happened at the turn of a pullback on the 5-minute chart. We could then say that the pullback on the 5-minute chart and the subsequent trend leg have taken control as the 5-minute chart becomes the dominant time frame. Perhaps the market eventually runs into a new resistance area on the 30-minute chart, at which point we could identify that as the dominant technical structure. This discussion could apply without any loss of generality to daily/weekly/monthly or to any other set of time frames, but the most important point is to avoid that naive assumption that higher time frames are always more important. Work instead to identify the dominant technical structures and to understand what time frame has control.

There are two broad areas to this study: the impact of lower time frames on higher time frames and the power of higher time frame structures to shape price action and market structure on lower time frames. In practical terms, higher time frame considerations can add confidence to trades, filter other trades entirely, or help to set targets for trades. Lower time frames can help to add precise entry points for bigger, higher time frame patterns, and lower time frame price action can suggest whether support and resistance are more likely to hold or to break on higher time frames. This is an oversimplification, but these factors are the core understanding of how most traders use multiple time frame analysis.

This is a difficult subject to teach because traders often attempt to move to multiple time frames before they understand the structures and implications of a single time frame. There is some justification for this attempt—patterns become much more powerful when seen in the context of multiple time frames, and a few simple tools can greatly increase the probability of winning trades. However, it is impossible to develop the intuition and skills needed to comprehend multiple time frames unless you can proficiently read the chart of a single time frame. It is important to fully understand the individual building blocks before trying to create elaborate structures.

The situation is complicated further because much of the written material on this subject lacks clarity. The trend seems to be either toward indicator-based oversimplification (e.g., look for long trades while an indicator applied to a higher time frame shows that the higher time frame is in an uptrend) or toward obfuscation and confusion. Neither is good. Multiple time frame trading cannot easily be reduced to a simple rule set, but there are some commonalities and structures that occur over and over again. This section examines a few recurrent patterns and concepts, and lays a foundation for further exploration.

Lower Time Frame Structures within Higher Time Frame Context

Earlier in this book, I outlined a useful, but rigid, three-time-frame structure in which the trading time frame was supported by both lower and higher time frames. "Lower time frame" always refers to the time frame below the one being traded, and "higher time frame" always refers to the time frame above the one being traded, with each time frame usually related to its neighbor by a factor between 3 and 5. For now, let's leave that structure behind for a minute and simply consider two time frames, a higher and a lower, in relation to each other, without designating one specific trading time frame.

To understand higher time frame influences on lower time frames, first consider what price patterns create the highest-probability trades on a single time frame. There could be some debate, but good places to start would be mean reversion in overextended markets, especially following climax moves; the interface between pullbacks and new trend legs, or the point where new with-trend momentum emerges out of a pullback; higher time frame drives to clear target areas; and failure tests at the extremes of a range, ideally with signs of accumulation or distribution. In the presence of one of these formations on the higher time frame, lower time frame price action and market structure will be molded as prices inexorably move toward a resolution of the higher time frame pattern. A few examples will help to clarify these vital concepts.

Higher Time Frame Mean Reversion   One of the main problems in technical analysis is distinguishing exhaustion from strength. Exhaustion is indicative of overextended moves that will soon reverse; real strength (or weakness) occurs with moves that should have continuation in the same direction. If it were always possible to tell one from the other, we would always know whether to fade moves or to enter pullbacks for continuation, but, of course, it is not possible to make these distinctions every time. Though there are characteristics associated with each, there are also many similarities and even our best tools work within the laws of probability. There is no certainty in trading; the best we can hope for is to find something that will give a slight, reliable bias or tilt. Some type of well-calibrated band or channel—for instance, the Keltner channels I use and discuss in this work—can provide a good visual and quantitative reference for overextension. On a single time frame, you would not want to make a standard practice of buying strength above the upper band or shorting weakness below the lower band.

Figure 7.21 shows a pullback on daily Wheat futures that might have been buyable, taken out of context: the market consolidated after a strong upthrust, put in a series of smaller-range bars, and eventually showed a return of upside momentum at the spot marked on the chart. However, the weekly chart shows a long tail and a clear exhaustion above the channel, greatly reducing the attractiveness of the potential long entry on the daily chart. Many traders think that a good analytical system will get them into more winning trades, but equally valuable is a system that will reduce the number of losing trades. Being aware of higher time frame overextension and potential exhaustion is one tool that can help traders avoid trades that immediately fail and collapse under the force of higher time frame mean reversion. (Note that in all of these charts the left pane expands on the highlighted section of the right pane. The lower time frame is in the left pane, the higher time frame in the right.)

Figure 7.22 shows another example, this time in the broad U.S. equities market. At the end of the daily chart, an aggressive trader could have justified taking a shot at a short. True, this was not the best possible trade setup, but the market had just completed a sloppy complex pullback after making new lows, and had been locked in a strong downtrend for many quarters. However, the weekly chart again puts this trade in context. After three pushes down, the last of which was on a glaring momentum divergence (i.e., price made a new low and the MACD fast line was unable to do so), it would have been unrealistic to expect a clean short. There are two valuable lessons here: First, the weekly chart does not clearly support a long trade, but it did offer enough upside

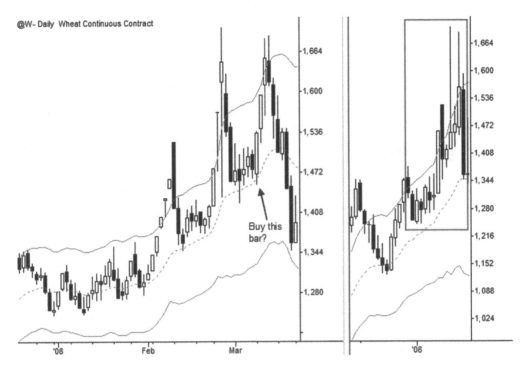

FIGURE 7.21 Exhaustion on the Weekly Chart Suggests Passing on This Buy Signal

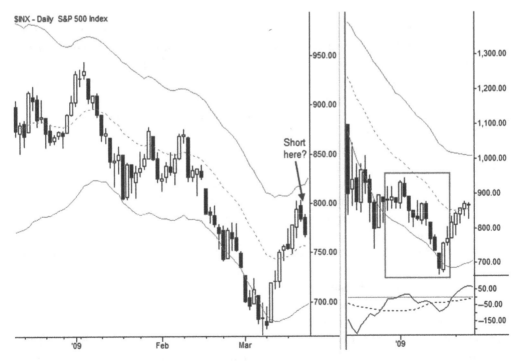

FIGURE 7.22 Several Factors on the Weekly Chart Contradict a Potential Short on the Daily

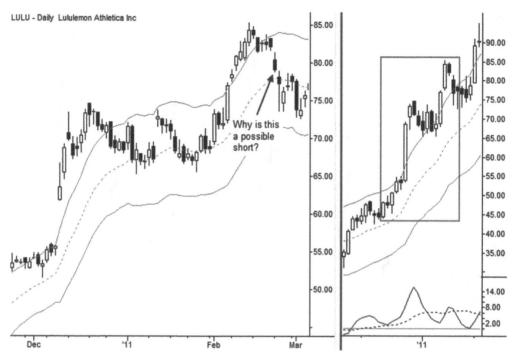

FIGURE 7.23 Why Short *under* a Bull Flag on the Daily Chart?

evidence to negate a potential short setup on the lower time frame. In this case, a set of conditions that might not have fully supported a long entry were enough to justify not taking a potential short setup. Second, most of the trades that are contradicted by higher time frames are also not excellent setups on one time frame. To some extent, focusing on the geometry of a single time frame will also wrap in some of the multiple time frame factors, though there is still valuable information to be gleaned from analysis of neighboring time frames.

Higher time frame considerations are not limited to providing filters to skip trades; sometimes they also can be motivation enough to justify trade entries. Figure 7.23 shows LULU, a market-leading stock in February 2011, extended above the upper band on the weekly chart, again with momentum divergence on the MACD. The tight consolidation on the daily chart might potentially be a place for aggressive longs to consider adding to positions or entering new positions. Looking only at the daily chart, we would *never* consider shorting under such a consolidation, because a high and tight flag is usually indicative of real conviction from buyers; furthermore, shorting an extremely strong market leader in any context is usually a recipe for pain. It is far better to spend your time and mental energy figuring out how to buy those market leaders and how to short laggards, in most cases. However, in this case, the weekly chart provided another layer of information, and the clear overextension made it possible to justify a quick short under the little range on the daily chart. There is also another lesson here: after a longer

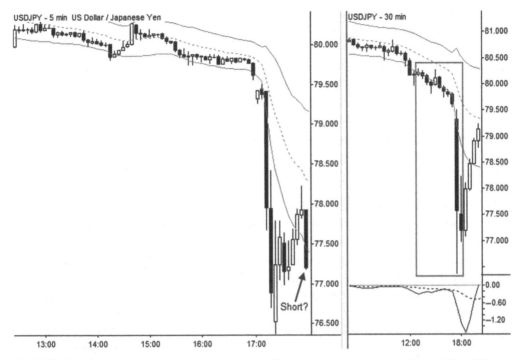

FIGURE 7.24 The Higher Time Frame Suggests That the Lower Time Frame Short Will Be Difficult

pullback, this stock spent some time consolidating and eventually headed much higher. Swing traders cannot be greedy. Your job is to take what opportunity the market offers and to be quick to realize when the trade is over.

These examples have focused on longer time frames, but the same principles apply to much shorter time frames as well. Figure 7.24 shows 5- and 30-minute charts of the USDJPY in the early evening (New York time) on March 16, 2011. The 5-minute chart shows a structure that could potentially be shortable for at least a retest of recent lows, though the presence of a selling climax, indicated by the overextension past the lower band, should give shorts pause for concern. In this case, the 30-minute chart provides context that is not as clearly visible on the 5-minute chart. The market is drastically overextended beyond the lower band on the higher time frame; this usually happens in response to a significant exogenous shock—in this case the aftermath of the 2011 Tōhoku earthquake in Japan.

In a situation like this, you may still choose to take the short trade, but you have to realize that the character of the trade, especially if you are wrong, will be different. There is a much higher probability of a dramatic failure and reversal when the market is overextended on the higher time frame, so a trade taken under these conditions has a completely different risk profile. Skip the trade altogether, take it and manage the risk with a tighter stop, or choose to get out at the first sign you might be wrong—these are all acceptable alternatives. What is *not* acceptable is ignoring the clear message of the higher time frame extension and taking an unnecessary large loss as you continue to short into the mean-reverting higher time frame.

Higher Time Frame Pullbacks To understand the effects of higher time frame pullbacks on the trading time frame, first review some of the characteristics that define high-probability pullbacks on a single time frame:

- Presence of a good impulse setting up further continuation.
- Market is not overextended.
- Market is not on the third (or later) trend leg.
- Absence of momentum divergence.
- Absence of buying or selling climax.
- Pullbacks show generally lower activity and volume than the trend legs.

These conditions and patterns, when they appear on the higher time frame, can provide motivation for and add confidence to trades on lower time frames.

Figure 7.25 shows a pattern on the daily chart of Crude Oil futures that might not be compelling by itself. It is obviously some form of a pullback, but the move up off the lows was maybe a little too far too fast to justify shorting; it could also be read as a potential setup for a long Anti trade, but it is not an example of the best possible trade

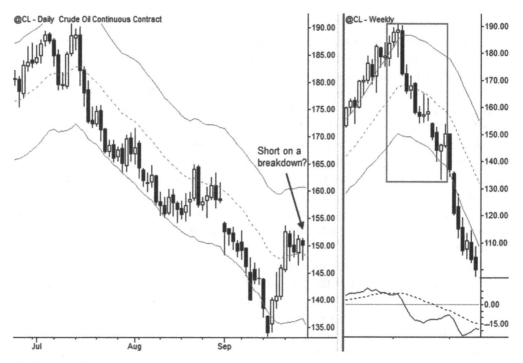

FIGURE 7.25 A Mediocre Pullback on the Daily Chart Is an Excellent Pullback on the Weekly Chart

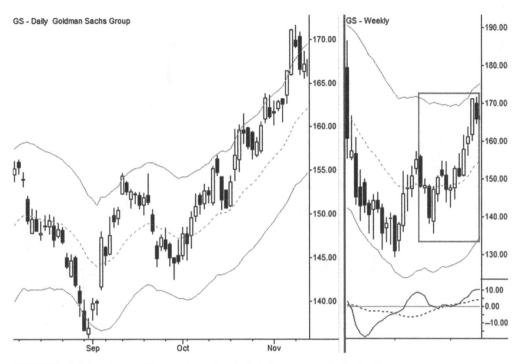

FIGURE 7.26 The Weekly Anti Provides Bullish Context to the Daily Chart

on this time frame. However, the weekly chart shows a clean bounce, which was the first reaction after the collapse from the overextended highs *and* the first pullback after a strong impulse move pushed prices below the lower channel. The weekly pattern added confidence to the daily consolidation, and justified a short attempt on a breakdown out of this pattern.

Figure 7.26 shows another example on weekly and daily charts of Goldman Sachs from October 2010. The pattern on the daily chart was anything but convincing: many large gaps and sudden reversals. Though the market was in an uptrend from the September lows, it might have been difficult to see this at the time. However, the weekly chart shows a pattern that we know well: several marginal new lows on slackening momentum followed by a sharp reversal off those lows. The upward reversal (not visible on the daily chart) made new momentum highs on the weekly chart and set up an Anti trade. This weekly chart pattern put a clearly bullish context on an otherwise difficult daily chart, and traders would have been justified aggressively pursuing long setups on the daily chart. In this case, there were many small bullish setups on this time frame: failure tests of support, breakouts of small daily flags, and, finally, an overextended climax just beyond the weekly measured move objective for the weekly Anti. At this point, realizing that the weekly chart had basically fulfilled its expectations for a measured move would have removed much of the bullish context from the daily patterns, justifying a reduction of risk or perhaps a complete exit from the trade.

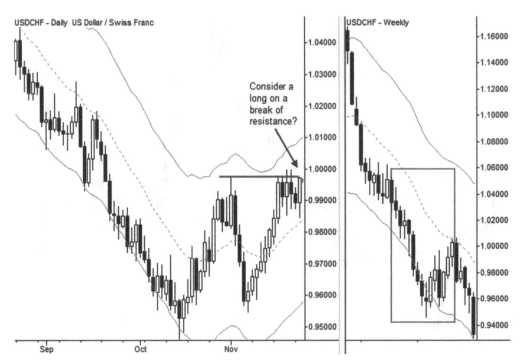

FIGURE 7.27 The Potential Breakout on the Daily Is Contradicted by the Weekly Complex Consolidation (Bear Flag)

Higher time frame pullbacks can also be a filter to skip trades that set up against those pullbacks. Figure 7.27 is an important example that shows what might have been seen as a good setup for a breakout on the daily chart: the consolidation up against resistance normally suggests the possibility of a strong break above that level, and is the opposite of the price rejection that normally accompanies a level holding. However, the weekly chart provided context, showing that the breakout was actually coming near the top of what was more likely to be bearish complex consolidation on the weekly chart. In this case, the higher time frame provides a bearish bias, which clearly contradicts the smaller pattern on the daily chart. The consolidation on the weekly could certainly fail, and it would do so through the success of the bullish breakout on the daily, but the probabilities favor downside continuation. There are a number of things you can do with this information, ranging from skipping the trade on the daily to taking it on smaller risk (which is not usually a good idea), or perhaps even watching for a breakout failure and entering a short trade on the daily. This last possibility combines a small pattern on one time frame with a bigger-picture bias from a higher time frame, which is an excellent use of multiple time frame information. At the very least, beware of patterns on one time frame that are clearly contradicted by strong patterns on higher time frames, especially when the patterns occur at potential inflection points.

Higher Time Frame Drives to Targets   In general, markets tend toward efficiency, and random walk prevails most of the time; when markets are more predictable, it is usually in short spurts of activity, which can sometimes be identified through specific patterns in prices. One common area of a more predictable spurt occurs when a pattern has broken into a move to a target—for instance, on the drive out of a consolidation pattern or following a strong break of support or resistance. These situations are not that common, but recognizing that a scenario like this is in play can lend support to otherwise uninteresting lower time frame patterns. Consider Figure 7.28, which shows several small consolidations on the daily chart of Finisar Corporation (NASDAQ: FNSR). These are perfectly acceptable consolidations (the first is an Anti, and the second is a simple bear flag), but the weekly chart provided strong tailwinds for these patterns and made them much more attractive than they might have been on their own.

Another possible use of this concept is to monitor evolving price action on *lower* time frames while a trade is underway on the trading time frame. If consolidation patterns resolve in the intended direction of the trade, all is well. If the trade should fail, it will usually do so through a failure of one of these lower time frame patterns. Being able to read evolving price action and market structure on the lower time frame can often provide excellent exits from trades, but it is necessary to balance this new layer of information against the possibility of being overly reactive to insignificant noise.

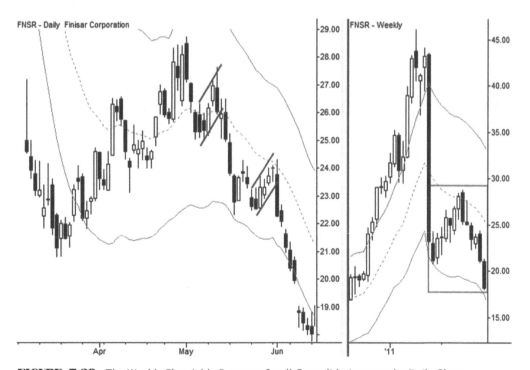

FIGURE 7.28   The Weekly Flag Adds Power to Small Consolidations on the Daily Chart

Higher Time Frame Failure Tests   Most traders who have studied multiple time frame interactions are comfortable with the idea that a market can be uptrending on one time frame, ranging on another, and downtrending on yet another, but there is another important consideration that few traders understand: the strongest trends often emerge in higher time frame consolidation areas. We know that price tends to respect support and resistance levels in trading ranges, oscillating back and forth between those levels. These levels are often rough and poorly delineated, and price action within the range tends to be more random and subject to sudden, large shocks. The irony is that what appear to be large shocks on one time frame are often strong, tradable trends on the lower time frame. Since one of the cleanest trades in a range is the test beyond the confines of the range that immediately reverses, as in the classic Wyckoff spring or upthrust, we can trade reactions off those higher time frame ranges with some degree of confidence.

Figure 7.29 shows a continuous chart of Gold futures. After an extended uptrend, this market ran into resistance, made multiple marginal highs, and eventually rolled over into a trading range at the beginning of 2011. The sell-off found support at a previous swing low (visible on the weekly chart in the right pane), and the subsequent move off that low was a strong uptrend on the daily chart. In this case, resistance eventually failed and the market continued much higher, but this is not the point. The point is that the daily chart showed a clean, strong uptrend off the support level defined by the weekly

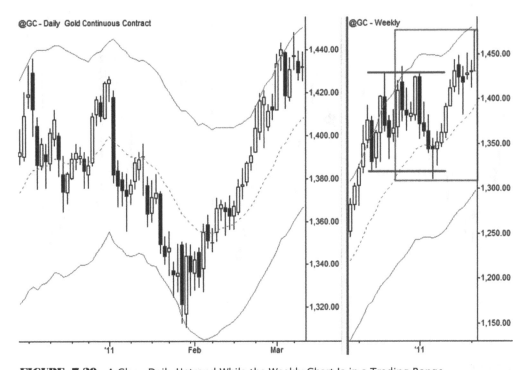

FIGURE 7.29   A Clean Daily Uptrend While the Weekly Chart Is in a Trading Range

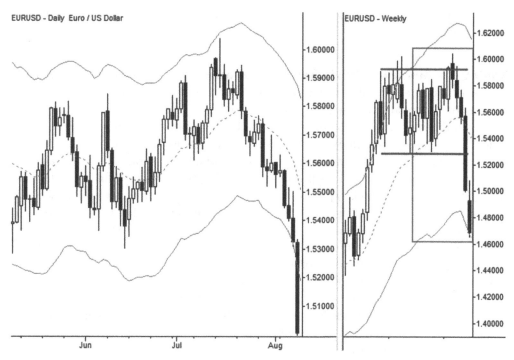

FIGURE 7.30 Another Example of a Lower Time Frame Trend While the Higher Time Frame Is in a Trading Range

trading range. Even if you are a trader who avoids markets in trading ranges, be aware that there may be opportunities in those markets on other time frames.

For another example of this concept, look at the EURUSD, pictured in Figure 7.30. The weekly chart was clearly in a trading range, while the daily chart shows a strong downtrend off the test of resistance in July. Some of the best and cleanest trends come within higher time frame consolidation areas. This is an important and often misunderstood element of price action that will repay careful study.

Timing Entries from Lower Time Frames

Remember the general three-time-frame structure: there is the time frame actually being traded (the trading time frame), and a higher and a lower time frame relative to that trading time frame. This is a somewhat arbitrary structure, but it is important for traders to define their intentions and the relevant time frames clearly. It is difficult to isolate cross-time-frame influences because, in reality, these flow both ways. The higher time frame (relative to the trading time frame) usually can suggest which trades are more likely to reach their targets and which are more likely to fail; the bigger-picture context provided by the higher time frame can be a valuable layer of information. In contrast, lower time frames are usually used in two ways: to time precise entries into trading time frame patterns or to monitor price action and conviction that may not be visible on higher time frame charts.

Timing Entries from the Lower Time Frame   There have been hints of using the lower time frame to find exact entry points in the previous section. For instance, an alert trader could have used the tests of support and resistance on the higher time frames in Figures 7.29 and 7.30 to enter at the beginning of strong trends on the lower time frame. This is a general plan for a powerful way to use the lower time frame as a timing tool into higher time frame patterns: at important structural points such as tests of support/resistance or previous pivots on the higher time frame. Think of it like this: If you stand on a chair and step off, you will very predictably fall a short distance and hit the floor—no big deal. All other things being equal, this is what breakouts on any time frame are like; an equilibrium level is disturbed and a predictable move of moderate size usually results. However, now repeat the experiment of jumping off a chair, but this time position the chair at the edge of a cliff. The step off the chair is still one small step, but now the result is out of all proportion to what you would have expected from that simple step. This is what happens when the moderate and predictable momentum from a lower time frame break feeds into a structure that is already at the tipping point on a higher time frame. These have already been formalized in some of the trade entries in Chapter 7, but this is a rewarding area of study for discretionary traders.

Reading Price Action on Lower Time Frames   Another way to use the lower time frame is to add depth and richness to market structure on the trading time frame. Traders who are watching order flow and monitoring markets closely during the trading session usually develop an intuitive sense for price action in those markets. However, there is a practical limit to how many markets can be followed this way, and some traders will be unable to devote full attention to price action while markets are open. A very skilled intraday trader might be able to track two dozen markets reasonably closely, but most traders, especially developing traders, will find it difficult to monitor more than half a dozen at a time. In addition, many traders prefer to trade higher time frames, and they make an effort to not focus on the short-term fluctuations in the markets they trade.

For traders in these situations, a careful analysis of lower time frame market structure can inform their understanding of price structures on the trading and higher time frames. For instance, if the trading time frame is trending, how is the lower time frame moving? Are there clear consolidations and good breaks that are indicative of a healthy trend? Are there potential overextensions and exhaustions on the lower time frame, or signs that momentum is starting to fail on that time frame? If the higher time frame is engaging important resistance, what is happening on the lower time frame? Is there evidence of price rejection, or are there consolidations near the higher time frame resistance that could presage a break of that level? This is definitely a blend of art and science, but these are key considerations for traders who do not monitor every tick of every market they follow—in other words, nearly everyone.

Summary of Multiple Time Frame Analysis

We have just scratched the surface here; to make best use of these concepts they must be internalized, which takes repeated exposure, deep thought, and dedicated study. However, we have covered most of the important core concepts, and, taken individually, they are not complex:

- There are not always meaningful multiple time frame considerations. The best examples are obvious and clear. Do not get too creative; if you have to work hard to see them, they probably are not there.
- When a higher time frame is trending, patterns that work *with* that trend direction on lower time frames will be reinforced. Win rates will be higher, and moves will be sharper and cleaner.
- When a higher time frame is trending, patterns that run *contra* to that trend on lower time frames will tend to abort. Though there can be impressive countertrend runs on lower time frames, these have limited expectations and they tend to resolve into with-trend patterns in the higher time frame. Trends that are countertrend to higher time frame trends tend to end at ideal entry points for with-trend entries in the higher time frame trend.
- When the higher time frame is ranging, expect sharp trends on lower time frames. Some of the best trends actually occur in the context of higher time frame consolidation.
- Breakouts that might be insignificant by themselves can be reinforced if they occur at critical tipping points in higher time frame structures. When this happens, we can time entries into the higher time frame trades with precision from lower time frames.
- Ranges on lower time frames are often continuation patterns on higher time frames. This can provide a bias for a directional breakout of these ranges.
- The character of price action on lower time frames often provides insight into the relative buying and selling pressure behind the market's movements. There is usually more noise on lower time frames, so be aware of this complicating factor.

Armed with these ideas and the examples in this chapter, start to examine markets and trade setups with these ideas in mind. These multiple time frame considerations can add confidence to some of your best trades and may give you justification to cut some losing trades more quickly.

Relative Strength

Relative strength is another way to understand the action and the convictions of market participants in related markets. In general, the idea is not complex: things go up in price because demand has, at least temporarily, overtaken supply—these movements are driven by strong buying pressure. It takes a lot of money to make a significant move in a major market, so when we see relative outperformance in an asset or assets, we can usually assume that informed traders are driving the move. It is the same idea that drives all technical analysis: significant buying and selling must leave patterns in prices. These patterns can be complex and they are obscured by background noise more often than not, but if we can learn to read them we can understand what the large players in the market are doing and how they are positioning for the future. If we are monitoring a group of related markets, we will usually see that a few of them are stronger than the rest, and one or two often emerge as the clear leaders. Conversely, it is usually possible to identify a handful of laggards who tend to move behind the group. Much of the literature on relative strength comes from the context of equity traders who have a strong long bias (many of whom do not short stocks at all) and are attempting to identify market-leading stocks, but the concept is equally valid to the downside. In bear markets, it is possible to identify relative strength leaders to the downside and laggards that resist the sell-offs. Do not be confused by the terminology—relative strength leaders lead the trend, whether that trend is up or down.

A rule of thumb is that, if you are trading relative strength ideas, you want to be long the strongest markets in an uptrend, and you want to be short the weakest in a downtrend. Be careful, because to many traders, the opposite play might seem to be attractive. They will focus on buying the weaker markets in uptrends, with the justification that they are cheap and that they have a lot of room to make up. This is human nature, but, unfortunately, it is usually exactly the wrong play. It is difficult, and somewhat counterintuitive, to be buying things that are already marked up more than average (this is the definition of a market leader), but resist the temptation to go bargain hunting in the relative strength space. It is far better to be in the markets that have the best institutional reinforcement and support, or, on the downside, to be short the markets the institutions are dumping.

If you choose to develop a systematic trading plan based on relative strength, you will also need to consider the impact of mean reversion. Consistently buying the strongest markets will often have you buying overextended markets that are poised for at least a temporary reversal. Depending on how you rebalance your portfolio and actually execute, you could potentially then rotate into the new leaders after booking losses on the first set, and repeat this process as long as capital allows. Systematic approaches to relative strength are possible, but these issues have to be addressed in development and through proper backtests. There is also a lesson here for discretionary traders: though you may want to focus much of your attention on relative strength leaders, blindly buying them is probably not a path to success.

There are many ways to track relative strength. The simplest is probably to simply take a number of markets and rank them by percent change from a fixed point in time, but there are a few potential issues with this simple measure. Most importantly, this measure is anchored to two specific points in time, and is blind to anything that happens in between. One market could appreciate 10 percent in a series of steady gains, while another could have extremely volatile swings and just happen to end the evaluation period also up 10 percent. Both markets will register the same relative strength readings, but they may have dramatically different trading characteristics. In a purely quantitative ranking this may not be an issue, but it must be considered before trades are actually made.

Choosing an arbitrary look-back window is not always a good choice, since the rate of change (ROC) calculation is also sensitive to what happens at the initial point. To standardize, it is possible to anchor the calculations to a fixed point in time, and to calculate changes for a wide range of related markets from those points. Significant swing highs and lows are ideal anchor points for this calculation. For instance, if tracking individual stocks, they can all anchor their ROC calculations to a significant and visible pivot on the weekly chart of a broad index. When the market structure of that index evolves, usually no more than once every other month, the ROC calculations can be updated to refer to the new pivot point. The same thing can be done with grain markets, currencies, or world equities, though the reference indexes are not always as clear in these situations. Another limitation is that, if we want to compare relative strength across disparate asset classes, it is usually impossible to find a significant anchor that makes sense for all of them. Why compare, for instance, European equities, grains, sugar, and cocoa to the same starting date, and how is this better than picking an arbitrary starting point?

One potentially attractive solution averages several different rates of change, perhaps with different weightings. Using a system like this, it is possible to create a measure that has a very long look-back window, but is also very responsive to recent data. Bill O'Neil has long been an advocate of such an approach, which has been used with some success in his funds and his writings. Traders who are interested in this concept can begin by simply averaging two different rates of change, comparing relative strength rankings, and then tweaking the measure via weightings or the addition of other look-back periods in the average. As always, each addition will bring additional complexity into the tool, so be sure that you are compensated with real value. Simple, parsimonious tools will usually outperform complex calculations in most market-related applications.

Trading Relative Strength Though the concept of being long the strongest markets by relative strength and short the weakest is sound, there are the twin forces of mean reversion and range expansion to consider. A campaign of simply buying the strongest markets will usually result in frustration, as your entries will often be at the apex of overbought markets. At the risk of oversimplifying, most successful relative strength trading programs follow some pattern like this:

- Understand the overall market trend, and decide whether you want to trade from the long side, the short side, or both. If trading from both sides, decide whether you wish to construct a true hedged portfolio or simply to hold both long and short positions as you deem them attractive.
- Identify the strongest and weakest relative strength candidates.
- Look to buy the strongest relative strength candidates, but buy them on weakness and using specific technical patterns as triggers. Conversely, look to short the weakest markets into strength.
- Once the leaders have been bought on weakness, monitor them carefully as they turn out of the weakness to see if they resume leadership. If not, exit or adjust the trade. If the weakness continues for too long, the leaders will no longer be leaders.

The actual execution of buying into weakness is not as difficult as it sounds—use the general technical rules for buying pullbacks. As long as the pullbacks do not develop extreme countertrend momentum (e.g., make a significant new momentum low reading on the MACD), they should be buyable for at least an attempt at making new highs. The reverse is true for shorting into pops. With some experience, it is not difficult to make these trades with some degree of reliability, but every piece of the puzzle matters: the relative strength measure, the frequency of evaluation/rebalancing, the actual execution triggers, whether you are executing off simple charts or spread charts, and your intended exit strategy. Change one part, and the others will have to adjust as well, as there is usually a fairly small sweet spot where everything comes together and the system works reliably. As long as you understand the core concepts, do your homework, and understand how these concepts play out in your chosen market, you can build a strong trading program around these ideas.

It is, however, very important to have a realistic sense of how these ideas work, rather than trying to trade an idealized model that has a loose connection with reality. Realize that relative strength leaders are usually a large group, and there is generally rotation within the group. In the case of stocks, there may be 50 to 150 different names vying for leadership on the rallies. In the case of the commodity metals, there may be only four to 10 names in the sector, but relative strength may pass between two or three of those regularly. The point is that you cannot say that "XYZ is the market leader" and then abandon XYZ the first time you notice another name has edged XYZ off the very top of list. In addition to its actual ranking in any quantitative scheme you develop, the trading patterns and integrity of trends in the leaders are also important considerations. Last, consider the actual instruments you will use for execution. A relative strength portfolio allocation model could focus on broad sectors or asset classes, though it may make little sense to consider relative strength between, for instance, equities and real estate. Shorter-term traders will probably find better success with individual stocks or futures contracts, but this analysis may be enhanced with an awareness of shifting relative strength in those broad sectors.

One of the recurring themes of this book has been that simplistic technical patterns, taken out of context, have very limited utility. The only reliable patterns are those that are truly driven by large-scale institutional buying and selling pressure, and technical traders have an edge only in the presence of a real buying and selling imbalance. The logical question is: how do we know when such an imbalance exists? Relative strength points the way to one possible answer: using a relative strength screen as the first step in a technical process that then focuses on individual patterns will usually have the trader focused on markets that are, by definition, experiencing an imbalance of buying pressure. Again, there is no holy grail, but this combination of well-researched technical patterns in a relative strength context creates opportunities for synergy and for a trading plan in which the whole truly is greater than the sum of the parts.

CHAPTER 8

Trade Management

Choices are the hinges of destiny.

—Pythagoras

T rade management is what you do after you get into the trade. These decisions are complicated because they deal both with mathematical realities and with trader psychology. One thing that you'll often hear is that it's your responsibility, as the trader, to find your own right way to trade. The implication is that basically anything works; you just have to make some choices from the giant menu of possibilities, experiment until they feel right, and then stick with them. There is some truth here, in that any rule set must be matched to the trader's personality and psychological makeup, but there is also a very important point that goes unsaid: it is exceedingly difficult to find an edge in the market. You must understand the impact of every decision and every adjustment.

Consider the simple case of a specific trading pattern that has an edge in predicting a small directional movement over the next few bars. Traders A and B decide to trade this pattern, but they both realize the importance of adapting it to their personalities. Let's simplify the problem they face, and consider only the choices in exiting at a profit and exiting at a loss, and furthermore restrict the options for those two conditions to "large" and "small." If we were trading our theoretical random walk market, these choices would not matter because the probability of winning would adjust to maintain zero expectancy (remember, no edge is ever possible in a random walk market), but the situation is different if the trading signal actually has predictive value in real markets—trading signals that have predictive value generally see that value limited to a specific time horizon and magnitude. This is fairly intuitive. No one would expect a signal on an intraday time frame to reliably have an impact many months out. In this theoretical example, assume that the signal is good for only a few bars following the entry.

Trader A finds that a combination of a rather wide stop and a fairly tight profit target works for him in trading this pattern. The losses are infrequent but large, and he appreciates the psychological reinforcement of having long strings of winners, so this strategy works for him. Trader B knows from past experience with other patterns that she has a different approach to trading. She prefers to have a few large winners, and doesn't care so much about having a high win rate. She is perfectly comfortable sitting through many small losses, knowing that the gains from the large but infrequent wins will more than cover those losses. However, she is about to make a serious mistake. Though this approach has worked well her with other types of systems (e.g., longer-term trend following), the signal under consideration in this example has predictive value for only a few bars. If she tries to squeeze large profits out of this pattern by setting a large profit target, it is unlikely to work because the signal has no power that far out; the market degenerates into random noise a few bars after each occurrence of the signal—the profit target must respect this reality.

Many traders struggle because they do not understand that these choices matter. They wrongly assume that they can make any decision regarding stop, target, and position management, and, as long as they follow a disciplined plan, they will make money. You must understand the nature of the patterns you are trading. Some, like the pattern in this example, require very close targets and would allow for discretion on the stop. Others might require both large stops and large targets. Consider the case of a long-term signal that has predictive value many weeks to months after the signal event, but is essentially random in the time period immediately following the signal. A tight stop or target would be hit in this random noise. In addition, markets do have a baseline level of random noise on any time frame. Stops must be set outside that noise level or they will be hit by normal, random fluctuations. In most trading methods, there is a fairly small sweet spot or combination of parameters across which the system will be profitable. If you tinker with or change any part, there may be unintended consequences. Systems can and should be adapted for each trader, but this work requires careful thought and testing; it cannot be done haphazardly.

PLACING THE INITIAL STOP

The placement of the initial stop is very important. First, it sets the ultimate risk point on the trade and so removes much of the emotion from the trade process. This point is also important because many traders will use this risk to set the trade size in a risk management/position sizing plan (see Chapter 9). From the outset, consider that there is an unavoidable trade-off between near and far stops. Closer stops allow larger positions, which, of course, means larger profits on winning trades, while farther stops will result in a higher probability of a win on a smaller position size. All of this is fairly intuitive, but it leaves an important question unanswered: where do we actually place these stops? There is no one right answer, but here are several common solutions to the problem, some better than others.

Fixed-Percentage Stops

Old-school stock traders, in particular, tend to do this: simply get into a position and give it 10 percent or 20 percent price movement against you. There is one good thing to say about this approach: it does define a fixed and clear hard loss limit. It is far better to have one, even if it is a not very well-thought-out level, than to have none at all. However, using the same fixed percentage across different markets is not optimal. Most importantly, different markets trade with very different volatility levels. For instance, most actively traded stocks trade with an average daily range that is a little under 3 percent of their stock price (based on 500 active stocks as of April 1, 2011), but many have a much larger average range that is 9 percent or more of their underlying price. Using a 10 percent stop on two markets, one with 9 percent average daily range and one with 3 percent average daily range, will give very different results; for the first market, a 10 percent stop is within the potential noise level of a single trading day so probably does not represent an intelligent stop point. Using a fixed-percentage stop is better than no stop at all, but not that much better.

Volatility-Based Stops

A simple refinement would be to use a percentage stop that is based on some measure of the market's volatility. For instance, a trader might use a stop that was N times a market's average daily range, or N times a single-day one standard deviation move. Stops for volatile markets will naturally be much farther away from the entry price, so position sizes will be smaller in volatile markets; stops calculated in this way automatically respect the natural swings of each individual market. These can be useful stops for discretionary traders, and often are ideal initial stops for algorithmic trading systems.

Market Structure

A third approach is to set the stops based on the structure of the market itself. This is definitely an art, and it can be difficult to learn, especially for the newer trader. It is not possible to reduce this to a set of simple rules, but here are some guidelines:

- The stop placement is determined by the location of pivot points. If entering a position with the short-term momentum, you do not want to see the market take out the closest pivot low (the solid straight line in Figure 8.1). It is also possible to step back to the penultimate pivot in many cases (the dotted line stop in Figure 8.1), but with the trade-off of a much smaller position size.
- In general, it usually makes sense to set fairly wide initial stops. As a rough guideline, it would be very unusual to set an initial stop that is less than two Average True Ranges (ATRs) from the current price, and the initial stop may sometimes be more than four ATRs away from the current price. (You may choose to actually calculate

FIGURE 8.1 Two Stop Levels for a Long Position Entered on the Last Candle of the Chart

the ATR, but it is also possible to judge it from a visual inspection of the chart for this purpose.)

- If buying against a sloppy support area with many shadows below, the only stop that makes sense is beyond the most extreme low. Furthermore, it is entirely possible that the stop will be hit on a drop to an even more extreme low. If this happens and you are stopped out of the position on a fakeout, it is necessary to rebuy with a new stop beyond the new, lowest extreme.

- In practice, if you are concerned about the particular market for some reason—for instance, an impending report or something else that could generate excessive volatility—you may want to have smaller size on the trade. One way to accomplish this is to set the initial stop farther away. This is a tool to be used only in rare, extreme cases.

There are many examples of my initial stops and subsequent trade management decisions in Chapter 10. In addition, the trade templates in Chapter 6 also feature discussions on initial stop placement for each of those patterns. These are specific examples, but the principles can be adapted to your own personality and your own trading style. The most important thing is that every trade, without exception, has a precise initial risk point defined at the time of entry. In other words, you always know where you are getting out if you are wrong, and you must always respect that level.

SETTING PRICE TARGETS

To set or not to set price targets, that is the question. Many traders prefer to not set price targets in an effort to follow the maxim "let your winners run." Other traders make the cogent argument that fixed profit targets are easy to test in the context of a trading system, and that smaller profits can be taken with a degree of regularity. Compared to the multiple trade management decisions that may go into an open-ended trade, it is relatively easy to quantify and test a system with fixed profit targets and fixed stops, and such a system may be amenable to an optimized sizing strategy. There is value in both of these perspectives, and some traders even combine the two by taking partial profits at a set target and holding the remainder of the position for a larger move.

In general, there are two approaches to getting out of profitable trades: with or against the trend of the trade. With-trend exits (i.e., selling into strength or covering into weakness) are usually done via limit orders and are often done at preset targets. Countertrend exits are usually done after some kind of give-back rule is activated and the trade has retreated from its maximum profit point. Let's consider a few variations of profit-taking strategies.

Fixed Profits at Risk Multiples

If the initial risk is always known at the time of trade entry, we can use multiples of that risk for profit targets. This is my personal approach: I usually exit between 25 and 33 percent of the position on a limit order at a profit equal to my initial risk in the trade. For instance, if I am buying a $50 stock with a $45 stop and my position sizing rules have me buying 10,000 shares, I will offer out between 2,500 and 3,000 of those shares at $55. As a matter of discipline, this order is entered as soon as the entry order is filled, and is left working *good till canceled (GTC)* in all sessions. From a practical standpoint, you usually do not want to work *stop orders* in premarket and postmarket hours, as they can be hit by strange off-market orders in those illiquid environments, but this is actually a *benefit* to your profit-taking orders. As much as possible, you want these profit-taking limit orders to be working in overnight, thin markets, because sometimes other traders will make mistakes and you should be happy to provide liquidity to them at these spots.

In addition, orders are prioritized in most electronic trading books in the order in which they are received. If there are 25,000 shares bid at a price and you join the bid for 500 shares, you will not be filled until 25,500 shares print at that price. However, modern order books have a tremendous amount of cancel-and-replace activity due to the presence of high-frequency electronic trading algorithms. Most of those 25,000 shares might be canceled and replaced thousands of times each minute. If you put a real order into the book (one that you do not intend to cancel), it will percolate to the top of queue as other orders are canceled and replaced. This is why it is so important to get your orders in as soon as possible. Even with daytrades, you will often find yourself filled first at prices if your orders have been in the book awhile—it is completely possible that 1,000 shares print at the high of the day, and all 1,000 of them will be yours if your order has been in the book for a couple of hours.

This concept can be extended to taking profits at two or three times your initial risk. This is very much a matter of personal preference, but I also make it a point to be down to between one-third to half my initial size at two times my initial risk, and then manage the remainder according to a different set of rules. Whatever you decide to do, first test it over a large set of trades to make sure it makes sense and that it works with your market selection and entry criteria. Once you have settled on a plan, be consistent. You may have multiple rules and qualifying conditions, but, within those rules, you must be absolutely, perfectly consistent. The market is random enough; don't make your results more volatile by adding random decisions to your process.

Market Structure Targets

A good argument can be made for putting profit targets at visible points in the market. You should generally assume that your limit order will have to be traded through to be filled. In other words, a limit to sell at $10.00 will certainly not be filled if the highest price is $9.99, and, in backtesting, you should assume it will not be filled even if a lot of volume trades at $10.00. However, in most electronic markets, you are guaranteed to be filled if price trades to $10.01, as this cannot happen until all liquidity (including your limit order) is taken at $10.00. Because of this, it makes sense to place your limits slightly inside the actual point in the market; if there is clearly visible support at $10.00 and resistance at $20.00, you would place a limit to buy above $10.00 (perhaps between $10.01 and $10.15, depending on the market and your time frame) and a limit to sell somewhere below $20.00. If you are a daytrader looking to take profits at the high of the day, your profit-taking order should be a few cents or ticks below the high. It rarely makes sense to put your orders on the other side of a visible chart point, unless you are counting on extra volatility from stop orders being hit in those areas. This is an obvious but often-overlooked point, and is something to consider if you tend to trade around those chart patterns.

It is not possible to create a comprehensive list of every chart structure that may provide a reasonable profit target, nor is it necessary to do so. Many are obvious: visible support or resistance; visible support or resistance on a higher time frame; big highs and lows like important 52-week highs and lows for stocks or contract highs and lows for commodities; high and low of the session for intraday trades; long shadows of accumulation below ranges or distribution above; and so on. In most cases, it is enough to be aware of the market structure as delineated by the pivot highs and lows of the swings. Don't over think. If you normally take profits at risk multiples and find yourself entering an order to buy or sell beyond one of these visible points, it probably makes sense to tighten the orders up a little bit and bring them inside the swings. This will slightly reduce your profit (though, theoretically, the probability shift will compensate), but there is no sense learning to read market structure if you don't make good use of the information it is giving you.

Trailing Stops

Many traders use some type of trailing stop approach to winning trades. Though there are many variations on this concept, they all define stop levels that move with the trade according to some rule set. They may adjust very infrequently according to simple rules. For instance, a trader taking profits at 1× the initial risk on the trade might then move the stop for the remainder of the position to a higher price, effectively locking in a profit on the trade. There are also many more complex, algorithmic rules for trailing stops that adapt to market conditions as the trade develops. Let's look at some variations of these rules.

Moving Averages and Trend Lines   Many traders will get into a trending trade and will then stop out when price touches or, in some cases, closes below a moving average. Traders often use 100-, 50-, or 20-period moving averages, but we have to ask: why not 103, 98, 49, or 17 periods? Why not 53? The choice of which moving average to use is arbitrary, and so the moving averages in general are arbitrary. Using a moving average for a stop is better than having no plan at all, but moving averages usually make poor choices for stop levels.

Another commonly used plan is a stop below an important trend line. There is some logic to this idea, but there are also some serious flaws. First, trend lines are unavoidably arbitrary; two traders will often draw two different trend lines on the same chart. This in itself does not compromise the validity of the tool, but the bigger problem is that trend lines are not suitable stop levels. It is extremely common to see a good trend line violated, and then to see price immediately recover. Some of the best entries into patterns occur when these trend line breaks are reversed, so why choose a stop plan that puts you on the wrong side of that tendency? If you want to use a trend line as a trailing stop, it might make sense to require significant price action under the trend line. How you define significant price action is up to you: multiple closes, consolidation under, multiple legs under, are all possibilities, but they all require price movement and leave the position open to larger losses. Again, there are better tools for trailing stops.

Wilder's Parabolic SAR and LeBeau's Chandelier Stop   Welles Wilder created a trading system he called *Parabolic Stop and Reverse (SAR)* in his 1978 *New Concepts in Technical Trading Systems*. The Parabolic, as it is usually called, was originally intended to be a complete trading system designed to keep traders always in the market, flipping their bias from long to short as the trend changed. It works by identifying the most extreme trend point (highest point in an uptrend or lowest point in a downtrend), and then placing a stop a certain distance from that extreme point. Each day, the stop is moved closer to that extreme point by an amount called the *acceleration factor*; this factor also increases every day so the stop is ratcheted in at an ever-increasing rate. If the market trends strongly, the Parabolic stop level will trail behind, but if the market reverses or goes flat, the acceleration factor will usually force a trend change indication very quickly. Originally, if this stop level was reached, the trend was deemed to have changed and you were also supposed to flip your position. Figure 8.2 shows an example of the Parabolic applied to a continuous chart of oat futures.

Though it is difficult to trade the Parabolic as a stand-alone system in the always-in context that was originally intended, it can be an extremely useful tool for discretionary traders who can turn to the Parabolic for trailing stop levels in trending markets. It is possible to initiate a position, take your first partial profit (if that is in your trading plan), and then use the Parabolic's levels as trailing stops. When the stop level is hit, exit the position but do not flip. The usual caveat applies: it is a mistake to use any trading tool that you do not completely understand. If you are going to use the Parabolic, do whatever you need to internalize its calculations. If calculating it by hand or in a spreadsheet helps,

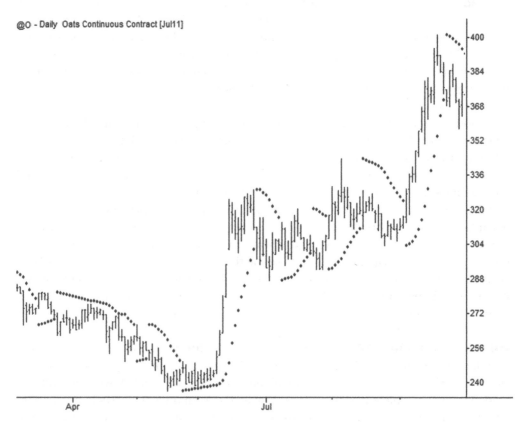

FIGURE 8.2 The Parabolic System Applied to Oat Futures

do so. I would highly recommend some kind of test environment where you can apply it to artificial data series you create (see Chapter 7) so that you can see how it reacts to every imaginable market situation.

A similar idea is found in Chuck LeBeau's *chandelier stop*, which basically hangs a stop a fixed number of ATRs from the extreme point of a trend, creating a stop level that is comceptually similar to the Parabolic without the acceleration factor. One of the problems with using the Parabolic on a strict, systematic basis is that the acceleration factor is constantly moving the stop closer to the market, even when there is no trend at all. While this is desirable behavior in some contexts, it also results in multiple flips from long to short while the market is chopping sideways. The chandelier exit usually gives the trade more room, which, though it may result in larger losses, will also allow you to stay in trades at the beginning of trends. Conversely, in mature trends the Parabolic will usually tighten stops dramatically compared to the chandelier stop, which may help to protect profits in open trades.

Other Price Action/Market Structure Stops It is also possible to use references to price action and market structure for trailing stop points. For instance, a simple plan might be to stop out of an uptrending market on the first down close, at the lowest low of three days ago, or on two consecutive downward closes. If you are going to explore these, also consider stops that limit your loss on any one day, perhaps stopping out a certain ATR multiple from the previous day's high, low, or closing values, and be certain that you understand the statistical tendencies supporting your stop plan. For instance, all other things being equal, stopping out after three consecutive downward closes in stocks would be a bad plan because the market is usually primed for a bounce at that point. Whatever you choose to do, it should be subjected to a battery of statistical tests if possible, and backtested by hand (so that you see each detail of each trade) on at least several hundred trades.

Any of these stops will work well in strongly trending markets, but there is an important point here—*anything* will work well on carefully chosen examples in strongly trending markets. If you do research and backtesting on trailing stop methodologies applied to strongly trending markets, you are preselecting the ideal environments for those stops, and they will all usually look fantastic. In actual trading, results will often fall short.

Another thing to consider is that it is possible to switch to these types of stops once you have used other techniques to enter and to manage the initial stages of a trade, but, at that point, we need to ask if these stops really add anything at all. The answer will be different for different traders at different stages of their development. My experience is that good discretionary traders will outperform any rule-based trailing stop methodology over a large set of trades. There will be exceptions, but discretionary traders will know when to stop out of trades before the rule-based level is reached, or will also know that sometimes they should let the trailing stop's level break without actually exiting the trade. Some discretionary traders will use a tool such as the Parabolic as a reference, incorporating it into the trade management process in various ways.

ACTIVE MANAGEMENT

Many trading systems are designed with fixed profit targets and loss limits that are entered at the time of the trade and not modified until one is hit and the other is canceled, and others use various combinations of dynamic levels calculated from tools like the Parabolic SAR. These are certainly valid approaches to trade management, but most discretionary traders will gravitate toward a more active style that allows them to make decisions while the trade is underway. This is, in fact, one of the main reasons for being a discretionary trader, but it raises some questions. First, are we adding value through this interaction? Psychological studies have shown that people performing a task with a random reward falsely attribute more of their results to their skill if they have more chances to interact with the process. The designers of slot machines and rub-off lottery tickets know this very well, but could the same thing apply to trading? Could traders also be vulnerable to this error? Could they develop a false sense of their ability if they can change indicator settings, look at different markets, and make many small adjustments to their trades?

The second important issue to consider is that decision making under pressure is difficult, and everyone is vulnerable to making mistakes. Even experienced traders struggle under the pressure of real-time position management; for the new trader, the task is almost impossible. The extreme highs and lows in any market are driven by the emotions of market participants—the last buyer finally dumps his position at the lows, or the last, stubborn short gives up and covers in desperation right at the highs. This last buyer or last seller phenomenon is one of the most important psychological drivers of price at extremes; one reason people trade automated or fixed systems is to avoid the possibility of participating in those errors. Anyone who has traded for even a short period of time invariably marvels at how many times their on-the-fly execution decisions were made at the worst possible point in the market. There is no possible way to completely avoid these kinds of mistakes, but, if you decide to adjust and actively manage positions, having a clear plan will reduce your vulnerability to making emotional mistakes under pressure.

Choices: Enter All at Once or Scale In?

Once you have determined the size to trade, you have the choice of entering the position all at once or in several pieces. There are times when that choice is constrained by market conditions or the type of trade setup. For instance, an order may be so large or the market so thin that it would be impossible to enter the whole position at one time. There are also kinds of trade entries—for instance, *scaling in* in anticipation of mean reversion—that may require multiple entries to be effective. The decision to scale in or enter all at once will depend as much on the type of trade signal as on the trader's inclination. There are many cases where it may make sense to buy into a decline or to short into a rally in a series of small trades, but there it is important to monitor your risk closely. It is very easy to scale into a trade, to keep scaling in, and to end up with more size and a larger loss than you had originally planned. This is unacceptable and dangerous. These larger-than-expected losses will add up, with the possibility of a catastrophic loss looming around the corner as well. (Remember, the fact that you can scale into the trade in the first place means that the market is moving the *wrong way*.) First, define an absolute dollar amount you want to risk on the trade. Next, define the ultimate drop-dead stop in the market past which you will not hold the trade, and then carefully track your size and average price so that you know, at all times, what the impact of a loss at that ultimate stop level will be.

Taking Partial Profits

Taking partial profits as the trade moves in your favor can make good sense; you are paying yourself as the market proves your trade idea correct. There is an unavoidable trade-off: taking partial profits will mean that you do not have your full size on for the trades that become big winners, so the trade-off is consistency at the expense of larger, but less frequent, wins. In the context of a well-planned trading program, either approach is viable. Some traders feel the need for activity, and will start exiting part of their positions without any plan soon after entry. If this is not well thought out, what usually happens is that these early exits simply remove some of the edge from winning trades, as the natural psychological tendency will be to lock in some profits, however small, on winners. In addition, short-term traders on all time frames are especially vulnerable to making executions in the noise level of the market. While they may believe that they are contributing something of value to the trade, this is often not true. Make sure that your partial profits are actually adding to the bottom line.

Taking Partial Losses

Another possibility is to take partial losses as the trade moves against you to reduce the size of the final loss if the trade hits your stop point. There are a few things to consider here; the same concern with making executions in the noise level of the market applies. If you are entering a $50.00 stock with an ATR of $2.00 on the daily chart, making decisions when you are up or down $0.25 on the trade probably does not make sense. More importantly, partial exits on either the profit or loss side of the entry will have the effect of anchoring the profit and loss (P&L) to that side. In the case of partial profits, this is what we are trying to accomplish, but taking partial losses may work against us.

One useful tool for visualizing this is to imagine two lines moving in time: one is the market you are trading, and the second is your P&L. If you have your full size on, the P&L line will track the market exactly; if you have half size on, then the line will move half as fast (change half as much) as the market, either up or down, and this pattern continues for different amounts of leverage. Imagine entering a full-size position, and then the market swings down to a loss, where you exit part of your position. The market

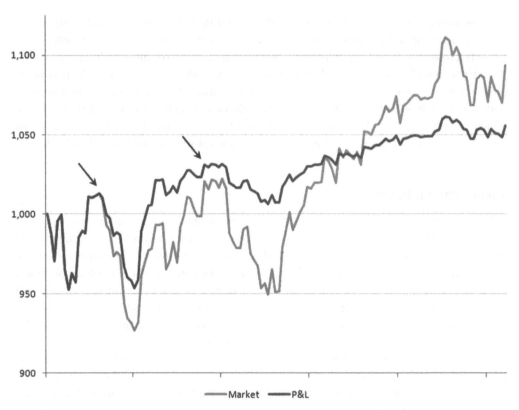

FIGURE 8.3 Partial Exits (Marked with Arrows) at Two Optimal Points Early in the Trade

turns back up, but your P&L line now lags the market because you sold some of your position at a small loss, in effect locking in that loss.

Figures 8.3 and 8.4 show two scenarios of a theoretical P&L with partial exits compared to the underlying market they are tracking. Both traders entered at the left edge of the chart with full trading size, but took partial exits of one-third of their initial position at two points early in the trade. The trader in Figure 8.3 obviously had a working crystal ball, because he knew to take his exits at the high points of the early swings. Conversely, the trader in Figure 8.4 made the worst possible decisions, and took off one-third of his position at the exact low points. The market eventually went higher, and both traders should have profited, but notice that partial profits taken on either side of the line that defines the entry price will tend to anchor the P&L on that side of the line. Locking in losses makes it very difficult to ever recover those losses. If you are ever considering taking partial exits at a loss, it may make sense to simply exit the entire position at a small loss rather than deleveraging your P&L in the loss space. Use this tool to visualize various scenarios and their impact on your bottom line, and carefully consider the impact of these partial exits at a loss.

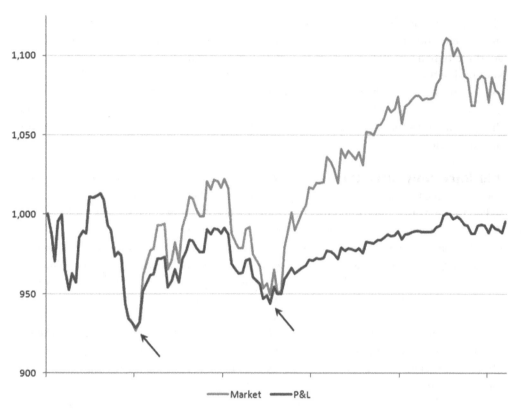

FIGURE 8.4 The Same Market, with Partial Exits at the Two Worst Points Early in the Trade

Adding to Existing Trades

There are a few different schools of thought on whether to add to existing trades. Be sure to separate these additions from the case of a normal, planned trade entry done in pieces. The normal scaling-in entry (if that is in your trading plan) is usually done as the trade moves against you, and with the idea of accumulating a maximum intended position size against a clear risk level. These additions are different from additions that come *after* the initial entry has already reached its maximum size, and they may or may not come after partial profits have been taken. In some cases, you may add to a full-size trade and so have on two or more times your expected exposure. In other cases, you may book partial profits (or losses) on an existing trade, and then add back only enough size to get back to your initial trading size and risk. There are too many possibilities here to consider every possible scenario, but let's consider some arguments for and against a few scenarios.

Never Add to an Existing Trade   Some trading systems are designed to simply enter on a set of criteria and exit on another set of criteria. In these systems, all we are playing for is the slight statistical edge that may come from the rule set, and some of these conditions have fairly limited influence with respect to both time (i.e., they are good for only a few bars) and price (small price movements). A trader working with a system like this, or with a discretionary approach that is similar, will find that adding to existing trades is usually a mistake because the statistical edge identified by the condition is usually strongest right at the entry point. Once again, note that this is not the same thing as an entry that requires scaling in to reach full size as the market moves against the entry price.

Add Back Only After Partial Exits   As another example, consider a trader who gets into a trade, takes half of it off at a 1X profit (where X is the initial dollar amount risked on the trade) and then finds the trade back at the entry price. This trader can add the half she already exited back to the trade; a stop-out at the initial stop point will now be only a half-sized loss because of the offsetting win on half the initial position. A trader establishing a position in an accumulation area could go through a process of selling part of her exposure at the top of the range and bidding to buy it back at the bottom, perhaps several times before the eventual breakout of the range. In effect, this trader is building up a profit cushion as the market oscillates in the range before the breakout. If she has misread the market, or if the trade doesn't work for any reason, her ultimate loss will be cushioned or even eliminated by the profits made in the range. There is always a trade-off, and in this specific scenario, if the market does eventually break out of the top of the range, the trader will have on less than full size because she was selling some of the position at the top of the range. This trader will be penalized on the clean, easy trade that breaks immediately out of the top of the range with no oscillations, but these trades are the exception rather than the rule.

Another case to consider is where a trader gets lucky and catches a well-trending market that extends for many trend legs after the entry. Though this is not common, there are opportunities to reap truly outsized profits from extended trends with the proper plan, so it is worth spending some time thinking about how to build positions in these trends while also managing the downside. One very good plan is to enter a full position and take partial profits at the appropriate targets. (For simplicity's sake, assume half the position is exited at a profit target.) Then, when another setup in the direction of the trend emerges, this entry is also taken on full size, so now the trader is holding a net position equal to 1.5 times the initial trading size. At the appropriate target for that trade (the second entry), half of that trade is exited, leaving a full-sized position, essentially for free, with locked-in profits. This can be repeated, trading the same size and gradually accumulating a larger, more or less risk-free position as the trend expands. Avoid the temptation to increase size on later entries—growing profits can lead to overconfidence, which is especially dangerous near the end of trends, where volatility can dramatically expand.

Add Without Taking Partial Exits   The classic *pyramiding plans* fall under this category; accumulated profits from one tier are used to fund the next tier. *Reverse* *pyramid* plans, for instance starting with one unit, next buying two, then four, eight, 16, and so on, are used in a lot of marketing literature for trading methods and systems; if you want to turn $2,000 into $2,000,000 in one, glorious trade, this is pretty much the only way to do it. It is possible to find historical examples of trends and show that, if you had pyramided aggressively and perfectly, you could have eventually ended up essentially cornering the market in some commodity or owning most of the float in a stock, even starting with a very small initial investment.

By this point in this book, we probably do not need to point out the other side, which is that your probability of success is vanishingly small. The problem with reverse pyramid plans is that the position is top-heavy and becomes increasingly so as more contracts are added. When you start with one unit and end up adding 20 at higher prices, it takes only a very small dip in the market to completely wipe out all accumulated profits since the average price on the position is so high. As you also know, extended trends tend to become more volatile, so reverse pyramid plans usually end up blowing out accounts or, in the case of leveraged accounts, even going significantly negative.

In the exceedingly unlikely chance that you do get lucky with a reverse pyramid plan, there is something else to consider—you would be totally unprepared for and unable to deal with the psychological pressures of trading the size dictated by the pyramid. Imagine you are a one-unit trader with a $20,000 trading account, and you're comfortable risking maybe $500 per trade. If you happen to catch a good trade and pyramid up to 50 units, your average daily swings could be hundreds of thousands of dollars. How likely are you to make good decisions under that kind of pressure? These reverse pyramid strategies have payoff structures very close to a lottery ticket, which is probably the right way to think of them—just imagine you are buying a lottery ticket equal to your full account value. They are not acceptable, professional trading plans.

Pyramiding should not be dismissed out of hand, however; there is another way. *Proper pyramids*, those that have the largest size at the beginning of the campaign, can be valuable in some situations. In a proper pyramid, the trader adds successively smaller units as the trend progresses. (For instance, you might start with 20 units, and add 16, and next add 12.) A pyramid built this way keeps its average price closer to the base, closer to the first units; it is not top-heavy so traders can weather volatility near the end of the trend better. There are many successful trend followers who use some variation of this plan, but it can cause some problems in conjunction with certain entry techniques and other trade management plans. In the worst case, it basically adds another random element to the risk and trade sizing equation. These additions almost always result in a more volatile bottom line, so make sure that the additional upside compensates on a risk-adjusted basis.

If you do decide to pyramid, size up, or aggressively add to trades when you know you are right, make sure you are actually adding value to your overall P&L. These are important questions that should be considered. You have to ask whether it makes sense to add to trades in the first place. Many traders do not consider this question in building their trading plan, but make a hasty decision the first time they are faced with an extended and very profitable trade. Without a good plan, that decision is likely to completely destroy the profit in that particular trade, and perhaps to even do more damage to the trading account. If you do decide that adding makes sense, then you need to consider exactly how to do it. There are few absolutes in trading, but it is very difficult to imagine a reverse pyramid plan that actually makes sense. With that possibility off the table, there are several other variations of adding size to trades that can be explored. From a practical trade management standpoint, the last thing to consider is whether the additions will be considered completely new trades so that each individual trade preserves its own entry and management rules, or you choose to think of them as one combined position with an average price equal to the cost basis of the group. The answers to these questions will depend on your trading style and your chosen approach to the markets.

Time Stops

Few technical traders get into a position with the plan of the market simply staying at their entry price. (The obvious exception would be option spreads or other derivatives that are short volatility.) The choice to actually enter a trade is usually made because we believe that an imbalance exists in the market and that this imbalance should cause a price movement within a short time period. If this movement does not happen quickly, it often suggests that much of the edge has gone out of the trade, and we are basically flipping a coin. This is why time stops can make sense. There are many variations of these rules, but they basically say that if a trade does not hit some kind of predetermined profit limit within a certain time, the trade will be exited after that time window expires. Time stops will also cut out some winning trades. This is unavoidable, but, even with the loss of some winners, the end result could still be a net gain to the bottom line. In addition, many traders find that their best trades work right away; this is a reflection of certain setups in certain markets and may not generalize to all situations. For these traders, even if a trade does end up being profitable after an extended flat period at the beginning, the resulting trade is often less energetic and less profitable than the ones that worked immediately, so a time stop will still make sense.

There are several choices for how to actually execute time stops. The obvious choice is to simply exit at the market once the time window expires. Another choice that is not often considered is to tighten the stop very close to current market prices, moving it closer as time goes on in a similar fashion to the movement of the Parabolic SAR's stop levels. This greatly reduces the open risk in the trade, though it does leave the position vulnerable to a large loss if an unexpected event causes an overnight gap. Furthermore, after reducing the risk, this technique leaves the possibility of gains intact if the market does move in the intended direction. This is probably not a technique for the newer trader who has not learned to deal fully with the emotions of trading and who would probably be better off with a simpler rule set. For the more advanced trader, this technique can offer a very attractive compromise between limiting risk in flat trades and still preserving the opportunity to profit from trades that take a while to develop. This is one of the most underutilized techniques available to the self-directed discretionary trader.

Tightening Stops

At first glance, it would seem that tightening stops is a simple and effective way to reduce risk in existing trades. However, the risk/reward/probability matrix always applies in all situations and to every action the trader makes. Inevitably, tightening stops reduces the probability of the trade working out, as a tighter stop is always more likely to be hit than a wider stop. Make sure that you are moving stops in response to developing market structure and to the shifting probabilities of the scenario, rather than in response to your own emotions or desires to avoid losses.

There is a trade-off between staying in a trade for the bigger move, which requires looser stops, and being unwilling to give back much profit with tighter stops. Traders using very loose stops (far from current market prices) have a much higher probability of staying in the trade and not getting shaken out by noise, but they must also be willing to give back large percentages of open profits. We often say "weak-hand longs" or "weak shorts" in a pejorative sense, but there are times when a smart trader will actively *choose* to be the weak hand. There are times when we want to be taken out of a trade by a very small adverse move, for instance when taking profits in an overextended trend or a parabolic blow-off.

Trade Reaches a Risk Multiple Target For many technical traders, once the trade has made a significant move into the profit zone, it rarely makes sense to take a full-sized loss on the trade. Traders can use their initial risk level as a reference point, projected at an equivalent distance on the other side of the entry, to define a significant move for the trade. For instance, assume you enter a long position in a $50.00 market with a $2.50 stop at $47.50. When the market reaches $52.50, it may make sense to tighten the stop to just under your entry point or even higher. If the initial stop was set correctly for the volatility level of the market, once the trade moves an equivalent distance in the other direction, the trade is working. At that point, the pattern is playing out as expected, and a failure from that level usually suggests a larger-scale failure—there is no need to take a full-sized loss on a trade in this situation.

Another scenario applies to traders who take profits at specific multiples of that initial risk (e.g., taking profits at 2X). Once this profit target is hit, it usually makes sense to tighten the stop on the remainder of the trade to the entry price, essentially working a breakeven stop on the rest of the trade. The same logic applies here: the trade worked in that it was able to reach the first profit target, so it makes sense to eliminate the open risk on the trade. Move the stop to a point where a stop-out will, at worst, result in a breakeven trade, as the loss on the open portion will be offset by the already locked-in gains on the closed portion. Be clear: this solution may not be the right fit for every trading style, but short-term swing traders will find that a plan like this will significantly reduce the volatility of their returns.

Sharp Momentum Develops Sometimes a trend will accelerate into a parabolic run with very sharp momentum. This is a somewhat rare but glorious outcome, and one that

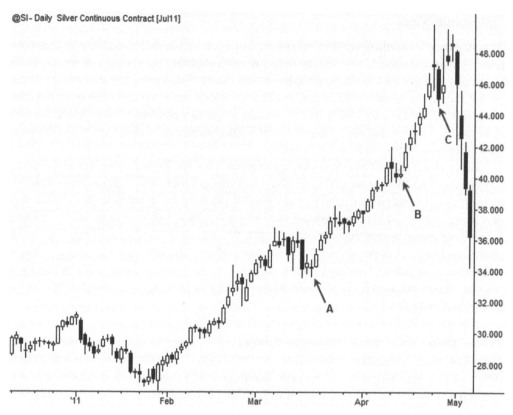

FIGURE 8.5   A Stop Under the Previous Day's Low Is Appropriate in a Parabolic, Runaway Trend

often justifies working very tight stops. Figure 8.5 shows a daily chart of Silver futures, which, after an already extended uptrend, broke into a parabolic expansion. A trader holding a long position in a runaway trend like this could have worked a stop each day below the previous day's lows. In this example, assume that the trade was entered somewhere around A on the chart; if you were working a stop under the previous day's low, it would not have been hit until the point marked C, the day after the extreme high of the run-up. This is a very aggressive stop technique that crosses the line into a profit-taking exit. Basically you are asking for the market to take you out of the position with a slight downtick so you can book the profit, but you are also leaving yourself open to continued upside in the unlikely event the market extends further. You *want* your stop to be hit in this case. Parabolic trends are a special example because they often carry very high risk of sharp reversals from climax points. Traders who are fortunate enough to be holding heavy exposure into such a move can become emotional and excited as they extrapolate the move into infinity, and this time of extreme emotion often results in very poor decisions. Use tight stops on at least part of the position to remove the emotional component from the decision process in parabolic trends.

The parabolic trend is an unusual and dramatic example, but even normal trends can often justify fairly tight stops, depending on the trader's plan and personality. Swing traders, who are clearly playing for only one swing with minimal giveback, will work much tighter stops than traders who plan to hold for the longer trend, if it should develop. Price action in trends is more directional and more predictable than price action in ranges, so we can get away with stops much closer to the market if the goal is to protect open profits. For example, in an uptrend, a tight stop could be trailed under the highest pivot low of the trend. Slightly wider stops could go under the second-highest pivot low, probably working both of these stops on a close-only basis to avoid the possibility of selling into a fake dropout. It is also worth considering that if you are stopped out by an intraday move that reverses on close, it may make sense to reenter the position with a stop under the new extreme.

It Is Difficult to Tighten Stops Against a Range   If it is easy to work tight stops in trends, it is much more difficult to work tight stops in consolidation areas. These areas tend to be much more random, and one of the dominant features of these structures is that they have large spikes outside the range. Volume and liquidity tend to be lower in these areas, reflecting the generally reduced trading interest, so medium-sized orders can have a very large impact on prices. Be aware that tightening stops on a trade in consolidation is usually effectively a time stop and a conscious decision to work toward being taken out of the trade. This is often justified, but if it is not what you are trying to accomplish, it may make sense to leave stops close to the initial risk point while the market is ranging. Once momentum and a new trend develop in the trade's favor, the stop can be significantly tightened in the new trending environment.

Widening Stops

The rules for this technique can be simplified to one word: don't. Most traders will be better off if they have a simple rule that says they will never move a stop in the direction of risk. In other words, never move a stop down in a long position or higher in a short position. For new trades, the reason is obvious: A trade is initiated against a fixed stop, and position size is calculated based on a loss at that level. If the stop is moved to allow for additional risk, then a larger than expected loss could result. Why even make rules for position sizing, initial risk, and initial stop placement if you do not intend to follow them?

I actually have a trading rule that says a stop can never be moved in the direction of risk, but there are two precisely defined exceptions to that rule. In both cases, the common factor is that the stop must remain inside the initial 1× risk parameter; this is a hard limit established at the time of trade entry that can never be violated. The exceptions are:

- When the decision to tighten the stop was clearly an error. In these cases I will move the stop back out, but not further than the day on which the error was made.

- When emerging market structure suggests the need for a slightly wider stop. Be careful because it is easy to justify moving the stop further and further away from the market as the market edges toward the stop. In my opinion, newer traders should never do this, because they do not have the experience to separate their emotional reactions from legitimate market feel.

There is actually a third, very rare case that justifies a larger stop. Imagine that you are scaling into a trade in a large move, and something happens that suggests the volatility may be even higher than expected. For instance, perhaps you are buying into a decline and then some news hits the market that causes ranges to expand. In this case, assuming you have on part of the intended position size, it may make sense to not complete your buying program, but to move the stop further away from the market. The total risk on the trade is equal to or less than the original intended risk, but the position size will be much smaller against a further stop. This is not actually an increase of risk in any way, as the total bottom line for the trade will be the risk that was initially allocated.

Managing Gaps Beyond Stops

Though many markets are moving toward round-the-clock trading, there are still cases where a market will gap open beyond a stop level. For instance, overnight news could cause a stock to open much lower, gapping under a stop on a long position. In a more dramatic example, a natural catastrophe could trigger a large shift in markets, causing many positions to gap beyond stop levels. In these cases, the initial losses on the open may be many times the intended risk on the trade. No doubt this event is a disaster, but the damage can get much worse. It is important to have a good plan that accounts for these possibilities, so that you are not put in the position of having to make emotional decisions on the fly.

There are two important factors to consider here. Understand your chosen markets' tendencies around the open. For instance, most gaps in equities are reversed; if a stock opens down, there is a good tendency for it to trade up into the gap. Second, consider the markets' tendencies in trading *off* the open print. The high or low of the day tends to be set in early trading. So, if you are holding a long position that gaps down and immediately starts trading up, it may make sense to set a new stop under the day's low to give the market a chance at recovery. However, if the market opens down and immediately presses lower, or breaks lower out of an opening range, there is a good chance that it could trend down all day. Long positions should be dumped immediately in the second scenario.

If you trade long enough, these gaps through stops *will* happen, and they will result in some stunning losses. Fortunately, you will be on the right side of some of these surprise events as well, but it is important to realize that your ability to make good decisions may be compromised in the face of very large, volatile market movement. In these cases, your best hope is to have a plan that already considered the possibilities and to follow that plan with perfect discipline.

PORTFOLIO CONSIDERATIONS

Active traders do not usually think in terms of building portfolios, but the reality is that any set of assets held at the same time in an account will behave as a portfolio. Much of the math and many of the assumptions of *modern portfolio theory (MPT)* are flawed, but investors and managers who are used to thinking in terms of portfolios usually internalize some sense of the risks and peculiar behaviors of portfolios. (MPT was created in 1952, so calling it modern is a bit of a misnomer.) Active traders may not have the same intuition, but these are important factors that can substantially alter the total risk a trader is exposed to. Anytime multiple positions are held, even for a few minutes, some of these portfolio considerations apply.

Correlated Positions

That correlated positions will tend to move together is obvious, but many people are not aware of how unstable correlations can be. Correlations between diverse and seemingly unrelated markets all tend to move toward 1.0 in times of financial stress or crisis. The traditional defense to correlation is diversification—holding many different assets with varying degrees of correlation so that losses in one asset class over a time period are cushioned by gains in another. However, long-term investors have been taught this important lesson time and time again: the supposed benefits of diversification are not there when they are most needed. An investor holding long equities, U.S. dollars, bonds, gold, crude oil, cocoa, and wheat would normally expect that some pieces of that portfolio are uncorrelated and some are usually negatively correlated. If the markets go into crisis mode, there will be periods when every asset in that portfolio loses value at the same time. In addition, correlations shift over time, both as a function of random noise and due to longer-term structural influences. *Changes* in correlations present a serious challenge to managers and investors who would build portfolios designed to weather the rough times; robust portfolio construction is a lot harder than many people think.

Short-term traders often tend to ignore correlations, assuming that whatever positions they have on are driven by price action dynamics that are unique to each of those markets. This is often true, but, when it is not, the losses can be catastrophic. Stock traders, in particular, do not have as many positions as they think. If you are an equity trader, consider the sum of the open risks in all of your positions and ask if you would take equivalent risk in a large single position in an index product. The answer, in almost all cases, will be no, but in reality, this is what you are doing. It's very simple: if the market makes a big move, your positions are going to move together. You will win or lose on the long and short sides of your book as two large blocks, regardless of what diversification you thought you had built into the equation.

For futures and forex traders, the situation is usually a little less complicated, though traders need to be aware of shifting correlations and unexpected influences in shocks.

For instance, a futures trader might expect that a portfolio of Gold futures, Sugar futures, and Wheat futures would be fairly uncorrelated, but there will be periods of time when those assets are more correlated than history would suggest. Monitor these shifting correlations from both a quantitative and a commonsense, qualitative perspective. Be clear on this: it is the *shifts* in the correlations that usually present the most danger to portfolios. Forex traders need to be aware of the obvious portfolio effects of their positions. A book that is long AUDUSD, JPYUSD, and EURUSD is very heavy on the short USD position, which may or may not be desired. The first step in wrestling with these problems is simply to become aware of them; most short-term traders do not invest significant time and energy thinking about these issues.

One practical rule set is equity-centric, and another applies to all asset classes. These are not heavily optimized rules, but they are a robust commonsense approach to managing correlated risk in an actively traded book. These are very similar to the rules I use in my own trading; you may prefer to use slightly different rules, but you *must* have rules like this in place before you begin trading.

- For equity traders, define X, the percentage of the portfolio to be risked on any one trade. Risk no more than 2X to 3X in highly correlated positions, for instance in multiple stocks in the same sector. Be aware that the correlations between all of your names, even across cyclical and defensive groups, are likely to be much higher than you expect. Furthermore, do not expect that long/short sides of your book will offset each other in a decline. Many technical traders find that their longs get hit in a sell-off, and the shorts hold steady because of the nature of the specific technical patterns being traded. Sometimes one side of the book is reduced by stop orders at the worst point, and the account suffers when the market turns. Plan for the worst.
- Risk no more than 1.5X to 2X in highly correlated groups (precious metals, petroleum products, grains, and so on for futures traders) or in currencies that share regional or economic influences. Assume that something bad could happen to the entire group and you could take a loss on that part of your book as the positions move in unison. Also be aware that the diversification effect you expect between noncorrelated parts of your book may not be there.
- The common thread here is to plan for the worst so that individual positions do not add up to an unacceptable risk to the overall portfolio.

Maximum Portfolio Risk

If you trade long enough, everything that can happen eventually will happen. It is also important to have a rule that limits the total amount of the damage that can be done to your account on any one day, assuming that every long and every short position hit their designated loss limit for that day. In reality, this may happen once every 5 or 10 years, but the psychological and financial impact of taking a 50 percent hit in a single day is irrecoverable. One way to deal with this kind of tail risk is simply to limit the total portfolio loss to a specific number, and, if that number is hit, exit all positions. This value could be an x multiple, as in total portfolio risk is 5x, or it can simply be a fixed barrier past which you do not want to lose. As you consider this number, think about the asymmetry of the gains required to recover a large loss. Too often, traders simply focus on the upside without really being aware of the risks they are assuming or the potential long-term effects of large losses. Manage the risk first and foremost, and the upside will take care of itself.

PRACTICAL ISSUES

This chapter has presented many ideas, but I hope a clear picture has emerged: There are many possibilities in how to manage trades. Ideas have to be adapted to your own personality and trading system, and not everything works. You cannot simply pick and choose random ideas, put them together, and expect good results; you must do the hard analytical work and be sure that you are crafting a rule set that really has an edge. Finding patterns to get into the market is only one small part of the picture; some traders would argue that it is one of the least important pieces. Once that is accomplished, trading size, risk, initial stop placement, and how to manage the evolving trade become very important—answers to all of these questions must be worked out in advance. In addition, the market is dynamic and will throw many surprises at traders. Field Marshal Helmuth von Moltke's statement that "no battle plan survives first contact with the enemy" is as applicable in trading as in war; experienced traders learn how to adapt and to make decisions within the framework of their rules as the trade evolves.

To make these ideas easier to apply, we need to connect the dots and consider some of the practical issues that traders will face. Many of the ideas in this section are directed to the trader holding overnight positions, but can be applied, with little modification, to traders who hold only intraday positions. Portfolio managers building portfolios and managing risk in the traditional models may also find some ideas that they can apply in their investment process as well. Newer traders should also be wary of trying to do too much at once and of trying to trade too many markets. It is far better to have on one or two positions and to know everything about those markets than to get lost trying to manage positions in eight different markets.

The work of monitoring and reviewing your positions must be done every day without fail. The less you want to do it, the more important it is. Traders usually will find excuses to skip reviews on days they have incurred losses, or after a string of losing days, but these are precisely the points at which you must do even more work. Of course, you may need to stop the bleeding in your account, but these moments are also exceptional learning opportunities. It is possible that you are simply suffering at the hand of a random market, but it is also possible that your behavior and your decisions have been suboptimal. Asking the hard questions is always painful, but the alternative is to keep losing. Every moment in the market is a learning opportunity; make sure you are doing the work to benefit from those opportunities.

Monitoring Tools

Another point to consider is how often you will look at your positions. If you are an intraday trader, you must be present at the screen every moment of the trading day. You will eat lunch at the screen and will reduce your break time to the bare minimum necessary for taking care of bodily functions, and there will be days you will even skip those. One of the advantages of being a trader with a longer time horizon is that it is acceptable to monitor your positions less frequently. For instance, a two-day to two-week swing trader can legitimately check in on her positions two or three times a day, perhaps on the open and again near the close, if there is a system in place for monitoring and catching unusual moves in her markets. Longer-term investors may well check in on their portfolios once a week, but it still behooves them to check daily for large and unusual moves in their holdings or in related markets. It is much easier to do this with some basic infrastructure in place to support these functions.

Position/Risk Sheet   Figure 8.6 shows an example of a daily risk and P&L sheet. For most traders, this is perhaps the most important daily record. After each session close, it serves the purpose of reviewing and summarizing the day's P&L and of measuring the intended risk for the next session. While the market is actually open, the stop levels and risk information on this sheet are important reminders and guides for behavior. Most traders get into trouble when they ignore risk parameters and end up taking large losses that are multiples of intended risk. Having this document and committing to following it religiously will insulate the trader from some of these catastrophic losses. Figure 8.6 is only an example showing the simplest and most basic information needed on this sheet. You can take this model and elaborate on it to fit your style and your needs.

Though some of the fields are self-explanatory, this sheet is extremely important, so it is worth the time to go through it in some detail:

- DateIn: This is the initial entry date of the first trade for the position.
- Patt: It is a good idea to have some way to distinguish among trades placed by different systems, from different patterns, or on different criteria. If you have only two or three positions, this may not be necessary, but it becomes important once you have on more than four or five. Furthermore, this classification is essential when doing statistical analysis of your trade results.

							P&L				Risk		
DateIn	Patt	Ticker	L/S	#	PriceIn	Close	OpenPL	ClosedPL	TotalPL	PL%R	Stop	Risk	PLStop	1StDev
6/14/11	PB	WX	L	800	72.08	71.63	(360)	0	(360)	−0.1X	67.25	(3,504)	(3,864)	1,328
6/13/11	Sup	CDE	L	1,000	41.43	41.62	193	(208)	(15)	−0.0X	40.05	(1,570)	(1,585)	740
6/10/11	Anti	ZZZ	L	750	11.05	12.55	1,125	2,865	3,990	1.1X	11.35	(900)	3,090	405
6/13/11	PB	ABC	S	375	105.89	106.64	(281)	0	(281)	−0.1X	115.00	(3,135)	(3,416)	(1,076)
6/10/11	PB	XYZ	S	2,750	29.93	29.19	2,032	771	2,803	0.7X	29.46	(742)	2,060	(2,200)
5/24/11	Res	BB	S	500	22.99	19.04	1,976	3,175	5,151	1.4X	20.50	(730)	4,421	(310)
						Total	4,684	6,603	11,287	3.0X		(10,582)	706	(1,113)

FIGURE 8.6   A Basic Daily Risk and P&L Sheet

- Ticker: This one is self-explanatory. If you are not completely comfortable with futures and options symbology, you might consider a field here in plain English.
- L/S: Long or short.
- #: Net size in shares, contracts, or units. This can be more complex than it seems, as it is common to have a position on and add and subtract to it as the trade develops. At any time, this number must reflect your net exposure coming into the day's session.
- PriceIn: The average price of the position. This can be surprisingly complicated, as it raises some accounting issues. For instance, imagine you buy one contract at $10, later buy another at $15, and then sell one at $20. Your net position is obviously $1 (1 + 1 - 1)$, but what is the entry price? There are actually two right answers, but the calculation has to be done correctly and consistently from an accounting standpoint. The two choices are first in, first out (FIFO) or average price. Using the example, FIFO would keep your entry price at $10 for the one contract, recording a $5 win on a closed trade for one contract. Average price would show the long position marked from $12.50 (average of $10 and $15), recording a closed trade win of $7.50. Both methods will show the same total P&L for the sum of open and closed trades, but it is important to understand which system is being used to mark open trades.
- Close: The settlement price for the instrument you are trading. Ideally this should be the same price that your broker's statement uses for settlement to make this P&L record match your broker's statement as closely as possible.
- OpenPL: This is the P&L associated with the open portion of the position. Again, there is an accounting issue to be resolved, because this will depend on how the entry price for the open position is calculated.
- ClosedPL: This is the closed P&L associated with the OpenPL position on this sheet. For instance, it would be possible to be carrying an open P&L of a $1,000 loss while having closed out $5,000 of the same position at a profit. The $1,000 loss, taken alone, would be misleading and must be considered together with the closed P&L. Also, the actual closed P&L will be different depending on the particular accounting system chosen, but the *total* of the open and closed will be the same, regardless. One more issue to consider is that sometimes a trade will be closed, and then another trade will be initiated that is a continuation of the first trade. Make sure you have considered these possibilities and planned for them in your accounting package. There is no one right way to deal with these issues, but you must be absolutely consistent.
- TotalPL: The total of the OpenPL and ClosedPL for this particular trade. This number will be the same regardless of the accounting method used, as the choices between FIFO and average price affect only the distribution of P&L between open and closed trades.
- PL%R: This is the P&L on the trade, expressed as a ratio of the amount initially risked on the trade.
- Stop: The stop-loss point for the trade. If the position carries multiple stops, you may need to create a sheet to show all of those points or simply display the one closest to the market (the highest stop level for a long trade or the lowest level for a short).
- Risk: The name of the column is slightly misleading, and should be the *intended* risk on the trade. This shows the size of the loss from the current price (closing price in

this case) to the stop-loss level for each individual trade, or the maximum intended loss this position would incur the next trading session. Be aware that an opening gap could result in a much larger loss than indicated on the sheet. It is also possible that market conditions such as liquidity or a sudden price spike intraday could make it impossible to execute the stop at the intended level. Just remember, it is certainly possible to have a loss that is larger than the intended risk.

- PLStop: This field shows the total trade P&L if the stop were hit. In other words, it is the current, total P&L (open and closed) for the trade minus the Risk field. Use this as a what-if scenario to judge your overall risk on the trade.
- 1StDev: It is helpful to have some sort of dollar-adjusted volatility measure that shows you how much the position is likely to swing on an average day. This helps to moderate expectations as a proxy measure of risk. The choice of volatility measure to use is a personal decision; I use 20-day historical volatility, but Average True Range, average absolute change, or any other measure could be adapted, depending on what you are trying to accomplish. (An excellent plan might be to use the higher of 20-day historical volatility or implied volatility.) If you are assessing risk, it probably makes sense to use a multiple of this number in your mental calculations—for instance, expecting that many markets could make moves 3 times this volatility measure while also remembering that extremely large moves (10 times or more) are possible. It is also a good idea to consider the sum of these numbers, or, more properly, a correlation-adjusted sum, as an assessment of single-day portfolio risk.

Use this sheet as a departure point for your own position and risk management system. It is relatively easy to build a P&L tracking system that incorporates your trades in real time into a spreadsheet that also updates with live market prices. Though brokerage software and execution platforms do provide position accounting, there is currently no retail-level platform that provides this degree of risk and position information. There is some value to having a hard-copy, printed-paper version of this sheet every day, but remember (obviously) that it will show positions as they stood at the end of the previous day. Active traders may find a real-time spreadsheet a more viable solution, or they may prefer to update the written sheet several times during the trading day. Last, some traders will find it helpful to *not* report P&L in actual dollars, but rather to standardize everything either for unit risked or as a percentage of the account equity. This could be done by reworking all of the fields on the sheet that show dollars to show risk multiples of the intended risk on the trade. As long as the risk levels are comparable, the P&L between trades will also be comparable.

Dynamic Tracking Tools   Very long-term investors who intend to hold positions for many months or quarters can safely ignore all but the largest single-day moves in their positions as noise. The rest of us do not have this luxury; even for the multiweek swing trader, a single large day can have a dramatic impact on the total P&L of a position. Many traders will not want to flip through charts of many positions every day. It is far better to have some kind of consistent screen that presents relevant data for movements in your positions and related markets. For futures and currency traders, I would recommend two sections to such a screen: markets in which you have positions and every other significant market, tracking front month or ratio-adjusted continuous contracts in all futures markets. This is, at most, 30 markets for domestic futures traders, so it is certainly a manageable number. Traders trading spreads can adapt this concept to track a number of spreads in addition to outrights. For equity traders, the situation is considerably more complex because of the number of moving pieces in the market. I would recommend that equity traders start with a screen that has four divisions: first, your actual positions; second, major broad market indexes representing three or four slices across market capitalizations (i.e., S&P 500, Russell 2000, Nasdaq Composite); third, 9 or 10 broad sector indexes (energy, financials, etc.); and fourth, perhaps 50 significant names drawn from various sectors. The list of significant stocks will change over time, but should be high-volume, high-visibility stocks in each sector so that you will see the impact of news on these leaders possibly even before it filters through to the broad sector. Once you have the selection of markets you wish to follow, consider tracking some of the following specific quantitative elements.

- The most obvious screen is one that is probably provided by your brokerage software, a *simple accounting of the P&L* for each position. I find it useful to track P&L in three pieces: the day's change or P&L marked from the previous close, any closed P&L related to the position, and the total P&L from inception. Some of this accounting will probably have to be done manually, and the risk sheet in the previous subsection shows one way to incorporate open and closed P&L into a total position P&L. It is also good to be able to track where, at any instant, each market is in relation to predefined stop and target levels. Ideally, this distance should be measured on some volatility-adjusted basis, for instance as an ATR multiple or a standard deviation. Comparisons made on a simple raw point or dollar basis are not very useful; everything must be adjusted for volatility.
- Particularly for equity and futures traders, some tool to monitor *gap openings* is very helpful. Of course, these can mean dramatic and immediate changes in the P&L for any existing position, but many gaps in related markets (e.g., stocks in the same sector or industry) can show an imbalance that might have a lasting influence through the trading session. More and more markets are moving toward becoming true 24-hour markets; gaps in those markets are not actual gaps but are the result of overseas trading in our off-hours. Most futures markets are technically at this point already, and currencies certainly are. In another decade, this focus on overnight gaps is likely to seem like a quaint anachronism, but, for now, the open of our U.S. session is still important for many markets.
- It is also helpful to have a tool that simply identifies markets that are making *large moves that day*, perhaps with large changes in volume if that is relevant for the market you trade. It is important to standardize these measures of large moves and volume for recent market history; many traders use ATR multiples, saying, for instance, a particular stock is up 1.5 ATRs while another is up only 0.5 ATR. My personal

preference is to use my volatility spike indicator, which simply expresses the current day's change (last print to previous day's close) as a standard deviation of the past 20 trading days. I have a screen that updates the day's change as a standard deviation for a number of markets and color codes any move larger than three standard deviations up or down. This makes it very easy to see, at a glance, what is going on even if I am looking at a quote screen with several hundred tickers. If you look at the board and see only white, it is probably a boring day. If you look back later and see a sea of red, then you know that something has changed and that long positions may demand attention.

Last, you may want to consider other measures of unusual activity in the markets and positions you are following. The simpler these tools are, the more robust and useful they are likely to be. It is easy to be seduced by the power of the programming tools available and to try to create elaborate, complex monitoring tools. In most cases, this is not necessary and is even counterproductive. You simply need to know when your positions or related markets are moving with unusual activity on the day.

A Tool for Tracking Positions Intraday

Some of the best ideas really are the simplest. For intraday position monitoring, I also use a tool that shows where the current price is in the day's range in a simple text graph format. This has proven to be an extremely useful tool for intraday traders to visualize order flow and relationships across many markets, and can even help longer-term traders read the flow in a market. Here is the basic eight-step procedure for creating this tool:

1. Calculate the *close as percent of day's range* = [(last print – day's low)/day's range] × 100.
2. Calculate the *open as percent of day's range* = [(open – day's low)/day's range] × 100.
3. Create a text variable that consists of 10 dashes = "- - - - - - - - - -".
4. Each dash is a decile. Replace the dash that corresponds to the *open as percent of day's range* with the colon (:) character.
5. Replace the dash that corresponds to the *close as percent of day's range* with the pipe (|) character. If the colon already occupies that space, overwrite it with the pipe.
6. If the current price is the absolute high of the day, replace the entire string with "= = = = = = = = = >".
7. If the current price is the absolute low of the day, replace the entire string with "< = = = = = = = = =".
8. Color code as desired. One idea might be to color code the entire indicator red for any values where *close as percent of day's range* ≤ 20, and green if ≥ 80.

Practical Tips on Execution

It is difficult to give guidelines on execution that will apply across many different asset classes and time frames, but there are a few commonalities to consider. First of all, you can choose to be either a price maker or a price taker—to add or take liquidity from the book. Particularly for very short-term traders who do a lot of volume, the rebates associated with adding liquidity to the book can help to offset a significant portion of their transaction costs, so it makes sense for these traders to execute on limit orders, adding liquidity as often as possible. However, it is also important to consider the adverse selection effect associated with limit orders, meaning that if you focus on limit order executions, you will always be in every losing trade, but you will price yourself out of some winning trades.

In general, be careful with market orders. True market orders have no price limit and you have no recourse in the event of a very poor fill. It is even possible, in some markets, to be filled outside the day's range at a price where the asset never traded. We refer to the difference between the intended price and the actual execution price as *slippage*, and it is a serious cost in some markets. Very large market orders will eat through a signifi-cant amount of the liquidity in the book, sometimes moving prices significantly. A mar-ket maker's biggest fear is running into an informed trader who executes a large order in the market, placing the market maker, by definition, on the other side of that order. Market-making algorithms monitor the way orders are hitting the bids and offers, and they identify large market orders taking a lot of liquidity as potentially informed traders. To protect themselves, the market makers then widen spreads and step away from the inside market, which further exacerbates the impact of these large market orders.

When and if you must use market orders, do so with discretion. Break up large orders into smaller pieces if possible and execute them over a longer time period. *Marketable limit orders* should almost always be used instead of pure market orders. A marketable limit order is an order that is placed on the wrong side of the market: a limit order to buy normally goes on or under the bid, but a marketable buy limit order is placed at or above the offer. A marketable sell limit order similarly goes at or under the bid. Marketable limit orders may well clear liquidity and result in slippage up to the limit price, but they avoid the possibility of a very large adverse fill with the trade-off that a marketable limit order may not be filled at all. If the order scares the market and sends price moving without completely filling the order, the remainder will continue to work as a limit order at the limit price. Perhaps the only time you may want to consider an outright market order is as a stop loss on a position, when you really want out at whatever cost. Otherwise, make the marketable limit order your standard tool.

Most traders, especially shorter-term traders for whom the spread represents a greater portion of their profit and loss, should think about executing at least one side of the trade on a limit order if possible. If you enter on a market order (marketable limit order), get out of your position on a limit order. If you enter via a limit order, you can use a market order for exit. Paying the spread on both sides of the trade can be a serious loss of efficiency. For instance, a short-term scalper may be playing for a profit of 0.10 with an intended risk of 0.10. If she gives up 0.02 on both the entry and the exit due to the spread, then her winning trades become 0.06 and her losers become –0.14. For higher-time frame traders, this factor is less important, but it is still good to build the discipline of trying to execute one side of the trade on limit orders as much as possible. Of course, when you are wrong, it is usually better to get out without messing around. Far better to simply hit a bid to get out than to offer at successively lower prices, as your offers will add pressure that will drive the price still lower. Most traders will find best results in not being too obsessive about execution prices in losing trades—just get out.

Large Orders, Thin Markets

Executing large orders in thin markets can be challenging, but it is often possible, with time and skill, to do even a multiple of the average daily volume in many markets without moving price too much. There is an unavoidable trade-off between urgency of execution and adverse price impact; the faster you must do an order, all other things being equal, the more you will move the market. Executing large orders is a specific skill that must be developed over time, and, like everything else in trading, probabilities apply—it is not possible to do this perfectly every time. There are three approaches to consider for these executions:

1. Break them up into smaller pieces and do them as much as possible on the bid or just in front of the bid. Use hidden orders whenever possible, and experiment with probing in between the bid and the offer to see if there are other hidden orders. For instance, assume that you need to buy 200,000 shares in a thin stock that does an average of 100,000 shares a day, is currently bid at 10.00 and offered at 10.20, and is not printing. Your first approach should be to place a hidden order at 10.02 to 10.05 and see if you are filled there. Once that order is working, you can try other hidden limit orders from 10.05 to 10.18, seeing if you will find any hidden orders there. You will usually have best luck placing very large orders so that if they meet another large order they will be filled. Be aware, if you do get lucky and print 50,000 shares at 10.12, the stock will probably adjust instantly and be bid at 10.20 and offered at 10.50 or something even worse. Be patient after these first fills and continue the process until the order is done. Above all, avoid paying the offer, as even a few hundred shares taken on the offer can send the stock bid well above those last prices. (Similar considerations apply in thin futures markets.)

2. This is highly counterintuitive, but many times thin books are a lot more liquid than they look. If you are trying to buy large size in a thin market, you may have good results showing most or all of your bid at a price near the offer. If you are unable to find any fills in the middle of the spread (10.00/10.20 as in the preceding example), you may want to show your full size at 10.15 or so. Being willing to give up most of the spread and showing your full size clearly tells the marketplace that you are a real, natural buyer. Yes, there will be times when the market instantly goes 10.40 bid, but these are offset by the times a natural seller will fill your whole order at 10.15.

3. Use an algorithm to do the execution. Most traders will start here, and this is probably the best plan for most situations. Most algorithms will follow some variation of the plan in the first bullet point, but they will do so with the advantage of being able to monitor many levels in the order book with constant vigilance. In addition, some algorithms have preferred access to various dark pools, and may be able to cross a significant portion of the order there.

Thin, illiquid markets are a double-edged sword. On one hand, illiquidity is *good* when you're on the right side of a trade. An illiquid market will usually move in the anticipated direction much faster, as there is less two-way trading and disagreement over price—the quest for the theoretical market-clearing price is much cleaner when there is less noise in the order book. Common sense dictates that partial exits in these cases should be taken in the direction of the price movement: sell existing longs into strength and buy back existing shorts on weakness. Yes, this means you will almost never sell the very top of a move or cover the very bottom, but you will, in general, be much more efficient if you do not pay the spread. The cost of getting out of thin markets when you are on the wrong side can be extreme. Even if you are watching the order book, you may not be able to execute against displayed liquidity, as it is pulled from the book far faster than you can humanly react.

One last thing to consider is the issue of mistakes. Everyone makes mistakes. Even if you are trading a completely automated system with little human interaction, there will still be some errors. You *will* make mistakes, and, while it is important to minimize the frequency with which they occur, it is equally important to accept that they will happen and to plan for how to handle them. Perhaps you buy instead of sell. Perhaps you mean to execute in one market but you actually execute an unintended order in another market. Perhaps you enter a stop or limit order with a wrong price and it triggers when you did not intend it to. Perhaps an exit order was canceled and you find yourself with a position you did not expect to have, at either a profit or a loss. The question is not so much how you make yourself mistake-proof as what you do when these things happen, and the answer is simple: fix the mistake immediately. Do not consider whether you are happy to have the position or whether you can trade out of it somehow. Do not think. Do not justify. Just fix the mistake. This is a matter of discipline and it must be enforced every time an error happens.

CHAPTER 9

Risk Management

*It is important to see distant things as if they were close and to take a
distanced view of close things.*

—Miyamoto Musashi, *The Book of Five Rings* (1645 CE)

Many of the problems of trading reduce to risk management. In most styles of
trading, the trader's job is essentially to manage the risk in trades, focusing on
exiting losing trades at the correct points, and letting the upside take care of
itself. Risk management is critical, as a few outsized losses can offset the profits from
many winning trades; it does not take many errors to completely erode a trading edge.
This chapter considers risk management from both practical and theoretical perspectives. We begin with practical, applied tools for risk management and position sizing that
traders in all time frames will find useful. Many large losses come from having trades with
inappropriate position sizes, and many traders do not understand the impact of trading
size on the bottom line. The chapter moves on to a higher-level perspective on risk, incorporating some ideas from modern academic thinking and focusing on a few specific
measures of risk, before concluding with a look at some of the less common risks that
self-directed traders often overlook.

RISK AND POSITION SIZING

From a practical perspective, there are three main questions to answer with respect to
risk. The first two have been addressed in the previous chapter, but the third is supremely
important:

1. Where do we place our initial exit orders, both for profits and losses?
2. How do we adjust the trade as it develops through time?
3. How many shares, contracts, or other units do we trade on each position?

First, Know Your Risk

There are few absolutes in trading. Most trading rules are flexible, and many master traders have a rule that basically says, "Know when to break the other rules." However, there is one rule that cannot be broken—it is perhaps the single most important rule in discretionary trading: *Always know where you are getting out of the trade if you are wrong, before you get in.* The choice of exactly where to place the stop will depend on the pattern, the trader, the profit target, the time frame, the specific market, and perhaps a number of other conditions, but the most important thing is that this level is defined at the time of entry.

As you consider your options, it is important to make sure that your stop is placed at a meaningful level that is outside of the range of the market's noise; with very few exceptions initial stops must not be placed too close to the market. A rough guideline is given by the average range of a single bar on the time frame you are trading. If you try to place your initial stops closer than one average bar's range, you are probably working within the noise level and have significantly impaired whatever edge you might have had.

%R and Position Sizing

Once this initial price movement risk level is known, the question of trading size must also be addressed. There is a large body of literature that deals with the theoretical ideas behind asset allocation and position sizing for individual traders. For the most part we will avoid these discussions and will simply limit discussion here to two points: some practical guidelines I have used with success in my own trading and an illustration of why consistent sizing is important.

Many traders are familiar with the *Kelly criterion*, which is a formula that gives the optimal amount to bet in a game of chance, assuming that a number of very important simplifying assumptions hold true. If these assumptions are met, then the Kelly formula will outperform all other approaches, usually dramatically.

> If you are interested in the theoretical background of asset allocation and position sizing for individual traders, good places to start are J. L. Kelly Jr.'s seminal 1956 paper "A New Interpretation of Information Rate" and Ralph Vince's *The Leverage Space Trading Model* (2009).

However (and for actual trading this is very important), if Kelly is applied in cases in which the simplifying assumptions do not hold, then it will all end in tears. For reference, the classic Kelly criterion gives f, the percentage of the account to risk on every trade, by this formula:

$$f = \frac{Odds \times Prob_{win} - Prob_{loss}}{Odds}$$

$$Odds = \frac{Size_{win}}{Size_{loss}}$$

The Kelly criterion and Vince's extension of it, called *optimal f*, are optimized approaches. In both cases, the objective is to maximize the geometric growth rate of the account while minimizing the risk of ruin, or a catastrophic loss of equity. Most optimized approaches like this are extremely aggressive, and large drawdowns must be accepted as a matter of course. In addition, and much more seriously, the theoretical assumptions behind these models are important and they rarely hold up in short-term trading. For instance, most optimized methods assume that each trade is independent of any other trade, but many trading systems experience strings of wins and losses while the market is locked in one regime (trending or trading range), and trade outcomes may show some degree of serial dependence. Furthermore, many of these optimized approaches require inputs like the largest trading loss, which must be based on historical data, and they are all dependent on the assumption that future results will look like the past. If you experience a larger loss in the future and you are using an aggressive, optimized position-sizing methodology, you could be in trouble. If you are going to use any of these approaches in actual trading, make sure you understand the assumptions and the risks involved in violating any of those assumptions.

Many traders find that the risks under an optimized position-sizing scheme are too great to bear. Another possibility could be to set aside a fixed percentage of your trading capital, and apply aggressive sizing rules to that portion while trading the remainder more conservatively. If you decide to do this, you should carefully consider whether the incremental gains offset the additional effort required to carry out this plan.

Fixed Fractional Approaches   My approach to position sizing is simple and robust. It is not an optimized method, nor is it meant to be. Rather, it is designed to do a few specific things:

- Define the risk from losing trades.
- Limit the risk from a much larger-than-expected losing trade.
- Limit the risk from a series of losing trades.
- Limit the total risk from a set of highly correlated positions.
- Limit the total amount of equity placed at risk at any one time.
- Allow easy scaling as the account balance changes.

Notice that the focus of this process is on limiting risk, not maximizing returns. This is how you stay in the game. Professional traders know that, if you are trading with an edge, the most important thing is to manage the downside so that no one risk can take you out of business. Profits, to a great extent, will take care of themselves; the first and most important job of any trader is to correctly manage the risk.

The rules are very simple: the risk for every trade is set at a consistent percentage of the account equity. I consider anything under 1 percent to be very conservative, and anything 3 percent or over to be extremely aggressive. When you are thinking about this risk number, it is important to consider the impact of a string of four or five losing trades in a row, or of a single loss five times your anticipated maximum loss. If you are risking

3 percent on a trade and have a disastrous situation where you have a 5× loss, you just lost 15 percent of your equity. In reality, a loss this much larger than expected should be extremely rare, but, even in this extreme case, the account would not be destroyed. If, however, you had been risking 10 percent of the account, you would be down 50 percent and in serious trouble.

Drawdown usually refers to the amount an equity curve, whether for a trader, system, or fund, has retreated from its peak. Drawdowns are a fact of life; there is always some natural fluctuation in an equity curve. Later in this chapter, we examine many of the traditional measures of risk and find them wanting on one level or another. It is easy to make an argument that drawdown is one of the best and one of the truest measures of risk, but, like many other elements of trading performance, future drawdowns must be extrapolated from history. If something changes in the future, the disconnect between historical performance and walk-forward projection can cause traders and managers to dramatically underestimate risk.

Recovering from Drawdowns

One of the mathematical realities traders face is the asymmetry between drawdowns and the percentage returns needed to recover. For some people, this is not always intuitive at first glance—for any given percent drawdown, it takes a much larger percentage return to recover. For any drawdown of D%, the return needed to bring the account back to breakeven may be calculated from this formula:

$$\text{Return needed for recovery} = \frac{D\%}{(1 - D\%)}$$

For small drawdowns, the return needed to recover is only very slightly larger. For instance, a 5 percent drawdown requires a 5.3 percent return to recover, but a trader in a 20 percent drawdown needs to make 25 percent just to break even. For larger drawdowns, the hole gets deeper very quickly—you would have to double your money, with a 100 percent return, to get back to even from a 50 percent drawdown. To put these numbers in perspective, very few traders make 25 percent a year with any regularity, and the chances of doubling your money, without excessive leverage and risks, are very, very small. An effective risk management strategy will focus on minimizing drawdowns, while acknowledging them as a natural and normal part of trading.

Another advantage of fixed fraction approaches is that the actual amount at risk grows or shrinks with the account size. A series of five losses of 4 percent each is not a 20 percent loss to the account because the account was shrinking after each loss. In this case, the actual net loss was 18.5 percent, slightly smaller. The *compound loss* resulting from a string of *t* losses of N% each is:

$$Compound\ loss = (1 - N\%)^t$$

Note also that this formula would be valid only for *consecutive* losses in an account trading *one position* at a time. If three positions are put on at the same time, they will all be risking N% of the same account balance, so a loss on all three of those *will* be equal to a single $3\times$ loss.

Calculating Trading Size   Once you have defined the percentage of account equity to put at risk on any one trade, the next step is to target that risk by having the correct position size (shares, contracts, or dollars invested) on each trade. Most trading patterns or systems will have more or less clearly defined stop points. If you want to risk more or less on the trade, you *cannot* accomplish this by moving the stop further or closer to the market. Essentially, you do not get to choose where to put the stop—that is dictated by the system, but you *do* get to choose how much money to lose by changing your trading size. An example will help to clarify this:

- Assume you are trading a $100,000 account and you want to risk 1 percent on each trade.
- Assume you find a trade to go long a $50.00 stock with a stop loss at $47.50. The difference between the entry and the initial stop is the *per-unit risk* that the trade requires: per share, per contract, per dollar, and so on for each respective market.
- The question is how many shares to trade so that a loss at the market price of $47.50 will equal a loss of 1 percent of the $100,000 account.

$$\text{Trade size} = \text{Desired dollar risk} \div \text{Per-unit risk}$$

In this case, we want to risk 1 percent of $100,000, or $1,000 on each trade, so $1,000 \div \$2.50 = 400$ shares.

Thinking in R multiples   This initial risk is very important because it is the base for the *R multiple* for the entire trade. Many traders will find it productive to think of all P&L generated by the trade in terms of this initial R multiple. For instance, if the trade loses the amount that was originally risked, this is a $-1R$ loss, or a loss equal to the initial risk. If the trade has a profit equal to half of this initial risk, we could say that it is a $0.5R$ trade, and so on. Thinking in R multiples is a valuable skill because it removes much of the pressure of thinking about actual money. Many developing traders find that they relate their initial wins and losses to real-life money situations, as in "I just lost enough on that one trade to make my car payment for three months." Experienced traders are more likely to think of the money as an abstraction or, in some cases, almost more of a score-keeping system. This is a subtle but critical psychological adjustment.

Traders also sometimes have trouble increasing their trading size because of the growing nominal risk. This is a problem for the individual self-directed trader, but can also be a problem on the institutional scale when new client funds come in. There is a big difference psychologically between risking $10,000 on a position and $100,000, but if they both represent the same percentage of different capital pools and are both the outcome of a 1R trade, it is possible to approach them with a degree of equanimity.

The Effect of Position Sizing

Evaluating the effectiveness of a position-sizing strategy is difficult because doing so requires a good understanding of probabilities in highly path-dependent situations. It is extremely difficult to build intuition in these scenarios, and it is very easy to make mistakes—we are not naturally wired to think about issues like this. Monte Carlo methods provide a useful framework for evaluating different strategies. Let's do a simplified analysis to see what the effect of different position-sizing strategies would be on the same trading system. Assume that you are trading a strategy that wins or loses with equal probability (probability of win = probability of loss = 0.5). When you win, you win 1.2 times the amount risked, and when you lose, you lose 1 times the amount risked; your winners are always exactly +1.2R and your losing trades are always exactly −1.0R. The first question is: would you trade this system? A quick check shows a positive expectancy of 0.1 per trade [0.5(1.2) − 0.5(1.0) = 0.1], so the answer is yes.

Let's further assume that you will trade this system for 250 consecutive trades, at which point you will stop and evaluate your results. It is important to remember that your actual P&L was just one realization of a nearly limitless set of possibilities. This is one reason that we have trouble thinking in probabilities: probabilities are meaningful over a large number of trials, but, in actual practice, we are usually dealing with the realization of one specific outcome. It is easy to focus on that one result and not to realize that it is one of many possibilities and, in some cases, may even be a highly improbable outcome. Our behavior and decisions must be governed by the *most probable* outcomes. *Monte Carlo modeling* or *simulation* can be a useful tool to help build intuition about these path-dependent situations. Each path on the tests that follow represents the outcome of one trader executing these 250 trades in a row; we will repeat the test for each of 1,000 traders. A useful mental trick is to imagine that each path is the P&L for one of 1,000 traders working in parallel universes, since it is difficult to imagine one trader trading the system 1,000 times. Last, most Monte Carlo tests are run on much larger numbers (by several powers of 10). Though the small sets used here may not be big enough to assure convergence to theoretical values, they are large enough to illustrate the relevant points.

So you have this system that you know has a positive expectancy, and you will be trading it in a $100,000 trading account. The only question left is how much to risk on each trade; you have to start somewhere, so let's begin by risking $2,000 on each trade. This seems like a reasonable compromise because it is a number that is significant, but is not extremely large relative to the account value. Before we jump into the Monte Carlo results, see if you can answer this question: What do you expect your winnings should be at the end of the run?

We can answer this by using the expected value of the system, which is 0.1 in this case. This means that, for every dollar wagered, we expect to make $0.10 per trade. (Another way to say the same thing is that for every dollar wagered, we expect to end up with $1.10 because the original dollar is returned.) Since we are risking $2,000 per trade for 250 trades, the relevant math is:

$$Ending \; P\&L = Expected \; value \times risk \; per \; trade \times number \; of \; trades$$
$$= 0.10 \times \$2,000 \times 250$$
$$= \$50,000$$

So, *on average*, we can expect to end up with $150,000 in the account ($100,000 starting value + $50,000 profit) at the end of 250 trades.

For each of the 1,000 runs, the final, ending P&L was recorded, and Table 9.1 presents summary statistics for these ending values. Most of the statistics in the table are self-explanatory. With one exception, these statistics are blind to what happens in the middle of the run. If a trader was up $5,000,000 at one point but the run ended up only $5,000, the only number evaluated is the ending $5,000.

The exception is that an account cannot continue to trade if it loses all its funds at any point in the trial, so each run is monitored for this condition. If, at any point in the series of 250 trades, a run reaches a zero or negative balance, it will cease trading and that value will be presented as the terminal value for that run. The number of the 1,000 traders who go bankrupt is recorded, and the percentage is presented at the bottom of the table.

Percent of accounts bankrupt = Number of accounts with terminal balance ≤ $0/1,000

We also will record the number of accounts than end up with a greater than 75 percent loss from the starting value. Though this is an arbitrary cutoff, it will serve to measure some of the downside risks in some of the more extreme scenarios later on. In reality, an account is in trouble long before it reaches a 75 percent drawdown. Consider the results in Table 9.1.

On average, we end up with $149,259, which is close to the theoretical $150,000 from the expected value equation. (Keep in mind that 1,000 test runs is actually a small number; had we done 100,000 or 1,000,000 runs, this number would almost certainly have

TABLE 9.1 Results of 1,000 Monte Carlo Runs Risking $2,000 per Trade in $100,000 Account

Mean Terminal Value	149,259
Median Terminal Value	152,000
Standard Deviation of Terminal Value	33,760
Coefficient of Variation	0.23
Mean of Maximum Value	159,070
Mean of Minimum Value	89,254
Highest Terminal Value	253,200
Lowest Terminal Value	50,800
Percent Terminal Drawdown ≥75%	0.0%
Percent of Accounts Bankrupt	0.0%

been closer to $150,000.) The standard deviation of terminal value tells us that 68 percent of the time, the terminal value should fall within +/−$33,760 of $149,259 *if* the terminal values are normally distributed. (Though not necessary in the context of Monte Carlo modeling, it pays to check assumptions of normality as a matter of course. In this case, they are, in fact, normally distributed.) The *coefficient of variation* is not particularly meaningful in this one case, but it gives us a quick tool to make risk-adjusted comparisons across different scenarios.

Make sure you understand the mean of maximum and mean of minimum terminal values: the average of the highest and lowest points reached by each of the 1,000 acounts over 250 independent trades risking $2,000 per trade. These are averages, and there will certainly be surprising deviations, especially in a larger number of trials. For instance, in this test we had one run in which the account balance reached $12,400 at one point. (This is not visible in the table because the account recovered significantly by the end of that specific trial.) At this point you should be saying something like, "What? I thought we were trading something that has a positive expectancy." Yes, this is a simple system with a clear positive expectancy, but one trader trading it would have experienced an 87.5 percent drawdown, purely due to the slings and arrows of outrageous fortune! This is an important reality check, and it gives us some sense of how much variation can exist within a positive expectancy framework. In this case, the account recovered to close at $55,200, but that also might not have happened in another universe. (Note that this is also not the lowest closing value of all accounts.) Is it possible that you can trade a system with a positive expectancy, make no mistakes trading it, and still go bankrupt? Absolutely. If so, how do we really evaluate our trading performance and separate skill from luck? This is an important question to think about—though there are no certain answers, Chapter 12 will offer some guidelines and helpful measures.

In Table 9.1, the highest and lowest terminal values are exactly what they say: the largest and smallest account values at the end of the 250-trade test; there will almost certainly have been significantly higher and lower values at other points in the run. (We already know that one of these accounts traded down to $12,400 before recovering to close much higher, and one of them traded up to $265,200 at one point during the test. (Neither of those values is shown in the table.)) Last, we see that none of the accounts ended in a greater than 75 percent drawdown, though we have no idea from this table how many may have crossed that barrier during their life cycles, and we see that none of the accounts went bankrupt (i.e., reached a zero or negative balance at any point during the trading, at which point trading would have been terminated).

So what conclusions can we draw from this? Well, first of all, math works—the theoretical expected value calculation gave a number very close to the mean of the terminal values, and the difference is easily explained by normal variation. However, this concept of expected value fails to capture the degree of variation possible within a positive expectancy framework. Few readers would expect to trade a system with a verifiable, valid trading edge and to lose nearly 90 percent of their accounts to random bad luck, but this can and does happen. There are also offsetting happy surprises to the upside, but it is very hard to develop an intuitive grasp of the contribution of randomness to our

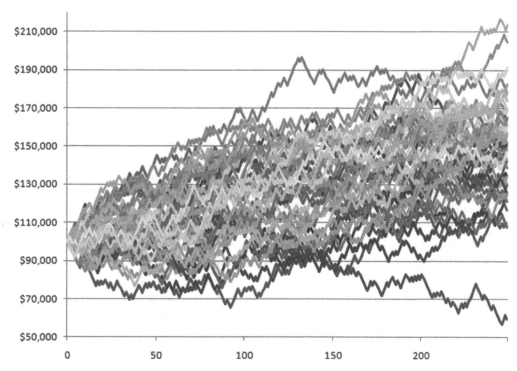

FIGURE 9.1 Fifty Sample Runs through the Monte Carlo Tree

trading results. Figure 9.1 shows the paths of the first 50 runs through this test. Though it is difficult to read such a crowded graph, notice that most of the paths do cluster around a rising central value, as would be expected. However, also notice that there are upside and downside outliers, some of which are quite extreme.

So, with that background, let's consider what would happen if we reran the test, changing only the amount risked on each trade. Table 9.2 shows results for several

TABLE 9.2 Monte Carlo Risking $x per Trade

	x = 2,000	x = 3,000	x = 4,000	x = 5,000
Mean Terminal Value	149,259	173,854	198,286	221,894
Median Terminal Value	152,000	178,000	204,000	230,000
Std Dev of Terminal Value	33,760	50,746	68,107	86,911
Coefficient of Variation	0.23	0.29	0.34	0.39
Mean of Max Value	159,070	188,604	218,139	247,448
Mean of Min Value	89,254	83,912	78,650	73,638
Highest Terminal Value	253,200	329,800	406,400	483,000
Lowest Terminal Value	50,800	(1,400)	(3,200)	(4,000)
Percent Terminal DD ≥75%	0.0%	0.1%	0.8%	2.3%
Percent of Accounts Bankrupt	0.0%	0.1%	0.7%	2.2%
Terminal Value − $E()$	(741)	(1,146)	(1,714)	(3,106)

different per-trade risks ($x = $). Note that the *only* thing that changed is this risk level; the trades for these runs were generated with a pseudo-random number generator, and the same random sequence was used in each set of 1,000 trades. The win/loss sequences are the same for the set of 1,000 trials and for each column in Table 9.2. (On a technical note, this kind of reproducibility is important in Monte Carlo testing, and is a strong argument against building these tests using Excel's built-in random number generator.)

What do we notice here? First, the simplistic understanding that some traders have that "the more you risk, the more you make" does seem to have some validity. As we increase the amount risked per trade, the average terminal value increases, as does the mean of the maximum value; risking $5,000 per trade gives us almost 50 percent more profit than our initial $2,000 risk. However, there is a cost. The standard deviation of terminal values increases faster than the mean, which can be seen by the steadily risking coefficient of variation. If we accept, for a moment, the standard deviation as a measure of risk, we are taking on additional units of risk and not being adequately compensated by higher returns. At the $5,000 risk level, we have a disturbing number of accounts that went bankrupt.

A new line has been added to the table that shows the difference between the terminal value and the expected value. The difference was very small at the $2,000 risk level, but it increases with the risk level. One reason for this departure is that the bankruptcy limit makes the test, and actual trading, asymmetrical. If an account hits this barrier, it is removed from the test and that value becomes its terminal value; this is also the reality of capital constraints in trading and money management. Otherwise, martingale betting strategies (where you double your bet size each time you take a loss) would work, but in reality, traders using this type of strategy invariably go broke if they trade long enough.

Emboldened by the observation that more risk equals more profits, let's say you decide to, as we kindly say in the vernacular, "go nuts." You increase risk to the reckless levels in Table 9.3, and finally some truths become very clear. At some point, with increasing risk, the party is over—the rising losses and risks of bankruptcy start to outpace

TABLE 9.3 Aggressive Risk Levels in the Monte Carlo

	$x = 6{,}000$	$x = 8{,}000$	$x = 10{,}000$	$x = 25{,}000$
Mean Terminal Value	243,140	281,387	314,822	463,980
Median Terminal Value	242,800	290,400	338,000	310,000
Std Dev of Terminal Value	108,326	153,502	200,806	519,633
Coefficient of Variation	0.45	0.55	0.64	1.12
Mean of Max Value	275,360	327,832	376,324	610,805
Mean of Min Value	68,993	61,058	54,662	28,480
Highest Terminal Value	559,600	712,800	866,000	2,015,000
Lowest Terminal Value	(5,600)	(7,200)	(8,000)	(20,000)
Percent Terminal DD $\geq$75%	5.2%	11.0%	17.6%	47.7%
Percent of Accounts Bankrupt	5.0%	11.0%	17.6%	47.7%
Terminal Value $- E()$	(6,860)	(18,613)	(35,178)	(261,020)

any incremental gains. Somewhere between $8,000 and $10,000 risk per trade, we finally reach a mean terminal value that is double what we have with our modest $2,000 trading risk, but we also have somewhere around 15 percent of the accounts going bankrupt. Though decisions have to be made within your own risk tolerance, it is hard to imagine this being acceptable. Consider the $25,000 per trade risk as a very extreme example. For one thing, you are risking a quarter of your initial account balance on each trade, which means you can be wrong three times before being taken out of the game on the fourth bad trade. What are the chances of that happening? It turns out the chances are pretty good, as nearly half of the accounts go bankrupt at this excessive risk level. Also, we are now risking 11.5 times our initial $2,000 risk, and the mean terminal value is not really *that* much higher—certainly not enough to justify the excessive risk of going bankrupt.

Consider one more thing about this $25,000 scenario: there was at least one account in this test that ran the starting capital of $100,000 up to over $2,000,000 (not visible in the summary table), at the same time that half the other accounts were going bankrupt. It is always possible to find one exceptional example.

Fixed Fractional Position Sizing in Action   Though risking a fixed amount on each trade is an improvement over having no system at all, there are some problems with this plan. For instance, if the account balance shrinks or grows dramatically, the initial dollar amount risked may lose some relevance. If your account doubles, why are you still risking the same amount per trade?

Fixed fractional risk is one solution to this problem: always risking a fixed percentage of the trading account's equity on each trade. Let's begin this investigation with a 2 percent risk, which, at the beginning of the run, will be the equivalent of the $2,000 risk in Table 9.1. Keep in mind that the amount risked will change on every trade, as the account balance waxes and wanes. As we have winners, the account gets bigger, so we are risking more on the next trade; conversely, as we run into a string of losers and the account shrinks, the risk on each trade will also shrink. Table 9.4 shows the results of this 2

TABLE 9.4   Fixed Fractional and Fixed Position Sizes Compared

	Fixed 2,000	2% of Equity
Mean Terminal Value	149,259	163,033
Median Terminal Value	152,000	158,317
Std Dev of Terminal Value	33,760	56,266
Coefficient of Variation	0.23	0.35
Mean of Max Value	159,070	179,236
Mean of Min Value	89,254	89,385
Highest Terminal Value	253,200	434,738
Lowest Terminal Value	50,800	57,654
Percent Terminal DD $\geq$75%	0.0%	0.0%
Percent of Accounts Bankrupt	0.0%	0.0%

percent fixed fractional sizing, and, though they are not directly comparable, reproduces the numbers from Table 9.1 for comparison.

A few things jump out here. First of all, these numbers do seem to be roughly comparable at first glance. We see that both the mean and the median values have increased, which is to be expected because, as the account grows—which, on average, it does with this positive expectancy system—fixed fractional sizing allows you to take on more risk. This is essentially a way to leverage your winners and to use accumulated trading profits to fund further risk. We note that the standard deviation has increased fairly dramatically; the coefficient of variation does not look good. In fact, if they were directly comparable, Table 9.2 suggests we should be able to hit a mean terminal value of around $200,000 for a coefficient of variation of 0.35 with a fixed dollar amount risk plan. Perhaps we are a little disappointed with the fixed fractional results, which seem to have increased volatility of returns without compensating for the extra risk. In fact, the fixed fractional approach would have a lower Sharpe ratio for a commensurate return. Naive rules would suggest that this is lower risk-adjusted return, but hold off on making any decisions for a moment. There just may be more to this story.

Digging a little deeper, we see that the mean of maximum value has increased fairly significantly, without any real change in the mean of minimum value. In fact, both the mean of minimum value and the lowest terminal value from the run have *increased*, and we also see that the highest terminal value is about 1.7 times what it was with the fixed sizing. Figure 9.2 gives some insight into what is going on.

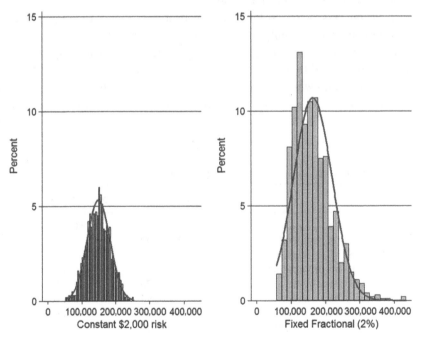

FIGURE 9.2 Distribution of Terminal Values for Fixed-Dollar and Fixed-Fractional Position-Sizing Plans

In Figure 9.2, the histograms also include a normal distribution curve for comparison with the returns. We established earlier that the constant risk scenario produced ending values that did seem to be normally distributed. However, even a casual glance at the fixed fractional distribution shows that it almost certainly is not normally distributed. (In this case, the returns have a skew of 0.95 and kurtosis of 4.3. The Shapiro-Wilk test confirms with a z value of 8.5, giving strong evidence of nonnormality. The returns of the fixed fractional plan are *lognormally* distributed.) The most obvious point about the fixed fractional distribution is that it is no longer symmetrical; the variation is concentrated in a long right (positive) tail. *This is critically important:* the asymmetrical risk profile compromises the relevance of simplistic measures such as the Sharpe ratio or the coefficient of variation. In this case, the increased risk from the fixed fractional approach is a good thing; nearly all of the extra variability is potential upside.

You Can't Go Broke? Really? Advocates of fixed fractional approaches often point out that it is mathematically impossible to take an account to zero using these approaches. As the account balance shrinks, you are risking an ever-smaller percentage of the declining balance. This is slightly reminiscent of Zeno's paradox in which you walk halfway to a fixed point, then half of that distance, then half again. Repeated into infinity, it seems as though you would never reach your goal. The people who say that fixed fractional approaches prevent the account from going to zero are absolutely correct (in the absence of commissions and other frictions), but, unfortunately, it is a completely meaningless argument. If we did 250 losing trades in a row, risking 5 percent of our equity on every single trade, our $100,000 trading account would not be completely gone—we would, in fact, have about $0.28 left. This is comforting if you consider a 99.9997 percent loss to be significantly better than a 100 percent loss, but the distinction is more than a little pedantic.

The advantage of a fixed fractional approach is expanded upside and dampened downside potential, not that it protects you from going bankrupt per se. This is also the reason for the pragmatic 75 percent ruined account barrier set in all of the Monte Carlo tests. In practice, most traders and investors will be uncomfortable with much smaller drawdowns, but this is a useful reference point across these tests.

Using Different Fixed Fractions We used a 2 percent fixed fractional size as a starting point without any real analysis or consideration; it is possible that other percentages could give better results. Table 9.5 shows the Monte Carlo results for several different fixed fractional sizes, including some that are a little crazy. When we were risking a constant $25,000 on each trade, nearly half of our accounts closed below $25,000, the average closing value was $463,980, and some lucky trader made over $2,000,000 at the end of the run. If we compare that to the fixed fractional 25 percent (again, not a direct comparison because that number changes with the account balance), we see the power of the adaptive bet size. Now, 66.5 percent of the accounts close with a greater than $75,000 loss, which is not good. (It's actually a little worse than you might think from the table. Only 281 of the 1,000 accounts actually made money. Over 450 of

TABLE 9.5 Several Fixed Fractional Monte Carlos

	4%	8.333%	10%	12%	25%
Mean Terminal Value	263,545	711,375	1,014,163	1,508,351	5,280,790
Median Terminal Value	222,225	307,825	300,832	262,485	5,630
Std Dev of Terminal Value	193,846	1,431,904	2,821,550	6,005,588	79,775,366
Coefficient of Variation	0.74	2.01	2.78	3.98	15.11
Mean of Max Value	316,875	1,046,380	1,636,924	2,781,394	62,017,391
Mean of Min Value	79,046	58,366	51,237	43,292	9,444
Highest Terminal Value	1,670,569	20,392,572	46,000,315	109,597,717	1,757,129,394
Lowest Terminal Value	29,561	4,647	1,967	629	0
Percent Terminal DD ≥75%	0.0%	4.6%	8.0%	15.6%	66.5%

the initial 1,000 accounts closed with less than $2,000—certainly a catastrophic loss by any reckoning.) However, the average closing value is well over $5,000,000, and one of the accounts made almost two *billion* dollars. This is not a bad run from a starting value of $100,000.

The 8.333 percent example in Table 9.5 is a special case: it is the Kelly number for this particular system. It is worth pointing out that this is exactly the kind of situation in which the Kelly criterion can be safely applied. The wins and losses are all the same size, and there are never any surprises in the form of larger-than-expected wins or losses. In addition, each trade is completely independent of preceding trades. In other words, there are never longer strings of winners and losers than you would expect to see in random data. The Kelly number produces some pretty impressive results, with mean and median terminal values far exceeding anything we were able to hit with the (reasonable) constant risk scenarios. In addition, the Kelly criterion opens the door to truly outstanding performance; one of our Kelly-sized accounts would have run the $100,000 initial investment up to over $20 million by the end of the run. As you might expect from an aggressive strategy, there is also significant risk of loss, as 4.6 percent of the accounts closed under $25,000. Even so, there may be situations in which a trader could accept the risks of an optimized strategy in return for the potential reward. This might depend on the trader's risk tolerance and investment goals for the account. For instance, is the trading account your entire net worth, or is it just a small subaccount that you intend to press aggressively? These questions go beyond the math behind the strategies, but they are important questions to consider before you actually put capital at risk in the market.

As you might imagine, since it is an optimized, aggressive number, bad things start to happen when we risk more than the Kelly criterion suggests. Though the general principle of "risk more, make more" is *technically* true, as you can see from the mean terminal values for the 10, 12, and 25 percent risk levels in the table, the declining medians tell a different story. We cannot see it in the table, but the distribution of these ending balances becomes unacceptable, and the payoff of our well-considered positive expectance trading strategy starts to look more like a lottery ticket as we risk a higher percentage of the account. Do not be misled by the sheer size of the winners, because, as you know by now, the extremely low probabilities associated with those outcomes moderate the expected value.

There is one last important thing to consider. Many traders like to change their bet size based on any number of factors. This can be a well-thought-out and disciplined element of a trading strategy or of trading certain markets. For instance, it might make sense to trade certain kinds of patterns on smaller risk (for instance, the failure tests in Chapter 6), and some traders might want to approach illiquid markets with smaller risk. Too many discretionary traders make emotional decisions about risk without any real analysis, varying their risk based on their impressions of how good a trade is likely to be. If you are making emotional decisions about risk, you are almost certainly making suboptimal decisions. If you are going to intervene and meddle with position sizing and risk, it is important that you do two things: One, understand the impact of random sizing on a system and a strategy. Two, keep careful records and do objective analysis to be sure that your actions are actually adding something of value compared to the unadjusted position sizing rules.

Table 9.6 shows the effect of randomly changing the bet size on each trade. The 4 percent column is reproduced from Table 9.5 for comparison, and then three other tests were run where each bet size was a random value between 0 and 8 percent (~Uniform [0, 8%]). On average, the random bets were still 4 percent, but they varied between 0 percent, where the trader skipped the trade altogether, to 8 percent, where the trader sized up and took on double risk. Notice that in all cases, the randomly sized bets underperformed the simple fixed fractional 4 percent. Of course, it does not have to be that way. The

TABLE 9.6 Examples of the Effect of Randomly Varying Bet Sizes

	4% Nonrandom	Rand1 [0%–8%]	Rand2 [0%–8%]	Rand3 [0%–8%]
Mean Terminal Value	263,545	262,190	257,249	254,106
Median Terminal Value	222,225	192,474	198,389	187,049
Std Dev of Terminal Value	193,846	239,548	211,231	220,697
Coefficient of Variation	0.74	0.91	0.82	0.87
Mean of Max Value	316,875	333,660	326,773	324,438
Mean of Min Value	79,046	74,116	74,063	73,836
Highest Terminal Value	1,670,569	2,062,297	1,886,388	2,001,251
Lowest Terminal Value	29,561	14,833	18,562	20,599
Percent Terminal DD ≥75%	0.0%	0.4%	0.2%	0.3%
Percent of Accounts Bankrupt	0.0%	0.0%	0.0%	0.0%

random sizer could have gotten lucky, but he *usually* will not be lucky, which is what matters. Note that in nearly all scenarios where the mean of the randomly sized scenarios is not much different from the nonrandom baseline, only the variability increases and it does so symmetrically, meaning that, in this case, standard deviations actually are a good proxy for risk. Changing bet sizes simply introduces another degree of freedom into the equation and brings more randomness to the bottom line. Most traders will find that their interventions in position sizing are actually harming their performance because they are making the wrong decisions at the wrong time.

Other Approaches to Position Sizing   There are other approaches and ideas for position sizing, which may be more appropriate for some situations than others.

- *Fixed-percentage allocation:* In portfolio construction and optimization, the values of various assets and asset classes are considered as a percentage of the overall portfolio. There are well-established formulas for understanding the theoretical contribution of each asset to the overall portfolio in terms of volatility, returns, and correlation. For the active trader, I would argue that this number is fairly meaningless. Depending on the risk profile of the market and the specific position, a position that is 5 percent of the portfolio might carry more risk than one that is 50 percent. This is rarely a meaningful measure of the risk associated with shorter-term, technically motivated positions.

- *Margin as a fixed percentage of account:* This is the futures trader's equivalent of the equity trader's percentage of equity allocation in a portfolio. Positions are sized so that the margin required for those positions is a consistent percentage of the account. Exchanges set margins based off their measures and perceptions of risk associated with each market, so, in theory, there could be some justification for this approach. In practice, though, it is a disaster waiting to happen. Volatility is a consideration in the margin calculation, but many other factors determine margins. There are much better ways to size positions.

- *Equivalent volatility strategies:* This strategy has received a lot of attention from portfolio managers and allocators over the past several years. Variations of this concept are sometimes called "equal risk" strategies, and it is also well known that Richard Dennis's and William Eckhardt's Turtles used a variant of this sizing strategy. Basically, you calculate a volatility measure for each market—Average True Range (ATR) is a good standard—and then size each position so that its daily contribution to the portfolio will be the same. You will trade a much larger size in a quiet stock or commodity and a much smaller size in a more volatile one. The point of this sizing is to equalize the impact of each market on the daily portfolio P&L, and it does that very well. It must be emphasized that this strategy does not truly measure and equalize the risk in each position, nor does it consider cases where volatility might be compressed and the market is overdue for a range expansion move. In the wrong hands, this kind of sizing is dangerous, as traders will be putting on very large size at points where the market is highly compressed.

There are many possibilities and choices to be made in position sizing. For the self-directed discretionary trader, this is an important element of the trading plan that deserves careful consideration and study.

THEORETICAL PERSPECTIVES ON RISK

Mathematically, risk is part of the expected value function, and can be defined as:

$$\text{Risk} = \text{Probability of loss} \times \text{Expected size of loss}$$

Though this is a simple equation, there is a profound truth hidden here: the key to properly understanding risk is that the magnitude of the risk depends on both the *probability* and the *size* of the loss (see Figure 9.3). Risks that are very rare and also carry no serious consequences are usually insignificant and can be ignored. However, make sure the consequences are really as small as you think they are; it is easy to miscalculate because these events are infrequent. In addition, consequences are not always consistent—is it possible that there is a small subset of these events that carry more serious outcomes? Risks that are common with low consequences demand careful attention and scrutiny. Traders tend to ignore these risks because they are clearly defined and seem small enough to be insignificant, but a large number of these can eat away at a trading account over time. Examples of these kinds of risks in trading might be normal slippage and transaction costs.

High-probability, high-consequence risks are also usually easy to avoid. These are risks that most people would characterize as stupid and inviting disaster. Most people will look at a risk like this and simply say, "Why would you do that?" Traders usually do not have issues with these risks because they effectively eliminate traders from the industry through a quick and efficient process of natural selection. If you take those kinds of risks as a trader, you will soon not be a trader.

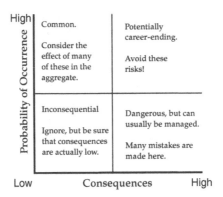

FIGURE 9.3 Probability/Consequence Risk Grid

In general, humans do not have a good internal framework for handling the calculus of risk and probability, especially in high-consequence, low-probability situations. The most dangerous risks for traders lie in this quandarnt. Some people obsess over these risks, but other times these risks are completely ignored. It is easy to mistake extreme improbability for impossibility. Take, for instance, the chance of the planet Earth being struck by an asteroid. It is difficult to imagine a more disastrous event—but the chance of it happening in our lifetime is vanishingly small. Should we be doing more to prepare for and to protect against this risk and at what expense?

I don't know the answer to that question, but I do know that many traders take risks with their portfolios that are, in a financial context, just as severe. A trader selling a lot of naked option premiums could have a single loss that wipes out decades of profits and puts him into personal bankruptcy, but the chance of that happening on any one trading day is very small. This trader probably thinks he can ignore the risk, and he is right, until it happens. Realize that the most serious dangers and risks are these risks that are extremely rare with dire consequences.

Thinking in Sample Sizes

One of the core problems is that thinking in terms of probabilities requires the ability to think in large sample sizes, while we are faced with the concrete realization of a single outcome in the real world. For instance, a common line of thought goes something like this: yes, the probability of that plane crashing might be very small, but that probability doesn't matter to the passengers who happen to be on a plane that *does* crash. This kind of thinking focuses on a single outcome only, not realizing that the true risk depends on both the severity of that outcome and the probability of it occurring. The true risk in this case is the risk present for millions of airline passengers, not those specific, unfortunate passengers who happen to be on a plane with a catastrophic mechanical failure.

It is possible that you play a game in which you have a positive expectancy and lose on several trials in a row, just as it is possible for profitable traders to have losing streaks. If this were your only trial, or if you made only one or two trades, you could end up with a loss due to the luck of the draw. It is counterproductive to focus on any specific outcome; some people say that you can't put probabilities in your bank account, but this is wrong—that is exactly what skilled traders do. Over a large set of trades, traders *do* put probabilities in their bank accounts. The outcome of any one trade, winning or losing, doesn't matter. What does matter is the sum of results over many trades.

Traders make these probability/payoff miscalculations all the time. One of the classic examples is the choice to use very tight stops because the trader wants low-risk trades, not realizing that a tight stop is often a very small but certain loss. Over a large set of trades, the risk of the those many small losses may actually be much higher than the risk associated with a larger stop, because the wide stop will be hit much less often. However, if that large stop happened to be hit on the very first trade, your perception would likely be skewed, and you would probably approach future scenarios with a different mind-set. The key here is to realize that your intuition and perceptions regarding probabilities are unreliable and must be backed up by logic, reasoning, and testing of relevant scenarios.

Uncertainty as Risk

One commonly used definition of risk in many fields of finance is that risk is uncertainty. For instance, when different assets are being evaluated, the standard deviations of their returns are often used as a proxy measure of risk. This raises a few issues that are often ignored: First of all, is this right? Is uncertainty an appropriate measure of risk? This is what is taught in business schools around the world, so it is often accepted by practitioners without question. True, there are applications in other fields of finance where uncertainty may be a good measure of risk. For instance, in corporate finance, managers often prefer a project that has a lower, more certain return to one that has much higher potential payout but with more uncertainty. Certainty of cash flows is the goal in some cases because it allows for the most efficient allocation of resources—surprises are not good. Though this is appropriate from the manager's perspective, it may not be the best standard to apply to trading and investment management, where strategies may sometimes be completely dependent on positive surprises and outliers.

This desire for certainty finds its way into investment management when portfolio managers use the standard deviation of an asset's returns, measured from past returns, as a predictor of *future* risk. This is potentially flawed on several fronts. First, there is no guarantee that future returns will carry similar variation to historical returns. In fact, it is easy to construct a study comparing standard deviations and distributions for assets across different time windows that will reveal the folly of this assumption. It is also entirely possible that an asset may carry risks that are not visible in the return series. For instance, the returns of a trader who simply writes option premiums every month are probably extremely consistent. A strategy like this may very well show many consecutive positive months (or years) with little or no variation, but there is no accounting for the hidden risk of an eventual catastrophic loss—execute this strategy long enough, and there will be a day of reckoning. Other examples might be complex derivatives, such as those that precipitated the 2007–2009 financial crisis, that have embedded structural risks; a return series is irrelevant for such an asset, especially if the market for them is illiquid and inactive. Quantitatively, there is no way to understand these risks from a simple examination of returns, but qualitative assessment might reveal some of the flaws and hidden risks in many of these cases.

Symmetry of risk is another issue that standard models may not capture very well. In the case of the short premium options trader, there is unseen large left-tail risk, but in other cases, the risks may be dramatically skewed to the upside. Which of these carries more risk: a fund that will return 5 percent annually with a 10 percent standard deviation or a fund that will return 5 percent annually with an asymmetrical risk profile extending 5 percent downward and 15 percent upward? The second fund has dramatically higher variability, but all of the extra "risk" is skewed to the upside—in this case, variability is opportunity, not risk, as we saw earlier with fixed fractional position sizing. Simplistic measures of risk will consistently misprice asymmetrical risks in the real world.

MISUNDERSTOOD RISK

If the academic world and market researchers are somewhat divided on how to measure risk, it is no wonder that traders are a little confused. One of the key skills of competent trading is excellent risk management; this can be achieved only if the risks are fully understood and accepted. It is important for traders to think deeply about the nature of the risks they are assuming, and to put them in the context of their expected returns.

Generating Positive Expected Value

We can redefine the expected value equation like this:

$$E = (Prob_{win} \times Size_{win}) - (Prob_{loss} \times Size_{loss}) \therefore$$
$$E = Reward - Risk$$
$$\text{Win ratio} = \frac{Prob_{win}}{Prob_{loss}}$$
$$\text{Reward/risk ratio} = \frac{Size_{win}}{Size_{loss}}$$

where the probabilities and sizes of wins and losses are averages over a large set of trades.

The job of a trader seeking to take consistent money out of the market can be simplified to making the E in this equation bigger than zero, or, more formally, to achieving a positive expected value over a large set of trades. It should be clear that there are two paths leading to this same end: the trader can get there through having either a high win ratio or a high reward/risk ratio. Any combination of the two that results in a positive expected value will make money in the absence of transaction costs. There is no inherent advantage to high-probability trading, and there is also no reason to think that "high risk/reward" trades are better.

The "Risk" of Risk/Reward

Mark Douglas (2001) makes a good argument that one of the major reasons traders struggle psychologically is that they are unable to fully accept the risk in any trade. I would go one step further and say that the reason they are unable to accept the risk is that they don't really *understand* that risk. This may be a radical idea, but, over a large set of trades, I would argue that the "risk" part of the risk/reward equation is not actually true risk.

We live in a world of probabilities, not certainties. No matter how good a trader you are or how good your system is, the outcome of any one trade is more or less a coin flip. You can be a great trader and have three or four losing trades in a row, but this is not *actually a risk*. The losses on those trades are not true risk; they are the cost of doing business. Consider the case of a retail business with a simple business model: the business buys things (inventory), marks them up, and hopefully sells them for a little more than it paid for them. If this were your business, would you consider the money you spent on inventory to be risk, or is it simply a planned expense? Certainly, there *are* risks associated with your business: you can buy insurance to guard against fire, theft, flood, or other damage, but inventory expense is a regular, recurring expense as are normal trading losses.

Some might call this an argument over semantics, but it is actually a very important distinction. When you enter a specific trade, you do not know if you will make or lose money on the trade, so there is a possibility of loss, but over a large enough set of trades, there is a near certainty of a profit *if* you are trading with a positive expectation. This loss is not, in the long run, a risk. (If you are not trading with a positive expectation, then you have a different problem.) Traders are paid for assuming the correct risks at the correct time within a larger-scale, positive expectancy framework. Until you fully assimilate this truth, you will struggle—this is probably the one belief the separates profitable discretionary traders from everyone else.

PRACTICAL RISKS IN TRADING

There are many very real risks in trading. Some of them are obvious, many of them are misunderstood, and some of them are unknowable. The purpose of this section is to get you thinking about these risks, some of which you will encounter every day, and some of which you may meet only once in your career. This is not an exhaustive list of all possible risks, but it does give you some ideas of things to think about.

Trading Without an Edge

One of the worst possible sources of risk must be acknowledged up front—perhaps the trader actually does not have an edge in the market. Larry Harris (2002) calls traders who trade without an edge *futile traders*, and has this to say about them:

> *Futile traders expect to profit from trading, but they do not profit on average. They cannot recognize the difference between their expectations and their results. They may be irrational, they may have poor information about their results ... or they may be of limited mental capacity.*

He goes on to define *inefficient traders*, saying:

> *Inefficient traders lack the skills, analytic resources, and access to information to trade profitably. They may do everything that profitable traders do, but they do not do it well enough to trade profitably.... [Their] profits are not sufficient to cover their losses to more skilled and better-informed traders. Inefficient traders generally make poor decisions about when to trade and when to refrain from trading.*

Without a real trading edge, everything else is a waste of time. Nothing will help; the trader is simply doomed to lose money because the markets are actually worse than our theoretical random walk zero-sum games—the markets are actually a *negative*-sum game due to trading frictions and transaction costs. It is impossible to make money trading without a real edge in the market, and, furthermore, if you don't know what your edge is, you don't have one.

A surprising number of retail traders operate without an edge, and they consistently bleed money. Why would anyone do that? As Harris speculated, perhaps they may be of limited mental capacity, but probably a more common reason is poor record keeping. Few retail traders keep professional-level records tracking every aspect of their performance over a significant period of time. Though record keeping seems like an incredibly mundane topic, the discipline of tracking performance is a core skill of professional trading. It is not uncommon to see working traders devote more attention to the process of record keeping than to actual trading. If you are keeping good records and carefully tracking your trade stats, the numbers will not lie.

Many traders fail and trade without an edge because they do not know how to do the correct analysis to understand their edge, or they make any of a number of mathematic errors in that analysis. (See Chapter 12 for some specific tools and a structured approach to this analysis.) Traders may work hard and sincerely believe they are trading with an edge, but they often are not, and they are confused by the fact that their trading accounts are continually decreasing in value. Many discretionary traders will resist the idea of a systematic, structured approach to trading, but I am not advocating that—I *am*, however, pointing out the necessity of that approach in analysis and in designing your trading system. Unless you do this analysis, how can you be sure you are really trading with an enduring edge in the market? Fail to do this, and you will lose.

Execution Risk

Execution risk is a topic that covers a number of events, including some that are out of the trader's control. Every trader should approach the market with a precise plan for when and where to enter and exit the market on every trade. Execution risk is the divergence between those intended points and the actual prices received. Though these differences will sometimes be in the trader's favor, on balance they will not be. *Slippage*, missed trades, and miscellaneous execution errors add up; collectively, these types of mistakes can become a trading friction that will significantly erode the trader's edge in the market.

The sources of these errors will vary from trader to trader and from market to market and will even be different at different points in a trader's career. For instance, newer traders often miss trades because they are nervous about the (false?) risk associated with the trade. They may hesitate or they may jump the gun and execute trades when their methodology does not actually call for an entry. Some traders randomly alter sizes, sometimes taking a few trades on much larger size, or they may try multiple entries with smaller size. The end result of all of this is that realized results will start to diverge from the theoretical edge.

Execution risk is, to some extent, a normal cost of doing business. Most executions that are time-sensitive will involve paying the spread on at least one, or maybe both, sides of the trade. In liquid markets, this is a negligible expense unless your strategy trades frequently, but for active traders, even the cost of paying a penny spread in and out can be a significant drag on performance. It is also important to consider what liquidity conditions may exist when you need to get out of a trade quickly. In some thin markets (e.g., illiquid futures, currencies, or small-cap stocks), slippage of 10 percent or more is possible at times. Though this is an extreme example, remember that slippage can be a much larger cost than the novice trader would expect. Another reason that execution may diverge from backtested results is that sometimes, in equities, it may not be possible to locate shares for a short sale, or other regulatory restrictions may interfere with the transaction. It is impossible to fully account for events like this in research and backtesting.

Execution risk can be minimized to some extent through experience and the acquisition of good execution skills. It is also important to invest money in technology, infrastructure, and relationships with the best brokers. A good broker should have competitive rates, but no trader should have to deal with a subpar platform or a poor Internet connection. Furthermore, new ideas in new markets should be explored on very small size to judge the difficulties of execution in the unfamiliar territory. If a trader normally risks $5,000 on a trade, perhaps a foray into a new market would be done in a minuscule size, risking $50 per trade. There may be issues as size is increased, but it is always a good idea to have your mistakes and errors on small size where possible.

Disaster Risk

Some *disaster risks* are fairly common, but some are almost impossible to plan for. Examples of fairly mundane risks are loss of power or Internet connection, a hard drive crash, or some other mechanical failure. It is important to have backup systems and to have a plan that extends several steps further than that. But there are many more serious risks that bear consideration. What would a natural or man-made disaster in a major financial center do to your trading program? What if you could not access your trading accounts for a period of days or weeks? Some of these risks are systemic risks and, frankly, cannot be managed very well. There is no point in obsessing over things you cannot control, but there is great value in being as prepared as you possibly can be.

Markets Evolve. Do You?

Throughout market history, there have been many ideas that have worked for a while or in one specific environment, and then they stop working, often after being published. Though we try to build our trading programs on principles that will not change, any trading plan is a specific expression of those tendencies expressed in one specific way. It is completely possible that what worked yesterday will not work tomorrow. This is reality. Stuff, as they say, happens. Markets evolve and erase certain kinds of trading edges.

This is why any system, including a discretionary one, should be subject to some sort of control process, similar to the ones used in manufacturing and quality control (see Chapter 12). The idea is to identify normal variation in the system and then to flag events that seem to violate that normal variation. This is not a simple task, as markets are subject to much more randomness than any manufacturing process, and large surprises are normal for many trading systems. However, with a little work and adaptation, it is possible. Monitoring your performance for severe changes or degradation can give early warning and allow time to make some adjustments. If you are trading an idea that stops working, you will incur some losses. This is unavoidable, but a control process will monitor those losses as they evolve and give a cutoff point at which trading should be terminated. The real danger is not recognizing that something has changed, and continuing to pour money into a trading system that has become a bottomless hole.

Event Risk/Tail Risk

Tail risk refers to extreme events in the tails of a distribution. We might observe a commodity trade for several years, and see that most of its daily returns fall within +/−2 percent of the previous day, with the occasional large move out to 4 percent. However, it is entirely possible that that same market could make a 25 percent move tomorrow, out of all proportion to anything in the historical record. Figure 9.4 shows a daily chart of Procter & Gamble (NYSE: PG) covering several months, including the day of the May 6, 2010 Flash Crash. This was a fairly boring blue-chip stock that was not prone to making volatile movements, but nearly an entire decade of price gains were erased in less than 30 minutes, only to be almost completely regained within the next few minutes. This was a move that most market participants probably thought was impossible, and yet it happened. There are other stocks that showed even more dramatic movements on this day, and this type of event happens several times a year in individual stocks.

In many cases, though not all, these large standard deviation events will be driven by geopolitical events or natural disasters and are completely unpredictable. It is the nature of these events that they are complete surprises. In addition, they are also more or less unhedgeable; appropriate hedges do exist for most of these risks, but the costs of applying them continuously will set a hurdle rate that would be difficult to overcome. For

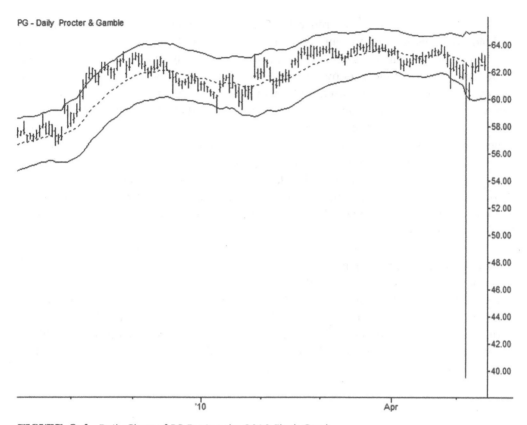

PG - Daily Procter & Gamble

FIGURE 9.4 Daily Chart of PG During the 2010 Flash Crash

instance, the cost of fully hedging a complex portfolio with options can easily run over 10 percent on an annualized basis. With that kind of haircut, you have to ask yourself just how good you think you are. Can you hedge, beat the hedge hurdle, and still make enough to make the venture worth your time? Not likely.

When most traders talk about tail risk, they refer to the kind of events that can put a trader out of business, but remember that tail events are not always bad. Sometimes the trader may be positioned on the right side of the surprise move, and it turns out to be a gift. Though some traders have tried, it is very difficult to structure strategies designed specifically to take advantage of these events, because they are so infrequent and volatile. Even if you are fortunate enough to be on the right side of such a move, there is no guarantee that you will find adequate liquidity to exit at a profit.

Correlation

Correlation is a major concern in portfolio design and analysis, but also may have a larger than expected impact on an active trader holding a handful of positions. Though correlation is usually considered in the context of longer-term portfolios, correlation risk cannot be ignored by the active trader. For instance, an equity swing trader who intends to hold positions for two to four weeks may often be holding five or more positions, distributed across various sectors and industries. Normally, these positions would be quite likely to each follow its own course, with some small degree of dependence on the overall index. A futures swing trader may hold positions in currencies, metals, and grains that turn out to be much more tightly correlated than expected. If a major event hits the market, they will all move together. In a nutshell, correlation is bad because it destroys diversification effects—diversification is not there exactly when you need it most. A trader may believe she is risking 3 percent of her portfolio on four different positions, but if they are highly correlated, it is much more like one large position risking 12 percent of equity. This is far more than most traders intend to risk on any one position, but they do it all the time when they underestimate correlation and risk, and the risk of *shifting* correlations.

There is a good reason to expect increased correlations in times of financial stress: large pools of money tend to move together in times of crisis. This has been well known and documented for decades, but the rise of ETF products has given more investors access to broad swaths of asset classes. Many of these assets are being pooled in various funds as general risky assets that will be dumped en masse in times of systemic stress. If this trend of aggregation continues, and it seems likely that it will, this effect is likely to intensify. Active traders must always consider the possibility that every position they hold can move against them at the same time.

Liquidity Risk

For most traders, the main danger of low liquidity is that you may be unable to execute at prices you intend. Even moderately sized orders can sometimes move markets far more than expected; if the order is time-sensitive, as in exiting a position at a stop point, heavy slippage can result. This is to be expected if the position represents a significant percentage, or multiple of, an asset's average daily trading volume. What might not be so obvious, and thus is more dangerous, is that lack of liquidity can pose a threat to much smaller positions in normally liquid markets. In addition, this effect has been exacerbated in many markets by the risk of high-frequency trading (HFT) programs that provide what is essentially predatory liquidity. Automated market makers are capable of bidding and offering tight spreads, and then widening those spreads when other orders take liquidity from the order book, at speeds far beyond human reaction time.

Regulatory Risk

Regulatory risk is rarely considered, but can have a catastrophic impact in certain market environments. In more mundane cases, a change to tax laws may impair the effectiveness of a hedge or an offsetting position. Sometimes, an increase in margin requirements for a futures contract may have implications for position sizing and leverage across a portfolio. It is not uncommon to see margin requirements adjusted by the exchanges after a

@SI - Weekly Silver Continuous Contract

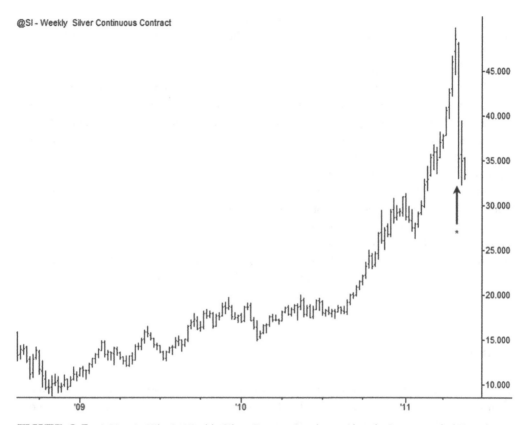

FIGURE 9.5 A Margin Hike in Weekly Silver Futures Breaks an Already Overextended Trend

large price movement, and sometimes these margin changes can break the back of an established trend. Figure 9.5 shows the effect of several margin hikes for Silver futures on the trend in mid-2011. Intuitively, you might expect that such a margin increase would be insignificant, but it can force liquidation and bring large-scale selling pressure into the market. The Hunt brothers' silver fiasco in the early 1980s is one of the best-known examples, but there have been many others as the regulatory environment continually evolves in response to the actions of traders and investors.

In equities, there are frequent restrictions on shorting that may cause actual trading results to diverge from theoretical tests, and there have even been examples where shorting has been banned altogether for a group of stocks or entire regions. In early 2011, some of the cutting edges of regulatory coverage are the issues surrounding HFTs, algorithmic trading programs, and the prevalence of computer-assisted trading programs that seek to capture the liquidity rebates across electronic communication networks (ECNs). It is quite likely that some regulatory move in the next few years will significantly alter the market microstructure and force traders to adapt.

It has also been fairly common to see trades broken in some environments. For instance, there are always traders who buy into large declines like the 2010 Flash Crash, and then sell their inventory into the rallies. Note to regulators and exchange officials: you want to *encourage* this kind of behavior. When markets are crashing, traders who take the risk of buying and potentially supporting markets should be rewarded for this behavior. Instead, in the Flash Crash, many trades were broken outside of arbitrary ranges that were not made up until the next day. This is capricious and random behavior on the part of the regulators. Imagine, for instance, that you stepped in to buy a stock that was down 40 percent, and you offered most of your inventory out at 30 percent, 20 percent, and 10 percent down. As the market recovered, the stock erased its sell-off, your sell orders were filled, and you went home flat. Now you wake up the next morning and discover that the exchange broke all trades more than, say, 30 percent down. What has happened? Your *buy* order was canceled as though it had never happened, but your sells stand, and you are now *short* the stock from 20 percent under the current price. If you are an individual trader, this kind of loss could put you out of business. This is not an isolated example; regulators and exchange officials make these random decisions several times a quarter in various stocks. There is no incentive for the individual trader to step into the breach and to provide liquidity in the event of severe declines, because your trades may simply be erased the next day.

SUMMARY

Risk management is the first and most important job of any trader. Traders must make clear distinctions between the normal risks associated with any trade and the more extraordinary risks that can potentially destroy a trading account or end a trading career. Many of the psychological struggles traders face come from not really understanding the nature of risk. The trader's job boils down to this: assume the correct kinds of risk at the correct times, and manage those risks appropriately; then, assuming the trader is working within a net positive expectancy framework, profits will accrue.

CHAPTER 10

Trade Examples

The main part of intellectual education is not the acquisition of facts but learning how to make facts live.

—Oliver Wendell Holmes

This chapter presents several examples of the trading patterns and ideas in this book applied to real-world market scenarios. Keep in mind that these examples reflect my trading style, which is a pure swing trader's approach that can be summarized as follows:

- Understanding bigger picture money flows between markets. In stocks this might mean understanding the difference in performance between domestic and foreign indexes, and then understanding which sectors offer the most attractive opportunities. This concept can be adapted to other asset classes as well, but the key is to start from a high-level perspective and to work top-down.
- Waiting for precise patterns that indicate the presence of an imbalance. These patterns also give risk points (stop levels) for each position.
- Executing trades to position with the statistical tendency behind that pattern.
- Managing the risk in the trade appropriately, perhaps adjusting the position as the trade develops.
- In almost all cases, I am playing for *one clean swing* in the market.

The last part of that is particularly important: a swing trader's job is to take money out of one swing, usually the next swing, in the market. Swing traders do not enter positions, add to them as they move against the entries, and hope for the best. Swing trading is a style of trading that requires precise entries and active trade management. In many of the examples that follow, you will see that it appears that a lot of money has been left on the table, as I advocate exiting positions when the market would, eventually, have continued to move in the trade's favor. Some traders will find success with an approach that tries to squeeze every penny out of every move. I have not. I focus on the best and the cleanest trades, and it is important to remember that even apparently profitable moves can be outside of the predictive horizon of the patterns traded. If so, they are simply the result of random noise, and may not represent repeatable opportunities.

The initial risk point and the disciplines surrounding it are perhaps the most important elements of these examples. Every trade, without fail, is entered with a predefined stop-loss point that must be respected without question. This risk point also sets the first profit target, the point at which the profit in the trade equals the initial risk. As a matter of discipline, I take profits on between 25 and 50 percent of the position at this first profit target. There is certainly room for discretion in trade management, and the size of this first exit is somewhat flexible. If I am feeling aggressive about a trade, I may, in rare cases, take as little as 20 percent; if I am concerned about a trade, I will book 50 percent at the first profit target. Aggressiveness means something different to me than it does to many traders. I do not risk more on trades I really like—every trade within a trade class is a consistent percentage risk to the net liquidation value of the account ("net liq"). An aggressive approach to a trade simply removes *less* risk and books less profit at the first profit target.

In writing this chapter, my first idea was to use only trades that I had actually executed, whether published in my Waverly Advisors market report or in my own trading account. In the end, pedagogical concerns won, and I made the decision to include some patterns that I did not actually trade. The point of this chapter is to give you the best examples of patterns, to replicate a little bit of the decision process at the right side of the chart; there were patterns I did not trade at the time that serve this purpose better than those I did trade.

Most of these trade examples are presented with two separate charts, the first of which shows what would have been visible to a trader at the actual entry point. Spend some time looking at that chart and trying to understand the market structure and context for the setup. Next try to visualize the most probable price paths that could follow the patterns. Move on to the following chart, which shows the outcome of the trade and the pattern resolution. This second chart also has a heavy vertical line at the point where the previous chart ended to help put the resolution in the context of the setup. It is remarkable how seeing further price action can completely change your perspective on a pattern at the right edge of the original chart. It may be constructive to spend some time going back and forth between the setup chart and the result chart, as well as thinking about alternate ways in which the pattern could have resolved. These are a handful of isolated examples, but they have been carefully chosen and provide a good foundation for learning these patterns.

This chapter is a departure from the existing trading literature because of its emphasis on pattern failures. Trading patterns that work is easy: find a bullish setup, buy, take profits, and move on. However, pattern failures are common, and too many traders have tunnel vision, envisioning only the price movements they expect. When something unexpected happens, they freeze and large losses can result. Understanding the failures and breakdowns of patterns is an essential part of building intuition about the dynamics supporting these trades. In your own work, focus more attention on the unexpected, on failed patterns, than on neat, perfect examples of successful trades.

Last, the discussions of these examples are, for the most part, kept to the most important and most obvious elements of the trade. In reality, any one of these trades could be the subject of deep investigation and could support a narrative running to hundreds of pages. If you think you see another way to understand or to read the patterns in some of these trades, you are almost certainly right. There is little discussion of other patterns and supporting factors (though the MACD and Keltner channels are reproduced on these charts, the text rarely discusses the patterns on these indicators). The trade-off was to provide you with many examples of relevant patterns and trade decisions.

TREND CONTINUATION

Trend continuation plays offer some of the best and most consistent trading patterns. Many traders find that these are their bread-and-butter plays, and that they are the backbone of a comprehensive trading program. All traders and analysts should be very familiar with the ways in which continuation patterns unfold, as a good grasp of these patterns leads to deeper insight into the strength and integrity of the trend.

Simple Pullback, Breakout Entry

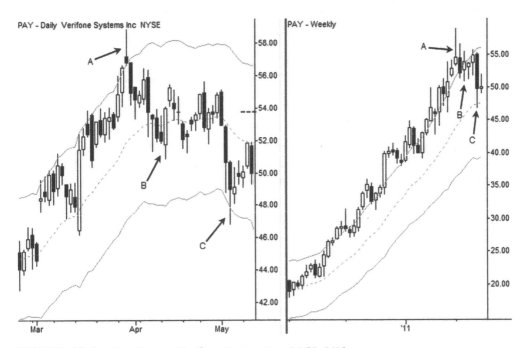

FIGURE 10.1 Short Entry in Verifone Systems Inc. (NYSE: PAY)

Setup

A: In Figure 10.1, a small climax on the daily time frame (left pane) caps a multiyear uptrend. Note that the weekly chart (right pane) is extremely overextended, with many bars pressing above the upper band and two free bars preceding A. This buying climax on the weekly chart provides the context for a potential short on the daily.

B: The daily chart shows a clear, two-legged complex pullback into B, followed by a failed attempt to resume the uptrend. Any trader contemplating buying this market at B should have been concerned that the weekly chart was still dramatically overextended at this point. An aggressive trader could have attempted a long entry at the bottom of this complex pullback, but should have been quick to reduce risk or exit the trade when the upswing failed a few bars after B.

C: A strong downswing brings the daily chart to the lower Keltner channel; the three days preceding C were a distinct change of character from recent price action. Note that the weekly chart has just now completed a complex pullback and has come into its (20-period exponential) moving average.

Entry   The actual entry was on the last bar of the daily chart, ideally when it broke under the low of the previous bar. This is a case in which information about the intraday chart can be inferred from the daily time frame. The penultimate bar on the chart was a small buying climax on the intraday chart (not visible in this example). The reversal the next day, our entry, reversed this buying climax and took out a number of support levels intraday. Also, this entry follows a small two-legged complex consolidation that would have been more clearly visible on an intraday time frame, but is also clear on the daily chart—the small full candle two bars following C represents a failed attempt to continue the downtrend, and the second leg of the pullback exhausts itself into that intraday buying climax.

Stop   An initial stop was established just under 54.00 (the small dotted line), with the plan to quickly adjust or exit the trade if there is no follow-through. A break like this should see immediate and sharp continuation.

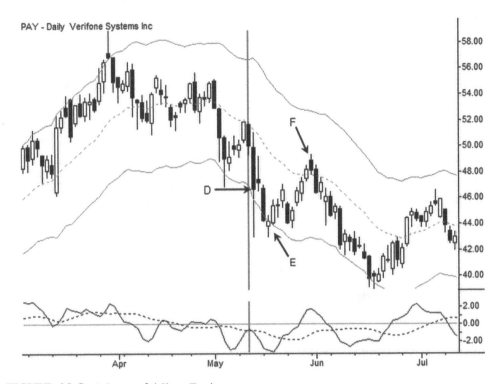

FIGURE 10.2 A Successful Short Trade

D: The next day (see Figure 10.2), a news item hit this stock intraday, driving it well through the 1× (one times the initial risk) profit target and within striking distance of the second. In an active stock like this, traders may use intraday patterns to manage risk and to time entries, but must guard against executing in the insignificant noise of those time frames.

E: An attempt to drive through the lows fails (note the failure test at E), and most swing traders would have been taken out of this trade a few bars after E, against a greatly tightened stop.

F: There was a possible second short entry after another larger complex consolidation, but this trade is slightly out of the scope of the swing trader seeking the simplest, cleanest possible trades.

Conclusions   This example illustrates what appears to be a simple, bear flag style pullback, but the context of the bigger-picture reversal from a parabolic higher time frame uptrend adds confidence to the trade. Furthermore, though there were opportunities for reentry and for longer holding periods, the swing trader's job is to be positioned for the single swing, taking partial profits around D, and most likely exiting the remainder completely on the failure test at E. This is a clean and simple trade, both in concept and in execution.

Simple Pullback, Breakout Entry

ZAGG - Daily Zagg Incorporated

FIGURE 10.3　A Simple Pullback Entry in Zagg, Inc. (Nasdaq: ZAGG)

Setup　Zagg, Inc. had been a market-leading stock for many months. Several previous examples of near-perfect pullback entries are marked on the chart (Figure 10.3), the second of which was a complex pullback. The current entry, at the right edge of the chart, has three warning signs: it is a divergence after at least the fifth leg in an uptrend, there is a momentum divergence on the MACD, and the stock is slightly overextended in a potential buying climax. In a very strong relative strength leader, it is permissible to take a trade with these conditions, which, in a more normal market, might be justification for passing on the trade.

Entry　The actual entry was on the close of the bar that broke above the previous day's high. There were other structures visible on lower time frames, but volatility was compressed, as evidenced by the smaller ranges on the preceding bars, and it was enough to take a simple breakout exit on close.

Stop　The initial stop was set somewhere around 11.25 (the small dotted line). It may seem like the stop could have been higher, for the pullback pattern would be decisively violated just below the recent lows, around 11.75. However, the placement of this stop was a risk management decision. Placing the stop farther away from the market results in a smaller position size; this is a prudent step in a potentially overextended market that could reverse on high volatility.

FIGURE 10.4 A Successful Pullback Trade

Overnight news drove the market to open around the first profit target (Figure 10.4). Many traders would have been tempted to not take partial profits here, or even to add to their positions, with the idea that the news could drive the stock into a new, steeper uptrend. While this is always possible, it is not what *usually* happens. Usually, large gaps like this lead to increased volatility; selling some of the position at the first target will mean that even though the stock may fluctuate wildly, your P&L will not.

A: After one very strong session, the stock began a pullback or a decline that ended in the volatile session marked A. Remember this pattern: A session with a long shadow in the direction of the preceding swing is often a small climax. In this case, a selling climax was clearly visible on intraday charts.

B: Though not the focus of this example, another long position could have been initiated on a breakout of the small days following the selling climax. Consider the bigger picture: this stock was driven higher on news, began a multiweek pullback that ended in a selling climax, and then spent two sessions in volatility compression. At this point, the stock was potentially primed for a directional move, and another long position was justified. Last, note that this leg ran into some resistance just under 16.00, which was approximately the high of the June spike.

Pullback, Lower Time Frame Climax Entry

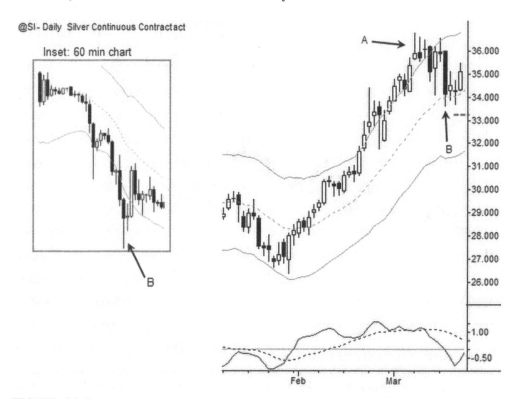

FIGURE 10.5 Lower Time Frame Climax Sets Up a Pullback Entry in Silver Futures

Setup Different markets have different tendencies to trend, and it is important to adjust your trade expectations based on these tendencies. Though it is a gross overgeneralization, currencies tend to trend longest and best, commodities are somewhere in the middle, and equities are more prone to mean reversion and reversal than long trends. Silver had just come from an impressive two-and-a-half-year trend, but this small climax and reversal (see Figure 10.5) were unlikely to be enough to end the trend.

> A: Again, note the buying climax evidenced by the free bars above the channel. There is *no* momentum divergence here, as there are no swings, only a steady grind up to A.
> B: The rule is to not buy pullbacks following a buying climax, and the bar preceding B is exactly why: fake-outs and false entries are normal in these environments.

However, notice what happens at B and the inset chart, which shows an intraday perspective on B and the bar before: a strong selling climax on the 60-minute time frame brings the market to the bottom of the daily consolidation.

Entry   This selling climax is most likely evidence that many weak-hand longs have been flushed out, and it sets up a potential long entry. After this much work, meaning time spent consolidating, the buying climax is effectively worked off. After two bars' consolidation (volatility compression again), the small breakout on the last bar of the chart is a reasonable spot to initiate a long trade.

Stop   A stop was established not far underneath the consolidation. If the trade is going to work well, the lower time frame selling climax should mark the bottom for the foreseeable future. There is no point giving a trade like this additional room to move against you after the entry, so a tight stop is justified.

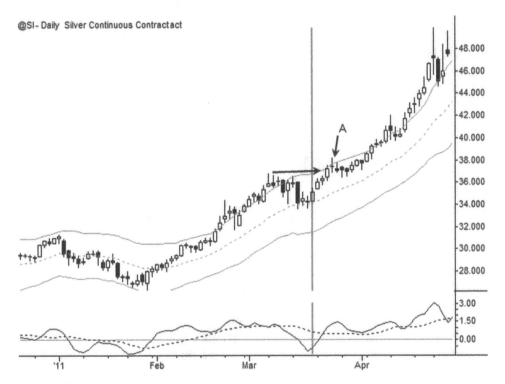

FIGURE 10.6   A Pullback Entry Leads to a Multileg Trend

There was no pain on this trade. Silver traded smartly higher, running into some resistance at A in Figure 10.6, just beyond the first profit target for this trade. Consider how a trading plan like this puts you in control. If you entered after the flush, took partial profits at 1× your risk or the previous swing high, and now hold a partial position against a raised stop, the worst possible outcome is a small profit. (Be careful with phrases like "worst possible outcome" though, because there is always the possibility of an outlier. But for all practical intents and purposes, this would be a risk-free trade at this point.)

Conclusions The outcome of this trade is an example of the best-case scenario in which the market accelerates into further trend legs. At the time of entry, the trend was already potentially overextended, but there were other factors that suggested the possibility of a continued advance. Buying blindly into such an overextended market is dangerous, as sudden, sharp reversals are to be expected, but a good technical pattern can provide a clear risk point.

The discipline of taking partial profits is important: pay yourself as the market makes profits available, and, in doing so, reduce open risk in the trade. Many traders looking at a chart like this try to find ways to pile in and maximize profits, but they will often find themselves with top-heavy positions at the points where volatility explodes. By reducing risk as the trade matures, the position will be able to endure elevated volatility without excessive swings or unnecessary risk.

Pullback, High and Tight

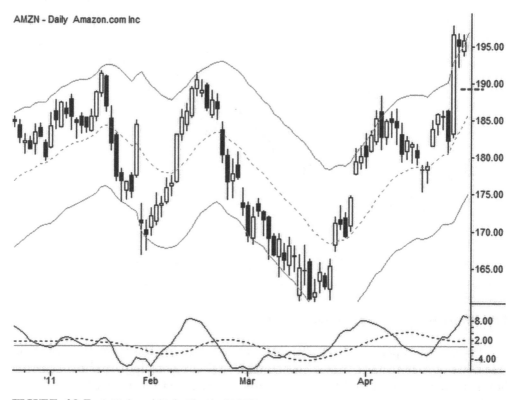

FIGURE 10.7 A High and Tight Flag in AMZN

Setup Casual inspection of a chart can sometimes give insight into the character of a market. In this case (Figure 10.7), Amazon.com, Inc. (Nasdaq: AMZN) appears to be a volatile and somewhat unpredictable stock—sharp reversals and gap openings are the norm. You have essentially two choices trading a market like this: either use very large stops and small position sizes or limit your involvement to the points where you have the clearest possible patterns. The high and tight flag at the end of this chart is such a setup. Look at this chart and consider what you will do the next day if the stock trades above the previous day's high. Though most traders will see that the breakout of the high of the last bar is a good entry, consider what you will do if the open gaps above that high. These patterns often build up a lot of pressure, and it is not uncommon to see opening gaps beyond the confines of the pattern. These can be difficult entries because you may find yourself executing at adverse prices, but these gaps often point to a powerful shift in the underlying dynamics.

Mark this example well. Two days before the end of the chart, the stock had one of its strongest up closes in recent history. At this point, it was potentially overextended (especially on lower time frames), but two days of tight consolidation worked off that condition and set up the potential for a good directional move. The fact that a market *can* consolidate near the highs of a large thrust (meaning that mean reversion has failed in this case) is strong evidence of underlying buying pressure.

Entry There are several ways to actually enter a pattern like this. The easiest is simply to pay a breakout (or a breakdown, for a bearish consolidation) of the small pattern. Expect volatility expansion. If the trade is going to work well, it should work quickly; be suspicious of markets that go dull and flat following an entry like this.

Stop You could make the argument for a tighter stop than the one indicated on the chart, which is just under 190. Would you really hold it to that point if the next day took out the last day's high, triggering a long trade, and then the stock turned and melted down? Few traders would, but again, the widened stop is a risk management decision. The proper stop for the pattern is much higher, probably around 191.50, but the wider stop, in this case, was seen to be a more prudent use of capital and risk given the prevailing volatility conditions and the risk of a large opening gap.

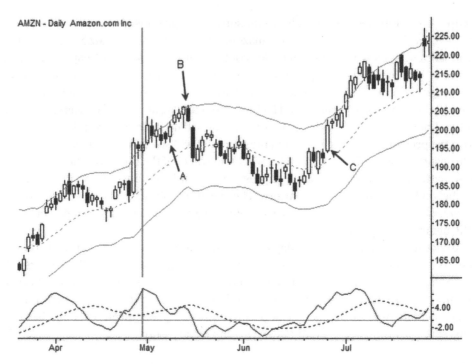

FIGURE 10.8 Targets Are Hit, but the Move Is Weak

If you had entered on the next open (see Figure 10.8), which gapped above the consolidation pattern, the first target would have been touched within the same session. Once again, reducing risk at this target is a key to effective position management.

A: The initial thrust out of the pattern did fail by going into another consolidation pattern. Depending on risk tolerance and the willingness to hold a flat position, a trader could have been justified in holding through this pattern, but it is not an example of best practice.

B: Another thrust to highs fails to see follow-through, and generates a glaring sell divergence on the MACD. Where should you exit any remaining long exposure? Though B is a downward close, it is a small range day and is still potentially consistent with consolidation. However, the next open gapped lower and traded down off the open with a vengeance. Any remaining longs should have been out long before the close of this day.

C: Another possible long entry, but not an example of one of the best setups on this time frame. A trade entered at this point would essentially have been a trade on the weekly time frame, as the long consolidation was required to work off the meltdown from B, following three pushes to a high. Appropriate stops for a trade entered at C are far away, perhaps under 175. Again, this large stop is consistent with a trade executed on the weekly time frame, but is far too large for the daily chart.

Conclusions   This is an excellent example of a high and tight flag. If a market makes a strong thrust in either direction (one to three bars) and is able to consolidate near the extreme of that thrust for a few bars, this sets up a good continuation play on a breakout of the pattern. This is potentially an aggressive trade that can lead to volatile swings both for and against the position, and it does require active management. This particular example had an anticlimactic outcome, though the setup and entry were textbook examples of the pattern.

Pullback, Nested

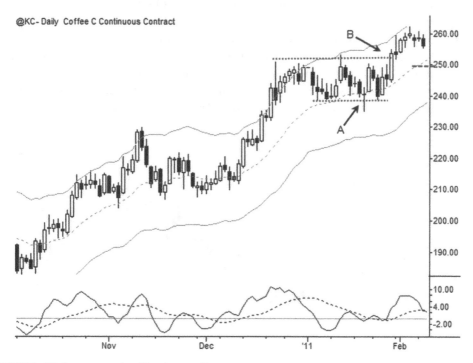

FIGURE 10.9   A Nested Pullback in Coffee Futures

A nested pullback is a small consolidation pattern that sets up in a drive from a larger, possibly higher time frame pattern. In some sense, it is simply a pullback preceded by the typical strong setup thrust, but the difference is that bigger-picture context and motivation are provided by the larger pattern. This particular example (Figure 10.9) is a breakout from a multiweek range that showed no signs of failure or reversal, so the first pause was a reasonable spot to increase long exposure. Note that there is some overlap between these setups, and this could just as well have been categorized as the first pullback following a breakout.

A: Though it was not clear at the time, A marks a classic Wyckoff spring. It is not always necessary to trade these patterns; much of the benefit comes from the information they add to the market structure. In this case, the presence of the spring pointed to accumulation in the range and suggested that the breakout might have some real strength behind it.

B: The actual breakout happened over several sessions and showed no signs of exhaustion or failure. At the end of this chart, the market was consolidating in a tight pullback.

Entry This is another type of very small pullback, and the same entry techniques that work for nested pullbacks will serve here. Look at the last bar on this chart and ask yourself: is there a potential entry on strength on the next bar?

Stop Some traders may prefer to use a very tight stop on a pattern like this, and it certainly is possible. My choice to use a slightly deeper stop is primarily a risk management choice that respects the tendency for volatility expansion following a contraction like this. There is also no rule that says you must hold a position to the stop level; in many cases, it makes sense to exit the trade once the pattern is decisively violated.

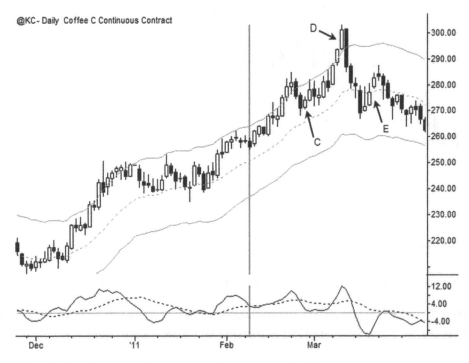

FIGURE 10.10 Two Strong Trend Legs Follow the Nested Pullback

Coffee broke out of the small nested pullback, and accelerated into an even stronger trend leg, as evidenced by the thrust above the upper Keltner channel in Figure 10.10.

C: This is an example of how a technical pattern may be used to manage an existing position, even if it is not strong enough to justify a stand-alone entry. It would have been difficult to initiate a trade on the small pullback at C, but traders holding existing longs could see that the pattern was unfolding according to expectations.

D: This is a classic example of a minor buying climax. Note the parabolic acceleration, the free bar, and the immediate sharp reversal. This is precisely the kind of pullback you *do not* want to buy, so existing longs should have exited their positions somewhere in this move. You will never sell the high tick of the move (D), but you will be able to limit losses on the reversals. This area also brings up the limitations of an indicator; the MACD did not show a momentum divergence, but the price structure was clearly climactic.

E: The downthrust at D was strong enough to set up a potential short (an Anti trade) in the pullback at E. At the very least, being caught long on a breakdown of this pattern is unacceptable.

Conclusions   There are many things going on in this example. Most important is the idea of using a small consolidation as an entry trigger into a bigger pattern. The successive price action at C, D, and E is also a good lesson in using these patterns to manage existing positions.

Complex Pullback

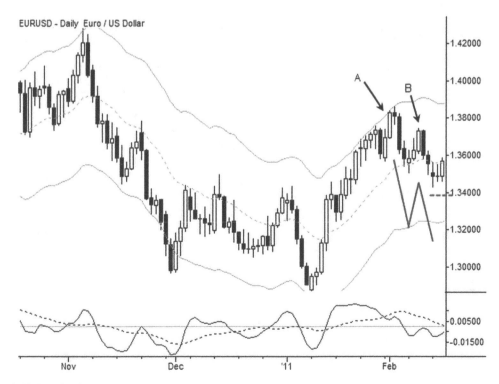

FIGURE 10.11   A Complex Pullback in the EURUSD

Setup

    A: After a month-long drive coming off a failure test of the lows in early January 2011 (see Figure 10.11), the EURUSD showed some signs of exhaustion near the upper band and rolled over into a pullback.

    B: It would have been a reasonable play to attempt to establish a long position following this pullback, but most long traders would have had a losing or, at best, breakeven trade following B.

Entry   After such a losing trade, many traders are tempted to move on and to remove the market from consideration. This is a mistake. A much better plan is to continue to monitor developing market structure, understanding that a complex pullback is likely. There are several possible entry techniques, ranging from buying tests of the pattern based on trend lines (not relevant in this example) to again paying small breakouts near the bottom of the pattern.

Stop   It is reasonable to establish tighter stops on these complex consolidations than on simple pullbacks. Moves out of these patterns should be both cleaner and stronger than corresponding moves out of simple pullbacks; a failure out of a complex consolidation is much more likely to lead to a sharp reversal and complete failure of the pattern, so further stops tend to result in larger losses with no compensating factors of probability or reward/risk.

FIGURE 10.12 A Complex Consolidation Leads to Significant Upside

If you executed the trade with this stop, there are several choices for targets. I set my first target at one times my risk in almost all cases, the only exceptions being when that target would be beyond a very visible chart point. In this case (Figure 10.12), there was additional volatility at C, but you should have already sold a portion of your exposure at the first target. Once again, booking partial profits and reducing open risk puts you in a position of strength and you can watch action at C and not be forced to react.

It is also worth noting that the long lower shadow on the candle at C suggests a lower time frame selling climax. Though it is an extremely aggressive entry, and not appropriate for most traders, adding or entering long positions over the high of C is a possibility to consider. (This is a variation of the nested pullback idea.)

D and E were both large drops against the uptrend, and should have been warnings that the trend was vulnerable. After a strong sell-off like E, it is difficult to justify holding long positions in the time frame relevant to this chart.

Conclusions   Again, much more data has been shown than was needed. Most swing traders, playing for only one clean swing, would have been out of their positions before D. Two other points to consider here: currencies do not tend to trade as cleanly as most other markets, so many technical traders will find better results trading them on higher time frames. Last, a complex pullback is usually a higher time frame simple pullback. This is why the moves following these patterns tend to be stronger—they are more correctly higher time frame drives.

Complex Pullback

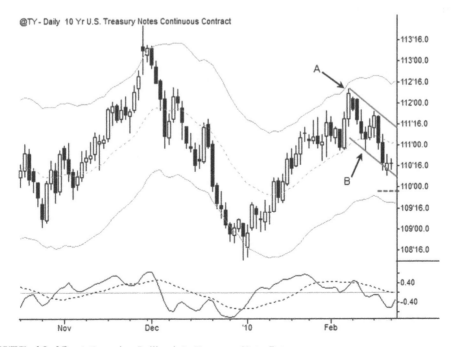

FIGURE 10.13 A Complex Pullback in Treasury Note Futures

Setup

A: After a small exhaustion on lower time frames, Treasury futures began a five-day
pullback.

B: Once again, a long entry was reasonable at the bottom of the first pullback, but
would have resulted in a losing or, at best, breakeven trade when the first pullback failed.

Entry   Another leg down brought the market to a potential entry for a complex pullback. Though only one time frame is shown in Figure 10.13, it is not difficult to visualize
the higher time frame: The long drive off the January lows would be a single thrust on a
higher time frame, and the complex pullback on the daily chart would resolve in a simple
pullback on the higher time frame. You want to avoid buying into the middle of a pullback like this. Focus attention on establishing positions either on breakouts, *with* the
anticipated momentum, or near potential support in the pattern.

This trade shows a hybrid entry technique. The last downswing pressed the pullback
below the parallel trend line, parallel to the standard trend line drawn across the top of
the pattern. This highlights a very small selling climax, and sets up a potential long entry
on strength in the next trading session.

Stop   Again, stops can be tighter in complex pullbacks than in standard pullbacks. A
reasonable stop is just under 110'0, and certainly no deeper than 109'12. There is no point
in holding a complex pullback through another countertrend swing. These structures do
exist, and they sometimes offer continuation in the direction of the trend, but they are
not great trading patterns.

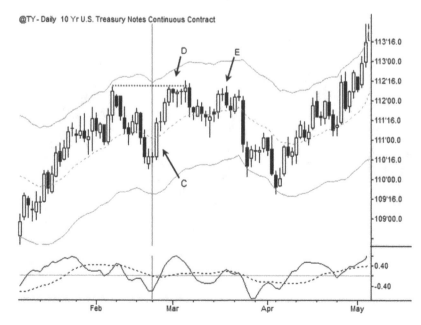

FIGURE 10.14 Is This a Failed or Successful Pullback Trade?

This example highlights the importance of trade location. Consider the entry bar C in Figure 10.14. If the actual entry was made on the close of that bar, the risk point may have been far enough away that no profit targets were hit before the move stopped near D. However, if the entry was done closer to the breakout of the previous day's high, first targets (at 1× risk) would have been reached on the second or third bar following C.

The consolidation at D is cause for concern for longs, but not necessarily justification for exiting the full position.

Pullback Failure at Previous Swing

FIGURE 10.15 A Pullback Failure at Previous Swing

The first common pullback failure is a failure near the previous swing that set up the pullback. Is this actually a failure? The answer depends on your expectations for the pattern. It is a failure if you were expecting another complete trend leg or legs to emerge, but the conservative target for a pullback *is* that previous swing point. Furthermore, if you have been able to establish a position near the bottom of a pullback in an uptrend or near the top of a pullback in a downtrend, the first 1× risk target may already have been hit. If this is a failure pattern, it is a failure that can often result in a profitable trade. The most common error here is to not recognize the failure, to continue to hold the trade, and to take a senseless loss on the position.

A: In Figure 10.15, this day provided an ideal entry into the small pullback, showing a small selling climax and subsequent failure on the part of sellers.

B: The swing falls short of the previous high. Consider the character of the move we expect to see out of ideal pullbacks: the best examples will show strong conviction, which this clearly does not. It would have been difficult to hold longs through the session following B.

C: No swing trader should still be long, but here is an actual failure test entry for shorts. If, by some chance, you are still holding a long position against a signal like this, exit immediately.

Pullback Failure at Previous Swing

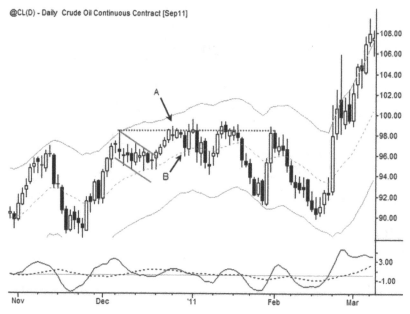

FIGURE 10.16 A Pullback Failure in Crude Oil

A: The same theme is in play here in Figure 10.16, except the pullback setting up the failure was not as deep, so first profit targets may not have been hit (depending on stop placement). Once again, the consolidation just under resistance at A is potentially constructive. Ideally, we would like to see more conviction and an easier break of resistance, but everything at this point is still supportive of the long trade.

B: There are several logical choices for managing a trade like this:

- Take partial profits at A, when the market runs into resistance, even though the 1× target has not been reached.
- Tighten stop under A, so that part or all of the position is exited on the bar marked B.
- Move stop to breakeven at A so that the worst intended outcome is a scratch. Remember that gap risk exists; the actual loss may be larger.

Whichever plan makes sense to you, the important thing is to execute it consistently. By B, it was clear that the pullback trade was not working cleanly and steps should have been taken to adjust or exit the trade. Also, remember the job of a swing trader is to take money out of one clean swing in the market. No swing trader, working on this time frame, would have been justified holding the trade through the multiple tests and failures of the resistance level, even though the market did eventually trade higher. Focus on finding and trading only the best and clearest opportunities.

Pullback Failure: Strong Momentum Develops

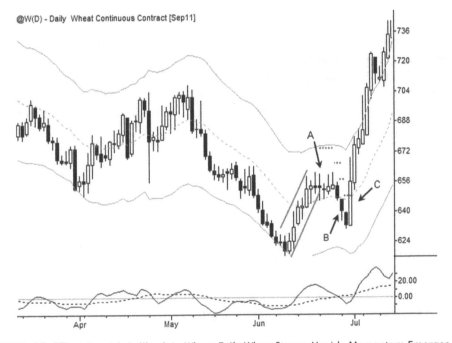

FIGURE 10.17 A Bearish Pullback in Wheat Fails When Strong Upside Momentum Emerges

Figure 10.17 shows a consolidation pattern in a downtrend. There were several spots to enter a short position:

A: The small bars in this area are evidence of volatility compression and justification to take trades in the direction of downside breakouts from this area. There were several spots to enter a short position somewhere around A, against a stop somewhere around the highest of the small dotted lines.

B: At this point, the second downward closing bar, the trade is working. This is a small, but very important point: once a trade is working, once the market is moving in the intended direction, tighten stops to reduce open risk. This is not a precise trailing stop methodology, but remember that once the trade begins to work, if it turns back up, a complex consolidation is a likely outcome. There is no point in booking a full-sized loss on a transition into a complex consolidation, and then possibly not having the capital or the will to attempt another trade in that pattern.

C: In this case, extremely strong upside momentum developed against the pullback. Though it was still possible that the pattern would develop into a complex consolidation, after momentum this strong it probably makes sense to move on to better opportunities—this is not what you, as a short or a potential short, want to see. Note that even though this appears to be a catastrophic pattern failure, the actual loss on the trade should have been very small against the lowered trailing stop.

This is a common pullback failure pattern, and a good reminder of the importance of moving stops. Trade management does not necessarily mean executing—everyone understands the idea of reducing position sizes to limit risk, but sometimes simply moving a stop is the right answer. Remember, your job as a swing trader is to take money out of the cleanest single-leg moves in the market. Never let a trade that is working turn into a full-sized loss.

Pullback Failure: Goes Flat After Entry

FIGURE 10.18 A Pullback in Live Cattle Futures Goes Flat

Every edge we have as technical traders comes from an imbalance of buying and selling pressure in the market. We get into pullback trades, such as the one in Figure 10.18, under the assumption that the pressure driving the trend will continue after the pause that creates the pullback. If this assumption is incorrect, the market may simply go flat after the trade is entered, without a significant move up or down. This is strong evidence that the market has temporarily found equilibrium and that whatever edge there might have been in the trade is now gone.

A: This bar offers an excellent entry into a pullback in a strong downtrend. After a strong down bar, the market consolidated with an inside day (a day which has a lower high and higher low than the previous day); this type of consolidation is perfectly consistent with the downtrend, but the next day broke to the upside. You have to decide how reactive you wish to be to small signals like this. In general, there is too much noise in most markets to trade every small movement, but at this point it is reasonable to say that this is not an example of the cleanest possible trade.

B: Even if you are prepared to trade pullbacks with a lot of patience, this is too long to sit in a simple pullback. The market is flat; the anticipated breakdown did not happen, so it makes sense to scratch the trade, exiting for either a small win or loss. Note also that B is a potential sign of distribution, a Wyckoff upthrust. Be careful of seizing on elements like this to justify overstaying your welcome in trades that are not working. This was a simple pullback trade that should have broken down long ago. Get flat.

C: In this case, the break was to the upside, but the point is that it was a coin flip—there was no point being in the trade by this time; your capital, both financial and mental, would be more profitably deployed elsewhere.

TREND TERMINATION

Trend termination plays are slightly more complex than trend continuation plays. There is more potential for extreme volatility and large surprise moves near the end of trends, so it may make sense to trade some of these on smaller size and portfolio risk. In addition, outcomes are not as clearly defined—there are many instances where the trend does terminate, but there is not enough play or price movement to give substantial profits. In all cases, the discipline of taking partial profits and managing risk on the remainder of the trade are essential skills for these types of trades.

Failure Test

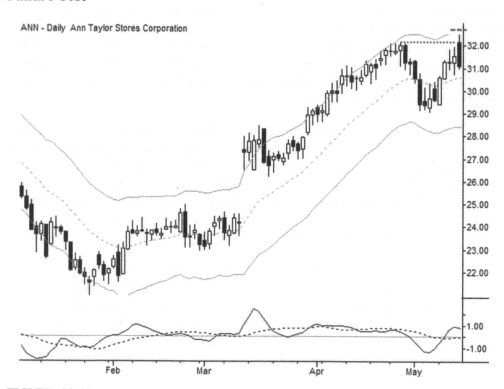

ANN - Daily Ann Taylor Stores Corporation

FIGURE 10.19 A Failure Test in Ann Taylor (NYSE: ANN)

Setup ANN had been in a multimonth uptrend, and was, in fact, a market leader for a substantial part of the advance shown in Figure 10.19. In general, it is difficult to find spots to short market leaders, so only the best and clearest trades are appropriate. A strong sell-off going into May broke the established pattern of the trend, putting with-trend traders on notice and giving countertrend traders warning to start watching for potential entries. This is an important and often overlooked aspect of countertrend trades: you must have some reason, some justification for even considering a countertrend trade, and the best justification is price action that shows a distinct change of character.

Entry The actual entry was on the day that pressed to a new high and immediately reversed, closing strongly lower. There is a trade-off between trade location and confirmation here. While an astute intraday trader may have been able to position somewhere near the high of the day, a trader doing so as a matter of course will unavoidably have many losing trades that reverse and take out the highs. A trader waiting for the close will give up significant price movement in return for the confirmation. Either plan will work if it is applied with discipline.

Stop   The stop in this trade should be located at or around (within a few pennies of) the previous trend high. Many traders will place the stop *outside* the previous trend extreme, but this can result in considerable slippage. Placing the stop inside the previous extreme will result in a rare stop-out where the trade is still valid, but the reduced slippage on nearly all exits will more than compensate.

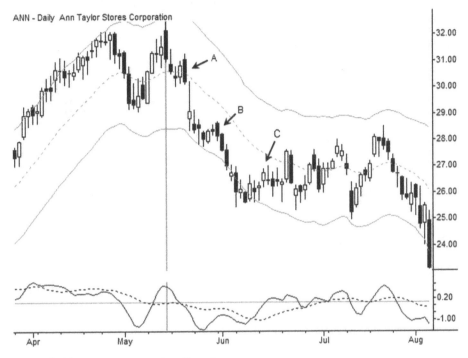

FIGURE 10.20   A Best-Case Failure Test Outcome

The chart in Figure 10.20 is an example of practically the best possible outcome from a trade like this. First (1×) profit targets would have been hit early on, and in this case, the failure test actually marked the extreme high point of the trend.

A: After a strong downthrust, a small consolidation like this often points to more downside—you can enter new positions here, add to existing positions, or just use the pattern as a reference to manage existing exposure.

B: Even if you do not choose to trade pullbacks, they are the fundamental structure of trends, and being able to read price action around pullbacks will give you great insight into the integrity of the trend. Many traders would have covered much of their trade by this point, but seeing small consolidations break down cleanly could give you justification for holding part of the trade.

C: Continuing with that theme, when you see these patterns *not* break down as cleanly or easily, it is a sign that something has shifted and the easy money in the trade is probably over.

Conclusions   This is admittedly a best-case example of a clean and simple failure test trade. It is absolutely essential to maintain the discipline of taking partial profits at the 1× target, because many of these trades will quickly reverse and continue the original trend. In addition, it probably makes sense to do these failure test trades on smaller risk for two reasons: stops tend to be very tight, often less than a single day's range, and there is increased danger of catastrophic gap failure through the old trend extreme.

Failure Test, Second-Day Entry

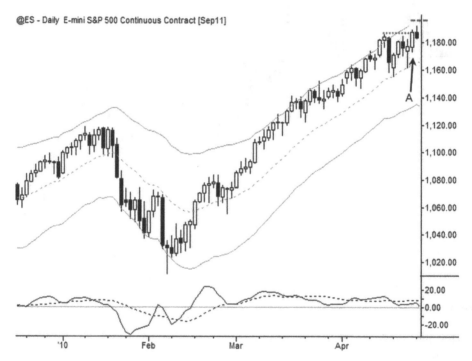

FIGURE 10.21   A Second-Day Failure Test Entry

Setup   The S&P 500 index, shown in Figure 10.21, had been in a yearlong uptrend and was showing signs of possible overextension on higher time frames. There was no strong down move setting up this countertrend trade, but there were multiple momentum divergences and failures on lower time frames that set up the possibility of a successful fade trade.

Entry

A: The actual entry is slightly more complex in this case. This bar presses to new highs and closes slightly above the previous resistance level. The next day trades high, then reverses to close under the old highs. Entry is on the close of the last bar on this chart.

Stop   The stop should be around the small, downward-closing candle's high, which is slightly less than an average day's range from the entry. It is appropriate to risk less on these trades; having a very large position size (required by the tight stop) near the high of a strong market in a strong trend is potentially dangerous.

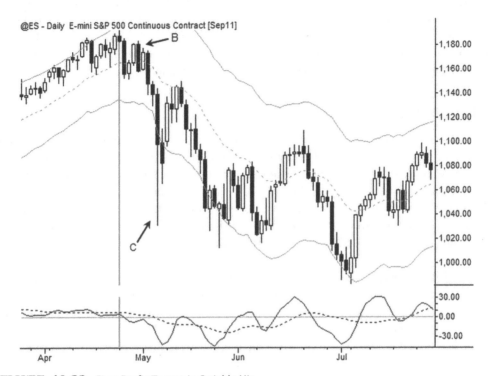

FIGURE 10.22   First Profit Target Is Quickly Hit

The next day (Figure 10.22) saw strong selling, and the 1× profit target was exceeded on this day. Again, even though the market may be very weak, maintain the discipline of these partial exits—this is absolutely crucial to your long-term success with these trades.

- B: The same concept at work as in the previous example: a brief consolidation breaks down into another down move. This is justification for continuing to hold part of the position.
- C: This is the May 2010 Flash Crash. If you are ever holding a position into such an exceptional move, cover part or all of the position into the move. Do not be greedy and do not play for a one-in-a-million event. On those very rare occasions when the market offers windfall profits, take them.

Conclusions   This is another exceptional outcome for a failure test trade, but does illustrate the power of this very simple trade entry. Traders who blindly fade trends will suffer loss after loss, while traders working with disciplined technical patterns like this can fade trends safely and effectively. There is also a lesson here in the interaction of intuition with disciplined technical rules. I had been writing in my daily research report that the market was overextended and that there was a dangerous degree of complacency. On the day of this entry, I wrote that the market was "vulnerable so that when a shock finally does hit . . . the effect may be out of all reasonable proportion."

This is not to say that this pattern predicted the Flash Crash. Far from it, for that was a completely unforeseeable outlier event, but the fragility of the market was apparent from an intuitive perspective, and this pattern provided a safe entry near the absolute high of the trend. We never know what opportunity a trade might offer—the best we can do is to enter on clear patterns, take partial profits, and manage the risk.

Failure Test, Other Variations

The failure test pattern itself is very simple, with only two significant variations: entry on the bar that makes a new trend extreme or on the following bar. The entry is probably best made on the close of one of those bars, but some traders will find success timing intrabar entries with a few potential trade-offs. (Note that both previous examples were shorts, but the trade is perfectly symmetrical for the buy setup.) There are a few common variations of patterns that set up this trade; the entry is consistent in all cases, the only difference being the preceding market structure.

Following a Long Consolidation   Many times a market will show a series of consistent consolidations (say five to eight bars), and then will consolidate near the trend extreme in a much longer consolidation, perhaps three or four times the normal length. Many traders would regard such a pattern as a sign of real with-trend pressure, but it often sets up a good countertrend trade on a failure test. Be on guard for failure out of these long consolidations. It is also worth considering what separates this pattern from a long prebreakout base. Though some of these long flags will function as a prebreakout base, the main difference is location in the trend. Consolidations tend to be near the trend extreme in a long trend, whereas breakout bases come after protracted trading ranges and usually not near an identifiable trend extreme.

Following a Climax   There are a number of patterns that point to a potentially climactic trend ending: three pushes, parabolic expansion, or multiple free bars. As always, it is usually counterproductive to try to get in front of these patterns and establish early countertrend positions in what could simply prove to be a very strong trend. It is better to wait for the potentially climactic structure, the first reversal off that structure, and then be on guard for a failure test at the previous extreme. This is a disciplined and relatively safe way to trade an aggressive countertrend trade.

As Entry into Higher Time Frame Structure   Some of the best trades come where failure tests market precise entries into higher time frame patterns. For instance, if the weekly chart is setting up bullish continuation patterns, failure tests of lows on the daily or hourly chart can provide outstanding entries.

FAILURE TEST FAILURES

On one hand, failures of the failure test pattern are simple—the market makes a new extreme and keeps going. However, this understates the potential damage and risk around these points. Some of these trades may fail with large gap moves, forcing the trader to exit far beyond the intended risk point. There is no perfect solution that can avoid all of these cases, but in addition to perhaps trading these with smaller risk, being aware of the patterns that typically set up failure of these patterns can provide additional insight into developing market structure.

Failure Test Failure by Consolidation

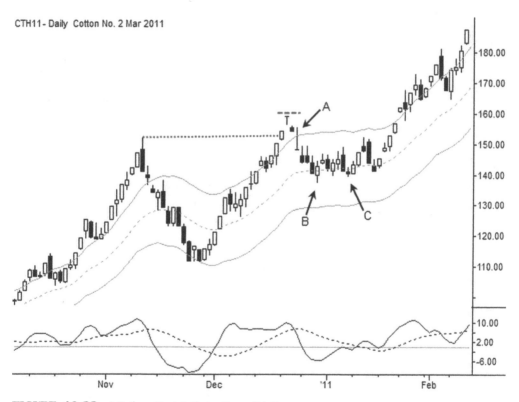

FIGURE 10.23 A Failure Test Fails by Consolidation

   A: This was an example of a slightly more complex entry on the *third* bar following a market high in Figure 10.23. This is an acceptable variation, particularly in the low-volume, preholiday environment of late December, but it is not a model entry.

B: This move falls short of the first profit target, which is a warning sign. In most cases, the stop and the first profit target on failure test trades are both relatively close to the entry price. You should not have to wait more than three or four bars for the profit target to be hit, and many times it will be reached on the first bar following the entry. It is justifiable to reduce risk in the trade (by exiting part of the position) somewhere following B because the trade is not working as well or as cleanly as expected.

C: Exactly how long you hold the trade is a personal decision, but somewhere following C holding becomes a matter of hoping rather than of positioning with a clean, working trade. In this example, the worst outcome should have been scratching the trade, exiting very near the entry price for a small gain or loss.

Failure Test Failure by Consolidation

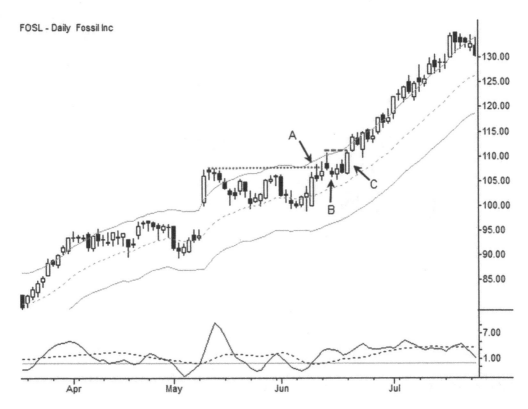

FIGURE 10.24 Another Example of Failure by Consolidation

A: The chart in Figure 10.24 shows also another nonstandard entry, but the less-than-perfect outcomes of these trades are probably not due to the quality of the setup patterns. Fossil Inc. (Nasdaq: FOSL) was a fairly illiquid momentum stock during this time period, so it did not trade cleanly around levels. An entry could have been attempted at A, but most traders would have wanted to see more decisive action above resistance to set up an entry.

B: The best entry for this trade is probably at B, but it may also have been a second entry for traders who booked a loss following A. Consider expectations for a trade like this, particularly in a market-leading momentum stock: If the trade is correct, the stock should immediately melt. There should be sharp and clean downward momentum away from the level.

C: This downward momentum did not develop, and the trade eventually failed at C. In this case, the preceding consolidation was small, only two or three bars. It is a challenge to make adjustments to the trade within this time period, so it is reasonable to expect that a trader might have booked another loss at C. This is another reason for doing these trades on half risk, relative to most other trade classes. In this example, a trader might have taken full losses following two entries at both A and B. Though unusual, this does happen, so it must be anticipated in the trading and risk management plans.

Failure Test Failure with Second Entry

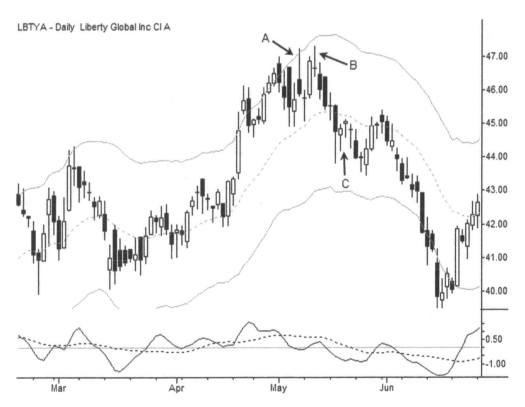

FIGURE 10.25 A Failure Test with Obligatory Second Entry

A: A simple, classic failure test entry in Figure 10.25, which also corresponds with a pullback failure via failure test. Assume that the entry was on the close of this bar so that the first target was not hit on the next bar.

B: The high of B slightly exceeds the high of A, so realistically, the short should have been stopped out. In this case, reentering on the close of B allows an excellent entry into a second trade that more than makes up for the loss on the first trade. Some traders look at trades like this and reason that they should not stop out of the first trade. This is a mistake—too many of these trades fail with dramatic moves beyond the high of A, so your focus must be on limiting risk and correctly exiting the losing trades.

C: Again, the small consolidation breaks down, confirming the health of the down-trend. When the ensuing thrust runs out of steam near the previous pivot low, it probably makes sense to close the trade and look for clearer opportunities.

There is an important lesson here. Though the first trade failed, the second entry is almost required. If you have let the first loss get out of control through inappropriate position size or poor stop discipline, it is very difficult to justify taking a second swing at the trade. Maintaining iron discipline *on every trade* is perhaps the most important part of building trading consistency.

Failure Test, Other Failures

There are a number of other possible failures for this pattern, but two deserve spe-cial attention. It is not uncommon to see these patterns fail at or near the first target. These targets may be touched overnight or in premarket, so it is important to have profit-taking orders working all the time, good until canceled and outside of regular trading hours. Sometimes other players make mistakes in those thin markets outside regular trading hours; it is your job to be ready to take advantage of those mistakes with well-placed profit-taking orders. One of the keys to trading these patterns well is to be very disciplined in taking profits at this first target. It is unacceptable to have a trade trade through the first target and then turn around and hit the stop, and for you to have taken a full-sized loss on the trade with no profits booked. This is not even techni-cally a *failed* pattern because it did hit the first target, so follow the rules and manage trades appropriately.

The second failure to consider is the possibility of a failure by a large adverse gap. Though not common, you are positioning countertrend near the trend extreme with this trade setup, so a trend-continuation gap can be a dangerous event. Gaps in the direction of the trade (i.e., through the first target) are more common, but plan for the possibility of a larger-than-expected loss on some set of these trades. Trading these failure tests on smaller size, perhaps half the size of normal, with-trend trades, is a prudent risk manage-ment step.

TRADING PARABOLIC CLIMAXES

Parabolic climaxes are disorderly, volatile areas. It is difficult to initiate positions in these conditions, either with or against the predominant trend, but they also present challenges for traders managing existing positions. The two biggest challenges are first, to recognize that a market is parabolic, and second, to stand apart from the emotional reactions of the crowd. In both cases, a rigid technical discipline is the answer.

Trading Parabolic Climaxes: Stand-Alone Entries

In general, trade entries within parabolic climaxes are problematic. It is usually impossible to find the precise turning point; wide spreads, low liquidity, and rapid price movement work against a trading plan that attempts multiple entries. However, these areas do give important information about the trend, and offer some attractive opportunities for countertrend trading. Two of the best plans use the parabolic climax as a setup for other countertrend entries.

Failure Test Entry Prices sometimes collapse after a parabolic entry, but it is also possible that the trend will continue following a more extended consolidation. Many players are focusing on this possibility; prices are already at dramatically extended levels and many traders are thinking only about catching the next big move. Furthermore, many of them will use a break to new highs (or lows in a downtrend) as an entry point. If they are wrong, there can be mass panic as they scramble to adjust losing positions in a market that rapidly snaps back.

This sets up an ideal opportunity for a failure test. Rather than dealing with the uncertainty and poorly defined risk limits in the actual climax, astute traders can wait for a failure test on a retest of the trend extreme. Of course, some of these trades will be failures—these are the set of failure test failures that tend to have exceptional slippage compared to normal failure tests. It is also important to manage trades appropriately; failure test entries following climactic moves should see immediate and sharp countertrend movement, driven by trapped trend traders. If this move does not develop, the probabilities start to tilt back in favor of consolidation and continuation.

Setup for Anti A parabolic climax can also set up an Anti trade. In this case, it is important to look for an initial sharp countertrend move that shows a distinct change of character. Position sizes may be smaller due to elevated volatility, but this can be a very attractive entry into the reversal following a parabolic expansion.

Trading Parabolic Climaxes: Managing Existing Positions

The example shown in Figure 10.26 is different from the others in this chapter. I am reproducing (edited) comments from my daily market report that show the evolution of my thought process and the risk management plan at different points in the move. Once Silver went fully parabolic, my plan was to basically stop out under the previous day's

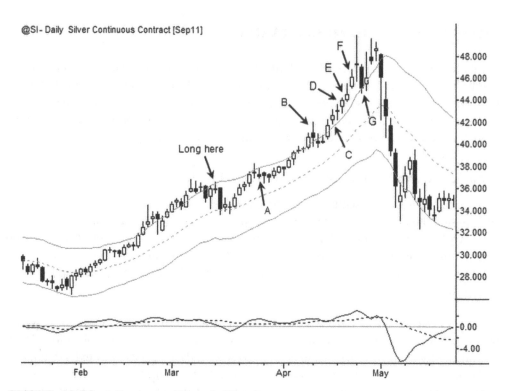

FIGURE 10.26 A Developing Climax in Silver Futures

low—a very tight stop in a volatile market, but also a reasonable risk point. In this case, the exit was fortuitous, coming on the day following the ultimate high for the move; not all trades will have outcomes this dramatic, but you must respect the potential for a very dangerous countertrend move when the climax finally turns.

A: "I have been . . . able to tighten the stop to above the entry price. I am still deeply distrustful of the trend . . ., but, for now, am positioned to take advantage of any continued upside." *This is a case of using a high and tight pullback to tighten the stop on an existing trade. Though no contracts were added in this pattern, a failure of the pattern would have been very bad for the trade, so a tighter stop was justified. Consider also that, even though I was uncomfortable with the potential in the trade, I did not exit and so was positioned to profit from the ensuing uptrend.*

B: "Silver is certainly overbought by any measure, but this is not a case where fading strength is justified." *Taken alone, the concepts of overbought and oversold are dangerous and are probably overemphasized in much of the literature. Strong trends reach overextended levels and just keep going.*

C: "My aggressive addition to Silver worked . . . stop [is now] just under yesterday's low." *The two small days provided another entry point to add additional exposure—yet another variation of the high and tight consolidation.*

D: "I have moved the stop to just below yesterday's low. In the intermediate term, everything suggests higher prices, and the possibility of extreme volatility. The challenge is . . . balancing profit taking . . . [against] holding a core position."

E: "The break, when it does come, could be dramatic. . . . I am working a tight stop very close to yesterday's low."

F: "I am ratcheting the stop very tightly every day. This is a profit-taking strategy, looking for weakness to take us out of the market." *Trade management does not always mean executing. In this case, tightening the stop reduced risk and locked in additional profits on a daily basis. Even though there were no executions, this is active trade management.*

G: "We were taken out of our long position in Silver futures yesterday, having booked a good profit for five weeks' work," *and the market immediately collapsed into a dramatic sell-off. Not all trades will be this dramatic, but rather than extrapolating the move and seeing virtually unlimited profits, always consider the possibility of a collapse like this. In this case, a simple technical pattern and a very tight trailing loss allowed our clients to sell Silver the day following the high water mark for the uptrend.*

Climax Failures

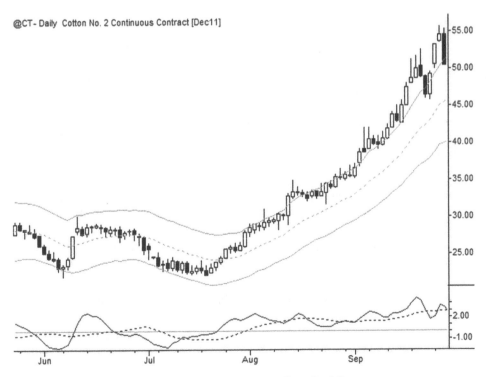

FIGURE 10.27 Does This Climax in Cotton Set Up a Short Trade?

The chart in Figure 10.27 has all of the signs of a classic buying climax: it is in a mature trend, the trend has accelerated into steeper trend legs, there have been multiple thrusts above the Keltner channels, the MACD shows a glaring momentum divergence, there are numerous free bars above the upper channel, and the last bar suggests a breakdown may have begun. In fact, the last bar on this chart is a standard failure test entry of the highs following a climax. Is this a good entry?

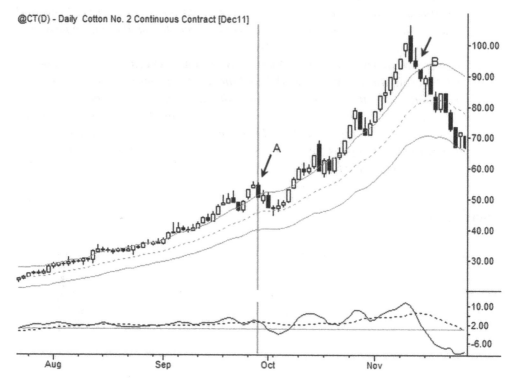

@CT(D) - Daily Cotton No. 2 Continuous Contract [Dec11]

FIGURE 10.28 A Parabolic Climax Can Extend Much Further Than Anyone Would Expect

A failure test entry at the point of A in Figure 10.28 would have failed after reaching the first target. With proper trade management, this trade would have been a scratch or a small profit. However, the point here is that countertrend trades initiated in climax patterns are subject to failure, and when they do fail, they will do so through trend continuation. In this case, after further consolidation, the trend continued, accelerating even more dramatically.

Note that there was no other entry on this chart, not even at the ultimate collapse at B. Many traders will look at a chart like this and try to find some way they could have entered a trade. This is a mistake. Your job as a trader is simply to trade well-researched patterns that are in alignment with the underlying tendencies of the market. There are many large moves in the market that do not offer an attractive entry point. This is one of them.

THE ANTI

The Anti is a pullback variation, distinguished by its position in the overall market structure. Most pullbacks come in established trends or following strong momentum moves that could lead to an extended trend. The Anti comes after a potential trend change and is an attempt to enter a new trend early in its formation. Risk management and correct profit-taking plans are important for correct management of this trade.

Anti 1

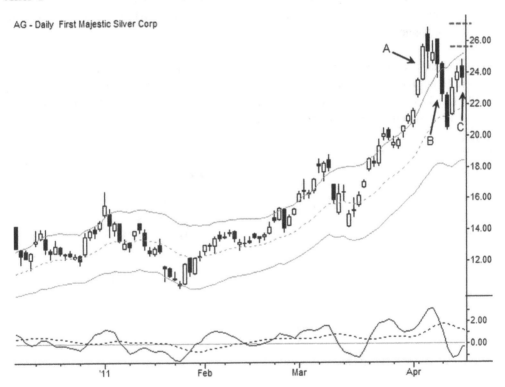

FIGURE 10.29 A Parabolic Expansion Sets Up a Sell Anti in First Majestic Silver Corporation (NYSE: AG)

Setup

A: Though not as dramatic as Figures 10.27 and 10.28, the chart in Figure 10.29 shows a small buying climax in AG. Note the multiple free bars, range expansion (large bars relative to prior history), and that this move is a radical departure from the previous trending history visible on this chart.

B: After a small consolidation, prices retreat from the highs in a very sharp sell-off. This sell-off is strong evidence of a change of character and suggests that the dominant group, the buyers, have at least temporarily lost control of this market. At this point, there is a much lower probability of the uptrend continuing, though markets will sometimes be able to absorb a shock like this and to continue.

Entry

C: The final nail in the coffin for the uptrend was the reluctant bounce here. Had the buyers been able to regain control, this move would have been much sharper and much cleaner and the stock would have quickly traded to new highs. This slow bounce is the Anti pattern, and is more likely to be a pullback preceding another leg down. The actual entry, in this case, was on a breakdown of the previous bar's low. This entry would have been justifiable on the bar marked C, but it did not trigger.

Stop   There are two possibilities for stop location, both shown on this chart. A near stop could be placed just above the extreme of the setup bounce, while the farther stop should be above the high of the trend. There is no point putting a stop in between as there is no compensation, in the form of higher probability, for the larger loss.

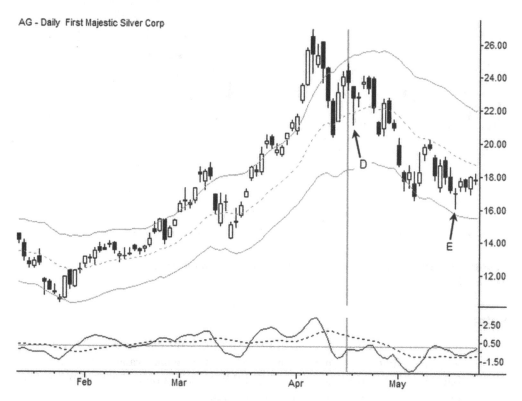

FIGURE 10.30 A Successful Sell Anti

D: Though the stock recovered to close above the midpoint of the session, this strong down day in Figure 10.30 is confirmation that the balance of power has shifted, and should add confidence to the trade. Note also that, depending on the exact location of the entry and the stop, the first target may have been hit on this first downward bar.

Do not expect that every one of these will be a clean trade with no retracements. In this case, there were multiple small pauses as the market traded lower. Maintain the discipline of profit taking, and avoid the temptation to add to the trade unless another pattern, such as a nested pullback, sets up. In this case, the small failure test at E might have been motivation to exit any remaining short exposure.

Anti 2

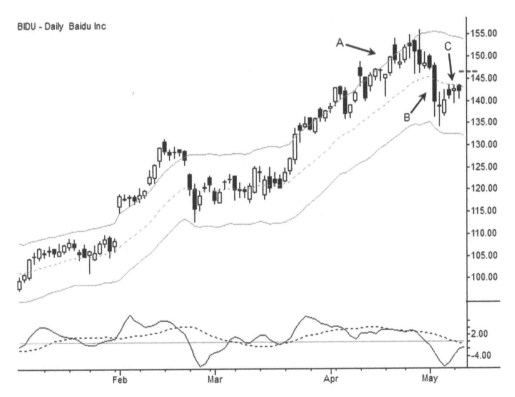

FIGURE 10.31   A Sell Anti in Baidu Inc. (Nasdaq: BIDU)

Setup

A: This "slide along the bands" trend in Figure 10.31 is a sign of a very strong though potentially overextended trend. Imagine the frustration that a trader attempting to fade this pattern would have felt—without any clear risk points, the trend continued to grind higher, rolling over any attempted short entries.

B: In this case, a single large bar completely shifted the technical picture. This bar was out of character with the recent price action and carried price well through the moving average. Note that the MACD registered a significant new low, relative to its recent history, on this thrust.

Entry

C: The actual entry would have been somewhere around C or the bars following, executing the plan of shorting intraday breakdowns or perhaps simply shorting below the previous day's low.

Stop   Only the near stop is shown in this example, though a much farther stop, above the extreme of the trend high, is also possible.

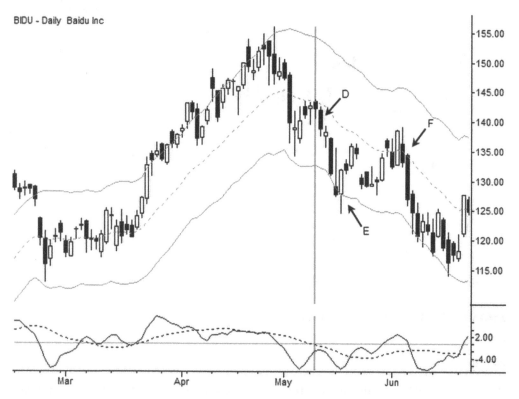

FIGURE 10.32   A Clean, Sharp Breakdown out of a Sell Anti

D: Whether this bar in Figure 10.32 or a preceding bar was the entry, the initial target was probably hit on the bar following D. Book partial profits here, and lower the stop to reduce open risk in the trade.

E: Remember, the swing trader's job is to take one clean move out of the market. Though there was more downside over the next four to six weeks, most swing traders would have covered their position on the sharp reversal at E.

F: This is essentially a higher time frame pullback and is not strictly part of the Anti trade, though it is an example of how a lower time frame structure (the Anti) can set up an environment that is favorable to a larger pattern.

Anti 3

FIGURE 10.33 A Buy Anti Setup in the EURUSD

Setup

A: This downtrend in Figure 10.33 was perhaps not as dramatically overextended as the uptrends in the previous examples, but multiple tests below the lower band, followed by a last-gasp sell-off that quickly failed, were warnings of a possible overextension and of a trend that was primed for reversal.

B: The bounce at B is out of character with the preceding price movement. The up-swing was longer than previous upswings, both in price and in time, and the MACD confirms with a new high.

Entry

C: This is a small complex consolidation (two legs down, separated by a failed rally attempt) nested inside an Anti. An Anti is, in fact, basically a pullback—the distinguishing feature is its location in the trend. An entry could have been at-tempted near the right edge of the chart, against a stop somewhere above 1.20.

FIGURE 10.34 A Strong Uptrend Develops off the Buy Anti

D: You have to pay attention with these entry setups, and cannot always wait until the end of the bar. In this case, if you missed the early entry on the previous day's breakout, it might have made sense to pass on the trade, rather than entering after such a large up day as D in Figure 10.34. However, this is a case in which the statistical tendencies for different asset classes matter. An individual stock or stock index might have been more set for a small reversal following day like D, but currencies do not show this tendency.

E: Though significant exposure should have been trimmed early, at lower profit targets, this small pullback is a justifiable second entry. Many traders will treat an entry like this as an entirely separate trade, perhaps continuing to hold part of the position from the Anti as well.

F: What is this? A potential setup for a sell Anti? In this case, the short trade following F would have been a marginal winner, but once again the message is clear: being able to read developing market structure and price action can give a great insight into trade management.

Anti Failures

The Anti is a specific variant of the pullback trade, characterized by its location in the trend and the specific strong countertrend thrust setting up the pullback. Because it is a pullback, when the Anti pattern fails, it does so through the same patterns in which other pullbacks fail. This section shows three common Anti failures: failure through consolidation, failure near previous swing, and finally, failure by strong momentum against the attempted trend change.

Failure Through Consolidation

FIGURE 10.35 A Buy Anti Fails into Consolidation in YGE

This point cannot be overemphasized: every edge any of these patterns has comes from an imbalance of buying and selling pressure. When a trade is entered, prices should quickly move from the entry price; if the market is able to trade around the entry price, this is more suggestive of balance between buyers and sellers. In this environment, technical patterns have no edge.

Figure 10.35 shows a buy Anti in Yingli Green Energy Holding Company Ltd (NYSE: YGE) at A. This was not an excellent example of an Anti because the preceding setup leg, the upswing, was only two bars and did not show a strong change of character. Not every pattern is textbook clear, and, though it may be counterintuitive, it is not necessarily true that better patterns have a higher expectancy.

In this case, after a long entry somewhere around A, the stock simply went dead and quiet. This is not what should have happened—if there were trapped shorts nervous about their positions, they should have covered aggressively and this buying pressure should have caused a sharp up move in the stock. When prices move contrary to what should be happening in a trade, it is time to adjust the trade: reduce exposure, tighten stops, or exit the trade completely.

Failure Near Previous Swing

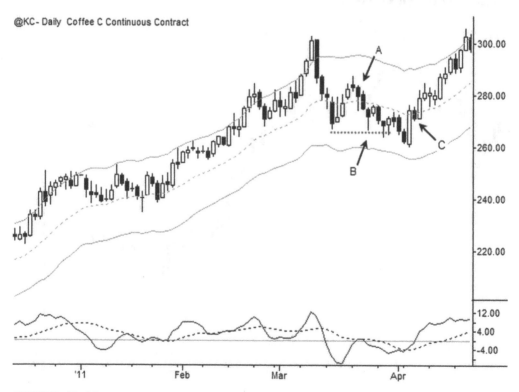

FIGURE 10.36   A Sell Anti Finds Support at Previous Swing

Figure 10.36 shows a good sell Anti in Coffee futures. After a parabolic climax, a sharp downdraft, and slow bounce, a short position could have been entered somewhere around A. Remember that in any pullback trade, the first, most conservative, target is the extreme of the move setting up the pullback. In this case, the market was clearly having trouble getting through this target at B. Depending on the exact entry point and stop location, point B may have already been beyond the first profit target. If not, it would have been prudent to reduce risk somewhere in the bars following the failure to trade below the previous swing at B.

Eventually, Coffee was able to slip below this support and appeared to be set to trade lower. However, a sharp failure at C swept price back above support. It might have been justifiable to hold a partial position through this large up day, especially if partial profits had already been booked, but there is no reason to endure any more pain following C. This small bar, consolidating at the high of the move back above support, is a lower time frame consolidation and a strong indication that prices are headed higher in the near term. Always respect the message of developing market structure.

Failure by Strong Momentum Against

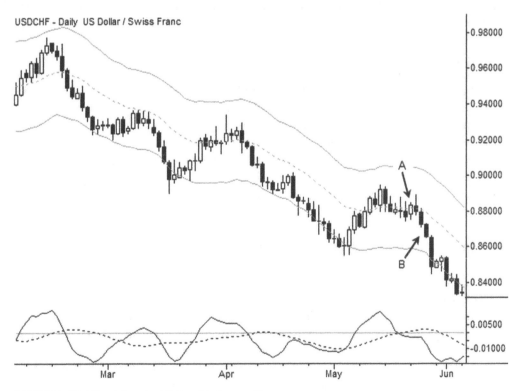

FIGURE 10.37 A Buy Anti Fails with Strong Momentum

The preceding failures may or may not be actual failures. The pattern did not carry through as expected and there were no further trend legs, but in many cases like those it will be possible to take profits at the first target. Once these profits are booked and risk is reduced, it becomes very likely that the trade will be breakeven at worst. However, not all Anti failures are this polite; Figure 10.37 shows an example of a failure that would likely have resulted in a full-sized loss on the trade.

After a protracted downtrend, the USDCHF bounced and set up a potential buy Anti. (Again, this is not a perfect example of a buy setup, as the setup leg did not display a strong change of character.) Long positions entered at A would have likely suffered full losses as the market turned back down and traded through stops around B. Further stops, located beyond the trend low, would also have been quickly hit in the ensuing downswing.

Though the Anti is a powerful pattern that sets up excellent trades, there are also some dramatic failures. There are even cases, not shown here, in which the market gaps dramatically against the position on the next open, resulting in a loss beyond the initial risk point. Do not focus only on positive outcomes. When you enter a trade, your attention should be on potential failures and on signs that the pattern can be failing. Failed patterns can often be more powerful than successful trades, and patterns often fail through other tradable patterns. Revisit the failure in Figure 10.35; is this a complex pullback? These patterns are far more than mere trade setups or entry triggers—they are a complete methodology for understanding market movements.

Conclusions

At first glance, the Anti might appear to be nothing more than a pullback—the market makes a sharp move, and, after a pause, another move in the same direction. However, the distinguishing factor is the location in the market structure, which allows traders to position near the end of one trend and the potential beginning of another; if the trade is correct, it will benefit from trapped traders scrambling to adjust their positions into the new trend. This pattern, with its precisely defined entry and risk points, is a powerful tool to play inflections and turning points in trends.

TRADING AT SUPPORT AND RESISTANCE

Trades made at support and resistance are plays for those levels either breaking or holding. To further simplify, breakouts are trades *through* support or resistance levels, while failed breakouts are trades that indicate the level is more likely to hold. Note that there is some potential overlap here: a failure test is a failed breakout, but it is usually a question of time frames. A failure test on the trading time frame will usually show one of the following section's failed breakout patterns on lower time frames. A good understanding of the ways in which breakout patterns unfold can add a valuable piece to the trader's analytical tool kit.

Breakouts: Early Entry in Base

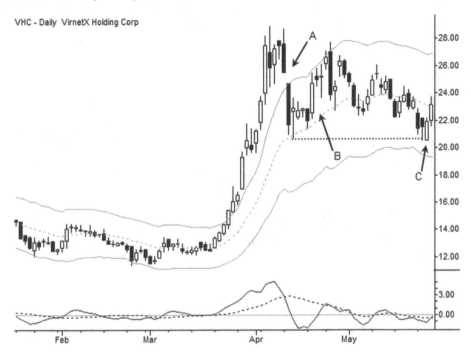

FIGURE 10.38 Buying a Spring at Support in VHC

Setup After a long run-up, VirnetX Holding Corporation (AMEX: VHC) rolled over into an extended consolidation, as shown in Figure 10.38.

A: The initial downswing, at A, might have set up a sell Anti.

B: However, at B, buyers stepped in and it became clear that there would be no easy downward momentum; the stock then traded in a multimonth range near the previous highs. This type of consolidation often sets up an attractive breakout trade, but the problem is finding a precise entry and managing the risk in the trade.

Entry One way to enter a breakout trade is to recognize the pattern setting up, and enter in anticipation of the breakout.

C: In this case, a failure test of the previous pivot at C offered an attractive entry. Note that this is a classic Wyckoff spring, though the best examples of springs should penetrate previous support more decisively.

Stop Initially, this entry is nothing more than a failure test at the previous pivot. The appropriate stop is just beyond the low of C, but the issue of potential slippage and a gap opening must be considered. One answer is to accept both of those risks as normal trade risks and to trade full size. It is also possible to initiate a smaller position near this low, planning to add to the trade later or to set the stop slightly lower. All of these are legitimate answers to these issues, but this question must be clearly addressed in the trading plan.

FIGURE 10.39 A Complicated Winning Breakout Trade

D: The stock immediately reversed off the spring and traded sharply back to highs in Figure 10.39. D marks the actual breakout, which failed on this attempt. Consider the difference between initiating a position at C or at D. The trader who enters at D is now in a position of weakness and must exit the position, while the trader who entered at C is holding substantial profits and has many more trade management options available. Will you exit part or all of the position on the failure, taking profits and looking to reestablish? Will you add to your position at D and then adjust it if the trade fails? Will you do nothing? These are all choices available only to the trader who positions somewhere near the bottom of the range.

E. The stock holds a tighter consolidation up against resistance. E is a small spring, and may not be a realistic entry as it penetrates previous support by only a few cents.

F: The actual breakout comes at F, as the stock finally clears resistance and trades sharply higher.

Conclusions Entering early in the base preceding a breakout is one way to sidestep the volatility and issues around the actual breakout point. Failure tests, lower time frame Antis, and small pullbacks call can offer attractive entry points within the range. If using some of these patterns, it may make sense to adjust the stop to respect the limits of the higher time frame pattern. In other words, if positioning in a daily range using a 30-minute Anti, perhaps set the stop outside the daily range. This will result in a much smaller position size, but it will be a position size that respects the reality of the higher time frame market structure.

This example also raised the possibility of adding to an existing position. This is a good plan in many cases, but it also makes sense to aggressively adjust the position if that second entry fails by exiting *more* than was added. In other words, if you were holding 5,000 shares from C and added 2,000 at D, you would exit *more* than 2,000 on the failure of D. Though it is difficult for some traders to maintain the discipline of a rule like this, it will add consistency to the bottom line.

Breakouts: First Pullback Following

A word on terminology: stock traders tend to use *breakout* for upside breakouts through resistance and *breakdown* for entries through support; futures traders are more likely to call both trades breakouts. Since all trade entries are more or less symmetrical, I have opted to simplify and to use *breakout* for both trades.

Setup

A: This example was deliberately chosen because it is much less clear than a textbook example. JPM had just come off a strong two-quarter uptrend (not visible in Figure 10.40), and seemed to be setting up for a further advance. Traders would have been justified in attempting to buy springs at support, as in the previous example. However, there are at least two important differences between this example and the best examples of long setups: One, successive bounces off support terminate at lower price levels—smaller upswings suggest that buyers may be losing conviction. Two, at point A price dropped cleanly below previous support.

Entry

B: Again, it would have been reasonable to be looking for a long entry on a failure test following A, as the third bar following traded strongly back above support. However, there was no upside momentum, and the market rolled over into a pullback at B. Though this proved to be the ideal entry in the breakout, it was extremely difficult to see this entry at the time; there was at least one other clear entry later.

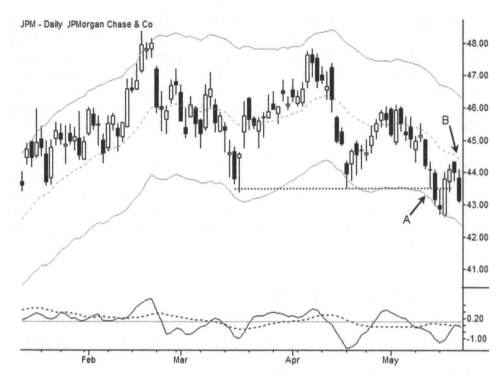

FIGURE 10.40 A Complicated Breakout Trade in JPMorgan Chase & Company (NYSE: JPM)

FIGURE 10.41 A Downtrend Follows a Downside Breakout

C: The entry at B, though obvious in retrospect, was much harder in real time. The entry at C in Figure 10.41, though, was a simple pullback and could have been traded like any other pullback. There is an important lesson here: Simple technical patterns become more powerful when they are put in context of bigger-picture market structure. In this case, the failure of the potential upside consolidation through a downside breakout could be expected to lead to several trend legs down. Taking bearish pullbacks in those conditions would have been an excellent trade.

D: This is probably the ideal exit for a trader looking to take one clean swing out of the market. A failure test at lows, on the third attempt to make new lows, tilted the probabilities slightly against the bears. In this case, the stock traded lower, but after more than a month of sloppy consolidation. Find the best trades, the cleanest trades, for that is where your mental and financial capital can best be deployed.

Conclusions   Another lesson here is that there is nothing magical about the breakout level. The pullback following breakouts can violate the pullback level (as B did in this example), can stop at the level, or can hold well clear of the level. In each case, price action is far more informative than the market's relation to a specific price level.

Breakout Failures

There are three common breakout failures. None of them need extensive analysis at this point, because they are pattern failures we have already considered elsewhere. However, for traders focusing on breakouts, it is important to have these possibilities in mind and to be prepared to manage the risk as the trade evolves.

At Breakout Point (Failure Test)

FIGURE 10.42 A Breakout Failure in Discover Financial Services (NYSE: DFS)

This failure pattern, shown in Figure 10.42, is nothing more than a failure test at the potential breakout level. (We could say that a failure test is a failed breakout.) A and C are classic springs (which are themselves downward breakout failures); each would have been an excellent entry for the potential upside breakout. There are also two failed upside breakouts here. B is a small failure test at the highs, and D is a large-scale failure.

These failures can be dramatic and they demand respect. Breakouts often encourage large groups of traders to enter overextended markets; the reversals from failures at these points can be violent. Note that the breakout may fail on the same bar or a few bars following the actual breakout. The main challenge here is differentiating between a normal breakout pullback, which may or may not violate the breakout level, and a more decisive failure.

At First Consolidation The first pullback following a breakout is often an excellent spot to enter a trade. If the breakout works and a longer trend develops, this entry will have been right at the inception of the new trend. However, there is still a possibility of a failed breakout, which, in this case, will fail through a failed pullback. Deep study and familiarity with all the variations of pullbacks and their failure patterns will help the trader to manage these potentially complex trades.

One point to consider is that these initial postbreakout pullbacks are rarely complex pullbacks. In general, simple pullbacks are a sign of some urgency in the trend, while complex pullbacks are needed to work off possible overextensions in further trend legs. In the best breakout examples, a strong trend will quickly follow and this strong trend will not generate complex pullbacks early on. Traders can trade these postbreakout pullbacks with fairly tight stops (not referring to the breakout level, but to the geometry of the actual pullback pattern) and usually need not consider the possibility of a complex pullback.

Failure in Base   Last, though entering in the base preceding a breakout has many advantages, there is one important problem—the breakout may never happen. For instance, buying in anticipation of an upside breakout in Figure 10.40 would have been a perfectly reasonable trade, but it would have been a losing trade. There is an eternal trade-off between confirmation and trade location. A trader positioning early has excellent trade location, but perhaps with a lower probability of the trade actually working. Traders waiting for the actual breakout often find themselves in a position of weakness because of poor trade location, but with a higher probability of the trade working.

It is possible to trade any of these patterns according to many different plans. The key, in all cases, is that the plan is clearly articulated and that it focuses as much on how to manage losing trades as on where to take profits.

SUMMARY

This chapter has presented many examples of the trading templates from Chapter 6. Though much deeper analysis was possible in every case, most of the comments focus on the most important and most repeatable elements of these patterns. These are not examples and models to be followed slavishly, but nearly all traders will find they can adapt these ideas and concepts to their own styles and techniques. In particular, the broad ideas for managing exposure in developing trades and for clearly defining the risk for all initial trade entries are nearly universal to all markets, time frames, and trading styles.

PART IV

The Individual, Self-Directed Trader

CHAPTER 11

The Trader's Mind

If you open yourself to insight, you are at one with insight and you can use it completely.

If you open yourself to loss, you are at one with loss and you can accept it completely.

—Daodejing (ca. 6 BCE)

At one point or another, everyone who has interactions with the market asks one-self, "Why is trading so hard?" There are legitimate reasons why trading *should* be difficult: markets are highly random; whatever edge we can find is eroded by competition from smart, well-capitalized traders; some traders work within various constraints; and markets are subject to very large shocks that can have devastating effects on unprepared traders. Even so, it seems like something else is going on, almost like we are our own worst enemies at times. What is it about markets that encourages people to do exactly the wrong thing at the wrong time, and why do many of the behaviors that serve us so well in other situations actually work against us in the market?

Part of the answer lies in the nature of the market itself. What we call "the market" is actually the end result of the interactions of thousands of traders across the gamut of size, holding period, and intent. Each trader is constantly trying to gain an advantage over the others; market behavior is the sum of all of this activity, reflecting both the rational analysis and the psychological reactions of all participants. This creates an environment that has basically evolved to encourage individual traders to make mistakes. That is an important point—*the market is essentially designed to cause traders to do the wrong thing at the wrong time.* The market turns our cognitive tools and psychological quirks against us, making us our own enemy in the marketplace. It is not so much that the market is against us; it is that the market sets us against ourselves.

These issues are particularly relevant to the individual, self-directed trader who has few limits placed on his or her behavior and is faced with the nebulous job description

347

of "making money." Traders in institutional settings have many advantages over the individual, not the least of which is that the institutional framework places many restrictions on their actions. These constraints, along with guidance from management and implicit mentoring from senior traders, provide a strong framework for shaping behavior and make new traders in these settings less vulnerable to some of the common psychological stresses and errors. Furthermore, many institutional traders have specific, clearly defined roles such as executing and managing complex sets of hedges, or managing inventory and flow resulting from customer orders. These traders are not faced with the broad task of beating the market and can become quite skilled at their jobs without fully conquering all of the psychological challenges of trading.

One word of warning: Though we now turn our focus to psychological elements of trading, positive thinking, meditation, visualization, and correct psychology can take you only so far. You absolutely *must* have an edge in the market to make money. For most styles of trading, it is impossible to apply that edge well without the proper psychological skills, but those psychological tools are not, by themselves, an actual trading edge. This chapter begins with a look at how the market turns some of our reasoning ability against us and how we become our own worst enemies in the market. Next, we look at intuition and flow, which are essential components of top-level trading for many traders. In particular, the flow experience is an important part of both performance and skill development. The chapter ends with some concrete suggestions for developing an environment that allows the developing trader to work to overcome some of the more common psychological errors.

PSYCHOLOGICAL CHALLENGES OF THE MARKETPLACE

The psychological demands of trading are almost unique in the human experience. First, there are serious consequences for making errors; trading decisions are high-risk decisions. Even if losses are limited so that no one trade can hurt us badly, it is a rare trader who can face 10 losses in a row without significant pain and suffering—even traders with secure institutional jobs may be in trouble after a string of losses. Furthermore, losses do not always result from bad decisions, and, even more ominously, bad decisions sometimes lead to good outcomes. This is a reflection of the randomness in the market environment, but it is very difficult to hone skills and to develop intuition when results cannot always be clearly tied to actions.

Furthermore, every trading decision you will ever make is *always* made with insufficient information. We never know everything there is to know about any trade, and, no matter how good our research is, there are many things that are simply unknowable. Even if you somehow could accumulate every relevant piece of information, known and unknown, there is always the possibility that a large order could be dumped into the market with unpredictable results—anything can happen in the market. In addition, many trading decisions must be made quickly and under pressure. There are certainly types of trading for which this is less true, but the actual decision to do *something* always comes down to one point in time. Someone has to pull the trigger, and risk management decisions sometimes have to be made on the fly in response to developing market action. This is the trading environment—high-risk decisions, made under pressure with insufficient information. Seen in this light, the reasons for some of the psychological challenges become clearer.

EVOLUTIONARY ADAPTATIONS

Many of the cognitive tools we possess may be relics from earlier times in our development as a species; though they might have been helpful in prehistory, they often fail us completely in modern life. For instance, the adrenaline flood associated with the fight-or-flight response might have been useful in fleeing from a saber-toothed tiger. It is easy to see how natural selection might have strengthened this response: If there were early humans who didn't have it, they became lunch. In modern life, this same response leads to road rage, bar fights, constant stress, and a whole list of endocrine-related diseases. This is who we are as a species. It is not possible to be completely free from these quirks, because they are part of the very fabric of our being; we are, and always will be, vulnerable to making certain kinds of mistakes in certain situations. The best we can do is to be aware of these biases and errors and to attempt to counteract them; but be clear on this point—you cannot *fix* them.

Perceiving Patterns in Randomness

Have you ever seen faces in clouds, or shapes in the wood grain of finished furniture? Ever heard voices murmuring, just out of the range of perception, when you hold a seashell up to your ear? These are universal experiences, and they most likely come from a slight misfiring of some powerful cognitive machinery. For instance, processing and recognizing faces is actually an extremely complex task, but nearly all humans can do this naturally and instantaneously. There are specific areas of the brain that have evolved to deal with this complex task, but the same areas of the brain will also take random patterns in clouds and force them into the structure of human faces. From an evolutionary perspective, there was no payoff for being able to properly process random data, no reason that natural selection would have preserved this skill. Instead, humans who could quickly process faces and manage social interactions with their peers were probably far more likely to survive in prehistory than were early humans who did not excel at these skills.

We are pattern recognition machines. Our brains are so good at recognizing patterns that they will readily create patterns where none exist. We attempt to make order out of chaos by imposing structured patterns on randomness. Traders often do not fully appreciate this fact—they do not understand that much of what they see in the market, no matter how convincing the pattern looks and feels, could simply be due to random fluctuations in the market. It is impossible to overestimate the seriousness of this bias.

Heuristics

A heuristic is a rule of thumb, a cognitive shortcut that can quickly find the answer to a problem that might otherwise be intractable. They are extremely fast and efficient; there are some problems that can be solved in seconds or minutes heuristically that would require hours or days of rational analysis. The root of heuristic thinking is the ability to relate new experiences to old, already processed information—"Oh, this looks like that." We learn, think, and deal with the outside world by generalizing and filing our experiences into broad categories, and when new situations are encountered we relate them back to these broad categories. In the market, we are likely to relate situations and patterns to groups of patterns that we have previously created or noticed, whether or not there is a valid link between the two sets.

Heuristics are useful or even essential for traders, but it is important that they are built from valid information and are carefully trained. Left unchecked, incorrect heuristics can be created and reinforced in the highly random market environment. For instance, one trader might have a heuristic that leads him to pay breakouts of the previous day's high in stock index futures, because he can remember many examples of good winning trades. Another trader, who has actually done the research, might have the correct heuristic, which in this case, would be to fade those highs. Both traders can make a trading decision quickly, but the trader whose intuition is based on correct principles of market behavior will make the *right* decision.

Shifting Blame

If you spend any time at all around traders, you will hear language like this: "Oh, *they* got my stop again." "That guy screwed me again. Can you believe that?" "Oh, *they* always do that. That's criminal! How can *they* always do this to me?" Traders tend to blame their losses on some great, nefarious, unseen *them* that is manipulating the markets behind the scenes—the U.S. government buying stock futures (the "Plunge Protection Team"), the floor traders manipulating markets, high-frequency trading (HFT) algorithms stealing from traders, or big banks heedlessly pushing markets around. Some or all of these things may happen, but here is the point: it doesn't matter. You would perceive this intentionality in the market whether it exists or not. You would feel a great unseen *them*, because of the way your brain is wired. *They* may or may not be real, but your perception of a third party manipulating the market says much more about your own cognition than about the market itself.

Markets are blatantly manipulated at times, of this there is no doubt. However, market action is the end result of the competing activity of tens of thousands of traders, across many time frames, with different objectives and perspectives; everything is folded into the patterns of market behavior and much of it nets out to noise. Rather than being angry when a market ticks your stop, either accept it as a natural event or, if your stop was placed incorrectly, modify your behavior. If this type of unwanted outcome happens frequently enough that you are this unhappy with it, you are probably doing something that is against the nature of the market. It is a simple choice: continue to deflect and to be angry at the way the market moves, or align yourself with it.

Fight or Flight

The fight-or-flight response is an amazing physiological adaptation. In times of great stress or danger, hormones flood our bloodstream, and our bodies and minds are transformed. Our breathing and heart rate speed up, and blood vessels contract in our extremities so that oxygen is routed to essential areas. This is the response that lets little old ladies lift cars off children or allows soldiers to continue in battle oblivious to grievous wounds. All of this is well known, but what a lot of people do not realize is that the way we perceive outside information also undergoes a profound shift under the fight-or-flight response—our hearing is impaired and our vision actually narrows. Tunnel vision is not just a figure of speech—it is a perceptual reality in response to stress.

In times of physical danger, this response can be a lifesaver, but the problem in modern society is that we have these same fight-or-flight responses to nonphysical stresses. There is only a flood of hormones, but it is not followed by fighting or running. Our bodies transform to prepare for action, but then we sit at our desk and *maybe* squeeze a stress ball if we're really worked up. Nothing in the history of our evolution has prepared us for this situation, and the hormonal flood becomes a constant stress on our systems. Traders experience dramatic emotional swings and the stress of this fight-or-flight response constantly, sometimes several times in a single hour, all through the trading day. The effects of this response on our minds are fairly well known, but the cumulative impact on our bodies is much less well understood. Traders must master their emotions well enough to minimize their exposure to this hormonal barrage that can impair perception, wear on the body, and cause great damage to trading accounts.

Aggression: The Good, the Bad, and the Ugly Most people believe that aggressiveness is a desirable quality for traders, and many outsiders have the impression that trading desks are populated exclusively by Red Bull–pounding, hyperaggressive 20-somethings. There is a grain of truth to this; these types are often attracted to the challenge and perceived glamour of being a trader, but there may be a difference between the kind of people who are initially attracted to the profession and those who survive. Aggression is a legitimate trading skill, but it must be disciplined and controlled.

If you find yourself in a situation where you are on tilt or otherwise out of control, the first step in fixing the problem is recognizing that you are there. This requires a degree of self-awareness than few new traders possess; it is the nature of this state of mind that it blinds you to everything except your anger and aggression toward the market. If you find yourself in this state, on the edge of losing control, realize that you are now in a very elite group of self-directed traders, the vast majority of whom will never achieve the clarity needed to evaluate their mental state. The first thing you need to do is to stop whatever you are doing; you cannot make good decisions when you are on tilt. Your brain is in a chemically compromised state—you are not in your right mind, and that is not a figure of speech. It is not just that you are making bad decisions; the situation is actually much worse—you *are incapable* of making good decisions in this state because the chemical balance of your body has been altered. As you mature as a trader, you will find yourself here less often, but it is good to have some concrete ideas and actions you can take when you find yourself on tilt:

- Stop trading.
- If you are a short-term trader, immediately exit any position that is showing a loss, and place breakeven or better stops on any other open trades. Even if you are a trader who does not normally place stops in the market, you do now. This is a special situation, and the objective is to remove yourself from the decision process for a period of time.
- Stand up and move around. Take a break, and go for a walk outside. If it is cold, maybe go for a walk without a coat. You don't want to be comfortable; you want to be jarred out of your mental state.
- Exercise. Go to the gym or do something physical.
- Have a non-trading-related conversation with another person. Trading is an isolating experience, even if you are surrounded by other traders. Sometimes we get so stuck inside our heads that a normal two-minute conversation can do wonders. Talk to the clerk at Starbucks. Call your mom. Do whatever it takes to break the cycle.
- Write something with pencil and paper. At least for me, there is some kind of magic in pencil and paper; it is not the same to type on a keyboard. As for what to write, it might be a good idea to write in your trading journal, but even a grocery list will work. Just write.
- Breathe deeply. If you can slow your body down and get control of your physiology, the mind will follow. Meditation can be another powerful tool.
- When you have cooled down and are ready to trade, do one insignificant trade of a very small size. Monitor your psychological reactions to that one trade. If you aren't ready to go back in the game, you will know.
- If you fail the previous test and are still rattled, take a longer break. There may be some cases where you need to take a break lasting weeks or months. If so, do not think about the lost opportunity; focus on the damage you will not do by trading when you are compromised.

These are guidelines, but they have been useful for me and for many of the traders I have worked with over the years. You will find your own list over time, but breaking the destructive cycle before it has a serious effect on your trading account is the key.

COGNITIVE BIASES

This chapter opened with the question "Why is trading so hard?" It seems that it should be easier than it actually is: we acknowledge that markets are extremely random and that there is a very small component of actionable trading signals in market data, but it is there. Why is it not possible to devise simple ways to capture this edge and watch profits accumulate in the trading account? This actually does describe the best high-level trading, but few individual traders ever get to that stage. One of the reasons is that the evolutionary adaptations and heuristics we just discussed result in some consistent cognitive biases. We are practically designed to make trading mistakes. Though these skills do serve useful purposes, unchecked they work just as effectively to ensure our failure as traders. Most traders enter the marketplace with no awareness of the handicaps and weaknesses they bring into the arena, and they are doomed to failure before they even begin. The first step in combating these biases is knowing that they exist and that they will unavoidably color every interaction with the market. A partial list of some of the more common cognitive biases follows.

Gambler's Fallacy

The gambler's fallacy stems from faulty intuition about random processes. After observing deviations in a random process, most people will be inclined to think that future deviations in the *opposite* direction are more likely. For instance, someone betting that a coin would flip heads might be inclined to increase the bet size after a few consecutive tails, or a trader might increase risk on trades after a string of losers. In both cases, they would feel that a win was somehow overdue. At the risk of oversimplifying, most of the problem comes from the fact that runs or streaks are much more common in random data than most people would expect; this single fact is responsible for many of the faulty intuitions we have about randomness.

It is also worth considering that there are cases in which the gambler's fallacy must be modified in market situations. The market is not always a flip of a fair coin. Markets exist in different regimes (e.g., trends or trading ranges, high- or low-volatility conditions, etc.) and certain kinds of trades will have strings of wins or losses in those conditions. It is important to understand the math and the theory, but it is equally important to understand where reality might deviate from those theoretical principles.

Biases Concerning Losses

Consider the following two scenarios. In each, you have a choice between taking the certain payout or loss and playing the game of chance:

1. You are given the choice between a certain $100 win and a 20 percent chance of making $1,000 with an 80 percent chance of winning nothing.
2. You are given the choice between a certain $100 loss and a 20 percent chance of losing (having to pay) $1,000 with an 80 percent chance of losing nothing.

In these cases, it is easy to evaluate the expected values, which tell us which are the correct choices to make probabilistically. In the first game, the winning game, the chance scenario has an expected value of $200 (0.2 × $1,000), which is twice the certain payout. There is no doubt that the correct course of action is to play the game of chance, rather than taking the certain $100. The same math applies for the losing scenario: a certain loss of $100 compared to an expected value of a $200 loss for the game of chance.

Logically, the correct course of action is clear: play the game of chance in the winning scenario instead of taking the certain gain, and take the certain loss in the second scenario. Most people, and even most traders, are inclined to do exactly the opposite in both cases. They will want to lock in the certain gain and will prefer to take their chances on the loss because there is *some* chance that they can avoid the loss altogether. This results in suboptimal decisions with respect to position management and exiting both winners and losers. Many traders will take small wins and will hold on to a loss in the hope that it will come back and they can somehow at least break even. There is good justification for the old adage to "cut your losers and let your winners run," but many traders find this difficult to do in practice.

Another related problem, especially for newer traders, is that many traders find it difficult to calibrate their perception of risk inherent in a stop. Nearly all traders would prefer a small stop on a trade to a wide stop, with the idea that it is better to take a small loss than a big one. If you are properly and consistently sizing positions, there really is no such thing as a low-risk trade; every trade will have a consistent impact on the bottom line regardless of the distance to the stop point, but there certainly are *low-probability* trades. A tight stop may have such a high probability of being hit that it is, for all intents and purposes, a nearly certain loss. Over a large sample size, this is actually a very high-risk stop, even though it might be a loss of only a few pennies at a time.

Overconfidence Bias

Psychological research shows, time and again, that people tend to have an inflated view of their abilities and skills. Most people believe they are better, smarter, and more skilled than average. (Of course, it is impossible for *most* people to be better than the average!) This problem is exacerbated because trading tends to attract competitive, confident people to begin with. Thinking that we are better than we are is a recipe for disaster and is probably one of the reasons why so few traders make it past the learning curve.

There are traders whose hubris extends to every aspect of trading, but the market usually eliminates those traders quickly and efficiently. It is far more common to find traders who believe they have a special skill or affinity for an asset class. Do you just *know* what a certain set of stocks is going to do? Do you have a *special sense* for the relationship between a currency and a commodity? Do you have a *touch* for a certain trade setup? Well, one of the great things about trading is that it is easy to evaluate performance: are you making money? If you have a special skill, the only way it matters is if you are making consistent money over a large sample of trades. There are no excuses. In many cases, traders are much more confident about their trading abilities, about their analytical abilities, and about the epistemological limits of market knowledge than can possibly be justified by their results. We are never as good as we think we are, and markets are far more random and far less knowable than we wished they were.

Confirmation Bias

Confirmation bias is the tendency to overweight information that reinforces our beliefs and to ignore or downplay information that contradicts. This bias is a key part of keeping many other biases alive. For instance, traders could not be overconfident in their ability with a certain trade setup if they were truly, objectively evaluating their results. However, when they remember two winners and forget about five losers, or come up with reasons why the five losers shouldn't matter, they are engaging in confirmation bias. Record keeping, both of trade results and of research, is critical, because this bias often distorts memory—you simply will not remember contradictory information, or it will be somehow fuzzy and obscured. In most cases, the confirmation bias is not a deliberate attempt to deceive or to manipulate data, but it occurs as a result of the fundamental ways in which we process information.

Anchoring Bias

Anchoring bias is the tendency to place undue weight on one particular piece of information and to ignore everything else. In the case of the overconfident trader, maybe she has made a trade 20 times with 18 losers, but one of the winners was dramatic. It is easy to find your entire perspective colored by a large outlier event, whether it was good or bad. Careful, objective analysis of trade results and pattern studies will guard against this bias. Paradoxically, though it is important for traders to spend time studying the market and its patterns, studying carefully chosen trade examples can actually be counterproductive; too many traders waste time trying to figure out how to reproduce the 1-in-10,000 trade. Do not spend undue time analyzing your big winners or losers; rather, spend time studying the entire set, and understand how those large outcomes fit within the framework of all possible trades.

Recency Bias

Recency bias is the tendency to overweight recent information, or information near the end of a series. Good public speakers know this and structure their speeches around this effect—always end with whatever you want the audience to remember. Good teachers know this when they review key information at the end of a lesson. Traders do not always realize how much they may be swayed by the most recent results of their trading system. There is a potentially nasty interplay between this bias and the tendency of the market to spend time in certain regimes or phases. Imagine a trader trading a good system that just happens to have a large loss due to a market distortion such as a large gap opening. On the next trade, the trader is probably going to be focusing on this loss rather than on the long history of the system. Once again, careful record keeping and broad studies of patterns are important; learn to see each event, regardless of where it falls in the time line, as only one of many possible outcomes, and avoid attaching too much significance to large events, good or bad, near the end of the series.

Hindsight Bias

"Coulda, woulda, shoulda"—these are the poster children for this bias. When you are evaluating a trade and think you should have seen something or you could have avoided a loss if you had realized a piece of information was significant, be careful. It is far easier to say this after the fact than it is to act on this kind of information in the middle of the trade. This is another reason to avoid putting too much emphasis on the outcome of any one trade. If you spend too much time reviewing large winners or losers, there is a temptation to try to see what you could have done differently as the trade developed.

Illusion of Control

Research has shown that, particularly in stressful and competitive environments, people are unable to distinguish between outcomes due to skill or chance. Langer (1975), who first coined the term *illusion of control*, showed that it was more prevalent in tasks when "skill cues" were present—competitive tasks with clearly defined and familiar outcomes where the individual seems to have the ability to make a choice. In an experimental setting, if you have someone sit and watch a box with randomly flashing numbers and tell them they win when the numbers increase, they are not likely to think their skill has any effect on their results. However, give them a button to push, even if the button does nothing, and their assessment of their skill and its relevance to the task goes through the roof. Casinos know this when they design games of chance; why else would thousands of people push a button or pull a lever attached to a random outcome, and one with a negative expectancy, for hours at a time? For traders, this can be fatal. Many of the other biases are wrapped into one powerful package here—overconfidence, attribution, hindsight, confirmation—and these all reinforce the illusion that traders are really better than they are, and suppress the role that randomness plays in the bottom line.

For traders brave enough to try it, Mauboussin (2010) proposes an interesting solution: can you lose deliberately? At first, you will think the answer is obviously yes, but think deeper. Are you really confident that you could, for an extended period of time, trade *against* your methodology trying to lose, and show results that would be significantly different than what you have achieved trying to win? If you cannot lose deliberately, then whatever wins or losses you are experiencing are merely the result of chance. In short, you are wasting your time. It is better to know you do not know—to know you do not have an edge—than to waste your time and money on a futile exercise.

THE RANDOM REINFORCEMENT PROBLEM

In the rational, sane world, correct actions are met with rewards, and doing the wrong thing results in punishment. This is simple cause and effect, but unfortunately, this is not the way the market works. Imagine a completely crazy teacher in a classroom, who without any rhyme or reason randomly screams at some students, ignores some, rewards a few, and punishes others. A student could hand in a perfect paper and get a failing grade, sometimes more than once, while a student who puts a big "X" in the middle of a single sheet of paper receives a perfect score for what was supposed to be a 25-page essay. It is not that the teacher is actively punishing the good students; there is no pattern at all to the teacher's actions. Can you imagine trying to learn in such an environment?

This is a problem for traders, because the market is like this teacher; it often rewards incorrect behaviors and punishes perfectly correct actions. You can do exactly the right thing on a trade and lose money several times in a row, or you can make a serious mistake and make a lot of money. The statistical edges in our trading setups become valid only over a large sample size; on any one trial, anything can happen. Especially for developing traders, this random reinforcement, coupled with the extreme emotional charge of both winning and losing, conspire to create one of the most challenging learning environments imaginable.

Random reinforcement is a profoundly powerful tool for behavior modification, and is frequently used to train animals. If you train dogs and reward them every time they obey, their good behavior will probably stop as soon as the rewards stop. On the other hand, if you randomly reward their obedience by sometimes giving a treat and sometimes not, the modifications to their behavior will usually be permanent. (Again, do you see any parallels with slot machines?) It may be counterintuitive, but random reinforcement is actually a much more powerful tool to shape behavior than consistent reinforcement.

There is so much random noise in the market that even excellent trading systems have a large random component in their results. Over a small set of trades, random reinforcement of both good and bad behavior is *normal* for our interactions with the market. Excellent decisions are just about as likely to be met with good results as bad results, and poor decisions will also result in a number of winning trades. Traders trying to be responsive to the feedback of the market and trying to learn from their interactions with the market are likely to be confused, frustrated, and eventually bewildered.

The market's reinforcement is not truly random; over a large number of trades, results do tend to trend toward the expected value, but it certainly can seem random to the struggling trader. The solution should not surprise you by now: evaluate your trading results over a large sample size, and use statistics to separate reality from your emotional perceptions. Learn from 20 or 30 trades, not one. Make decisions about changing your trading rules based on the results from 50 trades, not five. The market is a capricious teacher.

EMOTIONS: THE ENEMY WITHIN

As logical and rational as we try to be, there is no denying it: our decisions are made based on a combination of reason, intuition, and feeling, each in degrees depending on our personal makeup and the specific situation. Once again, this is a mode of decision making that has great utility in many situations, but it can misfire in the context of trading and markets. Emotions can create stress that unbalances the brain on a chemical level. Emotions can cause us to overweight and underweight certain factors, and sometimes to make decisions without any reasoning at all. Successful traders have many strategies for dealing with their emotions, but that is the common thread—they have all found a way to integrate their emotions into their trading process. Some deny and control them with iron discipline and try to become logical machines, some seek modes of trading that remove emotion from the decision process, and some embrace their emotionality and actually build their trading process around it; but in all cases, they understand their emotional balance and how to control it within the framework of their work flow.

Ego

We all have egos. (I am using the term *ego* here in the colloquial sense to mean self-image rather than in any formal, psychoanalytical context.) Everyone likes to be right, likes to be seen as intelligent, and likes to be a winner. We all hate to lose, and we hate to be wrong; traders, as a group, tend to be more competitive than the average person. These personality traits are part of what allows a trader to face the market every day—a person without exceptional self-confidence would not be able to operate in the market environment. Like so many things, ego is both a strength and a weakness for traders. When it goes awry, things go badly wrong. Excessive ego can lead traders to the point where they are fighting the market, or where they hold a position at a significant loss because they are convinced the market is wrong. It is not possible to make consistent money fighting the market, so ego must be subjugated to the realities of the marketplace.

One of the big problems is that, for most traders, the need to be right is *at least* as strong as the drive to make money—many traders find that the pain of being wrong is greater than the pain of losing money. You often have minutes or seconds to evaluate a market and make a snap decision. You *know* you are making a decision without all the important information, so it would be logical if it were easy to let go of that decision once it was made. For nearly all traders, this is not the case because we become invested in the outcome once risk is involved. Avoiding emotional attachment to trading decisions is a key skill of competent trading, and being able to immediately and unemotionally exit a losing trade is a hallmark of a master trader.

Being wrong is an inescapable part of trading, and, until you reconcile this fact with your innate need to be right, your success will be limited. Earlier in this book, I suggested that an appropriate way to look at normal trading losses is not as losses at all, but simply as a planned, recurring cost of doing business. Though many traders feel shame, anger, and hurt over losing trades, this is illogical—the market is so random that it is absolutely impossible to trade without losing. Many good traders are wrong far more often than they are right; trading is not about being right or predicting the future. All you can do is to identify places where you might have a small edge in the market, put on the trade, and open yourself to the possible outcomes.

Hope and Fear

Scylla and Charybdis were two sea monsters in Greek mythology situated in a narrow strait so that ships had to pass close to one or the other; captains had to choose because it was not possible for a ship to make the passage and to avoid both. For traders, fear and hope are the twin monsters, and no matter how experienced we may be as traders, we are unable to completely conquer them. What we can and must do, however, is to become aware of our weaknesses and our responses to these emotions. If we can monitor ourselves for susceptibility to errors, we can often intervene before the emotional reaction has resulted in a poor decision.

The reasons for fear are obvious. Most traders are afraid of loss, though this is probably rooted in a misunderstanding. It is wrong to be concerned about or to focus on the normal losses that accrue as part of the trading process, but there is certainly the danger of the unexpected and uncontrollable loss from an outlier event. Recent flash crashes have shown that stable markets can have unprecedented sell-offs; who would have thought that a big blue-chip stock could drop 80 percent in a few minutes? Many traders also face deeper, darker fears that are tied in to questions of self-worth, security, and personal finance. Even for a well-balanced person, trading can be a serious emotional challenge at times.

As powerful as fear is, many traders find that hope is actually more dangerous. Hope encourages us to take potentially reckless risks that we might not otherwise take. It can keep us in winning trades long after the profit potential is gone; many traders give back a lot of open profit because they are clawing for even more. Many traders are also loath to exit their losing trades, sometimes even at their predetermined stop level, because they are *hoping* that the trade will turn around and become a smaller loss. Once again, one of the distinguishing characteristics of successful traders is an ability to cut losers with minimal emotional attachment. No individual trader can succeed without mastering both hope and fear.

After many years and many mistakes fighting these twin monsters, I found a solution that works for me. It is deceptively simple, but it is difficult to do consistently. Here it is: *for every trade you put on, immediately assume you are wrong.* This is your baseline assumption, and, if you find evidence to the contrary (that you are right), be pleasantly surprised. This works because it takes all pressure off you and all hope out of the trade. Normally, once you have made a decision to buy a market, confirmation bias kicks in and you will start to subtly overweight information that supports your position. Instead, think, "I bought it thinking it will go up, but I'm probably wrong." There is no struggle, no fight against the reality of the market, and also no fear because you are *expecting* to be wrong. This is a subtle shift in your thinking, but it can produce a powerful change in your perspective and your behavior.

INTUITION

Intuition is an important part of the trading process for many traders and styles of trading. It is certainly more important to some types of traders than to others, but even highly quantitative work benefits from intuitive leaps at some points in the process. Though there is a lot of misinformation and misconception about intuition, the best working definition might be that it is a way of knowing that falls outside rational thought. Someone who arrives at an answer through reason can usually explain every step—how an answer led to another question, which led to another answer, in an unbroken logical chain. When someone arrives at an answer intuitively, the individual will often say that he or she "just knows" or "feels that it is right," and cannot explain much, if any, of the thought process behind the answer. Intuition works in leaps and bounds. This is not a sign of sloppy reasoning; it is a completely different mode of thought, another way of knowing entirely.

Many developing traders overestimate the importance of intuition, believing that it will cure all of their trading ills. They may think that great traders have a sixth sense that other people do not, that they just trade based on this gut feeling. Some people believe that great traders are born with market sense—either you have it or you don't. Other traders, particularly systematic traders, may believe that intuition does not really exist or that it is unreliable and mostly useful only in hindsight. As usual, all of these viewpoints contain an element of truth, but they are also wrong because they miss some essential points.

Developing Intuition

There is no magic in intuition. Rather, it is a normal problem solving skill that functions on a level outside of consciousness. As such, it cannot be forced, but it *can* be cultivated—there are things you can do to foster the growth and development of intuition. Everyone has had the experience of working very hard on a problem and being unable to solve it during the work session, and then the answer coming spontaneously after a break or a night's sleep. The answer seems to come easily and naturally, with no effort at all, but this is not quite true. The sudden flash of intuition is really the result of a lot of hard work and an extended period of focused effort that activated the cognitive machinery on another level. There are two important elements to building intuition. One is repeated exposure to consistently structured data, which is the focus of much of this book. Equally important, though, is that the work be approached in the right emotional context, which is basically an open, receptive, and almost playful attitude. This is something that is so profound, but is often ignored. Most adults understand the need for hard work and focus, but they are not so in touch with the need for novelty and play. Perhaps this is one reason why children find it easier to acquire new skills, particularly in the artistic/intuitive/right brain domain.

There is a large and growing body of research on neuroplasticity, which says that high-level skill acquisition actually depends on physical changes in the brain—the brain rewires itself to accommodate these new skills. There are structural differences, for instance, between the way a chess grandmaster's brain processes chess patterns and the way a typical person's brain works. They fundamentally see and think differently because their brains *are* different, and this difference is the result of intense training. This also explains why skill acquisition does not happen overnight: It takes time for the brain to build and reinforce these new structural connections, which requires intense work over a long period of time.

Teachers of high-level skills have known for generations that the correct emotional context and environment facilitate high-level skill development, but they did not realize that students were actually, physically rewiring their brains. Learning should be fun, not only because the student will be motivated to work harder, but because the emotional charge of this enjoyment actually encourages the physical changes needed for skill development. It is very difficult to excel at something unless you love it. This is a real problem for newer traders, for whom the market is an out-of-control emotional roller coaster. Until those emotions are brought under control, it is impossible to approach the market with the correct, receptive mind-set.

Where Does Intuition Come From?

There have been many studies in the social sciences and in psychology that have established the reality of human intuition. Focusing specifically on trading and market-related intuition, Bruguier, Quartz, and Bossaerts (2010) structured a set of experiments designed to "better define what is meant by 'trader intuition,' and to understand why some traders are better than others." They did this by creating a number of scenarios representing markets that both had and did not have trading by informed insiders, with the goal of seeing if novice traders could intuit the intentions of these informed insiders through price movements. Perhaps surprisingly, they found that uninformed traders with no experience in financial markets were quickly able to discern the intentions of these informed insiders, based on nothing more than information contained in price changes themselves.

The logical question, of course, is how did they do that? Bruguier et al. postulated a connection between traders' intuition in market situations and a specific ability known in the literature as theory of mind (ToM). ToM is the human ability (perhaps shared by some other primates) to read benevolence or malevolence through the patterns in one's surroundings—for instance, the ability to read another person's intentions through eye expression or through moves in a strategic game. Since markets with insiders represent an environment that may be deliberately manipulated against the uninformed trader, ToM becomes a potentially relevant skill. Not only did Bruguier et al. find that trader intuition in their market simulations was strongly correlated with tests for broader ToM-based abilities, but it was *specifically uncorrelated* with ability on mathematical or logical tests. Last, they confirmed in brain scans that subjects were activating areas of the brain that have been associated with ToM in previous tests and experiments. It appears that subjects were using highly evolved portions of their brains in new contexts and applications to drive market intuition.

(Continued)

This paper is one of many that confirm the reality of intuition, but these results are particularly interesting because they suggest a fairly mundane explanation for the phenomenon. Intuition is not some mystical skill that only supertraders have; it is a retooling and reapplication of normal human abilities built from our social interactions. However, the most important point is that intuition is not special. Even inexperienced, uninformed traders quickly begin to develop intuition about market patterns (a fact that has been confirmed in many other experiments.) If everyone has it, intuition cannot, in itself, be a source of a trading edge.

Using Intuition

A discretionary trader is someone who trades based on a strong understanding of the fundamental principles of price behavior. Many outsiders and developing traders assume that discretionary traders rely on a nearly supernatural sense of what will happen next. In general, this is not true, as most discretionary trades are placed according to more or less clearly defined rules. Good discretionary traders have a passion for understanding how the market really works and for what drives unfolding price movements, and they are also willing to let go of preconceptions and theories immediately if they are disproven by the market. All good discretionary traders are statistics junkies, whether they know it or not. Some are attracted to hard-core statistical methods, but many others spend hours studying charts and keeping records and journals of market behavior. What are they doing if not internalizing the patterns of the market? I would suggest that a rigid analytical framework has the advantage of objectivity and scope, but dedicated traders can accomplish many of the same goals with charts, records of their own trades, and pencil and paper.

Even though much can be quantified, most traders will experience periods of knowing that go beyond the statistics. Sometimes there is a strong gut feeling or emotional reaction associated with a pattern; maybe, for instance, you are considering a trade in three markets and one objectively is less attractive on the chart, but you keep coming back to it for some reason you cannot define. It is also common to experience intuition on a longer time frame. Maybe you have a trade that is working well, but you find yourself thinking about it when the market is closed and you are unduly concerned. In each of these cases, this could well be a message from some part of your mind beyond your conscious grasp. It takes an enormous amount of emotional balance and experience to separate the real messages from the noise; this is one reason why the learning curve for traders is measured in years and not months. New traders simply have too much emotion and too many conflicts to be responsive to the still small voice of intuition or to separate it from their rampant fear and greed.

Trusting Intuition

In general, the most important questions about intuition concern how to balance intuition against reason. There is no simple answer to this; the answer will be different for a trader at different points in her development, for different markets and market environments, and perhaps even for different kinds of trades. In addition, many traders find it constructive to weight intuition more heavily when considering exits from existing trades rather than entries into new trades. The reason is that most discretionary traders find it easier to read a market when there is a position and fluctuating P&L involved. These factors tend to be powerful cues for intuition, but it is also important to guard against emotional distortions due to fear and greed.

The interplay of emotion and intuition is poorly understood. Intuition often communicates its message through sensations in the body, which is why it is often described as a gut feeling. It is ineffable and ephemeral, and it operates on the margin between thought and feeling. The problem is that emotions essentially communicate on this same channel, and emotions can cloud and distort the message of intuition. It is difficult or impossible for an emotional trader to respond to intuition, which is one reason why new traders should actively ignore any intuitive sense and should instead focus on building a rational analytical framework based on the inherent statistical properties of the market. Once the emotional charge is gone from the trading process, intuition will become more trustworthy, and this will probably also come at a time when the trader has finally been exposed to enough market patterns to have begun to develop some valid intuition.

For most developing traders, the most important points to remember are as follows: Intuition is real, but it is not special. Everyone who has interactions with the market quickly develops some degree of intuition, so the presence of intuition is not a trading edge. There are far more people who have intuitions about the market's movements than there are profitable traders. Also, realize that intuition relies heavily on heuristics, so it is absolutely critical that it be trained correctly. Last, realize that it will often not be possible to walk through logical steps that fully explain your intuitive conclusions. In fact, intuition will be at odds with logic and reason at times, creating a dissonance that the trader will have to resolve. Intuition is fallible and will sometimes be wrong, so it is critical that all intuitive impressions are subject to rational review and evaluation.

Numbers to Leave Numbers

Josh Waitzkin (2008) uses the phrase "numbers to leave numbers" or "form to leave form" to describe his experiences building mastery in both chess and the Chinese martial art *taijiquan*. In both disciplines, students typically spend many years studying fundamentals and basics, focusing on the building blocks of mastery. The chess student may begin by studying endgames where there are only three pieces on the board, and eventually progress to memorizing full games of grandmasters. The novice martial artist spends a lot of time learning to do basic things like standing and shifting weight from one foot to the other.

The journey from fundamentals to mastery is a long one—true mastery does not come until many hours of work have been put in for many years and until fundamentals have been assimilated on an unconscious level. Students may show aptitude early on, but it takes a long time and a lot of hard work in the right environment for even the most talented students to reach their full potential. At the end of this work, intuition grows as a natural result of everything the trader has done to understand the market. All statistical and quantitative studies, every experience in every trade, and every contemplation of market action are folded into a holistic understanding that is true market intuition.

FLOW

Have you ever been so completely engrossed in an activity that you become lost in it? Maybe you had no sense of time and hours seemed like minutes—you forgot what you were doing, and even the normal, scattered wandering of your mind stopped and you were completely focused on the task at hand. Chances are, whatever you were doing, you did well, even though you might not have been able to explain exactly how you did it. This state of *flow* is a common thread in elite performance, regardless of the context or the field: the professional athlete who sees the whole field at a glance and effortlessly seems to be at the right place at the right time, the professional musician playing an hour-long concerto from memory with effortless perfection, the line cook in a busy kitchen balancing completion of a dozen dishes at a time for hours on end, the video gamer sitting in front of his screen, or the religious mystic sitting on a wooden floor praying for days on end—these experiences are united by a common state of mind. Mihály Csíkszentmihályi (1997) was the first psychologist to seriously investigate this state, though it has certainly been a part of the human experience for millennia. He has identified a few commonalities to the flow experience:

- We are completely focused and completely absorbed in what we are doing.
- There is a sense of great inner clarity.
- The task must have clearly defined goals, so we know what must be done and how much progress we are making toward accomplishing those goals. Feedback is immediate and direct, so that our activity can be readily adjusted to match the task.
- Though the flow experience is connected to complex tasks, we know that our skills are adequate—we are up to the task. There is a sense of easy self-confidence, sufficiency, and no worries.
- There is a loss of our sense of self. We may perceive ourselves becoming one with the task, or even lose sense of the boundaries where our consciousness ends.
- We lose sense of time, and, in some cases, have a feeling of standing outside of time. This, together with the loss of self, sometimes is described as an expansion of consciousness.
- It feels great. Actually, that is a dramatic understatement. Many people report the flow experience as being one of sheer ecstasy. There is an ineffability to the state; many times we are simply unable to find words to convey the experience and it defies all explanation.
- Because of this, activities that produce flow become their own intrinsic motivation. We are driven to excel in these activities simply to achieve the state of flow—flow becomes its own reward.

How to Get There

In the flow state, we are supremely competent. Someone observing our performance would remark that we make a complex task appear effortless and easy; this, in fact, is one of the attributes of true mastery in many disciplines. Elite performers do their best work in the flow state, so it is worth our time to consider the nature of this state, how to get there, and how to guard against events that could jeopardize the flow experience. To this end, Csíkszentmihályi, Abuhamdeh, and Nakamura (2005) identified three key conditions that must exist before flow is possible. (I have added a fourth condition based on my own experience.) The presence of these conditions does not guarantee that flow will be achieved, but, without them, it is not possible.

1. The activity must have clearly defined objectives and goals.
2. The task must offer clear and immediate feedback.
3. The performer must have confidence that his or her skills are matched to the task.
4. The experience rests on a set of foundational skills that are assimilated below the level of conscious thought.

Performance in any complex task contains a great degree of variation, even though this may not be apparent to an outside observer. For the athlete, changing humidity, lighting, or other environmental conditions will play a part in performance. An artist may encounter materials that have slightly different properties due to temperature or composition. Peak performance does not proceed in an unerringly straight line; there is no perfection, even though it may appear so to the outside observer. Constant and subtle adjustments have to be made. Good performers in the flow state make these adjustments easily and naturally—this is possible only because the task offers a constant stream of feedback.

Outside stress can jeopardize the flow experience. Performers in the flow state must be confident that they can handle whatever challenges the experience will throw their way. Figure 11.1 shows a chart adapted from Csíkszentmihályi's *Finding Flow* (1997) that considers performers' state of mind at the intersection of their skills and the challenges of the task. In the lower left quadrant, skills and demands are low, and the performer simply does not care about the task. This is the plight of an office worker who might describe the job as trivial and meaningless. If challenges increase without a commensurate increase in skills and abilities (moving along the vertical axis of the chart), the performers' stress increases as they realize that they are facing a task for which they are ill-suited, and that, at some point, they will be unable to accomplish it. If skills increase far beyond the challenges present, results may suffer as the performer could actually be too relaxed and comfortable. Interesting things start to happen when extremely high challenges are met with correspondingly high skills; it is here that the performer starts to have the potential to slip into the flow experience.

In my experience, peak performance, the kind of performance that facilitates flow, rests on a strong foundation of completely assimilated skills. The artist has held a brush

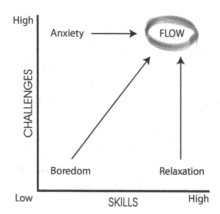

FIGURE 11.1 Csíkszentmihályi's Performer State as a Function of Challenges and Skills
Source: Adapted from Mihály Csíkszentmihályi, *Finding Flow* (New York: HarperCollins, 1997).

tens of thousands of times and understands the complexities of paper, paint, and mois-ture; he has mastered brushstrokes and color to the point where they are tools that he can draw upon without conscious thought. The master musician has assimilated the techni-cal requirements of her instrument through tens of thousands of practice sessions spread over many years. The expert rock climber seems to have a sixth sense, drawing on a deep understanding of torque, kinesthetics, and the properties of different types of rock that comes only from long experience. The trader has seen enough market action and has done enough statistical studies to know what usually happens when a market closes very strongly three days in a row, with a wider range the third day. There is nothing remark-able about any of these skills taken individually, but their deep assimilation into a whole that seems to be greater than the sum of the parts is one of the hallmarks of mastery.

Figure 11.1 also shows why the flow experience can act as a powerful guide for learn-ing and skill development. Being in the flow state is highly desirable; it feels good and we perform well in this state. Being in that space becomes its own intrinsic motivation and we will naturally do whatever is necessary to return to the flow state when we are pushed out of it. Imagine that you are in the area of the graph where your high skills are meeting moderately high challenges, but not sufficient challenges to fully absorb your attention. In this case, the performer can get back to the flow state by adding challenges and in-creasing the complexity of the task. Similarly, if the performer is in the space where high challenges are met by skills that might not quite be up to the task, increasing the level of those skills will move the performer back into the potential flow zone. It takes energy, attention, and focus to achieve this flow state, but its presence can be a powerful clue that the performer is in an optimal state to learn, to grow, and to develop new skills.

The Role of Attention and Focus

In the normal world, our minds are usually scattered. It is not unusual to be doing a task and to be thinking about several other things; in fact, multitasking is considered an asset in many professions. The problem is that we have only so much mental bandwidth, and it is hard to draw a line between multitasking and being distracted. There is the risk that when we focus on many things at the same time we will do many things, but do nothing well. Part of the beauty of flow is that we are completely focused when in this state. In fact, one of the mechanisms that have been proposed to explain the flow state is that it occurs when all available cognitive capacity is focused on one single point, a most unusual state of mind in our daily lives.

This state is not unfamiliar to meditators and religious aspirants. Many of the world's religions include a practice of repeating a mantra, a short phrase or prayer, over and over until it completely fills the field of awareness and much of the conscious mind shuts off. Mystics have reported that this is one route to achieving enlightenment and that a sense of religious ecstasy often accompanies this practice after many hours or days of this kind of focus. In the East, elaborate mandalas were created as aids to meditation. By focusing visual attention on one part of the image, the meditator was again able to enter into a state of higher consciousness. In yet another example, many meditative techniques revolve around ideas like focusing attention on a part of the body or on the breath as it goes in and out of the body; again, this is designed to achieve a single-point focus of attention.

One of the prerequisites for achieving flow is absence of distraction and complete focus on the task at hand. Whether this is evening chart review or screen time during the day, structure your environment to minimize distractions. Turn off the television, avoid Internet chats, do not check e-mail, and sequester yourself physically. It is important to do all of this with the right mind-set. Flow cannot be forced. You cannot try harder and work competitively to achieve the flow state. In fact, it flourishes in an almost playful environment of open-minded wonder, so it is not by chance that this is also the environment that is most conducive to learning and skill development. When we are in the state of flow, we are at our best, and our trading becomes something greater than the sum of the individual skills and parts.

PRACTICAL PSYCHOLOGY

Much has been written, here and elsewhere, about the psychological issues traders face and the right mind-set with which to approach trading problems. This is a complex subject because traders at different stages in their development will have significantly different challenges and needs. Different personalities will deal with the stresses of trading in significantly different ways, so solutions that might have relevance for one trader might fall well short for another—it is dangerous to make sweeping generalizations.

Psychological work is no substitute for actually having an edge, and proper psychology is not an edge in itself. No matter how hard you try, how much you focus, or how much you practice, you are not going to be able to flip a fair coin and make it come up heads more than about half the time, which is essentially what many new traders do.

Many new traders are trading methods and ideas in the market that do not have an edge and, rather than rectifying the real problem, they focus on the performance insights of trading psychology. Much of the time new traders spend on psychology would be better spent understanding the true nature of the market's movements.

For developing traders though, the situation is different. Once you have a method that has an edge in the market, it is impossible to apply that edge without having the proper mind-set and attitude. Traders find themselves making many strange mistakes that compromise their results, and these are often due to psychological issues. Dealing with the psychological stresses of trading is one of the core skills of competent discretionary trading, and it is something that requires ongoing maintenance throughout a career. No one is ever immune to psychologically driven errors. For more experienced and developing traders, it does make sense to focus on this area, perhaps even seeking the help of a qualified professional in the field.

Most of the suggestions that follow are for the self-directed trader working alone or in a team and, ideally, with a mentor. For institutional traders, portfolio managers, and quantitative system designers, your situation may be different. You will still be inclined to make these same errors, but the constraints of your job or the institutional framework may define your role well enough that your behavior is restricted. You may still find insight in understanding the issues self-directed traders face, because these reflect the psychology of the market and price movements at important inflection points.

Develop an Approach That Fits Your Personality

Who are you? It has been said that if you don't know the answer to this question, the markets are an expensive place to find out. This is true, and many millions of dollars and years of people's lives have been wasted because they were trying to trade methods or markets that were a poor fit for their psychological makeup. One of the secrets to managing yourself psychologically is to pick a trading style that plays to your strengths. So, once again, who are you? Some people make decisions intuitively and quickly, while others tend to prefer long debate and a careful weighing of all relevant factors. Some traders are naturally inclined to be more aggressive and active, while others prefer a more sedate pace. Some developing traders have serious constraints on their time and are not able to monitor markets intraday, whereas others can sit at the screen every minute the market is open. Some traders may have backgrounds and experiences that make certain markets more interesting or attractive to them. For instance, a trader who grew up on a farm will probably have natural inclinations toward agricultural markets that might be alien to a trader with a strong background in accounting and corporate finance. Every piece of their trading methodology and trading plan must be shaped by who the trader is.

Choose a Market   The choice of which markets to study and trade is an important one. Many retail traders are drawn to foreign exchange, but this is probably because of the extremely low account balances required to open a forex account. This is also unfortunate because the forex markets tend to be the most random and least predictable of all the major markets in many time frames—it is difficult to derive a quantifiable short-term edge in the currency market. One reason might be that a lot of the activity in the forex markets is driven by a complex web of factors and much of the activity in these markets is secondary.

Futures are also problematic for many new traders, because even with mini contracts, considerable risk capital is needed to navigate these markets. A stock trader might be able to start trading and, using odd lots (odd lots are less than 100-share lots), might be able to limit her entire risk to $10,000, risking perhaps $50 on a trade. It takes a long time to lose $10,000 in $50 increments, which is exactly how the beginner should be thinking. For most futures traders, $50,000 is probably a realistic initial risk to allocate to their learning period. Many traders are drawn to stocks because they come from investing backgrounds and owning stock is intuitive, but these traders are at a disadvantage because *shorting* stocks also needs to quickly become intuitive.

Choose a Time Frame   The primary question here is do you want to *day trade*, swing trade, or invest for the long haul? Details of whether you want to use 10- or 15-minute bars are considerably less important than this big-picture time frame decision. There are advantages to day trading, especially for the new trader. A swing trader might see a few hundred patterns in a year, but a day trader will see hundreds in a single week. The immersion and focus on pattern assimilation can result in a greatly accelerated learning curve, provided the trader can enter into the right psychological state to take advantage of the opportunity. In addition, the more times you apply a statistical edge, the more consistent and larger your profits will be; no other time frame offers as many "at bats" as day trading does.

However, the costs and challenges of day trading are severe; the impact of transaction costs alone presents an insurmountable barrier for many traders. For instance, imagine a trader with a $250,000 account who does 10 trades a day and who likes to trade stocks in the $150 to $200 range that might have, on average, $0.05 spreads. Furthermore, assume this trader pays $0.001 commission per share and no exchange or electronic communication network (ECN) fees on balance. (These are extremely favorable assumptions.) Last, assume the trader consistently bids or offers for his exits and enters trades with market orders, so he is paying the spread on 50 percent of the shares he trades. If he does 10 trades a day on 1,000 shares, transaction costs will total $502 a day, meaning that he has to make about $126,000 a year *just to cover costs*. This is a 50 percent annual return, again, just to break even. To put that in perspective, the Renaissance Technologies Medallion Fund, widely considered to be the best of the best, has averaged an annual return just under 40 percent since its inception; traders and funds that can make 25 percent a year are rock stars in this industry. This is a tremendous vig for the new trader, so consider this carefully.

The other issue with day trading is that the psychological demands are extreme. Day traders ride the complete emotional roller coaster from euphoria to despair, usually several times in a single trading day. Unless you have the emotional control of a Buddhist monk, day trading will play on every psychological weakness you have, and you will frequently find yourself under a degree of stress that challenges the open receptiveness needed for optimal learning. I am not saying that no one should day trade, but you need to be aware of the costs and challenges of this type of trading.

On the opposite end of the spectrum are *long-term investors* who intend to hold positions for years. For many of these players, a month is a short time frame and they consider anything on the weekly chart to be pure noise. At this level, infrequent trading and position adjustment become barriers to the trader who needs to assimilate patterns and to learn to make decisions. It is not that technical patterns do not work in the long term. The balance of mean reversion and range expansion is a little different in some time frames, but technical tools retain their validity even at long time horizons. The problem for the long-term investor is that you will not get to see them work very often and it is difficult to build intuition about the market's movements if you are making only a few decisions a year.

In the middle of the spectrum are the swing traders. Properly, the term *swing trading* does not define a specific time frame, but rather a specific style of trading—looking to target and to profit from one specific swing in the market, usually the next one, while tolerating as little pain as possible. A swing trader will attempt to position long as the market turns into an uptrend, and will usually not be interested in sitting through retracements in that trend. Some swing traders may aim for holding periods of two days to two weeks, while others may look to hold for two weeks to three months, and still others may focus on swing trading hourly charts with holding periods ranging from a few hours to two days. For many traders, the swing trading approach in an intermediate time frame of several days to several weeks offers an excellent balance: Trading is frequent enough that learning takes place quickly, and most analysis can be done outside of market hours, minimizing the decisions that must be made under pressure. This has the dual advantage of allowing the trader to enter into an open, receptive state, while also allowing time for deep reflection and analysis of the patterns being considered.

Choose a Style   Though there are a thousand subtleties to a trading style, and every successful trader creates a style that fits some key elements of his or her personality, there are two key questions to consider: are you a trend follower or countertrend trader, and do you want to be a scalper or hold for bigger moves? It is impossible for a new trader to answer these questions without some exposure to markets and to the actual trading process; the answer may change for a trader at different points in a career, but finding the answers to these questions is a key part of knowing who you are as a trader.

As a group, most traders have strong personalities, are opinionated, and are contrary to the extreme. As a result, they also tend to be distrustful of consensus and group-think, and most traders find that fading (going against) moves comes more naturally than following the trend. In addition, there is a tendency to regard markets that have made large, sudden moves as being mispriced, either on sale or ridiculously overpriced. However, traders who would focus exclusively on fading moves need to deal with an important issue: with-trend trades are usually easier and offer better expected value than countertrend setups. The most effective fade traders lie in wait until markets reach ridiculous emotional extremes on the time frame they are trading, and then they pounce. This requires extreme patience, discipline, and maturity. If you go into the market constantly looking for opportunities to fade, you will find them, but you will often be steamrollered as markets simply keep going. The crowd may be dumb, but they are often right and trends can go much further than anyone would expect.

There are advantages to trend following: with-trend trades tend to be less transactionally oriented, and it is possible for a single successful trend trade to make many multiples of the amount risked on that trade. However, trend traders will accumulate many small losses while they work to find the one market that will trend. It certainly is a viable strategy, but it is not the answer for all traders. There are strong statistical tendencies for mean reversion, and traders working a disciplined approach to fade trades may find that they can achieve higher returns and more effective deployment of capital, albeit at the expense of much harder work and many more transactions.

Scalping refers to a style of trading that focuses on a large number of very small trades. We usually think of this on very short time frames, but it is also possible to scalp on a daily or higher time frame; the key is simply that the expected profit or loss is a very small percentage of the average-sized move on that time frame. Scalpers are exposed to very high transaction costs, and are rarely involved for the big swing. Scalpers may take five cents out of an intraday swing that moves two or three points. So, why scalp? The best answer is that some people and some personality types are good at scalping, and it can offer these people consistent profits. If you believe you want to be a scalper, realize that these edges have been significantly eroded in recent years by more efficient market microstructure, and the game could well be completely over for the human trader within the next decade. Many traders choose to scalp because they lack the discipline to wait for actual trade setups—but this is not a good reason to scalp. If you choose to scalp, do so because it is the right answer for your personality, not because you are undisciplined and impatient.

Let me share my personal perspective on these questions: the best answer for most traders is to reach some kind of middle ground. Though traders should focus on a handful of patterns to trade, especially at first, it is probably best if some of those patterns are with-trend and some are countertrend. If you have only one set of tools, you will tend to force every market pattern into the context of that set of tools. If you trade only countertrend trades, you will always be looking for places to fade. If you trade only with the trend, you will ignore the spots when trends might be overextended and will always be focused only on finding the next spot to enter with the trend. In other words, if the only tool you have is a hammer, every problem you encounter will look like a nail!

Discretionary or Systematic?   The choice between *discretionary trading* and *systematic trading* is also important. This book has been written for the discretionary trader, but some traders may discover they are more suited for a systematic approach. They may find that they are not good at handling the stress of making decisions under pressure and that they function better in an analytical context far removed from the heat of battle. These traders are not doomed to failure, and they could be well-equipped to do quantitative system development. Some traders also find success with a hybrid approach, utilizing a trading system and making intuitive interventions in that system's decisions at critical points. A word of warning is in order here: If you are going to do this, carefully monitor your hybrid results and compare them to the raw system results to be sure that you are actually adding something of value. Many traders who do this intervene based on their emotional reactions to risk, and their actions are rarely constructive. Another point (which would seem to be obvious) is that your system must actually *work* and must actually show a profit after all costs are considered. If your system does not show a solid track record in properly done backtests and forward tests, it probably will not work in the market.

Also, if you choose to be a discretionary trader, carefully consider why you made that choice. Many discretionary traders avoid the systematic route because of laziness or because they lack the quantitative skills to really understand system development. This is a mistake. Discretionary trading is probably the *hardest* trading there is; it takes more work, more time, more analysis, more self-reflection, and more self-control to achieve success in this arena than in any other type of trading. In addition, if you are a discretionary trader, *you* are the most important element of your system. Any outside stress—whether it be illness, financial problems, relationship problems, sickness, or injury—that compromises your emotional balance can seriously jeopardize your trading results. Good discretionary traders who find success over the long haul develop a system to monitor themselves and their emotional state, and usually reduce their risk at times when they are not at their peak performance level.

SUMMARY

Though I have made this point repeatedly throughout this book, it bears repeating here: one of the most important keys to successful trading is consistency. Consistency applies to your actions and interactions with the market, but also to seemingly mundane points like your daily schedule, record keeping, analysis of your results, and review of your journals. Good trading is, to a large degree, boring and predictable. This is another key reason that many traders fail: they are drawn to the markets and to trading by what they perceive as a challenging, glamorous adventure, and are unable to make the adjustment when confronted with the reality of competent trading, which is very different. If you are seeking excitement in the market, you will find it. Trade too much risk on one trade, take reckless entries, skip a few days' review of your positions, put on large size before an impending economic report—any of these things will generate an exciting outcome, but probably not a good one. Creating excitement is often at odds with creating profits; good traders strive for consistency first and foremost.

Consistency is important from at least two perspectives. First, it is not possible to evaluate the efficacy of any trading system or rule set if you are not applying it with perfect consistency and discipline. Imagine that you have a trading system that is performing poorly but you are also trading it inconsistently; the bottom-line results are a combination of both the system's actual performance and your own inconsistent application of that system. It would be extremely illogical to make adjustments to the system rules based on this performance, but this is an error many developing traders make. The market is such a random environment that your first task should be to remove degrees of freedom affecting your results. If you are a self-directed trader, this should be the focus of your early development: remove degrees of freedom whenever possible. If you are an institutional trader, the confines of your job description will take care of this mandate, which is one reason that traders in clearly defined roles develop competence much faster than most self-directed traders. Second, for traders in both roles, consistency in your planned study times, review, and even specific screen setups will foster the rapid assimilation of market patterns on a deep level, quickly leading to the growth of real market sense and flow.

CHAPTER 12

Becoming a Trader

Intention, good or bad, is not enough.

—John Steinbeck

M ost of this book applies equally well to individual or institutional traders across a wide range of time frames and asset classes. The lessons of statistical tendencies and market structure are universal; ideas regarding trade and risk management are important for everyone, and can even be adapted to work in conjunction with Modern Portfolio Theory (MPT) in some applications. This chapter is different; it is written specifically for the individual self-directed trader trying to manage all of the complex tasks of trading on his or her own. The rest of the book has given you many of the pieces you need to be successful. Without a firm understanding of all of those pieces, you are not likely to be successful in the long run, but even if you are able to master the individual parts, success may still be elusive. Putting it all together into a coherent whole, building a trading methodology that fits your personality, and living through the learning curve make up a monumental challenge.

This chapter also is intended to be a reality check. If there is one message for new traders to take away from this book, it is this: trading is hard—very hard. It will challenge you in ways that you cannot imagine, and it will take much longer than you expect to reach a level of competence. Your success will be incremental and ephemeral at first. Expect an emotional roller coaster where progress is followed by errors and failures that erase most of that progress in the next period. Remember that most people who try to trade will fail, or trading will remain a marginal hobby that has no real financial impact on their net worth. If you are determined to make it something more, you have a long, hard journey ahead, and you must be prepared.

THE PROCESS

The challenges of becoming a trader are similar in many ways to those faced by doctors, lawyers, or engineers in that a period of education is followed by a grueling period of apprenticeship and on-the-job training. Many people give up and fail at some point in the process and move to other careers, but some make it through and become competent. Fewer still achieve real mastery and rise to the top of their profession—the elite in any discipline are rare. Trading differs from those careers in that the path to mastery is not as clearly laid out, and there are no prizes for second best. In many professions, people can develop the skills to become competent but not exceptional and can make a good living. In trading, especially for the individual trader, only the superstars make substantial profits over a long period of time.

In the interest of moderating expectations, it might be useful to lay out a rough road map of the typical path of trader development. In some ways, this is an artificial exercise because individual traders will have dramatically different experiences at some points due to differences in environment, innate ability, mentoring, or pure luck. Traders' development will also depend, to a large degree, on the specific market environment in which they begin their education—some years are more challenging than others. However, the following stages are a useful guide:

- *Pretrader.* Everything is new at this stage, and everything is difficult. This is the point where the trader is learning the very basics of charting and of market structure and is also just starting to explore the marketplace. A trader at this stage has no business actually placing trades, because the emotional charge will hinder the learning process, and losses are virtually assured. Most traders should probably spend three months or so in this stage. *Papertrading* (trading a simulated, not real money, account) has limited utility, but it can be useful at this stage to acclimate the trader to the process of making decisions under uncertainty and in response to market movements.

- *Novice trader.* This trader is still guaranteed to lose, so his maxim must be "Stay small." At this stage, traders are not trading to make money; they are trading for experience and to begin to deal with the emotional challenges of trading. Introspection and constant journaling are critical in this stage of development, which may last six months to a full year. Mistakes are common in this stage, but they are also learning opportunities, so trade size must be kept small enough that they are not too destructive to trading capital or emotional balance. If the trader neglects the process of journaling and trade review, these mistakes simply become losses and fall short of being the learning experiences they should be. One of the main signs of progress in this stage is that the trader will start to lose money more slowly than before. The novice trader is still losing, but losing less often and less consistently.

- *Early competent trader.* The first step toward making money is to stop losing money. A trader whose wins and losses balance out (before commissions) has taken the first steps to competence. Reaching this stage may take a year or more of very hard work. At this stage, the trader is still losing money every month due to transaction costs and other fees.

- *Competent trader.* The first stage of real competence is achieved when the trader is able to cover transaction costs with trading profits. Most traders find that they begin to develop emotional balance and control at this stage, and that they are not too attached to results and can focus more on the process. The trader will have an established routine for market review, execution, and trade review. Journaling is still important, but many of the psychological hurdles have been conquered and attention can shift to understanding how probabilities change while a trade is in progress. Reaching this stage may take a year and a half to two years for some traders. Consider this carefully—two years into the journey, a realistic expectation is to finally have accomplished the goal of being able to pay for your transaction costs. This may not seem like much, but very few individual traders ever survive to this stage.

- *Proficient trader.* Here the trader starts making money. Errors and mistakes are far less frequent, but when they do happen, they are corrected and reviewed, and the lessons are quickly assimilated. The trader has been exposed to the stressors of trading so many times that they have now lost most of their emotional charge and the trader is able to approach the markets in an open, receptive state. Trading returns are still variable and there may be significant losing periods, but the trader is able to match or beat appropriate benchmarks for most periods. As competence grows, the trader can look to manage larger and larger pools of money; developing the skills of trading larger size and risk becomes a focus at this stage. Most individual traders will be able to depend on income from their trading operation at some point in this stage, provided that they have access to sufficient capital. Expect that getting here may well take three to five years for the average trader.

- *Experienced trader.* It is difficult to imagine a trader becoming a true veteran without living through a complete bull/bear market cycle—about a decade in most cases. This trader has finally seen it all and has also become cognizant of the unknown and unknowable risks that accompany all market activity. It is possible for developing traders to gain much of this veteran trader's *knowledge* through study at earlier stages of development, but there is no substitute for experience and seeing events unfold in the market in real time. Even this experienced trader is not immune to losing periods. For instance, it is not uncommon for very proficient traders to stumble in the presence of an outside influence such as illness or family issues, but these traders usually have the control to know when to scale back their operations to limit the damage.

Requirements

With this rough road map in hand, we can next consider the prerequisites and necessities of trading. On one hand, the requirements seem to be minimal: anyone with a few thousand dollars and an Internet connection can open an account and place trades, but this does not mean that you can compete effectively, anymore than buying a football qualifies you to be in the NFL. Just because you have access to a market and can execute effectively does not mean that you can profit in an environment that immediately punishes any errors or inaccuracies. Many traders who fail do so because they have unrealistic expectations about what it takes to be a trader, and these misconceptions are reinforced by many authors and gurus. What follows is a brief but brutally realistic assessment of the basic requirements a beginning trader needs in order to have a chance of competing successfully in the marketplace.

Time   Time is important in at least two different meanings. First, you must be able to devote a sufficient amount of time on a regular schedule to building trading knowledge and skills. Within reason, the more time you can devote to the task, the quicker you will grow. It is important that you have a regular schedule for reviewing current market action and potential trades, and also important to have a time to review your own trades and your performance. It is better to have many repeated, regular work sessions than to work one marathon session infrequently. For instance, most developing traders will find that a half hour a day, every day, is more rewarding than a single 12-hour session on the weekend. Remember, part of the reason for the length of the learning curve is that you are physically restructuring your brain; this process works most efficiently in the presence of repeated and constant stimuli.

These physical changes in the brain also take time, and it is important to be realistic about the amount of time required for the entire learning curve. Most traders are unlikely to find any degree of enduring success in less than three years—a three- to four-year time horizon is consistent with what is required to achieve some degree of mastery in most other fields. It does sometimes happen that new traders start in exactly the right environments and have quick success, but this is probably the worst thing that can happen to a new trader. Many traders made quick and easy profits in the dot-com bubble in the late 1990s, as did those who began their trading adventures during the 2007 to 2008 financial crisis and crude oil bubble. Very few traders who begin in an easy environment like this have long and successful careers. When markets revert to more normal conditions, they are not able to adapt to the slower pace and to a trading environment that requires real skill and discipline.

You should be prepared to endure three years of trading with very limited success, especially if you are gauging success by the bottom-line profit and loss (P&L). It is entirely possible that the majority of your trading experiences in this period will consist of booking constant losses, but this is a normal part of the development process. You will have triumphs, breakthroughs, and successes, but do not expect to be profitable; no trader should make a call on his or her long-term ability in those first three years of trading. If you find you do not love trading as much as you expected, then consider it an important lesson learned and move on to something that does give you joy. On the other hand, if you find yourself captivated by the process but are frustrated by your lack of trading ability, persevere.

Capital It certainly *is* possible to trade for a living or to trade as a career, but there are significant constraints that must be considered. Most people do not have realistic expectations about the returns that professional traders make, so many of these traders believe they will be able to support their lifestyle with $100,000 (or less) of risk capital. At the institutional level, traders who can consistently make a 25 percent return on capital each year are very rare; these are the rock stars in the industry. Many competent traders are able to, at best, beat their benchmarks by a few percentage points; if you can do so by even a few *basis points* consistently, you can have a very successful career as a money manager. It is unrealistic to expect to consistently return hundreds of percents a year on your capital; it may happen in some extraordinary years, but this is not a realistic long-term plan. Do not go into this business as an individual trader expecting to dramatically outperform the industry benchmarks.

It is also necessary for the developing trader to have a sufficient amount of risk capital to fund the learning curve. You will lose money while you are learning to trade. Make no mistake about it—*plan* to lose money. Too many traders start off with very small (less than $25,000) accounts and plan not only to be profitable but to pay living expenses out of that account very quickly. This is unrealistic and is a formula that virtually assures failure. Plan for additional funds for educational expenses, books, and possibly even some graduate-level coursework, depending on your interests and educational background.

Working in a Team Many of the best professional traders work in a team, and some of them count it as an essential part of their success. For this to be most effective, the team must actually share both trading decisions and P&L; though is it scary, the reason this arrangement works is that your decisions will have an impact on someone else's P&L and vice versa. Traders working in this arrangement are essentially yoked together—they will succeed or fail *together*. There are many advantages to this arrangement, but the most significant of them deal with the issues of discipline and self-control. It is much more difficult to do something reckless or stupid if you know that not only will you have to be accountable to another person, but your mistake will actually cost that person money. Teammates who work together closely develop a sense of each other's rhythm, strengths, and weaknesses, so it is often easy to address behavioral problems before they have an impact on the P&L. In addition, there are obvious advantages of having two sets of eyes on trading questions and market data, and the camaraderie of a trusted teammate can counteract the isolation of trading.

This is not a relationship to be entered into lightly or halfway. It is important that you know and trust the other person, because you will be giving that individual full access to your trading capital. Firm, written contracts are also essential, outlining responsibilities and obligations for both parties. It is also worth considering that this arrangement is problematic for developing traders and may be much more suitable for established, consistent traders. Having another person in the decision process can compound the already severe emotional challenges developing traders face. In addition, two developing traders will grow at different rates and will have different sets of strengths and weaknesses.

There is great potential for reinforcement of weaknesses and additional confirmation bias if developing traders work too closely in teams.

It is possible to work an arrangement like this at a distance, though there are many advantages to working in the same office. If you decide to pursue this relationship, spend a lot of time considering how you will work with your teammate. Expectations must be clearly defined. Have a clear plan for how work will be divided; it makes sense to do some of the work together, but most teams find it useful to have done a good deal of individual work before bringing ideas to the team. Expect that you both will make errors, and expect to be called out on them. One of the reasons you are working with another person is to have the benefit of someone looking over your shoulder and monitoring your emotional state, but the first time you are on tilt and someone taps you on the shoulder to suggest that you need to step back is always a difficult moment in the life of a trader. It requires exceptional maturity and self-awareness to successfully manage a teammate relationship in the emotionally charged trading environment, but the benefits can be substantial. This element of teamwork is a secret of top-level professional trading that is not often available to the at-home individual trader.

Working with a Mentor   Most traders who achieve some degree of success owe much of that success to the guidance of a mentor. (Personally, I can think of three people without whom I probably would not have succeeded in this business.) There are many ways this relationship can work, ranging from one-on-one instruction over an extended period of time to much less frequent course corrections. In addition, a mentor can guide a new trader in many different ways. Some mentors are teachers who prefer to work with students who have little or no market knowledge, starting at the beginning and building a comprehensive approach to trading. Others may work more as coaches, preferring to take a student's system and knowledge and help to shape the application of that system.

There are at least three important issues to consider about the mentoring relationship. First, both parties must be committed and there must be a clear understanding of responsibilities and obligations. An effective mentor does not have to spend long hours with a student, but if the student expects that kind of time and the mentor does not, the relationship will not be successful. If a mentor expects to work only with full-time, professional traders, then a student working very hard to learn on evenings and weekends is probably not going to fulfill expectations.

Second, the question of fit is very important, both in style and personality. A mentor with a hard-core, drill-sergeant style approach will be completely ineffective with a student seeking a supportive, nurturing approach. A mentor who focuses on intraday trading will probably be less effective working with students who focus on longer-term trades—there certainly can be exceptions to these rules, but the issue of fit is paramount.

Last, the issue of compensation should be understood clearly by both parties. Mentoring can be a major investment of time and energy from the mentor's side, so it is reasonable for that person to be paid for the time, but too many mentors are not competent traders themselves. Anyone can claim to offer trader mentoring, but it is difficult for the student to truly evaluate the mentor's skill and ability.

Technology: Software and Hardware   It goes without saying that you must have access to good infrastructure: On the hardware side, you must have one or more good computers with data backup and fast, reliable Internet access. In terms of software, you need a few important tools:

- *Execution software:* Many traders base their choice of broker on the quality of its execution software. It should be easy to use, allow easy tracking of positions and open orders, and have excellent accounting support. Most traders find that it is a good trade-off to pay slightly higher commissions for better software and accounting—many of the lowest-cost brokers do not offer acceptable software interfaces, though this gap has closed in recent years.
- *Charting software:* Most execution packages incorporate some degree of charting capability, but many traders find it worthwhile to pay for specialized charting programs. Good charting software has fast access to data, all of the relevant data for markets you trade, and the ability to customize displays to fit your preferences. Most higher-level programs will allow you to write programs for custom indicators and customized data processing; some traders find this to be a valuable capability. Last, if you trade futures, make sure you understand how your vendor handles rolls and continuous contracts.
- *Record-keeping software:* There are several ways to keep the records you need, and each trader must develop his or her own system. Some will prefer to keep journals and trade records in a word processing document, while others will prefer more complex solutions like a database.
- *Microsoft Excel:* This deserves its own bullet point since nearly every trader will use it in some way. Invest the time learning to use it well and properly: be comfortable with formulas, references, and macros, and learn to use it without touching the mouse. (Keyboard shortcuts are literally five times faster than corresponding operations with the mouse.) Excel is adequate for many basic analytical and record-keeping tasks.
- *Analytical software:* If you intend to perform deeper analysis of market tendencies and create your own statistical studies, you will need to move beyond Excel at some point. Excel is capable of doing some fairly in-depth analyses, but it is not the right tool for this job. Some versions of Excel have small but persistent calculation errors that can cause serious errors in trading applications, and Excel's management of large data sets is cumbersome at best. Though it is a major commitment of both time and money, learning to use a software package like SPSS, SAS, Stata, or R is the only alternative for traders wanting to do their own deep-dive data analysis.

A Business Plan and Trading Plan   Always think of your trading as a business and treat it as such. No one would try to start a business with insufficient capital, with no plan for how to expand the business, and with no vision of where the business could be in one, five, or 10 years, but this is exactly how most people start trading. The challenge, of course, is that you do not know at the beginning if you will be able to develop the skills to trade successfully, or how long it will take. There are many more uncertainties than in most other areas of business, but there are parallels—imagine a company that is making a speculative bet on a new product that may or may not catch on, or a new industrial process that may or may not be able to take market share from existing competitors. In these cases, the companies would make very sure that they understood the competitive marketplace, that they had access to resources they need to succeed, and that they had sufficient capital to weather the start-up period, though their long-term success might be less than certain.

With this in mind, craft a business plan for your trading operations. This will be a plan that, hopefully, will mature as your trading abilities develop. In the beginning, perhaps this is a document that focuses on your development and provides a yardstick for measuring your commitment. As you actually start trading, the document can be modified to encompass risk parameters, markets traded, and new directions you are exploring. (Strike a balance between modifying this document often enough that it is relevant and having a good control document. If the plan is always changing, it is probably not very helpful.) Hopefully, at some point you will expand this plan and perhaps even use it to recruit partners or investors as your trading business grows. The sky truly is the limit, but you must approach this as an extremely competitive and difficult business.

While the business plan is the overarching control document, the trading plan is more dynamic and flexible. The trading plan defines exactly what you will and will not do in the market, and it will evolve as your trading abilities mature. It is not unusual to revise a trading plan at least slightly every month; each trader will adapt the concept of a trading plan slightly, but a good plan will include all of the following:

- Schedule for your daily or weekly research and trade review.
- List of patterns and ideas you will trade, similar to Chapter 6.
- Target activity and risk levels. How many trades a day/week/month will you allow? How many positions can you have on at the same time? What is the maximum percentage of your capital that can be at risk at any time? How and when will you use margin? Is there a loss level at which you will stop trading for the day/week/month?
- A clear plan for trade management. Will you enter all at once or scale in? Will you take partial profits? If so, where and how?
- How often will you make trading decisions? Are you able to make decisions in the middle of the day, or do you prefer to create a plan the night before and simply execute it as faithfully as possible during the trading day?

Once you have these documents, much of your work boils down to making sure that you are following the plan. Remember, any evaluation of your performance over any time period is an evaluation of both your plan and how well you followed that plan. Follow the plan as precisely as possible to remove extraneous sources of variation in your returns.

Commit to the Process

In many ways, the intellectual problems of trading are trivial. This may seem to be an ironic statement, given that it appears in a large book about trading, but the essential elements of market structure and trade management could fit on a single piece of paper. The elaborations, variations, and applications are much more extensive and will reward long study, but the core knowledge of trading is not complicated. Most traders rather quickly assimilate the foundation, but the gap between knowledge and execution must be bridged. The core *skills* of competent trading—and be clear that skill is not the same as knowledge—are primarily emotional. If traders have not mastered discipline and emotional poise in the face of volatile market movements, their trading will be forever plagued by errors that will erode whatever edge they may have had. Though it is possible to accelerate the learning curve in many areas, the only way to master emotional control is through actual trading over an extended period of time. The process of trading can be summarized as doing analysis, making decisions, putting capital at risk, and dealing with the consequences. Only by living through that loop repeatedly can the trader make progress; regular, repeated exposure is the key.

Stay Small   Again, while you are going through this learning curve, *expect to lose money*. This is what new and developing traders do—they lose money while they are learning. Therefore, it makes sense to keep your risk as small as possible on each trade until you have achieved consistency. The gain or loss on any individual trade should be so small that it is insignificant; the point of early trading is to gain experience and to learn about the trading process while keeping the losses as small as possible.

Granularity is an issue in some markets. For instance, equity and forex traders can usually trade small enough that they can risk a tiny amount, say $50, per trade. A trader who has a $25,000 to $50,000 trading account can lose $50 many times in a row before he has made a dent in his allocated capital. Futures and options traders, in contrast, may often find it difficult to risk less than $500 on a trade because of the size of the contracts. From a purely technical perspective, there are reasons why forex may be very difficult for shorter-term traders, but equities might offer a better learning environment than either futures or options for newer traders. This point cannot be overemphasized: keep your risk small enough that the win or loss on any individual trade is insignificant until you have shown many months of consistent profitability.

Periodic Evaluations   It is important to have a regularly scheduled time to evaluate your trading performance, both over the most recent period and over a longer time span. This would also be an appropriate time to check in with a more experienced trader, a coach, or a mentor if you do not work with someone on a regular basis. For most traders, the end of the month is a natural spot, but for other, longer-term traders, the end of the quarter might be more suitable. Find a balance between having frequent enough reviews to make useful corrections and having long enough periods of trading in between so that performance trends are meaningful. (Even for active traders, a week is too short a time for a serious reevaluation.)

This review does not have to be a complicated, painful process, but it must be done regularly. At a minimum, review your equity curve (perhaps without commissions for the developing trader), the performance of the various categories of trades you are trading, and each individual trade made over the period. It may also make sense to review psychological journals and performance, and most importantly, to note any recurring errors. The result of this periodic evaluation should be a written list of things to work on in the next period. This does not have to be a long list; in fact, many times it will be useful to identify only the two or three biggest issues the trader is facing. Note that there is an obvious tie-in with the quality of your record keeping and the ease with which this review can be done. If your records are a mess, then this review will be much less effective.

Dealing with Setbacks   If you are an individual self-directed trader, expect setbacks and failures, especially in the first two years. Expect that your triumphs may be promptly followed by dramatic failures, that you will make mistakes in areas you thought you had mastered, and that any positive P&L may be quickly erased next week. Furthermore, do not expect that your learning curve will be described by a straight, upward-sloping line. It is far more common for students of any high-level skill to find that their progress comes in a series of jumps interspersed with long, flat plateaus. It is often difficult to maintain motivation during the flat periods, because you will feel that you are working very hard and not making any progress, and then progress comes, seemingly overnight, in a blinding flash. The reason for the sudden spurts of progress is the hard work done on the plateaus, but it can be difficult to keep up very hard work for seemingly no reward.

You will hear various stats suggesting that somewhere around 95 percent of self-directed traders fail. The definition of failure, of course, depends on your definition of success. What is success in the market? Is it being able to make a living, pay your bills, and have enough left over for security? Is it having the satisfaction of being able to do something extremely difficult well, so that being able to manage the trading process is itself a degree of success? Is it as simple as beating the indexes by a few percentage points, consistently outperforming what a professional investment manager would be able to do for your account? Your definition of success will probably change as your trading ability matures and your personal financial goals shift, but trading success must be both financial and nonfinancial. Be clear that trading is about making money—whatever other motivations and satisfactions are tied into the process, at the end of the day there must be financial reward and it must be substantial. Trading is difficult, time-consuming, and emotionally challenging, and nearly all traders find that their trading income is highly variable, so a higher average (annual) income is required relative to other professions. However, it will be very difficult to succeed if you are not absolutely fascinated by markets and the process of trading. If you don't love it, you won't be a very good trader, so there must be motivations for trading that go beyond financial gain.

If we redefine success as making substantial financial gains on a percentage basis, then I suspect the success rate for individual traders is far less than 5 percent. In fact, probably fewer than one in a thousand, and maybe *many* fewer than that, really succeeds. If you are going to be in this elite group, you must prepare yourself, work hard, and have the emotional resilience to deal with setbacks along the way. It is very hard to find common personality traits that make people suited to be traders; most people can succeed in some capacity if they find a market and trading style that fits their personality, if they have realistic expectations and all of the prerequisites for success, and if they commit to enduring the learning curve.

One last thought on this subject: When we look at people who are very successful in any field, we find a very mixed group. They come from different backgrounds, have very different personalities and attitudes, and reached their success through interesting paths, some of which are far from straight. In most fields, it is impossible to find consistent predictors of success, but people who succeed have one thing in common—they did not quit. This is so simple that it seems trivial, but *is* the common thread tying all of these people together. As Mark Cuban said, "It doesn't matter how many times you fail. It doesn't matter how many times you almost get it right. No one is going to know or care about your failures, and neither should you. All you have to do is learn from them and those around you because ... all that matters ... is that you get it right once. Then everyone can tell you how lucky you are." Commit to the process. Never give up.

RECORD KEEPING

Good record keeping is an important part of skill development in many disciplines. Self-directed traders usually focus on two specific kinds of records: trading journals and trade-specific records. Trading journals may include narrative about the patterns in the markets and pattern research, or they may focus on psychological issues the trader is struggling with. Trade-specific records are P&L records with some deeper information on each trade: at least the type of trade and initial risk assumed on the position. If these records are done well, it is then possible to do deep performance analysis on them to understand how the trader's ability is growing and to target specific areas for further work.

There are many ways to create and format these sets of records once you understand the goals. With all of these records, the most important thing is to create a routine that you can commit to following on a regular schedule. There is a trade-off between complexity and ease of use; it does no good to create an elaborate system that takes so much time to maintain that you do not do it on a regular basis. On the other hand, an overly simplistic record will probably not contain enough information to be useful. Invest time at the beginning planning and creating a system that will work for you, be open to some revision as you use it, and once you have settled on a final plan, commit to keeping these records consistently. It is not unusual for traders to spend more time maintaining and reviewing these records than they do in actual trading.

Another issue to consider is whether the records will be kept on paper, in an electronic format, or in some combination of the two. Electronic records have many advantages, probably the most important of which is that they are easily searchable. If you want to find every instance of the word *slippage* in your trading journal, this can be done in seconds. They are also easier to read and to store, and if they are backed up in the cloud, can be accessed from any computer in the world. Even with all of these advantages, there may be some argument for keeping at least a portion of the records on paper. Many people find that the act of setting pencil to paper engages a type of thought—perhaps a part of the brain—that is different from the experience of typing.

Journal

A good journal is one of the trader's most important tools. For the developing self-directed trader, it is a concrete record of successes and failures; careful reflection on and analysis of this record can point out weaknesses and growing edges that can have an immediate impact on the bottom line. Having a good written record is essential, because memory is somewhat mutable after the fact. Highly emotional events, gains and losses, and large market movements will invariably color our recollection. Keeping this record is a difficult task that most traders have trouble sustaining over many years, but it is virtually impossible to progress from novice to expert without keeping a solid trading journal. For the proficient trader, the journal becomes a type of control document. Every trader's performance is subject to some variation as a function of the natural randomness in markets, but there are also performance slips that are due to some outside stress or psychological issue. If performance deteriorates, the trading journal becomes a valuable resource to answer the question "What has changed?"

Journaling about Yourself   As a self-directed, discretionary trader, *you* are a major component of your trading success and failure. Your attitude, emotional state, and energy level will all have an impact on the bottom line, and these things should be recorded in a daily journal. At the beginning, err on the side of too much detail. Though it might seem absurd, you should record such trivial points as what you had for breakfast, how much you slept, and anything unusual that happened in the morning. If you do not record those events in your journal, it is going to be difficult to tease out a pattern and to find influences that help or hurt your performance. Write down *everything* at the beginning, and modify the procedure only after you see how you will be using this document to improve your performance.

Journaling about the Market   In writing about the market, there are two aspects to consider. One, there is the objective reality of price movements and relationships between markets; over time, this journal will become a source and a reference for your own research into market patterns and trading ideas. Perhaps you observed four down days in the major indexes, followed by a large up day with strong buying. Maybe you think you see an interesting correlation between currency rates and the spread between two equity sector indexes. Traders who are truly committed to understanding how markets work maintain large backlogs of trading ideas and often work on many ideas at the same time. You will be surprised at the times you will think of something several years down the road, dig back into an old journal, and find a relevant observation that can be a revelation for a research project you are doing at the time. This record of observations and ideas about market action is an important tool for your learning and development.

In addition, you should also be journaling about your reactions to the market's movements, adapting this record to your stage of development and your function as a trader. Do you find that a period of small-range consolidation days near lows makes you nervous? Do you find yourself becoming extremely bullish during large-range multiday declines? Some of these reactions will be mistakes, and you will find some inclinations and biases that can be corrected before they become too costly in actual trading. However, other reactions will, over time, reveal facets of your trading personality that you might never have seen without this record. For instance, perhaps you will discover that you trade declining markets much better than advancing markets, or that you excel at positioning in consolidations before breakouts. Record keeping is an essential part of the learning process; without it, you may still progress, but that progress will be much slower and much more uncertain.

Daily Game Plan   It is important to have a written daily game plan for each market session. Even long-term investors will benefit from writing down important cues and planned reactions to price movements over the course of days to weeks; intraday traders will need a very detailed and specific plan for each individual day. This document can serve as a control to help the trader build discipline, and can provide a connection between dispassionate analyses done outside of market hours and the actual trading process. Developing traders will often find that their view of the market is clouded by their emotional reactions to price movements, and that it is often much easier to see clearly when the market is closed. Sometimes the best solutions are the simplest: in this case, simply writing down a plan while the market is closed can do wonders. Over time, this particular record becomes something of a hybrid between a diary and trade record.

How you create this game plan is up to you, but it should probably include at least three sections: observations on the overall market, points to watch on existing positions, and potential new entries. Ideally, this document should *not* be in narrative style; this is not a journal, it is an attack plan—bullet points are much more efficient. In the beginning stages of your development you will probably want to include more detail: not only what markets you are looking at but notes on specific setups, price levels, action in related markets, and comments across multiple time frames. Later, when you have mastered your setups and your style is more fully developed, the daily game plan can become much shorter and more succinct. Retaining these plans and periodically reviewing them will give you insights into your growth as a trader, and can highlight issues of style drift that you might not otherwise be aware of.

Profit and Loss (P&L) Records

The most important set of records are probably the actual P&L records. Though developing traders should not expect to make money, their P&L is still an objective measure of growth and performance. For the working trader, P&L is the bottom line. It is important to maintain clean, well-categorized, and accurate P&L records, and to have your own set of records to double-check your broker or clearing firm's accounting. Errors happen. Positions may be missing, may be sized incorrectly, or may end up in the wrong account. Corporate actions, buy-ins, dividends, rolls in futures, interest rates in forex accounts, currency conversions for assets held on foreign exchanges, and options assignments can all cause issues, so develop an obsessive habit of checking statements and records after any of these events. In many cases the customer has some liability in this type of error; treat your trading as a business and manage every aspect of it with discipline.

Though many brokers produce records that are adequate for most accounting and tax purposes, more resolution is usually needed. One of the most important tasks in record keeping is categorizing all trades and executions according to the setup or pattern that generated the trade. For instance, it is useful to be able to separate all pullback trades or all failure test trades, and then to do statistical analysis on that particular set of trades. Again, think carefully when you develop this system, because it is important to strike a balance between ease of use and sufficient detail. If you do not include enough detail, your analysis will not tell you anything useful about your performance. If you include too much detail, you may create an onerous task and eventually stop updating these records every day. In general, most traders might find it useful to have three to five main categories of trades corresponding to specific setups and patterns they trade. Each category could optionally have more information regarding the specific entry or exit technique used to allow for cross-referencing and deeper analysis. Excel is adequate for keeping these records, but many traders will find a database program better suited to the task.

It is very important that you create a process that is meaningful for your style and frequency of trading, and it is also important to get it right from the beginning. If, for instance, you change the way you categorize your trades, you may have to go back through several hundred or thousands of trades and recategorize them all. Not only is this a waste of time, but it compromises the integrity of the records; you may be inclined to push certain trades into certain categories in a subtle effort to skew the performance metrics on some classes of trades. In many cases it is possible to designate a trade several ways: Was that a pullback trade? Did you buy at support? Did you buy a failure test against support? Was it a selling climax trade on a lower time frame? What matters is what you thought it was *at the time you made the trade*, not some decisions you may make weeks or months afterward, so beware of making revisions to these designations after the fact.

STATISTICAL ANALYSIS OF TRADING RESULTS

There are so many subjective elements in discretionary trading, but your P&L is not one of them—you are either making or losing money. Correct analysis of your P&L can reveal hidden strengths and weaknesses. You may find you trade certain market environments or asset classes better than others, or that you are trading a specific pattern well but giving back all of the P&L in other, less successful trades. In addition, tracking performance over a period of time can give early warning of problems, can highlight style drifts, and can tie performance to certain market environments. For traders at all stages of development, the main questions to ask of this analysis are:

- Are you making money? Does your P&L show that you have an edge? Are your results better than what someone could have achieved flipping a coin or throwing a dart?
- Is your performance dependent on one class of setup more than others? Could you improve performance by eliminating certain setups from your trading plan?
- Is there a market, group of markets, or asset class that you trade better than others?
- How is your performance changing compared to other time periods?

These questions can be answered through some fairly simple procedures. Many brokers will supply statements that will answer some of these questions, but others will need to be addressed through your own work and records. Once these basic questions have been answered, the analysis and review can be extended with other questions, such as:

- Are you repeating certain mistakes often enough that eliminating them could have a very positive effect on your overall P&L?
- Are you achieving superior risk-adjusted performance?
- Are there other things that you are doing that are hurting your numbers?

This next section will walk through a theoretical analysis to show the basic concepts and math used. (The set of trades is available from the author's web site at www .adamhgrimes.com/ and in Appendix C.) If this type of work is new to you, you should repeat the analysis yourself and compare your results to those in this section.

Quantifying Your Edge

Table 12.1 shows summary statistics for an active swing trader trading four separate systems over three months in a $100,000 account. Number of trades ($N=$) and cumulative net P&L (Sum) are given, as well as means for all trades and both winning and losing

TABLE 12.1 Summary Statistics for Net P&L

System	N=	Sum	Mean	StDev	AvgWin	AvgLoss	Win%	p=
A	29	(2,531)	(87)	616	456	(528)	44.8%	0.226
B	17	5,109	301	515	557	(314)	70.6%	0.014
C	16	1,109	69	653	361	(1,194)	81.3%	0.339
D	6	(529)	(88)	479	468	(366)	33.3%	0.336
All	68	3,158	46	600	456	(538)	58.8%	0.263

trades separately. The percentage of winning trades is given as Win% in the table. In this example, losing trades are 1 − Win% for all categories, but in other cases there may be breakeven trades to consider. Standard deviation is calculated as an intermediate step to deriving the p value, which is a significance test (one-tailed t-test) for the mean P&L being >0.

First, consider the bottom line of the table, which gives summary statistics for all trades combined. Over this period, this trader made $3,158 on starting capital of $100,000. The first question to ask is: Is this good performance? Even a simple question like this may not have a simple answer. On one hand, $3,158 is not a lot of money, but if this is performance over one quarter, a 3.16 percent gain is perhaps not bad. Assuming this trader can repeat this performance regularly, 3.16 percent quarterly compounds to a respectable 13.2 percent annually: $(1 + 0.0316)^4 − 1$.

However, it is not so simple: The standard deviation of the trades is a staggering $600 compared to a mean trade of $46. This is not good, and suggests that the positive performance could have been nothing more than luck. The p value of 0.263 basically says that, given this set of trades, there is a 26.3 percent chance of seeing results at least this extreme due to random chance even if the trader did not actually have an edge. Figure 12.1, a running total of the individual trades, provides another check on consistency and edge. (Note that this figure does not mirror the daily account P&L that is marked to market; this graph simply sums each trade's closed P&L. Graphs like this can be ordered either by trade entry or by exit date.) Consider this P&L line and ask yourself how hard it is to believe that it ended above zero just due to chance. In this case, there seems to be little consistency and the line wanders about as far above as below the zero

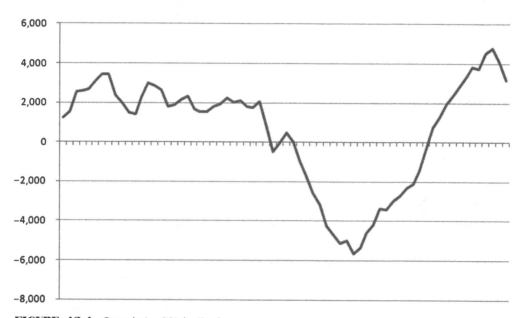

FIGURE 12.1 Cumulative P&L by Trade

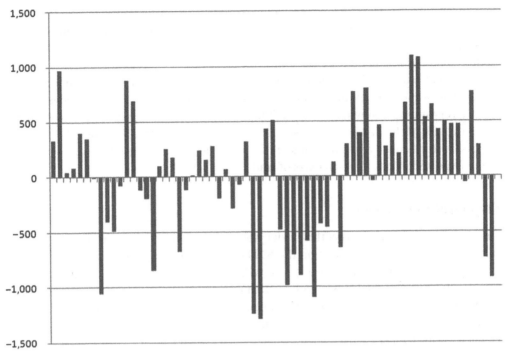

FIGURE 12.2 Trade-by-Trade Net P&L

line. This is not what we would expect to see if a trader had a strong edge. Though this is not an actual statistical test, visual inspection of a time series chart is a good companion to deeper analyses.

Yet another check comes from plotting the P&L of each individual trade (not cumulative) as in Figure 12.2. One of the most important aspects of this graph is the long runs of both winning and losing trades. There seem to be roughly three separate sections to this trader's performance: The first half of the graph shows winning and losing trades approximately equally matched, and then there is a potentially nasty series of losing trades as two large losses, followed by two small wins, lead to eight losing trades in a row. However, this period is followed by a nearly unbroken series of wins on the last third of the graph. There are questions that must be asked here that cannot be answered by this simple analysis: Why did this happen? Does the trader's style favor certain market environments over others, or is there an element of performance psychology here? Is the trader himself responsible for these streaks of losses or wins? Essentially all of the positive P&L comes from the long run of wins at the end, so is there some repeatable element in that set of trades? The answers to all of these questions may well be no. It is possible that these runs are just the normal expectation for the system, and that any tweaking would be counterproductive, but these are the kinds of questions to ask.

Though the trader's performance is not promising, all is not lost. The breakdown of trades by system (A, B, C, and D) in Table 12.1 shows that the B-class trades might have a stronger edge. These trades, taken alone, made $5,109 on 17 trades, showing a mean trade of $301 with a standard deviation of $515, achieving statistical significance as well. This trader should possibly consider these trades further, and ask if some of the other trades could be eliminated from the playbook.

This is also a vivid illustration of the fact that neither reward/risk ratio nor winning percentage is particularly important when taken alone. Consider the C trades, which have a very impressive win ratio of 81.3 percent, but an average loss more than three times the size of the average win essentially wipes out any edge. Note also that it is not necessary to calculate expected value in this analysis, as the trade means are equivalent to the expected values for each class of trade.

Standardizing for Risk

One complicating factor is that this trader was not consistent in his risk. Though not visible in Table 12.1, risk per trade on the $100,000 account ranged from a low of $199 to a high of $1,790. The nominal trade risk will vary under a fixed percentage plan (see Chapter 9), but this trader was not executing a fixed percentage plan as trade risks ranged from 0.2 percent to 1.8 percent of equity at the time of entry. Standardizing each trade's P&L as a percentage of the amount risked can provide deeper insight into the trader's performance:

$$\%R = \text{Actual dollar P\&L} \div \text{Initial risk}$$

Table 12.2 shows the result of this analysis.

This time, the results paint a very different picture. On average, the trader made 0.3 times the initial risk on every trade, with a standard deviation of 0.8; this is a much better ratio of return to standard deviation than in the first table. The t-test shows that this P&L is statistically significant at the 0.001 level, as there would be less than a 0.1 percent chance of seeing a result this extreme due to random chance. There is a very important point here: The trader's net P&L was a combination of both his position sizing choices and whatever actual edge he may have had. Standardizing for risk removes the position sizing effect and reveals that this trader actually *was* trading with a clear statistical edge, even though it was completely obscured by his position sizing decisions. This second analysis also suggests that there probably *is* an edge to the C-class trades, which

TABLE 12.2 Summary Statistics for %R P&L

System	N=	Sum	Mean	StDev	AvgWin	AvgLoss	Win%	p=
A	29	2.9X	0.1X	0.8X	0.8X	−0.5X	44.8%	0.249
B	17	13.5X	0.8X	0.8X	1.2X	−0.3X	70.6%	0.001
C	16	6.7X	0.4X	0.7X	0.7X	−0.8X	81.3%	0.013
D	6	0.1X	0.0X	0.6X	0.6X	−0.3X	33.3%	0.463
All	68	23.2X	0.3X	0.8X	0.9X	−0.4X	58.8%	0.000

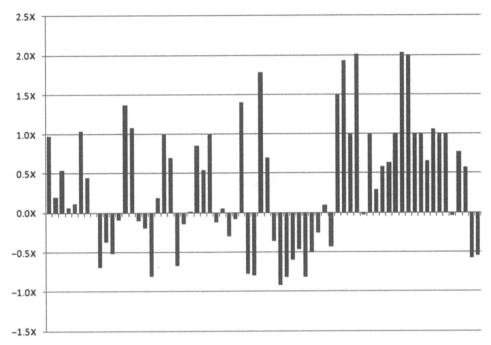

FIGURE 12.3 Trade-by-Trade %R P&L

returned an average of 0.4 times initial risk against a standard deviation of 0.7. Based on this analysis, A-class and D-class trades should be carefully examined, as it appears there may not be an edge.

Compare Figure 12.3, which shows the individual trade results as %R, to Figure 12.2. At first glance they appear to be similar, showing the same runs of wins and losses, but look again. Notice especially that the two large losses that stood out in the middle of Figure 12.2 are normal, insignificant losses when expressed as %R. Is it possible that the trader increased risk on those two trades, taking outsized risks and losses? If so, could those losses have unbalanced him psychologically and led to the series of losing trades? This cannot be answered from a numerical analysis, but these are the kinds of questions that must be asked. Note that, in general, Figure 12.3 is much more consistent—though the trader may have made poor decisions about his position sizing on each trade, it appears that he was working within and respecting his risk limits very well.

This analysis can and should be extended to more detailed investigations of the different classes of trades and different asset classes, if applicable. For now, let's leave this example with one more step. It is possible to generate a pro forma P&L, which assumes that the trader had risked a consistent percentage of account equity on each trade. Figure 12.4 shows this pro forma equity curve, assuming 1 percent fixed fractional risk, against the actual P&L. Note that you cannot simply add the %R results in Table 12.2 to get ending P&L under a fixed fractional scheme because the amount risked is always changing with each trade. In this case, the trader would have ended with $22,935 had he

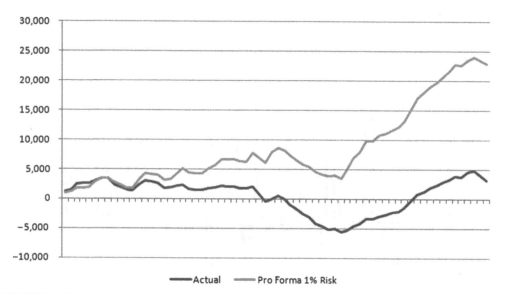

FIGURE 12.4 Cumulative Actual and Pro Forma P&L

simply used 1 percent fixed fractional risk, a stunning gain over his actual $3,158. The path of this pro forma P&L provides another, visual confirmation of what we have seen clearly in the %R analysis—the trader actually did have an edge, but did not apply it very well. The lessons, in this case, are probably simple: perhaps eliminate one or two of the trading systems and consider applying the rest with a fixed fractional risk approach in the next period.

Control Charts

Control charts are tools used in manufacturing to monitor physical processes for early signs of degradation or failure, and are an important quality control tool in diverse fields such as metalworking, electronics, and pharmaceutical manufacturing, among others. They are especially powerful in physical processes that can be tightly controlled, especially with large sample sizes. For instance, an automobile part produced on an assembly line might have tolerances measured in a fraction of a human hair; some variation, within tightly defined limits, is acceptable, but the production line needs a warning when products stray outside these bounds. The same concepts can be applied to trading, with the caveat that trading results are far more variable than manufacturing applications.

There are several different kinds of control charts used in manufacturing applications, but I am going to propose a simplified version that traders may find more immediately applicable. Many of the assumptions of distributions made in classic control charts do not hold in trading situations. For instance, one commonly used chart in manufacturing plots variations on both sides of an average, expecting that the variation should wander more or less freely above and below that average. The quality control manager takes note when four or five data points appear on one side of the average, and considers this to be an early warning that the process is potentially moving out of the control zone. This degree of control is very unlikely in trading, so the purpose of these charts is slightly different: to present trading results in a graphical format that displays the individual data points, a moving average, and some measure of variation. The first of these charts is the *Standard Deviation Control Chart*, and is produced by the following procedure:

- First, decide what the evaluation period is going to be. Many traders will find weekly analysis to be most applicable, but day traders should do this work on each trading day. (It is also possible to do a trade-by-trade analysis rather than a chronological grouping.)
- Collect a time series of individual (not cumulative) P&Ls for each period.
- Choose a look-back period. The example that follows is done on daily data produced by a day trader, so a look-back period of 20 trading days, which is approximately equal to one trailing calendar month, was chosen. In practice, look-back periods of 10 to 50 are probably most useful.
- For each data point, calculate a moving average of the look-back period as well as the standard deviation. Offset these by one day, so that today you are using yesterday's average and standard deviation. This is important because a large value today will influence the average and standard deviation and, particularly for short look-back periods, will give an understated view of the variation.
- For each data point, plot the raw data point as a bar, the moving average, and bands $+/-N$ times the standard deviation. Remember, it is very unlikely that this data will be normally distributed, so the usual rules of thumb for standard deviation do not apply. Rather, the standard deviation bands are used as a visual representation of the degree of variation in the process. The example that follows uses 2.5 for N, but values of 1.5 to 3.0 may be useful.

Figure 12.5 shows an example of this Standard Deviation Control Chart, based on 190 trading days of a model developing day trader's P&L. Though there is much to be gleaned from this analysis, here are some important points to consider:

A: The trader's variation has been steadily increasing, evidenced by the expanding upper and lower bands. Note that the average (the dark black line in the middle)

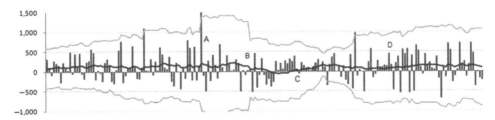

FIGURE 12.5 A Standard Deviation Control Chart

has been consistently above zero, suggesting that the trader is consistently making money. In addition, winning days are much larger than losing days. This is all good.

B: Something happens here. The average takes a turn down, and even crosses to the other side of zero. The trader would have been losing money during this period, but the variation also decreases. It is important to ask the right questions to understand why this happened. What caused the change in the average? Are there behavioral factors at work? Did something shift in the market? Was a new trading system implemented? Perhaps the trader was aware that he was not doing well and reduced trading size. The answers are not on this chart, but the chart can provoke the correct questions.

C: The average recovers after a series of winning days, but there may still be problems. The average is not as consistent, as it turns back down shortly after C, and there are not as many winning days above $500 as at the beginning of the chart.

D: Finally, the trader's P&L seems to be back under control, and the last part of the chart looks very much like the beginning, though the degree of variation (spread of the bands) is higher.

This chart will serve the needs of most traders, but another possibility to consider is the Range Control Chart. This chart, shown in Figure 12.6, can be a useful complement to other P&L analyses. The procedure for creating this chart is simple:

- For each period being evaluated (day, week, or trade), plot the raw data as a bar.
- Choose a look-back period (20 days was used in Figure 12.6), and also plot the high and low for the look-back period.

Consider the lessons of this chart in conjunction with the previous example:

A: Variation is increasing, but it is increasing because of more large winning days. This is good because it suggests that even though the trader's returns may be becoming more volatile, the variation is positive rather than being equally spread around zero.

B: The high/low bands contract, highlighting the reduction of variation already seen on the previous chart.

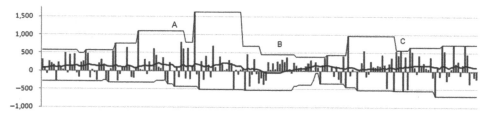

FIGURE 12.6 Range Control Chart

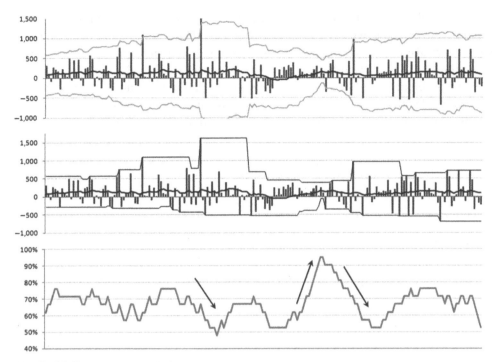

FIGURE 12.7 Three Control Charts

C: Variation is once again increasing, but now more symmetrically. This may temper our optimism at the end of the previous analysis a bit. The trader is making money, but why is more of the volatility to the downside in this period compared to the first part of the chart? Where have the large winning days gone?

One more chart that some traders find useful is a Win Ratio Control Chart, which is calculated by plotting a moving average of the win ratio over a look-back period. Though too much attention on win ratio is counterproductive, a *shift* in win ratio can be a harbinger of trouble to come, and it may be possible to identify problems before they become expensive. Figure 12.7 reproduces the first two charts, with the addition of a Win Ratio Control Chart also using a 20-day look-back period. Consider what information a careful analysis of these three together can give the trader. Note that there are two large declines in win ratio, all of which may point to some potential issues with trading performance. Again, the answers to most trading problems are not on these charts, but in many cases, the right questions are.

SUMMARY

Trading is difficult. Markets are highly random and nearly unpredictable, diverse and un-foreseeable risks crop up at every turn, and traders themselves are vulnerable to many psychological errors and weaknesses. In addition, the process of developing trading skill is a long one, fraught with hardship and obstacles. Many traders fail because they do not have realistic assumptions about the length and challenges of that process, or because they lack some essential requirements for success. This chapter addresses many of those problems, and gives valuable perspective and a much-needed reality check. A trader armed with these, and with the tools and techniques from elsewhere in this book, can develop a plan of attack and move along the path to trading mastery.

Trading Primer

At first glance, the process of making a trade seems to be simple. Someone wanting to buy an item meets with a potential seller, they agree on a price, and money is exchanged in return for the item. Even the most complex trading ideas begin with this concept. The mechanics may be much more complicated—perhaps the buyer and seller negotiate through a sophisticated electronic medium. Perhaps the item is actually a sophisticated financial instrument or set of instruments. Perhaps there are complications such as currency adjustments or financing costs to be considered, or perhaps the transaction is merely arranged to occur at a future point in time. Regardless, this basic meeting of buyer and seller—weighing of value against value— is the very essence and the root of all market activity.

Many books begin by saying that a trade occurs when a buyer and a seller agree on value, but this is not entirely correct. If this were so, if the parties truly agreed that the price represented the fair value of the asset, that one was equal to the other, wouldn't they each be willing to immediately unwind the trade and even to take the other side? This is almost never the case. In simple buying or selling transactions (excluding spreading and hedging, which we will get to in a minute) the buyer is willing to part with the money because he believes the asset will offer him more value in the future than the money he gave up. The seller has made a decision that the utility value of the money she will receive exceeds the value she would get from continuing to own the asset, so each participant has made an assessment of value that might be unique to his or her particular situation at that point in time. Rather than an agreement, each and every trade that occurs in the market represents a *disagreement* over the value of the money and the assets being exchanged.

THE SPREAD

We often hear language like "The stock of company XYZ is at $50," but even here we have an issue, for there is rarely only one price to consider; usually there are at least three. In active, liquid markets, there is a *bid* price at which buyers are willing to buy an asset, an *offer* (or *ask*, from *asking price*) at which sellers are offering to sell, and usually a *last print* (or simply, *last*) price where a trade was made. In a typical market, bids will be lined up below the market (more buyers are willing to buy at lower prices), and offers will be stacked at higher prices. The *inside market* refers to the highest bid price and the lowest offer, representing the best available price at any time, and the distance between those two prices is often referred to as the *spread*.

In the hypothetical case of XYZ that just traded at $50, we might find that the best available bid is $49.95 and the lowest offered price is $50.05. A trader would verbalize this situation as "49.95 bid, offered at 50.05," which is usually shortened in practice to "49.95 at 50.05." If the trader is reasonably sure the person he is speaking to knows the approximate price, he may drop the *handle* (the whole number) part of the price and just give the decimal pricing. As prices change rapidly, this can lead to a dialogue like "95 at 05 [meaning .95 and .05], at 7, at 9, 98 bid, now at 06." Though the last trade may have been at $50, there is a reasonable chance that we could not execute at that price in this situation with the market "95 at 05." In fact, it is even possible that the last print was 50.00, and now the market may have moved to 50.50 at 50.60. A buyer, in this case, has little hope of executing at any price under 50.50; the spread is often a better reflection of actual value than the last print.

Some traders glean a lot of information from the spread. For instance, the size of the spread is often a measure of the uncertainty in the market; when prices are changing rapidly, market participants often react by widening the spread. Buyers are not aggressive in paying high prices because they know the market could move against them in the next instant, so bids tend to drop lower. At the same time, sellers also react by lifting their offers to higher prices. There is other information in the spread: how rapidly it moves, exactly how it moves (do sellers lift offers higher or do buyers aggressively bid higher?), how much size is displayed, and many other subtleties.

If this seems like a lot of time spent on something very basic, you're right; it is, and it is also very important. The spread represents a very real cost of trading. Imagine that a buyer pays the offer, and then immediately realizes he has made a mistake and wants to get out of the trade. This can be done only by turning around and selling to the buyers on the bid, so the spread is a source of risk and a cost of trading in every transaction. It is also usually the best estimation of the actual market value of an asset. In the case of a very active stock that prints a trade every few seconds, the inside market is rarely very far from the last print, so the last trade is a very good approximation of value. (This kind of stock will usually tend to have a relatively tight spread as well.)

However, there are some instruments that may go days without trading (some stocks, options, distant months of futures contracts, for instance). In these cases, the last price may be completely irrelevant because it happened so long ago that the market has moved. To further complicate matters, very inactive, illiquid instruments will often have extremely wide spreads. If stock XYZ last printed 50.00 three weeks ago, but is now bid at 30.00 and offered at 49.00, what is it actually worth? Researchers studying price patterns need to be careful because printed price records in illiquid markets can be very misleading. As an interesting aside, a major factor in the 2007–2008 financial crisis was the importance of many financial instruments representing very significant financial commitments that did not have liquid markets. Spreads were wide, or in some cases, nonexistent, so it was impossible to derive a market value for many of these assets. In the absence of a market price, traders resorted to building complex models with many moving parts (if that sounds a lot like guessing, you're not wrong), and many of these models gave very misleading values for these instruments. This complete breakdown in understanding the value and risk of these instruments was one of the major contributors to the crisis.

Liquidity is a misused and often imprecisely defined term, but it usually means the availability of willing buyers and sellers. Liquid instruments tend to have tighter spreads and *deeper books*, meaning that there are many buyers and sellers at price levels beyond the inside market. Going back to XYZ, which is now 49.95 at 50.05, we might find there are 1,000 shares on the bid at 49.95, and many thousands at 49.94, 49.93, and so on for many pennies below the market. Imagine a very large sell order comes into the market. These buyers would easily be able to absorb that order, meaning that XYZ would trade on the bid at 49.95, then maybe 49.94 and 49.93—all in all, very little price change. However, imagine a second scenario where there are again 1,000 shares on the bid at 49.95, but now a few hundred at 49.91, a few more at 49.87, and so on. If a large sell order hits this market, it will "clear the bids" and the price will drop much lower.

Market makers are a specific group of traders whose job is basically to provide liquidity. A market maker will usually have both a bid and an offer in the market, though they are free to adjust those levels as needed. For instance, if market makers are getting hit on the bid so that they are accumulating large long positions, they may choose to still bid for the stock, but to drop their bid to lower levels. If they keep their offer price on the inside market (meaning that they adjust their offer so that it is the lowest offer), eventually they will be able to sell some of their inventory, and in this way manage their exposure. Floor traders in open-outcry markets were the original market markers. Early electronic markets had designated market makers, but this role has now passed to many firms who run computer programs (algos) that function as market makers.

Market makers incur significant risks at times because they will always be on the wrong side of big moves driven by informed traders. If a group of traders comes into the market with many buy orders, the market maker will be forced to short to take the other side of that trade. In extreme cases (e.g., the crash of 1987), market makers could be forced out of business by adverse price moves. Market makers are typically offered various incentives to compensate them for these risks; otherwise, no one would take this job! (As of this writing, in 2011, liquidity rebates, which pay the firm a very small fee for executing via limit orders, are one of the primary forms of compensation for most traders functioning as market makers.)

TWO TYPES OF ORDERS

Traders wishing to buy this market have, broadly speaking, two options. A buyer who is not really in any hurry might focus on getting the best (lowest) price he can get, so he can *bid* for the stock. (In this case, bid is used as a verb meaning "to place an order lower than current prices.") Consider the case of XYZ with the market bid at 49.95 and offered at 50.05; a buyer could *join the bid* and put his order at 49.95. Of course, the buyer can also place orders lower, but they will be filled only if the market moves down to the level where he is bidding. If the buyer is feeling a little more urgency, he can *step in front of the bid* and put his order at 49.96 or 49.97. Note that in this case, the inside market would now be 49.97 (still offered at 50.05). This is a natural force that tends to compress spreads as buyers bid slightly higher and sellers offer lower in competition for fills, and is one of the main reasons why active, liquid markets tend to have tight spreads. However, if the buyer is really motivated and must have stock XYZ now, he may choose to *pay the offer* (other common language is *take the offer*, and the reverse is to *hit the bid*). Though much simplified, these are the two options available to traders and they correspond to the two most commonly used order types.

Limit orders are orders where buyers try to buy at a cheaper price than the offer and sellers offer to sell at prices above the bid. A trader wanting to buy XYZ with a limit order might say, "Bid for it" or "Join the bid," as in "We're in no hurry here—just bid for it." A seller might say, "Okay, fine, offer it out. Put it up on the offer." *Market orders* are orders that will execute immediately. Buyers will pay the offer and sellers will end up hitting the bid. These orders usually reflect some degree of urgency—the order must be done immediately and a better price (trade location) is sacrificed for speed of execution. Though the buyer bidding with a limit order will get a better price if filled, the trade-off is that the order may never be filled if the market moves higher.

Now we have arrived at something subtle and very important. Imagine XYZ is again 49.95 at 50.05, and then it trades at 50.05. What just happened? A buyer wanted to buy the stock so much that he was willing to *pay the spread* or take the offer; we can say that this is a buyer-motivated trade. By analyzing the number of orders that hit the bid (seller-motivated trades) compared to those that take the offer (buyer-motivated trades), whether through computer-aided analysis or careful observation, traders can get a deeper sense of the conviction levels and urgency behind price moves. For instance, a stock may move from 50 to 51 in a series of back-and-forth motions with orders printing on both the bid and the offer. At another time, the same price change could occur in a straight line as buyers keep paying the offer and keep that buying pressure on the offer for the entire move. Simple observation would note that both moves began at 50 and ended at 51, and perhaps even occurred in the same amount of time and with the same amount of volume being done, but each of these moves suggests something different about the underlying conviction in the market.

A trader who buys something in anticipation of it going higher is said to be *long* that instrument. For most people, this is a natural and intuitive concept: buying something relatively cheaply, planning to sell it later for a higher price, and pocketing the difference (minus any costs of financing or insurance incurred in the interim). One of the divisions between professional and amateur traders is that professionals are often just as willing to *go short* (or just to *short*) a market, but the public often has a bias against shorting. There are several reasons for this; most equity traders have a natural inclination toward owning stocks, and think that shorting is a very complex transaction, or that it is somehow immoral to bet on a company's value going down. (In some markets it is theoretically complex, as the instrument must first be borrowed, then sold, later bought back, and finally returned to the lender.) This prejudice is unfounded and is one of the key differences between the public and most professionals. Shorting is nothing more than the opposite of being long. Whereas the buyer seeks to make a profit as prices rise, the short seller anticipates falling prices and hopes to *cover the short* (buy it back) at lower prices. Short selling is an important part of the trader's tool set.

Spread Trading

It is also worth considering that a certain amount of the buying and selling pressure in the market represents more complex interests than simple buying and shorting. Imagine a farmer who knows he will have a grain crop coming in September. This farmer might sell his grain in the futures market before the harvest comes in (technically, a short sale), but this does not in any way mean that he expects that prices will be going down. This is a simple example of a *hedging* transaction, and more complicated examples exist in all markets.

Spread trading is another type of transaction involving buying one asset and selling another, looking to profit from the change in value between the two. Imagine that a trader feels that Assets A and B should trade in a more or less predictable relationship, perhaps with Asset A at a premium due to production costs and so forth. This trader could track the spread, or the difference between Assets A and B. If she feels that the premium is too small, she can go long the spread by buying Asset A and shorting Asset B. This is not a bullish or bearish bet on either of the assets, but a bet that the spread between the two will widen. She will make money if A goes up and B goes down, if they both go up but A goes up more, or even if they both decline as long as B declines more. The key is that the percentage change of A must be greater than the percentage change of B (assuming an equal-weighted position) from the time the trade is entered. Conversely, if the trader felt the spread was too wide, she could short the spread by doing the reverse of this transaction.

This just scratches the surface of these complex, multileg transactions, which exist in and between all markets in virtually unlimited combinations. The message here is that much of the buying and selling we observe in markets may be part of spread trades like this. In this case, we might see the trader buying Asset A and assume she was bullish on it, when in fact, she does not care if it goes up or down—all she cares about is the spread relationship. Spreads can be created between different asset classes, regional markets, or international markets, and these trades can even be initiated with different timings on each leg. Do not assume that buying is always bullish and selling is always bearish; there may be much more going on behind the scenes.

CHARTS

The most basic language of the market is price changes, perhaps with associated volume. In the case of XYZ, we might see 500 shares done at 50.00, 300 @ 50.03, 500 @ 50.04, and so on. (A more complete record would include a time stamp and whether the order was executed on the bid, on the offer, or in between.) This record is sometimes referred to as the "prints on the tape" in memory of the old-style ticker tape machines, which really did print prices on paper tape. A very active instrument can "print" hundreds or thousands of trades in a single minute, so a trader would quickly become lost without some reference of historical activity. A chart of these price changes is the natural solution, and many discretionary traders find that charts present market information in a way that is both intuitive and useful.

Tick Charts

The most primitive type of chart would simply be the information in the prints plotted on a graph with price on the y-axis and trade number on the x-axis. The chart in Figure A.1

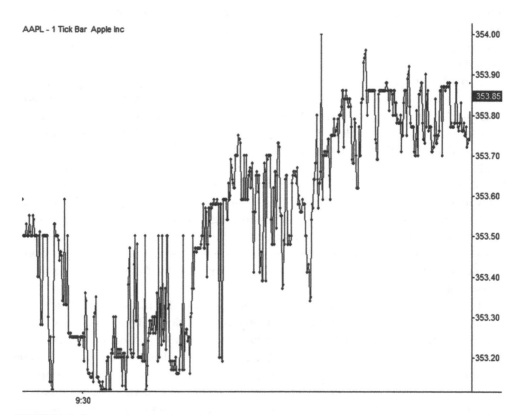

FIGURE A.1 A Single-Tick Chart of AAPL

is a *single-tick* chart of the market's opening for Apple, Inc. (Nasdaq: AAPL) on 7/12/2011 (trade numbers not shown). The single-tick chart is interesting from an intellectual perspective because it is the most fundamental language of the market—every single trade, every transaction that hits the *consolidated tape*, is displayed on the chart. From a practical perspective, a single-tick chart is not very useful, for the simple reason that it is difficult to fit much trading history on a single chart. This AAPL chart shows only the first 30 seconds of the trading day. In an extremely active stock, it is even possible that less than a single second's trading could fit in the same space; it is not possible for the human eye and brain to process this information in a meaningful manner.

The obvious solution is to aggregate many ticks into a single space on the chart. When this is done, we refer to the chart by how many ticks (trades) are put together into a single space on the x-axis. In Figure A.2, each bar represents 25 individual trades, and, now, approximately five and a half minutes of activity fit on the same chart space. It is important to remember that the x-axis is not scaled to time. This is one of the main advantages of aggregate tick charts: as the market becomes more or less active the x-axis expands or contracts to accommodate the activity. In many cases, this can

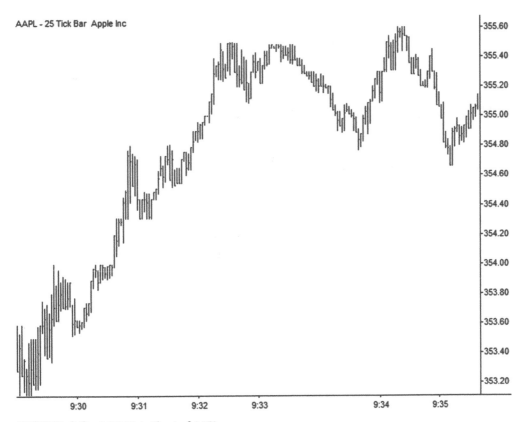

FIGURE A.2 A 25-Tick Chart of AAPL

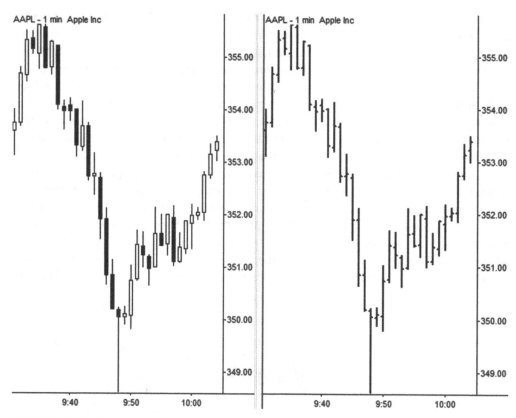

FIGURE A.3 Comparison of Bar and Candlestick Charts

create some advantages over simple time-scaled charts by making readable patterns out of very illiquid or extremely volatile markets.

Bars and Candles

Once we start aggregating trades on the x-axis, a graphical device is needed to explain the activity in that space. One logical solution is simply to plot a vertical bar, with the top and bottom of the bar representing the high and low extremes reached during the period (right panel in Figure A.3). Traders often find it useful to mark the first trade of the period with a tick on the left side of the bar (the *open*) and the last trade of the period with a tick on the right side (the *close*). These four data points, plotted like this, create the classical bar chart. An alternate format is the *candlestick chart*, which prints a wide body between the open and close of the bars, with thinner *shadows* (also called "tails" or "wicks") above and below the body, reaching to the high and low of the period (left panel in Figure A.3). Candlestick charts were first used in medieval Japan for rice trading, so much of the terminology associated with patterns of candles is also Japanese. Traditionally, the body of the candle is filled in if the close is lower than the open and left empty if the close is higher than the open. Modern charting software packages usually fill the body of every candle but change the color to something intuitive like red for downward-closing candles and green or blue for upward-closing candles.

Time Charts and Other Options

Though the strength of tick charts is their ability to adapt to activity levels in the markets, traders and analysts often prefer a format where each bar corresponds to a predictable unit of time. These time charts are by far the most commonly used in most applications, and are especially useful for traders looking at daily and longer time frames. The chart is referred to by the length of each time unit (as in a 5-minute chart), which may also be called the *time frame* of the chart. Many traders choose to look at different time frames (for instance, 5-minute, hourly, and daily charts) for the same market to get a better sense of the forces affecting prices at any time.

There are other possibilities for scaling the x-axis, but these tend to be less used except in certain specific contexts. It is possible to aggregate bars not by ticks (transactions) but by trading volume. In this case, a bar would contain a certain number of

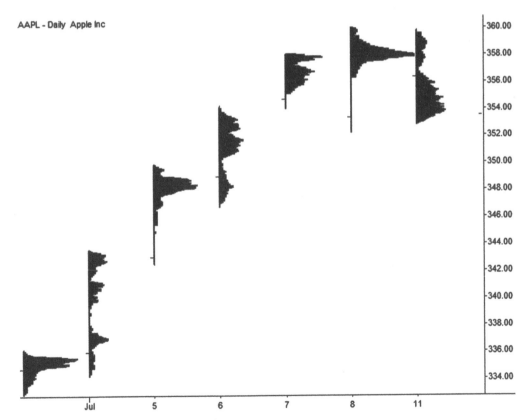

FIGURE A.4 Market Profile Chart of AAPL

shares or contracts, after which the next bar would begin. Another possibility is to have each bar end after a certain range is reached, so that, for instance, each bar would be 0.25 wide. (Be aware that the range bars created at the end of a trading day will be different from the ones created as the market unfolds. This makes backtesting and analysis on range bars virtually impossible.)

Other types of charts include swing charts, point and figure charts, kagi charts, line charts, and many others, but these are much less common and are outside the scope of this primer, with one exception. One other chart worth mentioning is Market Profile, created by Peter Steidlmayer in the 1980s. Market Profile charts essentially allow the trader to look inside the bar to see where most volume and trading activity occurred in the time period. Market Profile displays this information in a graphical format attached to the right of each bar, with wider horizontal bars indicating more trading activity at that price level. (See Figure A.4.) While most charting methods only reprocess the same open, high, low, and close (OHLC), volume, and open interest information, Market Profile is an important innovation—it adds detail and perspective that is not visible on a standard chart.

A Deeper Look at Moving Averages and the MACD

The charts and the discussion that follow may look a little strange, but the thought process is important. Too many times, traders use indicators or tools on their charts that they do not understand. Rules are developed based on the action of a squiggly line without fully understanding what that line measures and represents. Though some traders will find some success with an approach like this, it misses much of the potential in these tools. To fully understand a technical tool, it is useful to peer deeply into its construction, and to understand how it reacts to changes in the underlying market. One of the best ways to do this is to "feed" an indicator an artificially created dataset that focuses on specific types of market action. Think of this as a way to look at the indicator in a laboratory environment, isolating and controlling for various influences.

MOVING AVERAGES

If you want to really understand the tools you are using and how they will react to extreme situations, it helps to understand how they will react in the most simple, basic contexts as well. Of course, everyone grasps the basics of moving averages: add higher prices and the average will go up. When price flattens out, the average eventually will flatten, too. When price turns down, it will cut through the moving average, and, at some point, it will start pulling the average down with it. This is all simple, but it is not the point. The point is to build an intuitive and intimate understanding of the behavior of the average as it responds to changing market data. One of the best ways I have found to foster this intuition with any technical tool is to generate simple price patterns in artificial price series, and then to plot the indicator on this synthetic price data. (Nearly all charting packages allow users to import ASCII data, but if this is not possible, the indicator may be calculated directly in an Excel spreadsheet and graphed there.) Think of this as a controlled laboratory experiment: you are controlling the data that is fed to the indicator so you can begin to understand the details of the indicator's reactions to that data. This process, along with careful thought and reflection, will build an understanding that goes beyond a simple understanding of the patterns on the screen.

The charts that follow are examples of this process. There is value in these specific examples, but it is even more important that you can take the procedure and adapt it to your own use. These examples show both 20-period *simple moving averages (SMAs)* and *exponential moving averages (EMAs)* to compare their behavior and fluctuations. The formulas required to build these indicators are already available from many books or the Internet, so they will not be a focus in this chapter, but you must have a clear conceptual understanding of the behavioral differences between the two. The simple moving average simply averages the price over a look-back window. It is completely blind to any data outside of that window, which creates the first potential issue: a simple moving average moves *twice* in reaction to any single large event. The value of the moving average has a change both when the event occurs and when it passes out of the left side of the evaluation window.

The EMA is a considerably more complex animal. Recent data are weighted more heavily in an EMA, and, technically, no data points are *ever* dropped from the average. Rather than being dropped, past data is rolled off with an exponential decay. In actual practice, the effect of distant past data far out of the evaluation period of the average is so small that it is insignificant, but it is still there. It is important to realize, though, that this effect smoothes the left-hand side of the evaluation window—an EMA will not jump twice as a simple moving average will. This is one of the main advantages of the EMA over the SMA.

Comparing EMA and SMA Behavior

Consider first how the moving averages react to a sudden shock in the market. Figure B.1 shows an artificial data series that is flat, then suddenly breaks into a precise linear trend, which just as abruptly comes to an end as prices flatten out again. Both the SMA (dotted line) and the EMA (solid line) are 20-period averages, but the front-weighting effect of the EMA causes it to react more quickly to the initial price shock. After a period of time, both averages settle into a steady relationship to the price trend, but the simple moving average is much quicker to return to the center after the trend stops. This effect is due to the decay in the EMA, which sees *all* data to the left of the average; the SMA is just a simple average of the past 20 data points. Once the market has been flat for 20 bars, the simple moving average exactly equals the close. There are two important lessons here. Most traders know the first, but few know the second. For an SMA and an EMA of the same length:

- The EMA will react faster to a large price change because it front-weights the data.
- However, the EMA is also slower to react to stabilizing prices because it has a very long look-back window.

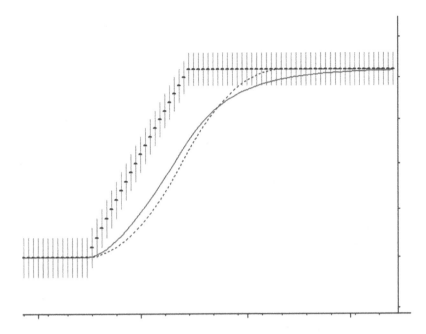

FIGURE B.1 Twenty-Period Simple (Dotted Line) and Exponential Moving Averages in a Market That Cleanly Shifts from Trading Range to Trend and Back

Many traders are convinced that moving averages provide support and resistance. Chapter 16 investigates this claim in some depth, and shows that there is no proof that any moving average is any better than any random number. One reason that so many traders remain convinced of this support/resistance effect is because it looks so convincing on charts. It is easy to find example after example of places where price touched a moving average and then shot away, but this is a result of two effects: One, we tend to attach more significance to lines on charts and to perceive patterns in random relationships. Two, there is a mathematical reason for this, as moving averages will approach prices as they pause in trends due to simple math. Figure B.2 illustrates this effect in an idealized market moving in stair-step trend legs.

If the rate of a trend is constant (arithmetically, not geometrically), a moving average will eventually settle into a consistent visual relationship with that market, tracking it at the same rate below, for an uptrend, or above in the case of a downtrend. If the rate of the trend increases, or if there is a shock in the opposite direction, the EMA will react before the SMA, but, as before, the SMA will react more quickly to stabilizing prices. It is also not well known, but the EMA will approach price more closely than a SMA in a stable trend, again due to the front-weighting in the EMA calculation. Essentially, the EMA catches turns a bit faster, but is much slower to come into the new, stable value when the trend ends and transitions into a new trading range. This is expected behavior, as the EMA should respond quickly to recent data while maintaining a memory of the long data history. Figure B.3 shows a trend with two inflection points and a clear ending

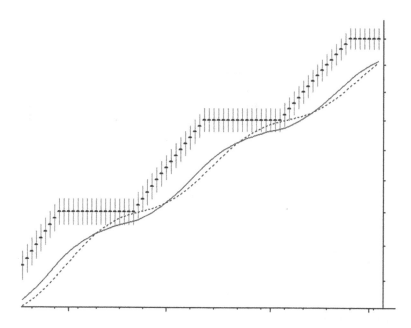

FIGURE B.2   Are the Moving Averages Supporting Prices?

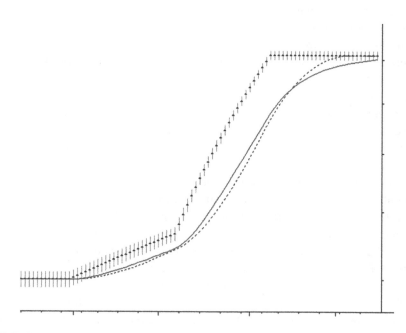

FIGURE B.3   Notice the Different Behavior of the EMA and the SMA at Inflection Points and at the End of the Trend

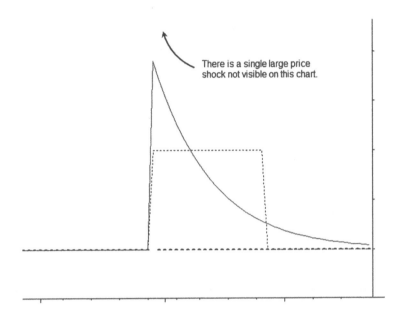

There is a single large price shock not visible on this chart.

FIGURE B.4 Notice the Different Behavior of the EMA and SMA in Response to a Single Large Price Shock

point. Spend some time thinking about how the SMA and EMA react differently at these inflections; if you are using the slope of a moving average, or a moving average crossover, to define trends, you need to be aware of these issues. One average is not better than the other, but you need to be mindful of the differences.

Figure B.4, which has a single price bar that is not visible far above the top of the chart, is useful for building intuition about how the averages react to a sudden shock. Note that the SMA shows *two* inflection points when there was actually only *one* event on the chart. The second inflection (the drop) in the SMA was merely an artifact created as the price spike moved out of the average's evaluation window. In this particular case, the EMA probably more accurately reflects what is going on in the market. Traders using an SMA in an intuitive fashion are not likely to be misled, because they are focusing on the bigger picture, but systematic approaches or tools (such as trend indicators) derived from an SMA may have some issues with outliers. Particularly in intraday data, where the overnight gap is significant, or longer-term equities, which have frequent price shocks due to earnings announcements, systematic tools based on simple moving averages are subject to distortion.

Few traders realize that simple moving averages are low-pass filters, meaning that they will filter out (eliminate) higher-frequency oscillations and cycles. Figure B.5 shows a situation that will probably not be encountered in actual trading: a market that is moving in an idealized 20-period sine wave, with 20-period SMA and EMA applied. Though it may be very counterintuitive, the SMA is completely flat. When the SMA length matches the sine wavelength, there are always as many values above as below the moving average,

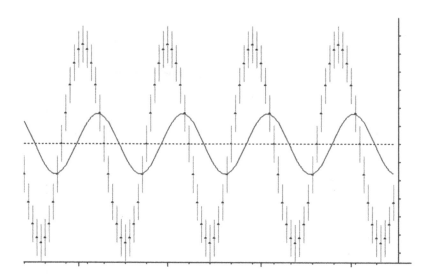

FIGURE B.5 Twenty-Period EMA and SMA Applied to a Theoretical 20-Period Sine Wave
Notice that the SMA (dotted line) is completely flat on the zero line.

so the average nets to zero—an SMA will always hide any cycles that are whole-number multiples of the SMA length. You might think that this is pure theory and that it would not have any application to a real trading situation, but extraordinary situations do occur. I once had a trader I was working with point out that his moving average on a 1-minute chart was not "working right" on part of the chart because it was not reacting to the market's movements. For about 45 minutes, this stock had settled into a very dependable cycle that just happened to match the length of the moving average he was using, so, while the market was oscillating fairly wildly, his average wouldn't budge. There are cycles in the market. It is difficult to trade them because they are ephemeral and they shift frequently, but they will sometimes line up with your moving averages with seemingly bizarre results. Trade long enough and you will see pretty much everything.

Let's end this section with an example that is important for longer-term investors to keep in mind. The natural language of the market is percentage changes and growth rates, which is why finance math is based on discounting cash flows and compound interest, and why the first task of any research project is converting prices into returns. Shorter-term traders tend to think in differences (e.g., "I made a point and a half in that stock."); longer-term investors think more often in percentages. Figure B.6 shows a market that is growing at a constant rate; each data point is a 5 percent increase over the previous one. On a linearly scaled chart, a market appreciating at a constant growth rate will describe a *curve*, not a straight line. On a linear chart, moving averages will seem to lag behind the price curve at an ever-increasing distance.

What is actually happening, however, is that the moving averages lag a *constant percentage* behind prices. The linear chart does not misrepresent anything, but it is not the right tool to look at percentage-based relationships. Figure B.7 is exactly the same as

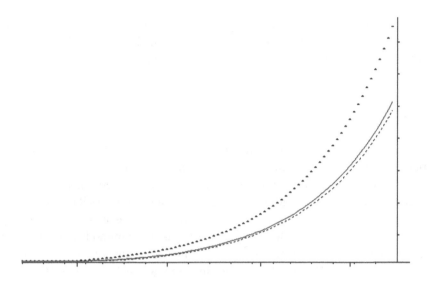

FIGURE B.6 Moving Averages Applied to a Market Growing at 5 Percent Constant Rate, Linear Scale

the previous chart; the only difference is that the y-axis is log scale rather than linear. Remember, log scale charts are designed so that equal distance intervals on the y-axis are equal percentage changes, not equal price changes as on a linear chart. Note the ticks on the right side of the y-axis, which are evenly spaced prices on the linear chart, become compressed near the top of the axis when log scaled. Be clear on this effect: straight lines on log charts are curves on linear charts. If you are drawing trend lines on

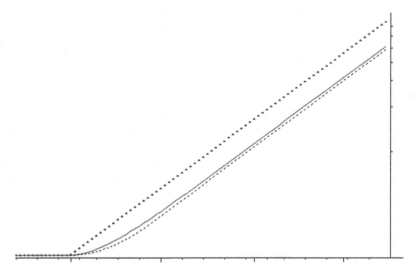

FIGURE B.7 Moving Averages Applied to a Market Growing at a Constant 5 Percent Rate, Log Scale

Note that curves on previous chart are straight lines here.

log scale charts, you are actually drawing curves on normal, linearly scaled charts. This may be perfectly correct in the context of a longer-term chart where the curve faithfully represents the growth rate, but it is something that must be fully understood.

THE MACD

Moving average convergence/divergence (MACD) was one of the early technical tools developed by Gerald Appel in the mid-1970s. As an interesting aside, this is one of the few commonly used indicators whose name actually says something accurate about the tool. Consider some other indicators: stochastics have nothing at all to do with stochastic processes; the Relative Strength Index (RSI) neither measures relative strength nor is it an index; the Commodity Channel Index (CCI) is not commodity-specific, nor does it deal with channels, nor is it an index. This is not an exhaustive list, but you get the idea. The standard MACD consists of four elements: a fast line (the MACD proper), a slow line (the signal line), a zero line for reference, and a histogram (bar chart) that shows the difference between the slow and fast lines. The standard MACD is constructed from exponential moving averages, but this modified version uses simple moving averages and dispenses with the MACD histogram altogether, resulting in a cleaner indicator.

Basic Construction of the MACD

The fast line of the MACD measures the distance between a shorter-term and a longer-term moving average. To understand exactly what this measure says about price action, think about how different periods of moving averages will respond to price movement. A moving average with a short look-back window (period) will track price movements more closely than an average with a longer period. Figure B.8 shows 3-period and 10-period simple moving averages applied to a daily chart of two-year Treasury notes. The line plotted below the price bars is the fast line of the MACD, which is simply the value of the slow moving average subtracted from the value of the fast average. When the fast average is above the slow average, this line is positive and vice versa. Notice the important behavior at the points marked A and B on this chart. Though price was higher at B, the distance between the moving averages was actually smaller, so the indicator registers a lower level at B. The distance between these two averages is one way to measure the momentum behind a market's movements, and this lower peak in the indicator suggests that the second price high was made on lower momentum.

Another important point is that the fast line of the MACD will register zero when the two averages cross; this highlights a condition of relative equilibrium on the time frame being measured. Figure B.9 marks spots where the fast line crosses the zero line, and shows that this happens when the moving averages intersect.

Figure B.10 shows the slow line (sometimes called the signal line) of the MACD, which is simply a 16-period moving average of the fast line. It is important to note that,

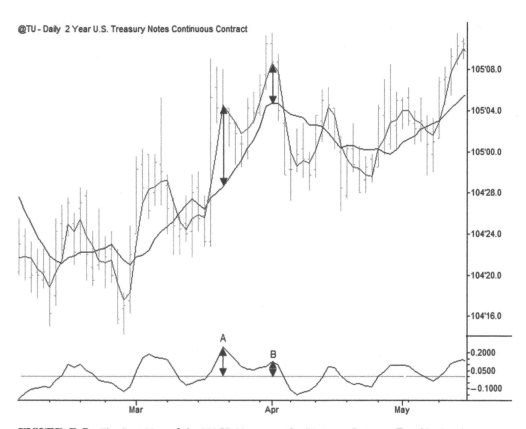

FIGURE B.8 The Fast Line of the MACD Measures the Distance Between Two Moving Averages

being a smoothed version of the fast line, it lags the fast line considerably, but also generally reflects the trend of the fast line—if the fast line is far above zero, the slow line will usually be sloping upward and vice versa. There are several ways to use the slow line, but the general concept tying them all together is that it reflects the trend on an intermediate-term time frame.

This is the construction of the particular variation of the MACD that I use. For each bar, calculate:

- Fast line: 3-period SMA minus 10-period SMA.
- Signal line: 16-period SMA of the fast line.
- Histogram: none.
- Plot a zero line for reference.

Using the same (3, 10, 16) settings in a standard MACD will give similar results, but, in my experience, the long memory of the exponential moving averages (EMAs) does make a difference at times. You will certainly be able to apply the same concepts to the standard MACD, but make sure you understand the differences between the two

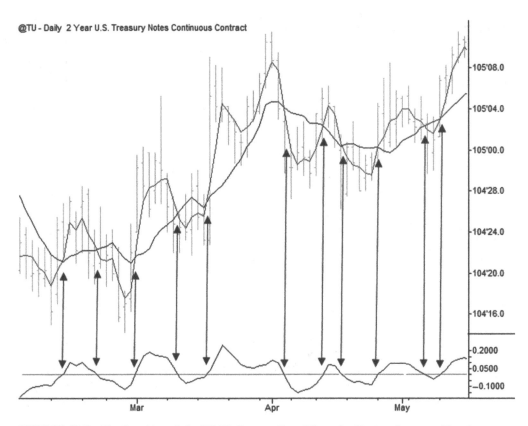

FIGURE B.9   The Fast Line of the MACD Crosses Zero When the Moving Averages Touch

indicators. Figure B.11 compares the modified with the standard MACD (3, 10, 16). Notice that the standard tool adds another plot, usually plotted as bars behind the indicator. This plot, the MACD histogram, shows the difference between the fast and slow lines of the MACD histogram, so it is actually the MACD of the MACD. Some traders find this to be a useful component, but it is possible to extract much of the same information from a careful reading of the fast and slow lines themselves.

A Deeper Look

The fast line is very sensitive to changes in the rate of change of prices. Read that again, carefully: the fast line swings up in response to the second derivative, or the rate of change of the rate of change of price. When we actually work with this tool, we usually think of it a little more loosely, as simply measuring the momentum of prices, but it is a good idea to be as precise as possible here at the beginning—this tool measures *changes* in momentum, not momentum itself. To begin to build some intuition about this tool, Figure B.12 shows a modified MACD applied to an idealized price series that breaks into

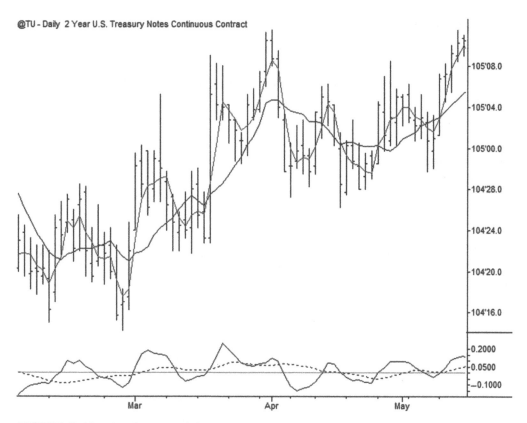

FIGURE B.10 The Slow Line of the MACD Is a Smoothed Version of the Fast Line

a steady-state uptrend and then cleanly transitions to a sideways market. Consider the inflections in the MACD:

- A: The fast line responds immediately to the change in the market by hooking higher on the first price bar of the uptrend.
- B: Everything between points A and B is an artifact of the indicator. Though the slope of the fast line changes in a curve, this does not reflect any change in the rate of trend in the market, which is trending steadily higher. At B, 10 bars into the uptrend, the 10-period moving average is now trending steadily with prices (remember, the fast line measures the difference between a 3-period and a 10-period moving average), so the indicator goes flat.
- C: The fast line again responds immediately to the shift in the market by hooking down on the first bar that breaks the trend pattern. Note that the MACD fast line going down does not mean that prices are going down, but that the rate of change of prices has gone down, in this case to zero.
- D: The fast line levels out, again 10 bars following the change in the market.

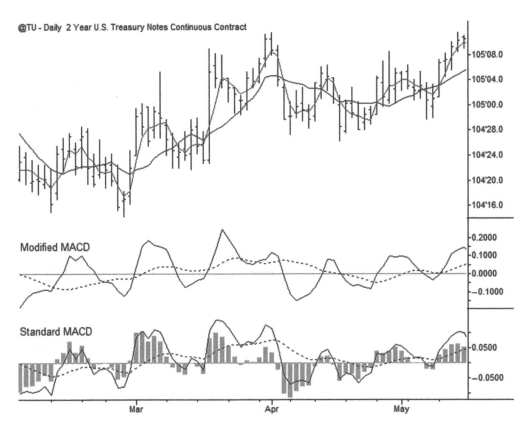

FIGURE B.11   Modified and Standard MACDs (Both 3, 10, 16) Compared

If you are looking at Figure B.12 and thinking that this could never be relevant in actual trading, consider the daily chart of Apple Inc. in Figure B.13. After a downtrend, the market transitioned to an uptrend at the point marked A, and the MACD fast line immediately responded by hooking upward, just as in the inflection marked A in the previous chart. Real market action, of course, contains much more noise and variation than our simplified example, but much of the downturn in the line at point B in Figure B.13 is due to this 10-bar artifact. A trader paying too much attention to the indicator's line at this point might surmise that momentum had turned downward. Prices did take a small pause at this point, but the indicator's reaction was out of proportion to that change. Point C is also interesting; a large move up is required to hook the fast line up after an extended trend. Half of the battle with using indicators is knowing when to use them and when to ignore them. If you are reacting to every jot of the indicator, you are missing the point. It is much better to use the tool only at potential inflections to add another layer of confidence to analysis that focuses primarily on the price bars themselves.

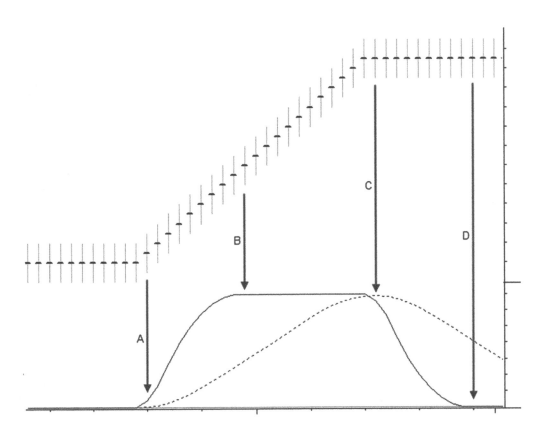

FIGURE B.12 Note That Inflections in the Fast Line of the MACD Include Some Artifacts Due to the Indicator's Construction

The modified MACD is constructed from simple moving averages, so it suffers from the problem of dual inflections to single price shocks. In fact, the multiple moving averages result in a complex reaction to single large events. This is rarely a significant problem when we are actually using the tool, but it can be an issue in some situations—for instance, in applying the tool to intraday data following a large overnight gap. Figure B.14 shows a situation that would be absurd in a real market: an otherwise absolutely flat market with a single large price shock, immediately reversed the following day. Note that the MACD's two lines have 12 inflections in response to this single bar! Again, this is not a tradable feature, but it does highlight the folly of trying to follow every move of the indicator too closely. In a real market situation, the indicator is nearly always irrelevant after a large price shock, and attention should be focused on other factors such as price action following the movement.

So far, these theoretical data sets have been so clean that it may be difficult to relate them to situations that are likely to occur in actual trading. Consider next what happens when the MACD is applied to a data set that begins to more closely approximate real market conditions, as in Figure B.15. This data set alternates uptrending and

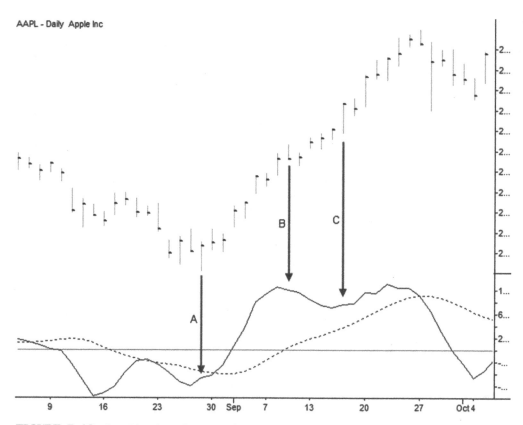

FIGURE B.13   Consider the Inflections of the MACD Applied to an Actual Market

downtrending legs, though it reduces them to consistent, idealized linear changes. Specifically, the down legs (BC and DA) are the same rate and length, while the up leg CD moves at a rate equal to 75 percent of AB's changes. The indicator registers a lower peak at D compared to B, which would suggest to many traders that trend leg CD, though it made a new high relative to the point B, did so on lower momentum; this is an example of a so-called *momentum divergence* on the MACD. This example shows precisely what lower momentum means for the MACD: here it means that the lower-momentum leg had smaller daily changes compared to the higher-momentum leg. Note that, in this case, both legs were the same length in terms of number of bars, so the lower-momentum leg, overall, covered a smaller range of prices than the higher-momentum leg. If the lower-momentum leg had continued for more days it would eventually have moved the same distance as the higher-momentum leg, but it still would have shown a divergence with the indicator at the second peak.

There is, however, another possibility, shown in Figure B.16, which has two uptrending legs (AB and CD) that both move with the same rate of change. Here, the second leg (CD) is shorter, including fewer bars than the longer leg, and the indicator again registers

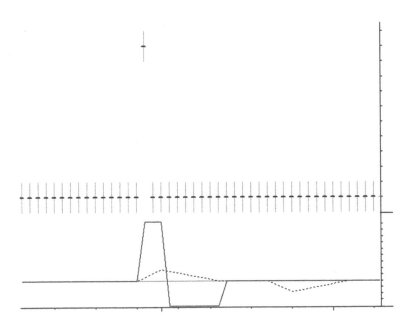

FIGURE B.14   Multiple Inflections on the MACD Following a Single Price Shock

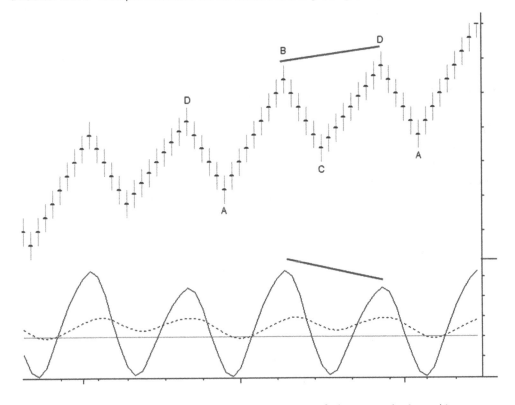

FIGURE B.15   Momentum Divergence Due to Lower Rate of Change on the Second Leg

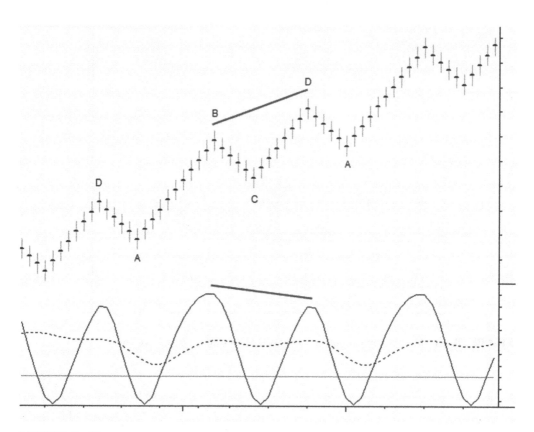

FIGURE B.16   Momentum Divergence Due to a Shorter Second Leg

a divergence. This is fundamental to divergence on momentum indicators: divergences will register with trend legs that either move at a lower rate of change or extend for fewer bars relative to the higher-momentum leg. In actual practice, the presence of additional noise and fluctuation obscures these simple tendencies, but this is the underlying truth of momentum divergence. Very few traders think about these concepts with precision.

Sample Trade Data

This table contains the trade data for the "Statistical Analysis of Trading Results" section in Chapter 13. These data, and the data for the control chart analysis in that same chapter, are available from the author's web site at www.adamhgrimes.com/ in CSV format.

Trade ID	System	Position Value	Initial Risk	Account Net Liq	Net P&L	P&L as %R	P&L as % Position Val	Pro Forma P&L
1	A	17,320	(1,260)	100,000	1,228	1.0X	7.1%	975
2	C	11,245	(1,655)	100,000	335	0.2X	3.0%	202
3	A	8,210	(1,790)	100,000	972	0.5X	11.8%	543
4	A	13,984	(736)	100,000	48	0.1X	0.3%	65
5	C	13,984	(736)	100,000	88	0.1X	0.6%	120
6	C	4,610	(390)	100,000	405	1.0X	8.8%	1,038
7	C	9,220	(780)	100,000	350	0.4X	3.8%	449
8	A	18,634	(1,154)	100,587	(5)	−0.0X	(0.0%)	(4)
9	C	53,563	(1,538)	100,829	(1,056)	−0.7X	(2.0%)	(693)
10	A	9,292	(1,068)	100,000	(400)	−0.4X	(4.3%)	(375)
11	D	18,189	(941)	100,000	(486)	−0.5X	(2.7%)	(517)
12	B	32,048	(884)	104,137	(80)	−0.1X	(0.2%)	(94)
13	B	26,959	(641)	103,406	878	1.4X	3.3%	1,417
14	C	26,959	(641)	103,406	694	1.1X	2.6%	1,120
15	B	16,250	(1,150)	102,016	(114)	−0.1X	(0.7%)	(101)
16	A	32,258	(1,018)	103,072	(198)	−0.2X	(0.6%)	(200)
17	A	14,091	(1,059)	102,706	(849)	−0.8X	(6.0%)	(823)
18	A	11,173	(511)	102,706	99	0.2X	0.9%	198
19	A	5,587	(255)	102,706	255	1.0X	4.6%	1,027
20	C	5,587	(255)	102,706	179	0.7X	3.2%	721
21	B	8,830	(1,008)	102,588	(676)	−0.7X	(7.7%)	(688)

Trade ID	System	Position Value	Initial Risk	Account Net Liq	Net P&L	P&L as %R	P&L as % Position Val	Pro Forma P&L
22	A	7,200	(850)	103,215	(120)	−0.1X	(1.7%)	(146)
23	A	17,888	(938)	103,215	15	0.0X	0.1%	17
24	B	5,242	(282)	103,215	240	0.9X	4.6%	878
25	B	5,242	(282)	103,215	152	0.5X	2.9%	556
26	C	5,242	(282)	103,215	282	1.0X	5.4%	1,032
27	A	35,552	(1,552)	100,605	(196)	−0.1X	(0.6%)	(127)
28	C	8,404	(1,196)	104,007	66	0.1X	0.8%	57
29	A	32,556	(956)	103,644	(284)	−0.3X	(0.9%)	(308)
30	A	25,103	(848)	103,162	(68)	−0.1X	(0.3%)	(82)
31	B	8,425	(225)	103,162	315	1.4X	3.7%	1,444
32	C	37,818	(1,602)	103,389	(1,242)	−0.8X	(3.3%)	(802)
33	C	14,340	(1,620)	102,812	(1,285)	−0.8X	(9.0%)	(816)
34	A	8,248	(243)	98,902	433	1.8X	5.2%	1,764
35	A	24,743	(728)	98,902	510	0.7X	2.1%	693
36	D	33,370	(1,350)	98,902	(480)	−0.4X	(1.4%)	(352)
37	A	54,095	(1,083)	99,862	(989)	−0.9X	(1.8%)	(912)
38	A	64,135	(865)	99,862	(705)	−0.8X	(1.1%)	(814)
39	A	29,880	(1,480)	99,862	(890)	−0.6X	(3.0%)	(601)
40	A	76,153	(1,247)	99,845	(581)	−0.5X	(0.8%)	(465)
41	A	63,936	(1,344)	98,076	(1,096)	−0.8X	(1.7%)	(800)
42	A	42,655	(845)	97,992	(425)	−0.5X	(1.0%)	(493)
43	D	29,970	(1,770)	97,992	(458)	−0.3X	(1.5%)	(253)
44	A	129,240	(1,470)	98,839	135	0.1X	0.1%	91
45	B	36,449	(1,505)	100,979	(645)	−0.4X	(1.8%)	(433)
46	A	4,801	(199)	98,238	298	1.5X	6.2%	1,471
47	A	9,602	(398)	98,238	768	1.9X	8.0%	1,896
48	B	9,602	(398)	98,238	398	1.0X	4.1%	982
49	B	9,602	(398)	98,238	802	2.0X	8.4%	1,980
50	D	53,445	(1,534)	97,640	(41)	−0.0X	(0.1%)	(26)
51	B	25,659	(466)	96,863	466	1.0X	1.8%	969
52	D	51,319	(931)	97,329	269	0.3X	0.5%	281
53	A	17,325	(666)	96,863	390	0.6X	2.3%	567
54	C	8,663	(333)	96,863	210	0.6X	2.4%	611
55	D	17,325	(666)	96,863	668	1.0X	3.9%	971
56	B	18,826	(539)	96,863	1,094	2.0X	5.8%	1,966
57	B	18,826	(539)	96,863	1,078	2.0X	5.7%	1,937
58	C	18,826	(539)	96,863	538	1.0X	2.9%	967
59	C	27,310	(650)	96,863	650	1.0X	2.4%	969
60	C	27,310	(650)	96,863	425	0.7X	1.6%	633
61	B	8,060	(470)	100,213	500	1.1X	6.2%	1,066
62	B	8,060	(470)	100,213	473	1.0X	5.9%	1,007
63	C	8,060	(470)	100,213	470	1.0X	5.8%	1,002
64	B	29,383	(1,547)	104,570	(57)	−0.0X	(0.2%)	(39)
65	A	16,676	(1,004)	102,317	772	0.8X	4.6%	787
66	B	8,338	(502)	102,317	286	0.6X	3.4%	583
67	A	63,520	(1,280)	102,484	(736)	−0.6X	(1.2%)	(589)
68	A	76,263	(1,662)	103,257	(912)	−0.5X	(1.2%)	(567)

Glossary

acceleration factor   In the Parabolic SAR, an input that controls how quickly the stop and reverse level is moved toward price. Normally, this factor increases with each bar, moving the stop closer at an ever-accelerating rate.

accumulation   One of the classic market phases in which large buyers establish positions without moving the market, but also can refer to the presence of underlying buying in other contexts. Accumulation is usually seen as constructive and supportive of prices.

adaptive markets hypothesis (AMH)   A theory of market behavior pioneered by Andrew Lo that proposes that markets can be described by a process of evolving efficiency.

always-in   A colloquialism for styles of trading that seek to always have a position in the market, reversing from long to short based on technical signals. Perhaps more useful as a research/backtesting methodology than an actual trading style.

Anti   A trade setup that attempts to enter the first pullback following a potential change of trend.

ask   Also called the offer. The price, almost always above the bid and often above the last print, in an order book at which people are willing to sell the market.

asynchronous trading   A problem in evaluating indexes, pairs trades, or some systems in which prices that occur together in the data series may not have actually occurred at the same time.

ATR%   Average True Range (ATR) as a percentage of the last price, or ATR standardized for price. This is a volatility measure that can be compared across assets with different price levels.

autocorrelation   The correlation of a time series to itself at different time points, as a function of the time between them. Autocorrelation can often cause trends in price series.

Average Directional Index (ADX)/Directional Movement Index (DMI)   Technical indicators that measure strength of trend.

average range   A simple volatility measure that averages the range of a set of bars. In practice, Average True Range (ATR) is more commonly used to capture overnight gaps, but average range may be more applicable in some intraday applications.

Average True Range (ATR)   A measure of volatility. True range is the bar's range (high minus low) plus any overnight gap from the previous bar's close.

backtesting Applying a rule set to historical prices to see how it would have performed in terms of returns, volatility, and stability. This is a complex and involved process; many traders who attempt it make some critical errors.

basis point One hundredth of a percent. 1 basis point (bp) = 0.01 percent.

bell curve An informal term for the shape of the normal distribution curve.

bid In financial markets, the price, often below the last price and always below the offer, where buyers are willing to purchase the asset.

binomial tree A useful tool in understanding random walks. A visual representation of the possible values a random walk or asset price could take at various steps in time.

black boxes A term usually reserved for completely computerized and rule-based trading systems.

breakout trades A class of trades that seeks to enter on moves above resistance or below support, looking for continuation in the direction of the break. Equity-centric traders are more likely to use the term *breakdown* for a move below support; futures traders tend to use *breakout* for both trades.

candlestick chart A type of chart that pictures the space between the open and the close of a period as an empty or full rectangle, depending on whether the close was higher or lower than the open, with thin "shadows" extending to the high and low of the period.

capital asset pricing model (CAPM) A model to determine the theoretical price of an asset as a function of the risk-free rate and market return. CAPM was an important step in the evolution of academic thinking about markets, but has little, if any, utility in actual practice.

causation In financial markets, it is very difficult to determine causative links between markets and exogenous factors. Classically, researchers in other fields try to isolate potential causative factors to understand their influence, but this is difficult to do in market settings. It is important to avoid assumptions and to learn to think carefully about this important issue.

central limit theorem A theorem that informally states that the outcome of many random events will tend to follow the normal distribution. For instance, if a set of dice is rolled many times and the rolls recorded, the data set will eventually approximate the normal distribution. The central limit theorem is very important to many statistical tests.

central tendency The term that describes how values in a probability distribution tend to cluster around one or more values. Mean, median, and mode are common measures of central tendency.

chandelier stop A trailing stop technique that hangs a stop a certain distance under the highest point the market has reached since the position was initiated. (The technique is mirrored to the downside.) Many variations are possible.

climax Usually refers to a move near the end of an extended trend in which the trend accelerates into a steeper move, usually accompanied by an increase in volume. Climaxes on higher time frames can mark major inflection points in markets, but smaller climaxes are common on lower time frames. One of the central problems of technical analysis is discerning climax from strength (or weakness, in the case of a downside climax).

close Many financial markets report official closing prices at the end of the session. These are usually not simply the last price traded (though they may be in some markets), but are set through several different methods. This price is important to traders because daily P&Ls are marked to this price. Also, many traders will use close to refer to the last price of any time interval (e.g., "the close of this current 5-minute bar or candle").

coefficient of variation Obtained by dividing the standard deviation by the mean— conceptually this is similar to the reciprocal of the Sharpe ratio with the risk-free rate set to zero. While not a meaningful measure by itself, it is useful when comparing different trading techniques, systems, or patterns, as it shows how much variability is being assumed per unit of return.

complex pullback A two-legged pullback that is a complete ABCD trend structure. These are common, especially in mature trends.

compound loss Compound gains or losses take into account the compounding effect of interest. For instance, two consecutive 10 percent losses do not total a 20 percent loss, because the second was made on a smaller capital base.

conditional probability If Prob(A) is the probability of event A occurring, then Prob(A|B) is read as "the probability of A occurring, given that B has occurred." Conditional probability is one of the techniques used to ascertain independence in trading systems and market patterns. Many traders make errors in thinking about probabilities because they do not understand this important subject.

cone of uncertainty A term that describes the future distribution of asset prices for a given level of volatility. Useful in a theoretical sense to visualize some specific problems relating to uncertainty, but most applications assume that the normal distribution holds. Since it almost never does in financial markets, there is limited practical utility for this tool.

confluence Some methodologies assume that support and resistance levels are more meaningful if levels from several different time frames line up at a specific price. This lining-up of levels is called confluence.

consolidated tape A high-speed system that electronically reports the last price and volume data on sales of exchange-listed equities.

consolidation A general term to describe a condition in which markets are not trending. In general, consolidation areas are seen as resting points in a trend, usually leading to continuation in the direction of the original trend. For practical purposes, pullbacks, flags, and consolidations are equivalent terms.

day trade A trade entered and exited on the same day and not held overnight.

demand line Richard Wyckoff's term for uptrend lines drawn below prices that show where buyers' demand has been sufficient to stop the downward movements of prices.

dependent variable In regression analysis, the variable whose values are assumed to change in response to the other variable(s).

disaster risks A term used to refer to risks from nearly completely unforeseeable events such as fire, flood, or a large-scale failure of the exchange network. These risks are extremely rare, could have catastrophic consequences, and are very difficult to hedge.

discretionary trading   A style of trading that allows varying degrees of human input in trading decisions.

distribution   The opposite of accumulation; traditionally, a price area where holders of an asset are seen to be selling their inventory carefully, so as to avoid causing prices to break down. In practice, often taken as a sign of impending price weakness.

drawdown   In trading system design or application, the amount lost from the high-water mark for the system/account. This is an underutilized measure of risk.

economically significant   Statistical significance is a reasonably well-understood subject, but there can be patterns that are statistically significant without being economically significant. For instance, perhaps a pattern shows a very consistent edge, but it would be impossible to capture that edge because it is smaller than transaction costs. It is often difficult to truly evaluate economic significance because costs will vary from firm to firm and from trader to trader—what might not be economically significant to one trader could be a steady income for another.

Efficiency Ratio (ER)   A measure developed by Perry Kaufman also known as the Fractal Efficiency Ratio, the Efficiency Ratio varies from 0 to 1 and is a measure of price movement compared to noise in the market. If price moves in an unbroken line for the period, the ER would be 1. If price returns to unchanged after moving away from the starting price, the ER would be 0.

efficient markets hypothesis (EMH)   Perhaps the cornerstone of academic thinking about markets, the EMH essentially says that all available information is immediately incorporated into asset prices, and that there is no edge available to traders doing analysis based on that information. The EMH is a useful theoretical construct, but rests on a number of assumptions that are severely violated in practice.

excess return   In general, the return of an asset or system minus the risk-free rate. (The most common proxy for risk-free rate is a Treasury instrument of similar duration to the investment's holding period.) In many of the tests in this book, excess return is used in a slightly different context: the mean return of a signal group (defined as having the entry condition to be studied) over the baseline return for the control group.

execution risk   A risk of trading in which the actual prices received for executions may differ from backtested results. In practice, liquidity conditions, execution skill, and trading size are primary contributors to this risk.

exhaustion   See *climax*.

expectancy or expected value   Mathematically, the expected payout of a scenario that has several possible outcomes is the sum of the probability of each outcome occurring times their payoffs.

exponential moving average (EMA)   A type of moving average that weights recent data more heavily than past data.

extension   In trend analysis, the third leg of the impulse-retracement-impulse unit that comprises the basic trend structure. Gauging the strength of the extension leg is one of the main ways to judge strength of the trend.

fading   A general term for styles of trading that seek to trade *against* the direction of price movements. A trader fading an uptrend, for instance, would be shorting into that uptrend.

failing Usually used in reference to a support or resistance level, meaning that the level is failing to contain prices. This term, and *holding*, are more often used to describe dynamic price action than static market structure. See *holding*.

failure test A type of trade in which price penetrates previous support or resistance, and then fails to continue beyond that level. This is a potentially volatile trade, but it also offers very clear risk points and profit targets.

fast Fourier transforms (FFTs) A mathematical technique for finding cycles in data.

Fibonacci ratios The idea that ratios derived from the so-called Fibonacci series {1, 2, 3, 5, 8, . . .} describe price movements in financial markets.

first-order pivots A pivot high is a bar that is preceded and followed by lower highs; a pivot low has higher lows before and after. These pivot points are called first-order pivots to differentiate them from more significant pivots in the market structure.

fixed fractional risk A position-sizing plan that seeks to always risk a consistent fraction of the account's value (also called "equity" or "net liq") on each trade.

flag Another term for a pullback or consolidation in a trend.

flow A term coined by Mihaly Csíkszentmihályi to describe the state reached by elite performers in many disciplines in which the performer's mental capacity is completely absorbed in the task. Flow is a characteristic of top-level performance.

free bars Bars that are entirely outside bands or channels set on price charts—that is, with the low of the bar above the upper band or the high below the lower band.

fundamental Traditionally, technical analysis is the discipline of understanding market movements based on information contained in the price changes themselves. Fundamental analysis is the discipline of using financial statements, economic data, or other information to try to determine what the fair value for an asset should be.

futile traders A term coined by Larry Harris to describe traders who do not make money in markets, and who have no hope of doing so. Harris speculates that one reason they cannot understand the difference between their expectations and their results could be that they are "of limited mental capacity."

good till canceled (GTC) A qualifier attached to an order to indicate that it should not be canceled at the end of the current trading session. A good till canceled order may not work indefinitely; some brokers cancel these at specific times (e.g., end of quarter).

handle A term used to describe the whole numbers in futures markets. For instance, a move from 1,038.00 to 1,040.00 in the S&P 500 futures is a two-handle move. The equivalent term in stocks is a point.

hedging A term with many meanings, but generally to hedge means to take positions to protect against risks in another instrument. For instance, buying a put option is a classic hedging strategy for long positions. Proper hedging is trivial and can be expensive.

high and tight flags A specific type of flag that holds near the high of a sharp up move (or near the low of a sharp decline) that often suggests strong buying (or selling) pressure behind the move. These often lead to sharp continuation.

higher time frame (HTF) The highest time frame in a normal lower/trading/higher time frames scheme. Time frames are typically related to each other by a factor between 3 and 5.

high-frequency trading (HFT) algorithms   Computer programs that rapidly execute orders, either for their own profit or to fill orders for clients.

histogram chart   A type of chart that is useful for visualizing probability distributions. Events are placed into bins, and the height of those bins is graphed to show the shape of the distribution.

historical volatility   Annualized standard deviation of returns. A common measure of volatility.

hit the bid   Vernacular for selling (whether initiating a short or selling an existing long position) to the price on the bid. This is usually done when a trader needs to sell quickly, because she could possibly have gotten a better (higher) price by putting offers in rather than hitting the bid.

holding   A term used to describe a market that is unable to trade beyond a specific level or point in the market, or to the action of that level on the market. See *failing*.

illusion of control   A term that describes a person's assessment of his own skill at a task that offers random reward. If the person appears to have some influence on the process, he will rate his contribution to the outcome as more important, even if there is no actual connection (e.g., a disconnected button that does nothing).

impulse move   In technical analysis, a strong movement in the market, usually sharp and in one direction. Also called a momentum move.

independent variable   In regression analysis, the variable(s) that is/are assumed to cause changes in the other variable.

indicator variable   A variable that assumes the value of 0 or 1 depending on some condition. For instance, an indicator variable could assume the value of 1 if today's close is higher than the previous day's, or 0 otherwise. Averaging this variable across the data set would then give the percentage of days that closed up.

inefficient traders   In Larry Harris's words: "Inefficient traders lack the skills, analytic resources, and access to information to trade profitably. They may do everything that profitable traders do, but they do not do it well enough to trade profitably."

interfaces   The areas between trends, trading ranges, or trends in the opposite direction. These areas can be difficult to read, but they offer some attractive trading opportunities if the risks can be properly managed.

interquartile range (IQR)   A nonparametric measure of dispersion calculated by taking the difference of the third and first quartiles. Also called the middle 50 because half (50 percent) of the data set's values will fall in this range.

Kelly criterion   A position-sizing plan designed to maximize equity growth if some simplifying assumptions hold. Violations of these assumptions can have catastrophic consequences, and violations are common in actual trading. If you choose to use a Kelly-style position-sizing scheme, make sure you understand the issues involved.

Keltner channels   Originally invented by Chester Keltner, these bands were drawn around a 10-day simple moving average of the *typical price*, and offset by a 10-day moving average of the bars' ranges. Various modifications exist today.

last print   The most recent transaction price in a market. May update very rapidly during the time the market is open. The last print of the trading session may not be the closing print in many markets.

limit orders   A type of order to buy or sell with a price limit attached. The order will be executed only at the limit or at a more favorable price (i.e., limit buy orders will be filled at or under the limit price, and limit sell orders at or above the limit).

linear regression   A mathematical technique for modeling the relationship between a set of variables.

linearly scaled charts   Price charts in which the y-axis (vertical axis) is scaled so that equidistant ticks are equal-sized price movements.

log scale chart   Price chart with the y-axis scaled so that equidistant tick marks on that axis are the same *percentage* distance apart.

long-term investors   Typically, individuals or firms that buy assets intending to hold them for multiple quarters or years. As a general rule (and one that is not entirely correct), these players tend to be more focused on fundamental analysis than on technical factors.

lower time frame (LTF)   In the standard three time frames scheme, the lowest time frame, below the trading time frame. Most traders use the LTF to time entries and to manage risk rather than for idea generation and analysis.

markdown   The classic Wyckoff market stage following distribution, corresponding to a downtrend in modern terminology.

marketable limit orders   Limit orders placed on the wrong side of the market. In other words, marketable buy limit orders will be placed *above* the offer. These orders will immediately execute at the offer, as would a market order. However, if they remove sufficient liquidity from the book to drive prices higher, they will not be filled higher than the limit price. This order offers a compromise between urgency of execution and protection from adverse fills. See *market orders*.

market makers   A set of market participants who, generally, are mandated to always be willing to buy and sell an asset in order to maintain an orderly market. Historically, many of these were floor traders, but this function is now generally fulfilled by computers and algorithms. Note that market makers have discretion to set the distance between their bids and offers, and they adjust this in response to market conditions.

market orders   A type of order that will be executed immediately, theoretically at the best possible price. In most markets, customers have no recourse in the event of a bad fill on a market order, so these should be used with caution. Nearly all traders will find *marketable limit orders* to be preferable.

market structure   The patterns of prices as revealed by swings connecting important pivot highs and lows. Skilled analysts and traders can use market structure to understand the balance of buying and selling pressure, and sometimes to derive an edge for the future direction and/or volatility conditions.

markup   In Wyckoff's terminology, the market stage following accumulation, corresponding to an uptrend in modern terminology.

mean   A measure of central tendency. In practice, this is what most people mean when they say "average": the sum of the values in a data set divided by the number of elements in that set.

mean reversion   The tendency for markets to reverse large movements and to come back to a middle or average value. This does not necessarily mean that markets will pull back to moving averages. Different markets display different degrees of mean reversion at different points in the market cycle.

mean-reverting   See *mean reversion.*

measured move objective (MMO)   A technique used to set an approximate price target for a swing out of consolidation, based on the assumption that future volatility will resemble past volatility. This, and all other ratio-based measures, is better used as a guide than a precise target.

measures of dispersion   Measures such as standard deviation, variance, range, and IQR that describe how data points spread out from a central value or set of values in a probability distribution.

median   A measure of central tendency. If a data set is ordered from smallest to largest, the median is the middle value in the set. If there is an even number of data points, the median is between the middle two points, and is the mean of those two points.

Micro Trendlines   A term used by Al Brooks to describe very small, short-term trend lines usually drawn between two to five bars.

Modern Portfolio Theory (MPT)   A mathematical concept that deals with diversification and risk in a portfolio context, seeking to maximize portfolio return for a given unit of risk. The term *modern* in the name is a misnomer, because MPT comes from work Harry Markowitz did in the 1950s.

modified MACD indicator   The moving average convergence/divergence (MACD) is a standard technical indicator. This book advocates the use of a simplified, modified MACD based on 3/10/16-period moving averages.

momentum divergence   There are several variations of this technical tool, but most of them look for a new high or low in price (relative to its recent history) that is not accompanied by a new high or low on a momentum indicator, such as the MACD. The assumption is that there was less conviction behind the move, so it is more likely to fail to continue.

momentum move   See *impulse move.*

Monte Carlo modeling or simulation   A mathematical technique, particularly useful in situations with many uncertain inputs that have many degrees of freedom or that are highly path-dependent. Monte Carlo methods essentially run multiple simulations and evaluate the results. A working understanding of these tools can help traders to bridge the gap to thinking in probabilities.

motive force   A term used to describe the tendency of price to move from one level to another. This appears to be offset by the resistive force. Though there are no easy applications of these forces, they provide the theoretical backdrop for all technical analysis and technically motivated trading. In some sense, these two forces are the purest expression of buyers' and sellers' intentions in the market.

moving averages   Tools used in technical analysis and signal processing that average values over a look-back window, called moving averages because the window moves forward with each new data point. There are many variations of moving averages used in technical analysis.

multiplicative rule of probability   The probability of two independent events occurring is the product of their individual probabilities. This can also be adapted for dependent events, but in this case the relevant math is: $Prob(A \cap B) = Prob(A) \times Prob(B|A)$.

next trend leg   The trend leg following a consolidation.

noise traders   Traders who have no reason or motivation for trading, and whose interactions with the market are irrational and erratic, known informally as the "idiot traders." In reality, the actions of many small traders essentially resolve into noise on most time frames, and cause slight deviations between price and value, even in efficient markets.

normal distribution   A probability distribution that describes many events and conditions in the natural world. Unfortunately, it is also frequently applied to market situations, with potentially disastrous results. Normal distributions rarely hold in asset prices or returns.

null hypothesis   In statistical hypothesis testing, the null hypothesis is the default assumption, usually that there is no effect or relationship in the data being examined. Note that this hypothesis can never be proven. Rather, the technique is to look for information that would contradict this hypothesis and cause it to be rejected in favor of the alternative hypothesis.

0%Rng   A measure of where the open lies within the trading session's range, expressed as a percentage of that range. For instance, 0%Rng of 100 percent means the open is at the high of the day's range, while 0 percent indicates the open is the low tick of that session.

offer   See *ask*.

open   In intraday data, the first tick of the bar. In daily data, opens are usually set by an auction process and may not be the first trade of the day. Also, most markets have electronic sessions that precede their official opens, so the instrument may have traded for many hours before the opening print.

opening range   A term used to describe the range price trades within a specific time following the open. Traders may use opening ranges from a few minutes to an hour.

opening skew   The tendency of the opening print to cluster near the high or low of the session, rather than to be somewhere in the middle. This is commonly assumed by traders to be evidence of a market inefficiency when in fact, it is completely explainable by the properties of random walks.

optimal f   An alternative to the Kelly criterion. Optimal f is another answer to the position-sizing problem. Developed by Ralph Vince, it may be more robust in some trading applications than the Kelly criterion.

out-of-sample testing   In system development or backtesting, part of the data set is usually held back for an out-of-sample test once development is complete. For instance, if you have 10 years of price data, perhaps you would do development on eight of those years and hold the last two for an out-of-sample test. Note that out-of-sample testing can be done only once; after that, the data set is contaminated and should be considered part of the sample.

outliers   Events that fall far outside the range of normal events.

overbought/oversold indicators   A class of technical indicators that try to identify markets that have moved too far in one direction and are poised for reversal. These indicators could provide entries for mean-reversion trades, but careful testing is needed.

pairs strategies   A term usually reserved for spread trades between different stocks. See *spread trading.*

paper trading   A tool sometimes used by developing traders that involves placing trades in a simulated environment. (The term does not imply literal use of pencil and paper.) Paper trading has limited utility because it cannot replicate the psychological challenges of having money at risk.

Parabolic SAR   A trading system originally developed by Welles Wilder that was designed to always be in the market, reversing long or short according to signals generated from price movements. (SAR stands for stop and reverse.)

path-dependent   Refers to a scenario that can have different values or outcomes depending on decisions or outcomes at different steps in the process.

pay the offer   A term that means to buy an asset directly at the offered price, without attempting to bid for a lower (better) price. Market orders should equivalently pay the offer, but there is the danger of large and uncontrolled slippage.

per-unit risk   The difference between the entry and exit price on a trade, or the risk to be taken on one unit (share, contract, etc.) of the instrument.

pivot high or pivot low   See *first-order pivot.*

pivot points   See *first-order pivot.*

point and figure charts   A charting technique, mostly obsolete, that charts reversals from pivot points. The x-axis is not scaled for any fixed unit; rather, it moves forward when the specified reversal from the pivot has occurred. This was a technique historically used by floor traders that still finds some applications in computerized trading.

population   In statistical testing, usually considered to be the set of all possible events or items with the characteristic being studied. The population is usually unseen and unknowable, so the central problem of inferential statistics is to try to understand the characteristics of the population based on samples taken from that population.

positive expectancy   See *expectancy* or *expected value.* A positive expected value suggests that a trader is likely to make a profit over a large enough sample size of trades, provided there is good execution and the expected value is larger than transaction costs.

post hoc   From the Latin term meaning "after this." Refers to events usually defined after the analysis or experiment is concluded.

preceding trend leg   In the impulse/consolidation/impulse framework, this is the initial trend leg that sets up the consolidation.

price action   A term that refers to a formalized understanding of how prices move. Price action is usually most visible on lower time frames, and price action creates market structure. In the terminology of a certain subset of retail traders, "price action trading" refers to trading without any indicators or moving averages, but this is mostly a meaningless distinction.

price rejection   The characteristic pattern of support and resistance holding: price makes an immediate (in the context of the time frame) and sharp move away from the level. The absence of price rejection suggests a higher probability of the level breaking.

profit target   Some technical systems set profit targets for part or all of the position. In general, traders using systems like this should develop the discipline of entering their profit-taking orders as soon as the trade is initiated.

proper pyramids   Pyramids that start with the largest number of units they will ever have at a level. These strategies can usually endure volatility at the end of a trend much better than reverse pyramids.

pullback   A general term for a consolidation pattern in a trend. Many of the traditional distinctions of technical analysis (flag, pennant, box, etc.) are not meaningful, as all pullback patterns can be traded according to similar rules.

pyramiding plans   Plans for adding additional units to a trade once the trade has moved a specific distance into profit.

random walk hypothesis (RWH)   A theory that says that asset prices can be described by random walks. Various forms and dimensions of random walks exist. In practice, the RWH seems to hold reasonably well for some assets and some time frames.

range   The high-low of a bar or trading session.

range expansion   A term to indicate more directional movement in markets. A market undergoing a range expansion phase will probably trend in one direction, the range of bars will probably expand, and measures of volatility will increase on some time frames.

real trend line (RTL)   A technique for drawing a trend line that marks the important inflections in trends, usually best-suited to application on longer time frames.

relative strength   A term used to describe relative price movements between markets. Skilled traders and analysts can find clues to institutional conviction and large-scale money flows in relative strength.

Relative Strength Index (RSI)   A technical indicator that seeks to identify overbought or oversold markets by measuring the relative distribution of up and down closes. Note that it does not measure relative strength, nor is it an index.

resistance   A term attached to price areas that may provide a barrier to advancing prices, or areas where sufficient supply may exist to stop prices.

resistive force   See *motive force.*

retracement   Another general term for consolidation, pullback, or a pause in an established trend.

return series   Most financial markets generate data as a series of price changes. It can be difficult to compare price changes across different price levels (e.g., a \$5 change in a \$10 asset is very different from a \$5 change in a \$1,000 asset). The first task of any market analysis is usually to convert the price changes into a return series. This can be either a percent return $(P_{today}/P_{yesterday} - 1)$ or a continuously compounded return: $\log(P_{today}/P_{yesterday})$.

reverse pyramid   A type of pyramid plan common in marketing literature for trading systems, but unacceptable for practical application. In these plans, the trader starts with a small position and then adds more units as profits from the trend allow the trader to pay for new units. For instance, a trader might start with one contract, adding two, four, and then eight at successive steps. These plans incur unmanageable volatility and drawdowns.

reward/risk ratio This ratio has many uses and applications, but a few points must be kept in mind. First, much of the literature uses "risk/reward ratio" when authors actually mean reward/risk ratio in nearly all cases. This book's terminology, while perhaps slightly awkward, is precise. Second, there is no innate bias to high reward/risk trades; this ratio must be understood in the context of expected value. Last, it is meaningful only over a large set of trades.

risk-adjusted returns It is possible to increase returns in a portfolio or trading system by increasing leverage, but true outperformance must come on a risk-adjusted basis, meaning that returns increase more than risk. Simplistic measures like the Sharpe ratio can help to build intuition about this concept.

risk-free rate In finance, the rate an investor could have realized in a theoretically risk-free investment. In practice, a U.S. Treasury bond, bill, or note with a maturity approximately equal to the intended holding period of the investment is usually used as a proxy for the risk-free rate. An investor must achieve higher returns than what she could have attained in a risk-free investment, so this is used as a hurdle rate in many applications.

R multiple If the risk (R) for every trade is known before the trade is entered, the profit and loss (P&L) can be expressed as an R multiple. For instance, $1\times$ (one times R) would mean that the profit was exactly equal to the initial risk taken on the trade.

R-squared or R^2 In a regression or correlation analysis, a measure of goodness of fit that shows how well the line fits the data. Often understood to be the percentage of the dependent variable's changes that are explained by the model.

rule of alternation In Elliott wave theory, the idea that retracements in trends tend to alternate between simple and complex consolidations.

sample In inferential statistics, samples are smaller sets taken from populations.

scaling in Refers to a style of trade entry where the trader builds a position, usually as it moves against the intended trade direction. For instance, a trader scaling into a long trade will usually be buying small pieces (perhaps 20 percent to 33 percent at a time) of the total position size into declines. This can be an effective entry technique for some styles of trading, but firm risk management rules are essential.

scalping A style of trading that takes very small but consistent profits. Scalpers need to focus on low transaction costs and on avoiding sizable losses, as a single large loss can wipe out many profitable trades. This term is also sometimes generalized to other time frames and styles of trading if the profits and losses are a small percentage of the average range on that time frame.

scatterplots A tool used to visualize the relationship between data sets.

seasonal Many markets exhibit somewhat predictable tendencies at certain times. Traditionally, this term applies to, for instance, grains at harvest time or natural gas spreads at certain times of the year. However, it can be generalized to time of month (are some markets strong or weak near the beginning or end of the month?) or even time of day for some markets.

second-order pivot A pivot point that is preceded and followed by lower *first-order pivots* for a second-order pivot high (reversed for pivot lows).

semistrong form EMH A variant of the efficient markets hypothesis that postulates that all publicly available information is incorporated in price. If this is true, it would not be possible to achieve superior risk-adjusted returns based on any publicly available information.

setup leg Another term for the preceding trend leg, or the leg that sets up a retracement.

Sharpe ratio A simplistic measure of risk-adjusted performance.

short To short or sell short is to sell an asset with the idea of buying it back later at a lower price. For most new traders, buying and selling higher is intuitive, but most professional traders are as comfortable shorting and buying back lower. (In this case, the sequence is "sell high, buy lower," which is still profitable.)

significance testing A statistical testing technique that attempts to evaluate the probability that the results could be due to chance and not to the presence of an actual signal in the market. (*Note:* This is a complex topic. This explanation is market-specific.)

simple moving average (SMA) A tool commonly used in technical analysis that averages prices over a lookback window, moving this window forward with each trading bar. For example, a 20-period SMA would average the past 20 bars' prices.

size effect Smaller stocks (in terms of market cap) tend to outperform larger stocks, but there may be offsetting risks.

slippage The difference between the intended and achieved execution prices. A cost of trading or an element of transaction costs.

spread This term is used in two different contexts: First, it is the distance between the bid and the ask in markets; wider spreads usually indicate less liquidity and higher costs of trading. Second, see *spread trading*.

spread trading A type of trading strategy that seeks to profit from changes in the relative value of a set of markets by being long and short different assets. This technique is an important part of most professional traders' tool kits.

springs The opposite of upthrusts: Price trades below support and immediately fails to carry lower. The quick recovery shows underlying buying pressure and potential accumulation.

standard deviation A measure of dispersion, also used as a (potentially poor) proxy for risk in many financial analyses.

Standard Deviation Control Chart A tool to visualize the variation in a trader's returns over time. Can be used to highlight potential problems and issues with changing performance.

standard deviation spike An indicator that standardizes each bar's price change for current volatility conditions.

stationary In a stationary time series, the properties of the distribution do not change over time. Note that this is not the same as saying prices do not move or trend;

stationarity refers to the shape and location of the return distribution. There is debate about whether financial markets exhibit stationarity.

Stoller Average Range Channels (STARC)   A modern variation of the Keltner Channel concept.

stop and reverse   A trading strategy that, rather than exiting the market, flips from long to short and vice versa when a stop level is hit.

stop-loss point   An initial point for directional trades, established at the time the trade is entered, where a loss will be booked on the trade. Stop-loss points must be placed outside the noise level of the market and at price levels where the trade is decisively wrong. Setting correct stop-loss points is a combination of art and science.

strong form EMH   A form of EMH that states that all information, even secret inside information, is incorporated in the price. Used today as a theoretical concept only, and well refuted by a number of events and empirical studies.

supply line   Another name for a downward-sloping trend line, drawn above prices. So-called because it represents an area where supply has been sufficient to meet demand and stop the upward movement of prices in the past.

support   A price area where it is anticipated buyers might offer enough buying interest to hold prices above the level. The study of how price acts around support and resistance is one of the building blocks of technical analysis.

survivorship bias   Survivorship bias covers a range of logical errors and mistakes that may come from examining the surviving members of a game of chance or another selection process. It is almost always better to examine the entire group before the selection process, as the survivors can give misleading impressions about the process and the probabilities involved.

swings   Price movements from one level to another. This is an imprecise term with some overlap between swings and trends. (Chapter 2 offers a structured approach to defining swings based on pivot points and market structure.)

swing trading   Formally, a style of trading that seeks to profit from the next swing in the market. Swing traders generally do not scale in, and do not attempt to hold through large, adverse price movements. Informally, many writers use this term to describe the trader who focuses on three-day to two-week holding periods, but this is a faulty definition of the term.

systematic trading   Usually refers to a style of trading that is rule-based and that could be at least partially computerized.

tail risk   The risk of large outlier events at the tails of a probability distribution. These risks are mostly unhedgable except at great cost, and they create serious problems for traders and risk managers.

technical analysis   Technical analysis is the discipline of gauging the probabilities of future price movements and/or volatility conditions based on information contained in price changes themselves.

theory of mind (ToM)   The ability to attribute mental states and emotions to others, and to understand that they have beliefs, desires, and intentions different from our own. Some researchers postulate that this theory also forms the basis for market intuition.

three pushes A typical end-of-trend pattern consisting of three symmetrical (in both price and time) pushes to a new high or a new low, followed by a reversal that shows a distinct change of character.

time frame Usually means the time period of the bars on the chart. For example, the 5-minute time frame would refer to a chart with 5-minute bars. Can also be used to describe a scheme where a trader looks at several time frames of the same market, and refers to them as lower, higher, and trading time frames.

trading time frame (TTF) In the three time frames scheme, this is the main, or focus, time frame. Lower and higher time frame charts may support decisions made based on the trading time frame.

trailing stop A system of trade management that moves the stop to lock in profits as the trade moves in the intended direction.

transaction costs The costs involved in participating in a market. They cover all financing, commissions, fees, the bid-ask spread, and any adverse effect your own order has on prices. Most traders, particularly retail traders, have a poor understanding of transaction costs.

trend continuation A class of trades that seeks to enter an established trend in the direction of that trend. Many trend continuation trades are based on entering in consolidation areas or pullbacks.

trend following An entire industry has been built around the term *trend following*. Many adherents of this school claim that trend following is far superior to other methods of trading, that it is easier than other types of trading, and that it essentially is the holy grail. None of these things are true. Trend following is a style of trading that usually attempts to position with a trend, with the idea that the trader may have to sit through significant whipsaws and drawdowns.

trend termination A class of trades that seeks to enter an established trend *against* the direction of that trend, with the idea that the trend is coming to an end. Note that these trades are not simply plays for trend reversal, as many of them will simply transition into trading ranges.

true range The range of the bar plus any gap from the previous close. In other words, if the low of the current bar is above the previous bar's close, the *range* of the current bar is the high-low. The *true range* of the bar is the range + (current bar's low − previous bar's close).

***t*-test** A common statistical significance test.

typical price The average of the high, low, and close for any trading bar.

upthrusts The opposite of Wyckoff's springs: price thrusts above resistance and immediately fails to carry through. This is also a type of failure test and a sign of classic distribution.

variance The square of standard deviation, and a measure that is not particularly useful in most market applications because the units are units squared. (For instance, variance of price changes in USD would be in units of USD^2.)

volatility clustering The tendency of high and low volatility areas to cluster together in market-derived time series. This is also a reflection of markets moving through different volatility regimes.

walk-forward testing A complement to backtesting, in which rules are applied to historical prices. In walk-forward testing, the rules are applied to fresh market data as it is generated. This is essentially a form of papertrading.

weak form EMH A form of the EMH that holds that information contained in past prices cannot be used to predict future prices. If this form of EMH is true, then the discipline of technical analysis is invalid.

whipsaws The tendency for many technical tools, systems, or indicators to accumulate many small losses while markets chop back and forth in trading ranges. For many of these systems, whipsaws are an unavoidable fact of life and must be offset by profits from trending markets.

z-score Also called a standard score, normal score, or a z-value: the number of standard deviations above or below a mean that a variable lies.

Bibliography

Acar, Emmanuel, and Robert Toffel. "Highs and Lows: Times of the Day in the Currency CME Market." In *Financial Markets Tick by Tick*, edited by Pierre Lequeux. New York: John Wiley & Sons, 1999.

Brock, William, Joseph Lakonishok, and Blake LeBaron. "Simple Technical Trading Rules and the Stochastic Properties of Stock Returns." *Journal of Finance* 47, no. 5 (December 1992): 1731–1764.

Brooks, Al. *Reading Price Charts Bar by Bar: The Technical Analysis of Price Action for the Serious Trader.* Hoboken, NJ: John Wiley & Sons, 2009.

Bruguier, Antoine Jean, Steven R. Quartz, and Peter L. Bossaerts. "Exploring the Nature of 'Trader Intuition.'" *Journal of Finance* 65, no. 5 (October 2010): 1703–1723; Swiss Finance Institute Research Paper No. 10-02. Available at SSRN: http://ssrn.com/abstract=1530263.

Campbell, John Y., Andrew W. Lo, and A. Craig MacKinlay. *The Econometrics of Financial Markets.* Princeton, NJ: Princeton University Press, 1996.

Collins, Bruce M., and Frank J. Fabozzi. "A Method for Measuring Transaction Costs." *Financial Analysts Journal* 47, no. 2 (March–April 1991): 27–36, 44.

Conover, W. J. *Practical Nonparametric Statistics.* New York: John Wiley & Sons, 1998.

Crabel, Toby. *Day Trading with Short Term Price Patterns and Opening Range Breakout.* Greenville, SC: Trader's Press, 1990.

Csíkszentmihályi, Mihály. *Finding Flow.* New York: HarperCollins, 1997.

Csíkszentmihályi, M., S. Abuhamdeh, and J. Nakamura. "Flow." In *Handbook of Competence and Motivation*, edited by A. Elliot, 598–698. New York: Guilford Press, 2005.

DeMark, Thomas R. *New Market Timing Techniques: Innovative Studies in Market Rhythm & Price Exhaustion.* New York: John Wiley & Sons, 1997.

Dimson, Elroy, Paul Marsh, and Mike Staunton. *Triumph of the Optimists: 101 Years of Global Investment Returns.* Princeton, NJ: Princeton University Press, 2002.

Douglas, Mark. *Trading in the Zone: Master the Market with Confidence, Discipline and a Winning Attitude.* Upper Saddle River, NJ: Prentice Hall Press, 2001.

Drummond, Charles. *Charles Drummond on Advanced P&L.* Self-published, 1980.

Edwards, Robert D., and John Magee. *Technical Analysis of Stock Trends*, 4th ed. Springfield, MA: J. Magee, 1964 (orig. pub. 1948).

Ehlers, John F. *Cybernetic Analysis for Stocks and Futures: Cutting-Edge DSP Technology to Improve Your Trading.* Hoboken, NJ: John Wiley & Sons, 2004.

Elder, Alexander. *Trading for a Living: Psychology, Trading Tactics, Money Management.* New York: John Wiley & Sons, 1993.

Faith, Curtis. *Way of the Turtle: The Secret Methods That Turned Ordinary People into Legendary Traders.* New York: McGraw-Hill, 2007.

Fama, Eugene F., and Kenneth R. French. "The Capital Asset Pricing Model: Theory and Evidence." *Journal of Economic Perspectives* 18, no. 3 (Summer 2004): 24–46.

Feller, William. *An Introduction to Probability Theory and Its Applications.* New York: John Wiley & Sons, 1951.

Fisher, Mark B. *The Logical Trader: Applying a Method to the Madness.* Hoboken, NJ: John Wiley & Sons, 2002.

Grossman, S., and J. Stiglitz. "On the Impossibility of Informationally Efficient Markets." *American Economic Review* 70 (1980): 393–408.

Harris, Larry. *Trading and Exchanges: Market Microstructure for Practitioners.* New York: Oxford University Press, 2002.

Hintze, Jerry L., and Ray D. Nelson. "Violin Plots: A Box Plot-Density Trace Synergism." *American Statistician* 52, no. 2 (1998): 181–184.

Jung, C. G. *Psychology and Alchemy.* Vol. 12 of *Collected Works of C. G. Jung.* Princeton, NJ: Princeton University Press, 1980.

Kelly, J. L., Jr. "A New Interpretation of Information Rate." *Bell System Technical Journal* 35 (1956): 917–926.

Kirkpatrick, Charles D., II. *Technical Analysis: The Complete Resource for Financial Market Technicians.* Upper Saddle River, NJ: FT Press, 2006.

Langer, E. J. "The Illusion of Control." *Journal of Personality and Social Psychology* 32, no. 2 (1975): 311–328.

Lo, Andrew. "Reconciling Efficient Markets with Behavioral Finance: The Adaptive Markets Hypothesis." *Journal of Investment Consulting,* forthcoming.

Lo, Andrew W., and A. Craig MacKinlay. *A Non-Random Walk Down Wall Street.* Princeton, NJ: Princeton University Press, 1999.

Lucas, Robert E., Jr. "Asset Prices in an Exchange Economy." *Econometrica* 46, no. 6 (1978): 1429–1445.

Malkiel, Burton G. "The Efficient Market Hypothesis and Its Critics." *Journal of Economic Perspectives* 17, no. 1 (2003): 59–82.

Mandelbrot, Benoît, and Richard L. Hudson. *The Misbehavior of Markets: A Fractal View of Financial Turbulence.* New York: Basic Books, 2006.

Mauboussin, Michael J. "Untangling Skill and Luck: How to Think about Outcomes—Past, Present and Future." *Mauboussin on Strategy,* Legg Mason Capital Management, July 2010.

Miles, Jeremy, and Mark Shevlin. *Applying Regression and Correlation: A Guide for Students and Researchers.* Thousand Oaks, CA: Sage Publications, 2000.

Niederhoffer, Victor. *The Education of a Speculator.* New York: John Wiley & Sons, 1998.

Plummer, Tony. *Forecasting Financial Markets: The Psychology of Successful Investing,* 6th ed. London: Kogan Page, 2010.

Raschke, Linda Bradford, and Laurence A. Conners. *Street Smarts: High Probability Short-Term Trading Strategies.* Jersey City, NJ: M. Gordon Publishing Group, 1996.

Schabacker, Richard Wallace. *Technical Analysis and Stock Market Profits.* New York: Forbes Publishing Co., 1932.

Schabacker, Richard Wallace. *Stock Market Profits.* New York: Forbes Publishing Co., 1934.

Schwager, Jack D. *Market Wizards: Interviews with Top Traders.* New York: HarperCollins, 1992.

Snedecor, George W., and William G. Cochran. *Statistical Methods*, 8th ed. Ames: Iowa State University Press, 1989.

Soros, George. *The Alchemy of Finance: Reading the Mind of the Market.* New York: John Wiley & Sons, 1994.

Sperandeo, Victor. *Trader Vic: Methods of a Wall Street Master.* New York: John Wiley & Sons, 1993.

Sperandeo, Victor. *Trader Vic II: Principles of Professional Speculation.* New York: John Wiley & Sons, 1998.

Taleb, Nassim. *Fooled by Randomness: The Hidden Role of Chance in Life and in the Markets.* New York: Random House, 2008.

Tsay, Ruey S. *Analysis of Financial Time Series.* Hoboken, NJ: John Wiley & Sons, 2005.

Vince, Ralph. *The Leverage Space Trading Model: Reconciling Portfolio Management Strategies and Economic Theory.* Hoboken, NJ: John Wiley & Sons, 2009.

Waitzkin, Josh. *The Art of Learning: An Inner Journey to Optimal Performance.* New York: Free Press, 2008.

Wasserman, Larry. *All of Nonparametric Statistics.* New York: Springer, 2010.

Wilder, J. Welles, Jr. *New Concepts in Technical Trading Systems.* McLeansville, NC: Trend Research, 1978.

About the Author

Adam Grimes has nearly two decades of experience in the industry as a trader, analyst, and system developer. He began his trading career with agricultural commodities, a reflection of his roots in a Midwestern farming community, and traded Chicago Mercantile Exchange (CME) listed currency futures during the Asian financial crisis. Later, he managed a successful private investment partnership focused on short-term trading of stock index futures, and swing trading of other futures and options products. He spent several years at the NYMEX, and has held positions for a number of firms in roles such as portfolio management, risk management, and quantitative system development.

Adam is the CIO of Waverly Advisors, LLC, an asset management and advisory firm specializing in tactical allocation and risk management in liquid markets. Adam is an expert in applying quantitative tools and methodology to market data, particularly in modeling volatility and complex intra-market relationships. In addition to his ongoing research and trading, Adam is also a prolific writer and educator. His personal website and blog (www.adamhgrimes.com) extends the work of this book with examples and applications to live market data. He has been a contributor on CNBC's "FastMoney," and his work and research have been quoted in major media outlets such as the *Wall Street Journal*, *Investor's Business Daily*, TheStreet.com, SmartMoney.com, *SFO Magazine*, and many others.

Index